Growing Rhododendrons

Richard Francis

Kangaroo Press

Acknowledgements

For editorial assistance
Margaret Barrett, Sam Bornsztejn, Lyn Craven, Peter Dainter, Lionel Marshall, Geraldine Roelink, Graham Snell, Alistair Watt.

Nurseries
Boulter's Olinda Nurseries, Davidson's Nursery, Green Valley Nursery, Kenny Lane Nursery, Leegray Azalea Nursery, Mount Boyce Nursery, Olinda Nurseries, Vireya Valley Nursery, Vireya Venue Nursery, Toolangi Wholesales Nurseries.

For photography
Malcolm Campbell, John Colwill, David Francis, Mary Moody, Dr John Rouse, Graham Snell and members of the Australian Rhododendron Society.

About the photographs
All photographs and line drawings are by the author unless otherwise stated. Most were taken in various private and public gardens in Victoria and Tasmania. Many of the species rhododendrons were photographed at the Lavers Hill Arboretum, Lavers Hill, Victoria. Other gardens include the Geelong Botanic Gardens, The National Rhododendron Gardens, Olinda, Victoria, The Royal Melbourne Botanic Gardens and the Royal Tasmanian Botanical Gardens.
ARS = Australian Rhododendron Society.

A key to the abbreviations used in the rhododendron tables is given on page 162.

© Richard Francis 1997

First published in 1997 by Kangaroo Press
an imprint of Simon and Schuster Australia
20 Barcoo Street (PO Box 507)
East Roseville NSW 2069

A Viacom Company
Sydney New York London Toronto Tokyo Singapore

Printed in Singapore by Toppan Printing Pte Ltd

ISBN 0 86417 898 0

Contents

Introduction	4
1. What is a rhododendron?	5
2. Landscaping with rhododendrons	11
3. Rhododendron culture	20
4. Good neighbours	27
5. Rhododendrons in containers	32
6. Protecting rhododendrons	37
7. Creating new plants	45
8. The species rhododendrons	57
9. The hybrids	73
10. Evergreen azaleas	117
11. Deciduous azaleas	140
12. Vireya rhododendrons	150
About the plant lists	162
Glossary	163
Rhododendron societies	167
Index	168

Introduction

> So fair, so sweet, withal so sensitive,
> Would that the little Flowers were born to live,
> Conscious of half the pleasure which they give.
>
> *William Wordsworth*

What makes the rhododendron so appealing to so many? For some it is the brilliance of a spring display of flowers that are among the most dazzling known to horticulture. For others it is the rich, sumptuous cloak of luxurious foliage as magnificent in their eyes as the blooms themselves. Or perhaps it is the mystique of plants that have come to our humble gardens from misty mountain landscapes in exotic places most of us can only dream about.

Two hundred years ago the rhododendron was little more than a botanical curiosity in the West. Then came the planthunters, with their stories of exploration rivalling Indiana Jones, in search of new treasures for the conservatories of the nouveau riche of the Industrial Revolution. Generations of dedicated hybridisers have bred the species into the huge variety of hybrid rhododendrons that are available in nurseries today.

Few garden plants offer so much. Within the genus *Rhododendron* are tiny, ground-hugging, prostrate and dwarf plants clinging to rocky outcrops with trusses of flowers as small as a centimetre in diameter. There are handsome trees, growing deep in the forests of the Himalayas, with gnarled and twisting trunks and leaves reaching as much as a metre in length, and shrubs of every size between. There are deciduous azaleas with brilliant flowers that inject life and colour to a bare late winter landscape and foliage that changes colour dramatically throughout the season. There are epiphytic rhododendrons that perch, orchid-like, high in the forks of trees, seeking just a glimpse of light from tropical jungle canopies. There are flowers of just about every colour, bold or subtle, and fragrance to equal that of the finest roses.

The rhododendron is seen by some as being difficult and exacting in its requirements – a feeling that plants with such splendid blooms and foliage would need an expertise beyond that of most gardeners. I would argue strongly against this view. All garden plants require certain conditions for success, and those of the rhododendron are not hard to understand or provide. Once established, the rhododendron in all its diverse forms is one of the easiest shrubs to care for. There is no need for annual pruning; the plants are afflicted with few ailments; and in return for the little care they do demand, they reward the grower with many years of pleasure, enhanced only with age.

1
What is a rhododendron?

A good first step towards an understanding of the conditions needed for any plant to succeed in the garden is to become acquainted with the family to which it belongs, and to look for the characteristics that are common to most, if not all, of the plants in that family. Then we must consider the locations in which the plant grows naturally and the conditions to which it has adapted in its natural environment. As far as possible we need to try to emulate those conditions in the garden if our plants are to do their best.

The family Ericaceae

Rhododendrons belong to the large and diverse group of eighty or so genera of woody plants that comprise the family Ericaceae. This family is widely distributed from temperate regions north into Arctic regions, although it extends southwards only as far as the tropics and then only at higher altitudes where it is cooler.

The family includes dwarf plants, such as the heathers and ericas, to medium-size forest trees like the strawberry trees (*Arbutus* spp.) and some of the larger rhododendrons. All genera within the family favour moist but well drained and acidic soils containing plenty of humus or decaying organic matter. Many members, such as the common Scottish heather (*Calluna vulgaris*), benefit from a symbiotic relationship with mycorrhizal fungi which greatly aids the plant's intake of nutrients, particularly on the poorer alpine or moorland soils that ericaceous plants often grow in.

The flowers of many of these plants often have petals that are joined at the base, giving that distinctive bell-shaped or tubular corolla that is very evident in many of the rhododendrons and the heathers. Most, including the rhododendron, bear pods or capsules containing many fine seeds, although some have drupes or berries, such as the strawberry-like fruit of the *Arbutus* genus.

Other plants in the Ericaceae family well known to gardeners include the mountain laurel (*Kalmia latifolia*), the lily-of-the-valley shrubs (*Pieris* spp.) and the cranberry (*Vaccinum* spp.), while in Australia the family is represented by members of the *Gaultheria* genus. Any environment where these plants are known to thrive should also be hospitable to the rhododendron, so long as the individual requirements of the particular species or hybrid, such as levels of sun, wind or drought tolerance, are taken into account. This is particularly true with ericaceous plants when considering soil conditions, but also more generally correct when assessing the overall environmental conditions we need to provide for successful growth.

The genus *Rhododendron*

As well as the popular garden shrubs displaying the dazzling, colourful spring flowers and rich, luxuriant foliage we associate with the rhododendron, this large and complex genus also includes the various types of evergreen and deciduous azaleas, once classified as a separate genus. A third group rapidly gaining in popularity are the vireyas, sometimes still referred to as Malesian rhododendrons, and often less than accurately called 'tropical' rhododendrons.

There are over 800 known species, including plants that are evergreen, semi-evergreen and deciduous, and they vary widely in form and size. This number has appeared to fluctuate a little over the years, as a number of previously separate species have been grouped together as varieties or subspecies of other species, and this process continues. At the same time, it seems certain there are more species remaining to be found and identified, especially in largely unexplored areas such as the island of New Guinea.

At one end of the size scale are ground-hugging prostrates such as the red-flowering *R. forrestii* from north-east Myanmar (formerly Burma) and China's Yunnan and Xizang provinces, and *R. prostratum* from Yunnan, Szechuan and Xizang. There are also miniature shrub-like species such as *R. trichostomum* (syn. *R. ledoides*), from Yunnan and Szechuan. The smallest of all rhododendrons is probably the vireya *R. rubineiflorum*, discovered in New Guinea in 1981.

At the other end of the scale are medium-size forest trees, like *R. arboreum* from the Himalayas, and *R. giganteum* and *R. protistum* from the Yunnan region and north-east Myanmar, which grow to as much as 30 metres in their natural mountain habitats. There are even a number of epiphytic species, such as *R. nieuwenhuisii* and *R. stapfianum*, vireyas found in Borneo, which germinate and take root in the decaying organic matter that accumulates in the forks of rainforest trees.

Foliage varies widely in form, determined largely by environmental factors. Some dwarf species like *R. serpyllifolium,* a deciduous azalea from Japan no longer known to be in cultivation, have tiny leaves often no more than 8 mm in length, which have evolved to withstand exposure to harsh, frosty winds on impoverished, gravelly soils. At the other extreme are the huge, broad, languid leaves of some of the larger-growing species habituating damp, protected valleys, plants such as *R. sinograde,* from Xizang, Yunnan and Myanmar.

The flowers of the rhododendron are always carried in terminal or lateral racemes, known as trusses, which bear varying numbers of florets from one to two dozen or more. These are usually 'single' in form, although there are occasional semi-double or even double forms. The colour range is vast, from shades very close to, but not quite, blue, through the violets, crimsons, reds, pinks, oranges, yellows and pale green to pure white forms.

While the foliage of rhododendrons is unpalatable, if not toxic, to some animals, the nectar produced by many species can be quite poisonous. The leaves of some species have been used to paralyse fish for an easy catch, and in the Western Highlands of New Guinea the flowers and other parts of *R. macgregoriae*, widespread in the region, are pulped and mixed with sweet potato and set out as rat baits. The poisonous substance is a narcotic known as andromedotoxin or actylandromedal, and the first symptoms of poisoning are itching and 'pins and needles', followed by numbness, laboured breathing, reduced blood pressure, paralysis and, in extreme cases, respiratory failure resulting in death. While the level of toxin is variable and there seems little information available as to which species in particular are dangerous, it is obvious that there is a risk. Great care should therefore be taken when handling the plants, particularly the flowers.

Habitat and distribution

The largest number of species of rhododendron are found between the tropics of Cancer and of Capricorn. However, the genus extends northwards into Arctic and tundra regions of Asia, Europe and North America, where possibly the hardiest of all rhododendrons, *R. lapponicum*, crouches beneath ice and snow for many months, while the southernmost species are found in the far north-eastern tip of Australia. These plants tend to favour the cooler temperatures and higher rainfall and humidity of mountain areas, particularly in the warmer climates where most of them grow. Africa and South America are the only continents not to have indigenous rhododendrons.

Most species are found concentrated in two areas. The best-known group, consisting of some 400 of the hardier, broad-leaved rhododendrons that were the first to be introduced into Western horticulture, are found in the Himalayas, including Nepal, Assam, Bhutan and parts of northern India, and stretching eastwards into northern Myanmar and the south-western Chinese provinces of Yunnan, Szechuan and Xizang (formerly Tibet). This area, marked by its continuous high humidity, summer rains and deep winter snows, is where the genus appears to have originated around 50 million years ago. From here it spread out to colonise other areas where similar conditions allowed it to gain a foothold, adapting itself on the way into new forms that suited local environmental variations.

The second major concentration is the vireya group of species, which are found in Malaysia, the island of Borneo (particularly the Malaysian states of Sarawak, Sabah and Brunei) and the surrounding islands, with the majority – more than 200 species – coming from New Guinea alone. The two quite similar red-flowering vireya species which grow in the far north-east of Queensland, *R. lochiae* and *R. notiale*, found their way south when Australia and New Guinea were joined together as one land mass.

A few species are found in Europe, ranging from the Pyrenees in the west through to the European Alps and into Greece. Among these is *R. ferrugineum*, the original 'alpine rose', which occurs across the European and Austrian Alps and the Pyrenees and has been in cultivation since the middle of the seventeenth century. There is also one deciduous azalea, *R. luteum*, found mostly in the Caucasus Mountains, but also scattered across much of eastern Europe. *R. luteum* has been used extensively in breeding along with North American species in the development of the Ghent hybrid azaleas.

The evergreen azaleas are mostly concentrated around the Sea of Japan, particularly the Japanese islands themselves and Korea. However, so much hybridising has occurred in Japan over several centuries that azaleas have become domesticated to the point where many of the original species are no longer found in the wild. There are also some species found in China, the Philippines, Taiwan and Vietnam.

Twenty-seven species of rhododendron come from North America. Particularly notable is the broad-leaved evergreen *R. catawbiense*, which has found its way into many hybrid lines. It grows in the wild in Virginia and North Carolina and is quite similar in form and appearance to *R. ponticum*, the sturdy, purple-flowering species from the Mediterranean region that has become something of a weed problem in parts of the United Kingdom since its introduction there. Seventeen of the North American species represent the largest concentration of deciduous azaleas, including *R. canadense*, which is found in the east of the continent from Labrador to Pennsylvania, and the delightful, fragrant *R. occidentale*, found from Oregon to southern California.

Altitude is as significant as latitude to the distribution of rhododendron species, with the majority of species found in tropical regions growing in mountain areas where night temperatures can often fall below freezing. Frosts are not uncommon at night – even in New Guinea – while during the daylight hours, which are longer at higher altitudes, temperatures will be 10–15°C lower than those found at sea level, where plants would not survive the heat. Rainfall and humidity are also greater at high altitudes, tempering the effects of the high temperatures, particularly during the monsoonal summer months.

Growing conditions in mountainous areas vary widely over relatively short distances, from full shade to open sun, protected or exposed, with soils varying in structure and organic content. These variations go some way towards explaining the huge number and variety of species, with some restricted to a relatively small geographic distribution. A species growing in one valley can evolve over time into a distinctly different form in an adjacent valley, its further spread prevented by the mountain barriers.

Rhododendrons growing in harsher conditions tend to be low-growing and hardier forms, while in more sheltered situations with deeper soils, such as rainforest valleys, the species are less hardy and tend to grow taller with larger foliage. Typically, below 1500 m/4920 ft the species will be smaller and they can sometimes be epiphytic tree and rock crevice dwellers. Between 1500 m/4920 ft and 3000 m/9840 ft is where the shrubs and tree species of rhododendron predominate, while above 3000 m/9840 ft to a maximum of somewhere below 5000 m/16 400 ft, exposure to colder, harsher conditions has encouraged the evolution of very hardy compact, dwarf or prostrate forms.

This ability of the rhododendron to adapt its form to suit the latitude is one of the keys to the success the genus has had in colonising new environments. Where conditions are ideal, rhododendrons of one or more species can be the dominant plant, smothering competing trees and shrubs and forming a spectacular massed display of colour when flowering.

Altitude can also affect flowering time considerably, with the same species flowering at different times according to the altitude and aspect of each plant. Flower and leaf formation normally occurs after the last risk of frost damage has passed.

History

Although we tend to associate rhododendrons with hidden, misty hilltop habitats in central and tropical Asia, it was in Greece that the rhododendron first entered historical records under rather tragic circumstances. Unfortunately for Xenophon (434–355 BC), Greek historian, soldier and follower of Socrates, *Rhododendron luteum* was in flower when he and his soldiers camped on the shores of the Black Sea around 400 BC. His campaign collapsed when the party consumed a sweetly flavoured honey collected from bees that had visited the plant, a native of the area. The honey and nectar were powerfully toxic, rendering all who consumed it thoroughly stupefied and demoralised. We can also thank the Greeks for naming the genus, although the word 'rhododendron', which means 'rose' (*rhodon*) and 'tree' (*dendron*), was applied to the rose-flowered *Nerium oleander* until the sixteenth century when it was first noted as describing the present genus of *Rhododendron*.

The rose, possibly the most revered of flowers across many cultures, has been cultivated and bred for thousands of years. Along with many other old-world plants, both horticultural and agricultural, it has a heritage that goes back into recorded history. But, like its good neighbour the camellia, the rhododendron is a relative newcomer to Western horticulture, its introduction arising from colonial exploration and exploitation and raised to full bloom by the spending power generated by the industrial revolution. We have the Chinese tea trading of the East India Company to thank for the first garden camellia, introduced through the 'accidental' substitution of a tea plant, *C. sinensis*, with its ornamental relative in an attempt by the Chinese to stop the Company using the local variety in its other plantations overseas. The rhododendron has no such commercial connection, only its attraction as a botanical specimen and later the thirst of newly wealthy industrialists for exotic conservatory treasures.

As confidence in alpine exploration increased and climbers ventured higher into the Alps, the first European species of rhododendron was identified: *R. ferrugineum*, the so-called 'alpine rose' found across the western European Alps and the Pyrenees. However, *R. hirsutum*, which is found from the eastern Alps and Transylvania, was to be the first species cultivated in Britain, by John Tradescant, son of the court gardener to Charles I, during the early 1600s. It was still almost a hundred years before *R. ferrugineum* was introduced into British cultivation.

The first American species to be brought to Europe, arriving in 1734, were two deciduous azaleas, *R. viscosum* and *R. calendulaceum*, with the most widespread of that continent's species, the evergreen ponticum rhododendron, *R. maximum*, being introduced from the east coast two years later. Known locally as the 'Rosebay of the Carolinas', *R. maximum* is rarely grown now as it offers little in floral value for its large size. In 1763 *R. ponticum*, a close relative of *R. maximum*, was introduced into Britain from its Mediterranean colony of Gibraltar, where it was growing wild. This vigorous and generously flowering Mediterranean species, which takes its name from the Pontic region of Turkey, has naturalised so well in some areas of the British Isles that it has become quite a weed problem.

By the end of the eighteenth century only about twelve *Rhododendron* species were being cultivated in Britain and no hybrids had been bred at all. It was the introduction of a further twenty or so species in the first decades of the nineteenth century that finally offered unforeseen combinations of characteristics, opening up new breeding possibilities, and triggering an interest in hybridising rhododendrons that continues today. These new arrivals included *R. arboreum*, the tree rhododendron from the Himalayan foothills which introduced the most brilliant red blooms yet seen (1811), and the Chinese azalea, *R. molle*, introduced from China in 1823 and later to become a parent of the Mollis group of deciduous azaleas. Others from this period to prove valuable in hybridising include *R. caucasicum* from central Asia (1803), and another close relative of *R. ponticum*, *R. catawbiense*, from Virginia and North Carolina (1809).

In the second half of the nineteenth century, the urge of the burgeoning class of rich manufacturers and industrialists to compete for the acquisition of new and exotic species to show off in their conservatories and greenhouses fuelled an era of unsurpassed excitement in botanical discovery. Expeditions of plant hunters were dispatched to the newly found treasure-houses of the colonies and beyond in search of undiscovered plants to be exploited. Glass in which to house these tender newcomers was now plentifully available and serious gardening offered people a means of acceptance into higher social circles. Enthusiasts vied fiercely with one another for the size, flamboyance and sheer curiosity value of their trophies.

Before the 1830s the only viable means of transporting plant material was as seed or pressed specimens, which meant a considerable delay before shrubs such as rhododendrons could be seen in their full flowering glory. The solution to this problem came with the Wardian case, developed by Dr Nathaniel Bagshaw Ward, a medical practitioner and amateur naturalist. This was a wooden-sided container with a pitched glass roof, totally sealed other than for a couple of small ventilator grilles. It became an invaluable aid in enabling plants collected overseas to withstand the long sea journeys involved.

Operating on much the same principle as a modern-day terrarium, more ornamental cases were used in Victorian drawing rooms to displays ferns and other plants requiring a humid environment.

The first real enthusiasm for rhododendrons as garden plants was kindled by a visit the botanist and plant collector Sir Joseph Hooker paid to the northern Indian state of Sikkim in 1849–51. Sir Joseph succeeded his father, Sir William Hooker, as Director of Kew Gardens, and the two worked together to publish *Rhododendrons of Sikkim-Malaya*. Sir Joseph sent back to his father the seeds of some thirty or forty new rhododendron species. Among those that expanded the possibilities for hybridising were *R. campylocarpum*, *R. wightii*, *R. falconeri*, *R. cinnabarinum*, *R. griffithianum*, *R. thomsonii* and the fragrant *R. maddenii*.

In 1856, plant collector Robert Fortune sent back from China the seed of *R. fortunei*, which offered hardiness as just one of its valuable ingredients in the breeding of plants for the cooler climates of Britain and North America. Fortune made a number of visits to the Far East, on behalf of the Horticultural Society (now the RHS) and the East India Company, principally to collect tea plants, and is credited with the introduction of a wide variety of plants including species of *Anenome*, *Lonicera*, *Weigela*, *Lilium*, *Primula* and, of course, *Rhododendron*. Later in the century the Irish collector Edward Madden, whose name is honoured in Hooker's discovery of *R. maddenii*, made further valuable discoveries, as did French missionaries working in various parts of Asia.

At the turn of the century, around 300 species of rhododendron had been identified, but these included over 200 vireyas from the New Guinea area unsuited to cool climate cultivation. All this changed dramatically in 1899 with the first of four plant-hunting journeys by Ernest H. Wilson on behalf of influential English nurserymen James Veitch & Sons to an untapped wealth of plants waiting to be discovered in central and southern China and the north of Myanmar.

Of greatest interest was a mountainous area where three great rivers, the Yangtze Kian, the Salween and the Mekong and their tributaries run within 80 km/50 miles of each other, cutting deep gorges through misty and humid rainforests. Here Wilson found a dazzling number of species that had adapted themselves to cope with a wide variety of local environments, from the still protection of valley floors to bleak and exposed rocky outcrops. In the first two years he sent back nearly forty new species, and over twenty years of exploration discovered many rhododendrons of value for breeding and as garden plants. Among these were *R. yunnanense*, *R. williamsianum*, *R. sargentianum*, the fragrant *R. auriculatum*, the prostrate *R. fastigiatum* and *R. augustinii*, the purple-flowering rhododendron to come closest to a 'real' blue.

Wilson was followed by the Scotsman George Forrest, who travelled to wetter and warmer areas of China, south of Wilson's territory, to find a huge variety of mostly more tender species ranging from the red-flowering prostrate *R. forrestii* to large-leaved varieties like *R. sinogrande*. Funded by nurseries and syndicates of serious collectors, Forrest eventually made seven expeditions to the region over twenty-eight years, mostly in the Chinese provinces of Yunnan and Xizang. Among the 1200 species of plants he discovered, he is credited with the introduction of over 300 rhododendron species alone, including *R. griersonianum*, *R. bullatum* and the dwarf species *R. tsarongense* and *R. russatum*.

From 1911, Francis Kingdon-Ward spent over thirty years plant-hunting in Assam, Western China and Myanmar, giving us such valuable garden plants as the dwarf pink *R. pemakoenese* and the scarlet *R. elliottii* as well as two breathtaking yellows, the large-leaved *R. macabeanum* and the rhododendron named after him, *R. wardii*. In a little over half a century, these and many other intrepid adventurers between them brought home more than 600 new species of rhododendron. And the search continues to this day. The adaptability of the rhododendron and the remoteness of many of its habitats guarantees that new species will continue to be unearthed for some years yet.

Taxonomy

To cultivate and enjoy rhododendrons, the grower really need not be too concerned about the efforts of botanists to classify the genus into various groups of closely related species. When one comes to consider the breeding of rhododendrons, however, an awareness of which group each species being considered for breeding belongs to is of paramount importance, as breeding between the major groups, known today as subgenera, is generally impossible, if not extremely difficult.

There was little logic or order to the classification of plants, which were named in random isolation until 1753 when the Swedish botanist and physician Carl Linnaeus wrote his *Species Plantarum*. In this seminal work of botanical classification, Linnaeus established the binomial system that remains the basis of botanical nomenclature to this day. The system uses one Latin name for the genus and a second latinised name to identify each particular species. This species name is usually derived from some distinctive physical characteristic of the plant or the name of the person who discovered or first described it or perhaps the location of its discovery. Linnaeus also described and classified all of the plants known to man at that time, including five species of *Rhododendron*. He grouped the azaleas into a separate genus, and it remained as such until the 1930s, when five of his six *Azalea* species joined the *Rhododendron* genus. The sixth (the alpine or trailing 'azalea', named *Azalea procumbens* by Linnaeus) was reclassified as *Loiseleuria procumbens*.

Earlier this century rhododendrons were classified into forty-three series by Sir Isaac Bailey Balfour of Edinburgh University, whose classification lingers on in many texts today. While Balfour's classification is still relevant in relating each series to a particular distinctive species to which members of the series can be botanically related, it was seen around the early 1980s that all the species could be grouped more simply into eight larger groups known as subgenera, with subsections allowing for diversity of form within each subgenus. The sections and subsections used to divide the larger subgenera in the current classification in most cases roughly correspond to equivalent series in Balfour's earlier grouping.

The subgenera Rhododendron and Hymenanthes contain all the species we know as the 'true' rhododendrons, also known as 'broad-leaved' or 'Asiatic' types, including the all of the lepidotes, such as the vireyas. The remaining six subgenera contain the azaleas and a few species of little horticultural significance.

The most important distinction in rhododendrons is between the lepidote species, whose leaves have tiny scales on their undersides, and elepidote species, whose leaves lack these scales. These scales are in fact almost microscopic structures that vary enormously in form from mushroom or funnel-shaped to globular scales. Careful examination of these tiny structures, which aid in the process of transpiration, can help identify the particular subsection to which a species belongs. They are more often than not golden brown in colour, although they can also be pink, purplish or grey. These scales should not be confused with the distinctive velvety coating (known as an indumentum), a characteristic of the leaves of many species, that is created by the presence of dense masses of tiny hairs.

The subgenus Rhododendron contains all of the lepidote or 'scaly' rhododendrons, including the vireyas, while the remaining subgenera contain the elepidote or scaleless species including the azaleas. As interbreeding between lepidotes and elepidotes is virtually impossible, all of the 20 000 or so hybrid rhododendrons can be classified into one of the two major groups.

Originally, azaleas were regarded as being a separate genus, having five stamens instead of the rhododendron's usual ten or more, and deciduous foliage, at least on the first species to be discovered and introduced into Western horticulture. However, when the evergreen azaleas were introduced, with botanical characteristics remarkably similar to those of the genus *Rhododendron*, the gap between the two types was bridged. The number of stamens and the lack of persistent leaves no longer seemed to be sufficient justification for the azaleas to continue as a distinct genus.

In the currently accepted classification of rhododendrons, deciduous azaleas are now grouped within the subgenus Pentanthera, while the evergreen, or more accurately, the persistent-leaved azaleas are grouped within the four sections of the subgenus Tsutsutsi.

The subgenus Azaleastrum or 'false azaleas' contains just two evergreen species rarely found in cultivation. *R. ovatum* is a shrub reaching about 5 m/16 ft. It has white to pale purple flowers and is found in central and southern China and Taiwan. The larger *R. stamineum* is a small tree from western China that grows to about 15 m/50 ft in height.

The remaining three subgenera each contain only one rarely grown deciduous species. *R. albiflorum* from the Rocky Mountains represents the subgenus Candidastrum and is an attractive white-flowered shrub growing to 2 m/6 ft; it has considerable ornamental potential.

The subgenus Mumeazalea consists of *R. semibarbatum*, a shrub from the Japanese islands of Honshu, Shikoku and Kyushu that reaches 3 m/10 ft. *R. camtschaticum* of the subgenus Therorhodion is a prostrate shrub found in the Alasakan islands and adjacent areas of Russia.

The genus *Rhododenron*

Lepidote (with scales) species

Subgenus	Section	Subsection
Rhododendron	rhododendron	Afghanica
		Baileya
		Boothia
		Camelliiflora
		Campylogyna
		Caroliniana
		Cinnabarina
		Edgeworthia
		Fragariiflora
		Genestierana
		Glauca
		Heliolepida
		Lapponica
		Lepidota
		Maddenia
		Micrantha
		Monantha
		Moupinensia
		Rhododendron
		Rhodorastra
		Saluenensia
		Scabrifolia
		Tephropepla
		Trichoclada
		Triflora
		Uniflora
		Virgata
	pogonanthum	
	vireya	Albovireya
		Euvireya
		Malayavireya
		Phaevireya
		Siphonovireya
		Solenovireya

Elepidote (without scales) species

Subgenus	Section	Subsection
Hymenanthes	hymenanthes (*ponticum*)	Arborea
		Argyrophylla
		Auriculata
		Barbata
		Campanulata
		Campylocarpa
		Falconera
		Fortunea
		Fulgensia
		Fulva
		Glischra
		Grandia
		Griersoniana
		Irrorata
		Lanata
		Maculifera
		Neriiflora
		Parishia
		Pontica
		Selensia
		Taliensia
		Thomsonia
		Venatara
		Williamsia
Pentanthera	pentanthera	deciduous azaleas
	rhodora	
	viscidula	
	sciadorhodion	
Tsutsutsi	brachycalyx	evergreen azaleas
	tsusiopsis	
	tsutsutsi	
	tashiroi	
Azaleastrum	azaleastrum	*R. ovatum*
	chioniastrum	*R. stamineum*
Candidastrum		*R. albiflorum*
Mumeazalea		*R. semibarbatum*
Therorhodion		*R. camtschaticum*

2
Landscaping with rhododendrons

The delights rhododendrons have to offer are available to virtually anyone who can garden, whether you have an acreage, a suburban block, an inner-city courtyard or even a balcony with just enough room for a few plants in pots. With careful selection and placement, there are varieties of rhododendron to suit just about every situation.

Some will cope with full sun if no shade can be provided, while others would much prefer to be kept in the shade. There are dwarf varieties ideal for containers and some of these – along with many azaleas – can be used as bonsai specimens. Rhododendrons are fairly tolerant of city pollution and can live happily for years in pots, so a collection of a few favourite varieties is easily accommodated on a patio or small courtyard. Those gardeners blessed with more space have the scope to create a woodland or rainforest garden that can include larger species and hybrids.

Recreating nature

Rhododendrons growing in the wild are found in a variety of situations, from shaded, humid, misty mountain forests to the light, sun-dappled woodlands. Surrounding trees can range from the deciduous birches of the Himalayas to rainforest trees and conifers throwing heavy year-round shade.

As often as not there will be a mixture of evergreen and deciduous trees, so that the levels of light will vary. We should try to emulate these conditions in the home garden if our rhododendrons are to not only grow well, but also to look 'at home' in their setting. We need, then, to consider the garden as a whole and provide a backdrop and environment that both looks good and can develop into an ecological system in its own right.

A woodland setting is possible in even the smallest courtyard garden, with a couple of well-placed small trees providing dappled light for the plants sheltering underneath. A light evergreen tree canopy sufficient to prevent frost damage, but still allow the entry of sunlight, can even allow gardeners in cooler, frost-prone climates to enjoy vireya rhododendrons.

Garden structure

Planning a garden should not be just a case of coming up with a flat ground plan, but should be an exercise in three dimensions and involve designing a vertical structure as well. Any garden comprises a series of vertical and horizontal layers. One needs to define what plants and features will constitute the background, middle and foreground or borders, as areas to be filled in a horizontal plane. It is this horizontal structure that is defined on the traditional planting plan, which is a bird's-eye view of the garden.

The vertical layers in the structure consist of the upper canopy of tree cover, the middle layer of feature shrubs and bushes, and the ground covers and smaller plants between the shrubs. These vertical layers can be visualised if one imagines a cross-section through any point in the garden showing the profiles of the planned shrubs and trees.

Preparing a plan

Whether you are starting a garden from scratch or renovating an existing one, drawing a plan on paper offers many benefits. By estimating the anticipated spread of shrubs and trees, the gardener is able to design planting beds and accurately position plants, avoid overcrowding, plot focal points, and estimate the approximate fall of shade.

A good plan becomes a permanent record of what has been planted and what is proposed. Anyone who has attempted to label all the shrubs in a garden will understand the frustration of labels that seem simply to disappear, no matter what method is tried. A better approach is to give each plant a number which is marked both on its label and on the plan, and to keep a separate record of its origin and planting date. This provides a permanent record of all plantings which doesn't rely solely on a label that may easily become lost or damaged.

You don't need years of training as a draftsman to prepare a useful plan of an average garden. It is easiest to work in metric measurements when preparing scale drawings, and a scale of 1:100 will usually allow sufficient detail and can accommodate most suburban gardens on one or two sheets of A3 paper. A plan of a rectangular block is the most easily drawn as you can take all the measurements from the fencelines. Imagine two sets of lines measured at one metre apart spread across the garden, one parallel to the front boundary, the other parallel to one of the sides. If the block is irregular in shape, measurements can be taken, working outwards, from any rectangular structure, usually the house itself.

For our scale of 1:100, lines drawn at one centimetre intervals will represent distances of one metre in the garden. Our garden plan now consists of many squares with sides of one metre and it is then a straightforward process to observe what falls within each square and mark it on the plan. For those preferring to work with traditional linear measurements, a close equivalent is the scale of 1:96 or 1/8" to the foot, which can be represented on the plan by squares 3/8" across representing one yard in the garden.

It's a good idea to ink in on the plan any permanent features such as paths, buildings and existing shrubs and trees, but to indicate new or planned plantings in pencil, as there will always be inevitable failures, replacements and transplants. Several different plans can be maintained for different purposes, such as a plan for shrubs and trees, a plan for annuals, bulbs and perennials, and another to record the layout of an irrigation system. This will help prevent the plans from becoming too cluttered. If they are drawn on tracing paper they can be superimposed on each other for you to view the relationships between the different elements.

Many households now boast personal computers, and a number of inexpensive software programs available enable the gardener to design a garden on the screen and try out a variety of scenarios before turning a single sod. Some of the more sophisticated programs include a library of popular shrubs and trees with their potential dimensions, while others will require you to provide that information yourself. Some will also allow you to see a cross-section of the garden so that you can visualise the vertical structure as well as the horizontal plan. Your computerised plan can be linked to a database where you can record any amount of information about the species or varieties you have planted, such as their history, breeding parentage, or details of the particular shrub itself, such as origin, purchase date, or any observations. When thoughtfully applied, the computer can be a great help to the gardener.

Structure

If you have inherited an established garden and wish to alter its structure, it makes great sense when commencing redevelopment or renovation to take account of existing elements that are worth retaining. Keeping any useful mature trees that can be worked into the new plan will save a lot of growing time. The cart may sometimes have to come before the horse if you are keen to keep particular plants that may are necessarily in ideal positions. I don't see this as a restriction so much as a challenge. The positioning of plants and topographical features in nature is a largely random thing, and elements we wish to retain may be used as a starting point for considering how to approach the rest of the garden. Many gardeners find it easier to be limited or even inspired by existing factors than to have to start with a totally bare piece of ground.

The plan is limited and determined by the boundaries of the block, the shape and relationship of any buildings, drives and paths, and existing garden features such as ponds, pools, pergolas, patios and barbecue areas, as well as the trees and shrubs the gardener would like to retain.

The upper level

Trees, large and small, are an essential component of any garden using rhododendrons as featured shrubs. They provide the shade vital for the successful cultivation of many rhododendron varieties and are one of the principal structural elements in any garden. Try to keep a sense of scale, selecting your trees in accordance with the size of your garden. Giant forest trees are obviously unsuited to the average suburban block, but the same effect of a high canopy can readily be achieved by careful selection, placement and pruning.

Every species of tree offers a different level of shade density, and a balanced garden will exploit this diversity, providing open and more exposed pockets, areas of dappled light, and stretches of fairly continuous unbroken shade. There are rhododendrons to suit every light level from open sunlight to all but the deepest of shade.

The choice between evergreen and deciduous trees is critical. A balance of the two is probably best. Carefully chosen and placed deciduous trees are a great ally to gardeners in warmer climates seeking cool respite from the hot summer sun, while maximising exposure in the cooler months and giving warmth to the soil and encouraging spring growth of plants beneath their spread. Many varieties of rhododendron will tolerate the weaker full sun of the winter months but relish greater protection from it once tender new growth has emerged in spring.

Evergreen trees and shrubs will provide year-round foliage, shade and vital wind protection. At least some of the trees in any garden should be evergreen, and by placing them in the perimeter planting, there will always be a background of interesting foliage and year-round wind protection.

On the other hand, too much persistent shade throughout both the day and the seasons will force plants to stretch out in search of life-giving light, becoming leggy and sparse. Under these conditions, pruning the plants to encourage more compact growth will not help much. They'll continue to grow in a leggy manner as they seek more light. Strategically reducing the number of trees or lopping selected branches to open the canopy and allowing more light onto the growing areas is the best option.

Roots are another factor limiting the size of trees and their proximity to dwellings in the smaller garden, and some species should be avoided at all costs – for example, some of the willows, lilacs and the notorious English elm, *Ulmus procera,* which will sucker vigorously well beyond the area of its leaf canopy. The surface-rooting habit of rhododendrons means that their supply of nutrients is usually not threatened by the deeper roots of any adjacent trees. With the decline of terra cotta in favour of PVC (polyvinyl chloride) drainage pipes, the likelihood of root invasion is reducing, so long as the drains remain well sealed and watertight. Any gap at pipe junctions will be found by the roots of many species exploring for water.

Agricultural drains laid to take away excess moisture among garden beds can also be a great invitation to the subterrestrially adventurous, so try to avoid trees and vigorous shrubs that have a reputation for having invasive root systems. As a general rule, keep *any* trees a reasonable distance from stormwater and sewerage drains, at least beyond their anticipated leaf canopy.

The spread of root systems can be restricted if necessary by pruning, though this is an arduous task best avoided. The roots of any tree, like its branches, can be periodically pruned by digging a deep trench every few years along a line set by the limit to which one wishes to restrict root growth.

The middle level

The middle garden level consists of medium-size shrubs and smaller trees. It is this level that is the focus of attention in any garden that depends for its character and scale, as most do, on a well-balanced association of mixed shrubs.

The lower branches of larger shrubs and small trees can be pruned away to create a sort of subcanopy giving smaller pockets of protection, ideal micro-environments for rhododendrons. When exposed in this manner the trunks of many shrubs can become a feature in themselves, with their twisted, irregular skeletal shapes often combining with interesting bark textures and colours, to provide a subtle, shaded backdrop to the lush foliage and flowers of the rhododendrons.

Consider the relationships between the shrubs you plan to use, among rhododendrons themselves and between them and their companion plants, keeping a view of the structure in mind all the time. Try to avoid too many shrubs of the same height and form, but cluster them into focal points, creating waves of rising and falling accents.

When first brought home from the nursery, potted rhododendrons will rarely be higher or wider than a metre, although the average budget will often not allow the purchase of such advanced and expensive plants. With a theoretical mature size for each plant in mind, you will consequently have a lot of bare, empty areas of open ground between the shrubs when they are first planted. And who is to say quite how we determine the optimum size of a rhododendron shrub? Like the conifers, rhododendrons have a way of steadily growing so that, with the right conditions, and over a couple of decades, a shrub once thought of as compact can sprawl endlessly.

As rhododendrons accommodate being transplanted, one solution to this problem is simply to overplant and plan to thin out the shrubs progressively as they demand more room. Another option is to grow 'disposable' shrubs between the specimens. These could be quick-growing and short-lived plants that enjoy similar conditions to rhododendrons. Vigorous perennials can also help to reduce the gaps for much of the year.

A third option is to look to ground level, and to cover much of the open surface with prostrate plants, creeping groundcovers and accent plants such as grasses, lower-growing perennials and bulbs, all of which can ultimately be moved out of the way as our specimen shrubs progress.

Quick-growing companion shrubs in the rhododendron beds can also serve the purpose of providing wind protection and some beneficial shade. Take care not to plant anything so close as to hinder the rhododendrons, especially in terms of competition for nutrients. Remember that rhododendrons resent any disturbance to their shallow roots. Avoid any planting of plants, like annual flowers, that demand repeated cultivation, and don't plunge bulbs into the root mass. The roots can be regarded as extending at least as wide as the leaves, and that area of soil should simply be mulched well and left undisturbed as far as possible.

Ground level

A well-balanced garden design demands variety. Areas of detail and spreads of ground-covering plants are needed to relieve the gaps between shrubs and to create borders of interest alongside pathways. Where possible, aim for multiple plantings of bulbs, perennials, dwarf plants and groundcovers rather than just planting one or two of each specimen. This will avoid a confused jumble of plants that are individually interesting but detract from the overall harmony you are trying to achieve.

The narrow, vertical detail of the foliage of grasses and bulbs can be used to provide contrast with the broad, bold leaves of the rhododendrons. Good choices here will depend very much on climate but could include hostas, mondo grass, sedges, bamboos, and a selection from many of the non-invasive grasses.

Bulbs of various kinds enjoy the mulch needed for rhododendrons, but usually prefer sunnier spots. Bulbs such as daffodils, tulips and freesias will flower under deciduous trees before the leaf canopy is fully established in spring. However, for most of their season above the ground all we see of bulbs is their foliage, so we are really considering them as part of the interplay of foliage between quite different types of plants rather than for their flowering attributes.

As well as playing an ornamental role in filling gaps between larger shrubs, spreading or creeping evergreen groundcovers can make a useful mulch, suppressing weed growth and helping to moderate temperature and moisture levels in the soil beneath their spread. Be wary, however, of using any potentially invasive plants, particularly those that set down permanent roots as they spread, like the common English ivy (*Hedera helix*) or periwinkles (*Vinca* spp.).

Rock gardens

There are many dwarf species and cultivars of rhododendron below a metre in height that lend themselves well to the alpine or rock garden. The term 'alpine' implies an exposed sunny aspect, simulating the conditions found on rocky, windswept outcrops at higher altitudes. An area designed to accommodate alpine plants can provide an alternative to the more heavily shaded areas offered for the larger, broad-leaved rhododendrons and like-minded shrubs. Local climate may dictate that we cheat a little in the plants we choose, but they qualify if they conform to the low-profile, ground-hugging habit we expect of alpines. Many nurseries have 'alpine' sections that offer a range of appropriate small plants, including many herbs useful in the home.

Exposure to the full sun means a great dependence on mulching to maintain moisture levels in the soil. Finely crushed gravel or stone mulches can be used to simulate the eroded rock of an alpine environment, and an irrigation system may be more necessary here than in other parts of the garden.

Sloping sites lend themselves well to alpine or rock gardens, allowing small terraced beds to be supported by thoughtfully placed rocks as retaining walls. The relationship of scale between plants and rocks in the alpine or rock garden is the opposite of that which applies to the rest of the garden. To emulate the erosive effect of the wind, plants and rocks need to reduce in scale the further up the slope they are. As in nature, prostrates that hug the ground tightly will be found at a higher level than dwarfs and compact shrubs at 'ground level'. On flatter sites, greater consideration will have to be given to using plants of varying height, size and form to provide structural elements, avoiding a look that is too horizontal.

Large rocks used as intermittent features, with much of their bulk buried below the surrounding soil level to give the appearance of being revealed by years of erosion, will look a lot more natural than a trailer-load of smaller rocks scattered on the surface.

Consider including some sort of water feature in the rock garden. A sloping garden will offer the opportunity to include a streamlet meandering between small ponds among the rocks and plants. Rhododendrons planted around a garden pond will enjoy the bonus of extra humidity as the water evaporates.

Size and shape

The ultimate height and growth habit of just about any plant can vary enormously for a number of reasons. The siting, level of cultivation, fertilisation, irrigation and pruning applied to a plant, as well as the climate and soil in which it is grown, can all affect its overall size and shape and the density of its foliage and flowering. Texts may list the growing characteristics of a species in its natural environment, which may be quite different from those of a plant grown with devotion in a home garden. A rhododendron nestling in its misty remote valley in Western China, for example, may accurately be described as attaining a straggly 6 m/20 ft or more in height as it struggles to reach the light. The same species, when cultivated in a home garden, regularly fed, carefully mulched and occasionally tidied and pruned, and with an aspect that provides more light in quite a different climate, may also be described realistically as reaching a typical garden height of around 2 m/6 ft. Plants growing in shaded situations will tend to grow taller, with less dense foliage, than those which do not need to fight for their light.

Evergreen azaleas growing in cultivation rarely reach more than 1.2 m/4 ft or 1.5 m/5 ft in height, and are more often somewhat lower, but with a spread much broader than their height. Deciduous azaleas are usually more erect in growth, sometimes reaching 3 m/10 ft or more. The trend this century has been towards breeding shrubs of manageable size for suburban gardens, so that the majority of evergreen rhododendrons, including vireyas, range from dwarfs and prostrates to shrubs rarely exceeding 2.5 m/8 ft.

Although there are no hard and fast rules, a plant's size can also have some bearing on its siting. Dwarf and prostrate plants with smaller leaves will usually be more tolerant of exposure to the sun, making them more appropriate for the rock garden or foreground beds. Taller-growing species or varieties have usually evolved larger and more sensitive foliage to catch the weaker light of the more shaded positions to which they are better suited.

Flower colour

When it comes to the selection of plants for flower colour, there seems little point in asserting that one colour scheme is superior in some way to any other. This is where gut feeling and instinct come in, and, as with so much in gardening, personal taste should be the first guide. If you like yellows, for instance, start with the yellows in the catalogues, and try to assemble a group of plants that will support those first yellow choices.

Try to contrast or complement in your colour selection rather than choose colours that are too close to each other. Such shadings will tend to detract from one another, undermining their own individual strengths. This will not be a problem, of course, if adjacent plants do not flower simultaneously, and timing is an additional critical factor to be borne in mind when planning your planting. There is obviously no sense in determining a wonderful colour scheme if the plants we are trying to mix simply do not flower at the same time.

Conversely, clashes can be avoided just as easily by staggering the flowering times carefully. Thus, two favourite rhododendrons that could be a disaster if they flowered simultaneously can be enjoyed in the same area. The character of any part of the garden will slowly, although sometimes dramatically, alter as different shrubs come in and out of leaf and flower. Focal points will shift around the garden throughout the flowering season as different specimens take their turn in the spotlight, then fade as others come on to take the centre stage.

Some colours are best left on their own if possible. Particularly difficult to place in relation to other colours are the strong pinks and magentas, which can overpower just about anything within reach. About the only colour that can be made to work in combination with the hot pinks are whites and some shades of yellow. White, of course, can be guaranteed to coordinate perfectly with any other colour. Shades of cream and yellow are also capable of integrating well with most other shades, but you must try to avoid a smorgasbord of colour. The most successful garden palettes are restricted to one dominant colour and others that will support rather than clash.

Deciduous azaleas offer the cooler-climate grower a range of vivid yellows and oranges in their spring flowers, followed by the excitement of young bronze foliage, capped off by a spectacular flush of foliage colour in autumn before the leaves finally drop.

While most other colour shades are represented well, there are no 'true' blues in rhododendrons. The closest is that of *R. augustinii* and *R. scintillans*, which are a violet-purple close to royal blue. There is nothing, however, approaching the strident blueness of genera like *Lithodora*, gentian or the florist's cineraria. Therefore, if you do want blue accents in your colour scheme, look to your companion plants to provide it.

Foliage

Although rhododendrons are among the more prolific flowerers of our garden shrubs, they do not have a long flowering season. For the rest of the year we have just the foliage, although that in itself delivers quite a show, with the contrast between the exciting new young growth

Rhododendrons worth seeking for their foliage

Non-vireya species
arboreum
campanulatum
degronianum
elegantulum
fastigiatum
grande
macabeanum
niveum
ovatum
ponticum 'Variegatum'*
rirei
thomsonii
wallichii
wightii
degronianum ssp. yakushimanum

arizelum
coelicum
edgeworthii
falconeri
fulvum
lutescens
makinoi
nuttallii
pemakoense
pseudochrysanthum
sinogrande
ungernii
wardii
wiltonii

Small hybrids
'Australian Cameo'
'Australian Sunset'
'Blitz'
'Bow Bells'
'Bronze Wing'
'Coral Velvet'
'Hello Dolly'
'Hydon Dawn'
'May Day'
'Potlatch'
'Redwax'
'Scarlet Wonder'
'Thor'

'Australian Primrose'
'Bad Eilsen'
'Blue Tit'
'Bric a Brac'
'Cilpinense'
'Fire Prince'
'Hotei'
'Kimberley'
'Odee Wright'
'Ramapo'
'Ruby Hart'
'Surrey Heath'
'Valerie Kay'

Medium hybrids
'Alison Johnstone'
'Award'
'Bruce Brechtbill'
'Chikor'
'Cup Day'
'Fire Walk'
'Gibraltar'
'Grace Seabrook'
'Ibex'
'Jean Marie de Montague'
'Lady Chamberlain'
'Madame Doumier'
'Noyo Chief'
'President Roosevelt'*
'Satin'
'Scintillation'
'Success'

'Aunt Martha'
'Boule de Neige'
'Canary'
'Crossbill'
'Dr. Stocker'
'Fusilier'
'Goldflimmer'*
'Harvest Moon'
'Jan Dekens'
'Johnny Bender'
'Lady Clementine Mitford'
'Matador'
'P. J. M.'
'Rocket'
'Scarlet King'
'Sir Charles Lemon'
'Witchery'

Large hybrids
'Anna'
'Antoon van Welie'
'Cearuleum'

'Anna Rose Whitney'
'California Gold'
'Walloper'

Vireya species
brookeanum
ericoides
orbiculatum
phaeochitum
sessilifolium

christi
malayanum
pauciflorum
phaeopeplum
zoelleri

*variegated foliage

and the older leaves from previous seasons. Companion planting with other flowering shrubs and perennials will relieve that monotony, but one should also consider selection of different varieties for their individual foliage qualities.

Contrast larger-leaved varieties against those with smaller foliage, and include selections that offer an attractive surface coating (known as an 'indumentum'), or fascinating new shoots, or deeply textured or ribbed leaves. The foliage of rhododendrons varies from thin spiky leaves no more than 10 mm long to the monstrous foliage of species such as *R. sinogrande*, whose leaves can exceed a metre in length. Species with such immense foliage, however, are unlikely to be practical for the home garden, because they require plenty of protection and room to grow.

The new growth of foliage on rhododendrons is always a great attraction as the new shoots follow the flowering. On most species and varieties, this new growth contrasts for some months against the previous years' leaves, in colour, texture and form. They are often covered with a luxuriant fawn or silvery indumentum – a dense covering of fine hairs – that disappears with maturity on some species, while remaining on others, and is often easily rubbed off. The young foliage grows upright, resembling Christmas tree candlesticks before unfolding, while older leaves tend to hang out or down.

Leaf shapes vary widely, ranging from the long narrow foliage typical of plants descending from *R. griersonianum* to the roundish or oval leaves of *R. williamsianum* and its offspring. Leaf surfaces can be smooth, nearly glossy or richly textured.

Foliage colours range from deep bluish greens to bright greens. Some plants offer superb bronze foliage, particularly on younger growth. Deciduous azaleas also turn bronze as their foliage matures before their autumn colour sets in and the leaves drop, while many evergreen rhododendrons and azaleas display bronze foliage during the winter months. It is also during the cooler part of the year that the foliage of many of the larger-leaved evergreens droops, hanging almost vertically from the shrub. This should not be confused with any ailment, but could have a lot to do with plants that are used to a blanket of winter snow in their original habitat.

Although they are not noted for it, there are a few rhododendrons that have variegated foliage, the best known probably being the popular and striking 'President Roosevelt', 'Goldflimmer' and the variegated form of *R. ponticum*. Some notable companion shrubs with variegated foliage include some varieties of *Pieris* and the variegated form of winter daphne, *Daphne odora*. Variegated foliage is indicated with an asterisk in the following lists.

Trunks and bark

With age, many of the larger species and hybrids develop wonderfully twisting thick trunks that writhe about under a heavy foliage mantle. They are often cloaked in bark that becomes an endearing feature in itself, improving with age. It can be smooth and skin-like, in shades of greys and pale browns, peeling and flaking, but can also be rough and deeply textured.

Fragrance

While not contributing to the visual impact of a garden, fragrance is a factor that still has to be taken into account when siting plants. Keeping in mind the other considerations for siting, fragrant varieties obviously need to be located where their fragrance can be enjoyed – close to pathways, for example, and near seats or other resting spots where lingering visitors may enjoy the scent. As the fragrance can often be fairly subtle, some consideration should be given to grouping a number of scented plants together to reinforce the impact. Fragrance in rhododendrons is genetically linked to paler flower colours, normally restricted to whites and paler pinks.

Perhaps the best known of the fragrant evergreen rhododendrons is the old hybrid 'Fragrantissimum', which is not, however, a particularly attractive shrub, tending to be rather straggly in form. Members of the Edgeworthia subsection, particularly *R. edgeworthii,* and its hybrids, such as 'Princess Alice' and the compact 'Suave', offer better form than 'Fragrantissimum', as do some species of the Maddenia subsection and their hybrids. Many other species and hybrids, including vireyas and a number of deciduous azaleas, offer varying levels of fragrance.

It's not just the flowers that can be fragrant. A characteristic of *R. cinnabarinum* that is passed on to its offspring is the cinnamon-like aroma of its foliage when rubbed against or crushed.

Species worth seeking for their bark

ambiguum	arboreum
arizelum	barbatum
cubitii	dendricola
elegantulum	falconeri
fictolacteum	fortunei
grande	griersonianum
griffithianum	hemsleyanum
lutescens	maddenii
niveum	nuttallii
pseudochrysanthum	sinogrande
spinuliferum	taggianum
tephropeplum	thomsonii
ungernii	veitchianum
wallichii	wardii
wiltonii	xanthostephanum
zeylanicum	

Rhododendrons worth seeking for their fragrance

Fragrant species
ciliicalyx
decorum
edgeworthii
fortunei
hemsleyanum
maddenii
nuttallii
scopulorum
veitchianum
dalhousiae
dendricola
falconeri
griffithianum
johnstoneanum
megacalyx
rigidum
taggianum
virgatum

Small fragrant hybrids
'Daviesii'
'Princess Alice'
'Suave'
'Dora Amateis'
'Sesterianum'

Medium fragrant hybrids
'Admiral Piet Hein'
'Award'
'Countess of Sefton'
'Lavender Girl'
'Mount Everest'
'Tyermanii'
'Wedding Gown'
'Anne Teese'
'Countess of Haddington'
'Fragrantissimum'
'Loder's White'
'Mrs A. T. de la Mare'
'Van Nes Sensation'

Large fragrant hybrids
'California Gold'
'Faggetter's Favourite'
'Irene Stead'
'Mother of Pearl'
'Satin Glow'
'Coronation Day'
'Geoffrey Millais'
'Janet Blair'
'Puget Sound'
'Sir Frederick Moore'

Fragrant evergreen azalea hybrids
'Alba Magnifica'
'Fielder's White'
'Schryderii'
'Exquisite'
'Magnifica'
'Schryderii Mauve'

Fragrant deciduous azalea species
arborescens
luteum
prinophyllum
atlanticum
occidentale
viscosum

Fragrant deciduous azalea hybrids
'Balzac'
'Buzzard'
'Exquisita'
'Lady Jane'
'Berryrose'
'Carat'
'Irene Koster'

Fragrant vireya species
carringtonii
konori
loranthiflorum
multicolor
phaeochitum
jasminiflorum
leucogigas
luraluense
orbiculum
phaeopeplum

Fragrant vireya hybrids
'Aravir'
'Bold Janus'
'Christopher John'
'Dr. Hermann Sleumer'
'Elegant Bouquet'
'Gardenia Odessy'
'Great Scent-sation'
'Highland White Jade'
'Jean Baptiste'
'Laura Kate'
'Lochmin'
'Magic Flute'
'Pastenello'
'Princess Alexandra'
'Sweet Amanda'
'Sweet Seraphim'
'Bob's Crowning Glory'
'Cherry Liquer'
'Craig Faragher'
'Eastern Zanzibar'
'Esprit de Joie'
'Gossamer White'
'Highland Arabesque'
'Iced Primrose'
'Johannes'
'Little Pinkie'
'Lovey'
'Moonwood'
'Pink Pizazz'
'Robert Bates'
'Sweet Rosalie'
'Sweet Wendy'

Flowering times

All species and hybrids will have their own set flowering times in relation to each other, more or less determined by the length of day. In most types this flowering will be concentrated in the spring months, between the spring equinox and the summer solstice. Many evergreen azaleas, however, can flower, if sparsely, in autumn as well as spring, triggered often by a burst of mild weather. Vireya rhododendrons are much less seasonal in their flowering patterns, depending more on rainfall and temperature. They can bloom at various times of the year, often in winter.

A variety of geographic and climatic factors, such as seasonal variations, altitude, latitude and proximity to the sea, will cause flowering times to vary widely from area to area and year to year. It will be the first random burst of warmer spring weather – not a date on the calendar – that triggers earlier flowering one year, or a long, cold, wet winter that retards the opening of those same buds the next.

Any suggested flowering times can therefore only be seen as an approximate guide, but they can be very useful when developing a planting plan, enabling us to consider the garden in a fourth dimension – time. Where they are indicated in the lists, these suggested flowering times give an idea of the relationship between the flowering of different varieties. For example, one hybrid will always flower before another, even if those times vary from year to year. Thus a succession of flowering can be planned to provide a flow of ever-changing harmonies and moods throughout the season, avoiding dead spots when there could be flowering and potentially disastrous colour clashes can be sidestepped.

Care must be taken in the selection of early-flowering varieties in areas prone to late frosts. Conversely, the blooms of late-flowering plants, particularly hybrids developed for cooler zones, can be damaged by the hot summer sun of warmer climates.

Cold hardiness

Most plant species have succeeded by adapting physiologically to the climates in which they are found and thrive. Most plants that come into our gardens originate from foreign climates, often differing vastly from our own. A number of steps can be taken in cultivation to compensate for these differences – for instance, the use of mulches or the provision of additional water, or by creating artificial climates in a glasshouse or shadehouses.

Although the term 'hardy' can also be used to describe a plant capable of tolerating drought conditions, the hardiness of a plant is more normally used as a rough guide to the minimum temperature it can survive before its sap freezes and it dies. Conversely, a plant unable to tolerate cold temperatures is referred to as 'tender'. The freezing of soil moisture in very cold climates can inflict drought conditions that are just as debilitating as extended hot, dry weather can be. Plants adapt to both climatic extremes in various, and sometimes similar, ways. These can include the presence of anti-freezing oils and crystals in their sap, thickening of the bark and the growth of a protective hairy indumentum over stems, and leaves that are reduced in surface area to lower transpiration.

In the horticultural heartlands of northern America and Europe, sustained low winter temperatures, frequent frosts and blankets of snow in many areas dictate that hardiness becomes a critical factor in plant selection. Hardiness is, however, not simply a matter of minimum temperatures, the type of climate being an equally critical factor. Plants growing in oceanic or maritime climates, such as close to the American seaboards and in much of Britain, can generally tolerate low temperatures better than those growing in the sustained cold of continental climates such as are experienced in much of mainland Europe and inland North America. Plants growing in drier climates are generally better able to cope with low temperatures.

Climatic zone systems, based usually along the lines of isotherms, have been developed for both areas, but are regarded sceptically by some authorities as being too simplistic. The relative hardiness between a choice of otherwise similar plants, can, however be used as a deciding factor in selection.

Once established and growing, plants seem to increase their hardiness with age. As nursery stock has been raised under protection, it makes good sense to 'harden off' plants in their containers for one season, to allow them to acclimatise before planting.

The tender flower buds and leaf shoots of some early flowering species and hybrids can be burnt by late frosts, although the plant itself may be rated as being quite hardy. This indicates that care should be exercised in frost-prone areas, particularly inland, when selecting and siting early flowering varieties. Plants should be sited to avoid early morning sun, slowing the rate at which the plant thaws out from freezing.

The use of a heavy mulch can help to prevent deep freezing of the moisture in the soil and thus raise hardiness by several degrees. Careful selection and placement of companion plants can provide screening and shelter from frosts and cold winds. Siting plants against a sunny wall that will absorb and reflect the sun's heat can permit the growth of more tender varieties, while raising beds to ensure good drainage allows frost to flow away from plants.

There are no heat tolerance ratings available for plants in the same way that there are hardiness ratings, so local experience and nursery advice should be relied upon where there is doubt as to the ability of plants to survive the heat. The deciduous azaleas and cool climate broad-leaved rhododendrons will generally succeed in those areas where winters are cool enough for deciduous trees to thrive.

Evergreen azaleas vary widely from type to type in their tolerance of heat. The hardier Kurume and Kaempferi hybrids are better suited to outdoor growing in cooler climates, while the Indica hybrids, developed initially for indoor use in the northern hemisphere, can thrive even in subtropical gardens as close to the tropics as humidity will allow.

Vireyas could be seen as perhaps the most versatile of all rhododendrons. As well as making excellent greenhouse specimens in cooler climates, they can be planted in the garden anywhere they can be protected from frost.

Tolerance of sunlight

The ability of rhododendrons to tolerate direct sunlight varies widely, depending on the species or hybrid and the local climatic conditions. In the wild, species are found that are rarely touched by the sun, growing as understorey plants in deep forests. These plants may well still tolerate periods of sunlight, and their growth will tend to be more compact as the need to reach out to the light is reduced.

Other species naturally inhabit open situations, exposed relentlessly to the elements. There is a general, although by no means inflexible, rule that the larger the leaf size, the more intolerant of sunlight the species or hybrid will be. The effects of the sun are lessened at higher altitudes as temperatures reduce, so that the same plants can be grown in more open and exposed positions in these areas than is possible closer to sea level.

Where there is doubt as to the vulnerability of plants to sunlight, restricting exposure to mid-to-late morning sunlight is advisable, or providing plants with dappled or partial shade, particularly in warmer areas. In cooler areas with the likelihood of frost or heavy dews, plants should be allowed to warm and dry out as gently as possible, so they should be sited and sheltered to avoid the dawn winter sun.

Sun-tolerant rhododendrons

Species
degronianum
  ssp. yakushimanum
maddenii
ovatum
ponticum
rupicola
scintillans
spiciferum
virgatum
webstrianum
yunnanense
falconeri
griersonianum
nuttallii
pemakoense
pseudochrysanthum
russatum
scopulorum
tephropeplum
wallichii
wightii

Small hybrids
'Augfast'
'Blue Tit'
'Dora Amateis'
'Fred Hamilton'
'Margaret Mack'
'Myrtifolium'
'Olinda Bells'
'Princess Alice'
'Rose Elf'
'Sir Robert Menzies'
'Sonata'

'Blitz'
'Cary Ann'
'Elizabeth'
'Jingle Bells'
'Moonstone'
'Oceanlake'
'Patty Bee'
'Ramapo'
'Scarlet Wonder'
'Snow Lady'
'White Flare'

Medium hybrids
'Abby Boulter'
'Arthur J. Ivens'
'Australian Rainbow'
'Blue Diamond'
'Blue Peter'
'Butterfly'
'Christmas Cheer'
'Dame Pattie Menzies'
'Diane Titcomb'
'Emasculum'
'Freckle Pink'
'Helene Schiffner'
'Jean Marie de Montague'

'Anah Kruschke'
'Aunt Martha'
'Belle Heller'
'Blue Jay'
'Bonfire'
'Caramel Coffee'
'Corinne Boulter'
'David Gable'
'Elizabeth Titcomb'
'Fire Prince'
'Halfdan Lem'
'Jan Dekens'
'Lady Clementine Mitford'

'Lavender Girl'
'Lord Roberts'
'Mahmoud'
'Markeeta's Prize'
'Mauve Bouquet'
'Mrs E. C. Stirling'
'Nova Zembla'
'P. J. M.'
'Purple Splendour'
'Rocket'
'Ruby F. Bowman'
'Souvenir of W.C. Slocock'
'Trude Webster'
'Vulcan's Flame'
'Yellow Hammer'

Large hybrids
'Alice'
'Antoon van Welie'
'Boddaertianum'
'Cynthia'
'Eleanore'
'Everestianum'
'Ivery's Scarlet'
'Madame Cochet'
'Mrs G. W. Leak'
'Sir Robert Peel'
'Stead's Pink'

Evergreen azaleas
'Alba Magnifica'
'Concinna'
'Elizabeth Lawrence'
'Fielder's White'
'Jean Alexandra'
'Magnifica'
'Pride of Dorking'
'Rose Glitters'
'Waka Kayede'

'Loder's White'
'Madame Doumier'
'Manderley'
'Maryke'
'Mrs A. T. de la Mare'
'Mrs Furnivall'
'Old Port'
'Purple Opal'
'Purpureum Elegans'
'Rubicon'
'Scarlet King'
'Spring Glory'
'Unknown Warrior'
'Winter Beauty'

'Anna Rose Whitney'
'Arthur Bedford'
'Cotton Candy'
'Doctor Arnold W.
  Endtz'
'Fastuosum Flore Pleno'
'Lighthouse'
'Mrs Charles E. Pearson'
'Our Gem'
'Souvenir de Dr. S. Endtz'

'Alphonse Anderson'
'Duc de Rohan'
'Exquisite'
'Glory of Sunninghill'
'Jill Seymour'
'Pink Lace'
'Purple Glitters'
'Splendens'
'White Lace'

3
Rhododendron culture

The right spot

The first step when preparing to plant rhododendrons – or just about any other plant, for that matter – is adequate planning. The value of careful consideration of the planting site in terms of availability of light, proximity to adjacent plants, soil conditions and drainage is often underestimated, but it will pay dividends handsomely with many years of successful growth.

You really only get one chance to provide the ideal conditions for your shrubs. Although rhododendrons will tolerate transplanting better than many garden shrubs, any move resulting from an error of judgement or lack of foresight at planting time will still set a healthy plant back for a season or two. The extent of this setback will also increase with the age of the plant and therefore, if a mistake is feared, it is wise to move earlier rather than wait in doubt.

What is needed is an appreciation of the rhododendron's requirements with regard to soil structure and drainage in particular and an assessment of the amount of effort required to bring your own garden soil into line with these needs.

Soil

To understand the soil conditions needed to grow rhododendrons successfully, one needs to look at the way they grow in the wild. Most species occur in a habitat that is protected and shaded beneath a canopy of foliage in misty woodlands or forests in areas of high rainfall and humidity. Here they are growing on relatively thin layers of mountain soil covered by a deep and permanent mulch of decaying leaves and twigs. These are conditions where moisture is abundant and nutrients are available in regular supply close to the surface only. The mulch not only includes decaying plant material, but the droppings and corpses of all manner of forest wildlife, slowly rotting into a rich feast of nutrients. Some species are in fact epiphytic, germinating and seeking their nutrients in pockets of moss or mulch that collect in tree branches or rocky crevices, requiring no true 'soil' at all. Some moisture from the rain and mist is taken up by the leaves, and vital nutrients are derived from water that has collected minerals and organic solutions as it passes over rocks and through the surrounding mulch and gravel.

Rhododendrons and other members of the Ericaceae family have adapted to these conditions by evolving a thick, dense mass of fine roots that spread out into the surface mulch and whatever topsoil there is rather than searching deeper for moisture and nutrients. This root system also provides great structural strength, having an effect similar to the reinforcing of concrete or fibreglass, and enables many varieties to stand up surprisingly well to the strong winds often found in their original mountainous habitats.

To the home gardener this should indicate that any soil in which rhododendrons are to be grown should be capable of providing a continual and plentiful supply of water. This moisture needs to be available in combination with air, otherwise waterlogging – a frequent cause of rhododendron failure – may occur. To achieve this the soil therefore needs to be very open in its structure, fibrous and very well draining, and with a very high content of organic matter.

Once planted, the rhododendron will resent any disturbance to its roots, which should be free to spread out into soil that remains undisturbed. It is then too late to attempt to alter the soil's structure, other than with mulches applied to the surface to percolate downwards through the activities of earthworms, fungi and the other organisms that transform organic matter into new soil.

Stubborn soils

Soils containing a high proportion of clay pose the greatest difficulty for the rhododendron grower. Although clay soils are normally high in valuable mineral content, their dense structure results in a lack of air spaces between the soil particles. This restricts the activity of vital microorganisms that interact with the roots, and reduces their ability to spread out and take up nutrients. Clay soils also tend to absorb and hold water rather than allow the free drainage these plants demand.

Clay can often turn up unexpectedly in patches of otherwise useful soil, having been brought to the surface during earlier excavations for building, landscaping or installation of drains.

All is not lost, however, if you have a high clay content in your soil and are still determined to grow rhododendrons. There are a number of ways that the structure can be opened up to improve the drainage and availability of air to the roots. A traditional method is the application of gypsum, which makes the soil particles congregate into larger 'crumbs'. Calcium, including various forms of lime, is a useful soil conditioner as well as an essential element. Gypsum, or calcium sulphate, makes the soils more friable while having little effect of making the soil more alkaline as applying lime would. Commercially prepared kelp-based 'claybreakers' act in a similar manner to gypsum and should not affect the pH balance. They can be convenient for the home gardener, requiring simply to be diluted in a watering can and applied to the soil surface.

Such treatments are not a permanent solution on their own, but can be made more effective by following the applications with a large amount of decayed or partially composted organic material dug well into the soil. A small proportion of coarse sand can be added as a lasting inert aid to opening the soil structure.

Drainage can be greatly assisted by installing subsoil drains, an operation which should be undertaken before planting. A trench is dug to a depth of about 30 cm. Coarse gravel is placed at the bottom of the trench and flexible black polythene drainage pipes with fine slots along their corrugated sides, are laid with a further layer of gravel on top. The pipes can be wrapped in weed restricting matting to reduce the likelihood of the drains slowly filling up with silt or being invaded and choked by foraging roots.

Another option is to raise the planting site by using a technique known as 'mound planting'. This technique also aids in protection against frost, because cold air tends to flow downwards, off the mound and away from the plant. A gently rounded hill of a good quality garden loam is mounded up over the existing soil surface to a height of at least 30 cm, or at least deep enough to ensure the base of the new plant's root ball is above the level of surrounding soil. The soil beneath the mound must be dug over and mixed with the new soil to allow a gentle transition from one soil type to another. Do not be tempted to dig out a planting area in dense soil and fill it with a more open soil – this will serve to create a dam, leading to the risk of waterlogging. Most landscaping suppliers can offer a selection of soils, sometimes already mixed with compost or other organic matter.

Siting plants on sloping ground rather than on flat areas will also provide better drainage. The principal consideration is that while a high moisture content is required by rhododendrons, this water, either from rainfall or irrigation, should be constantly replenished rather than being able to lie, and the soil structure or planting technique should allow that to occur.

Acidity and alkalinity

Garden soils and their underlying subsoils or rock vary widely in their dissolved chemical and mineral content. The availability of these chemicals and the ability of individual plants to take them up and use them as nutrients is closely linked to the acidity or alkalinity of the soil. The level of alkalinity in any soil is expressed in numbers ranging from 0 to 14, known as the 'pH' scale. The term pH stands for pressure of hydrogen and is an indication of the pressure of hydrogen ions in any given soil sample. As this pressure increases, the more alkaline the dissolved chemicals become, resulting in a less acidic soil.

A reading of pH 7 is considered 'neutral'. The pH levels of soils in any country will vary as widely from area to area as will their other properties such as structure and drainage. It is rare to find soils where acidity or alkalinity is so far removed from the neutral that successful gardening is restricted. Many plant groups, however, require a higher or lower level of acidity than may be naturally found and it is common garden practice to adjust the pH level accordingly.

Rhododendrons and other members of the Ericaceae family are best suited to acidic soils with pH readings of between 4.5 and 5.5. Members of the onion tribe and a number of other vegetables, for example, are best suited to a more alkaline soil of around pH 8 for optimum growth.

When the pH level of a growing medium falls outside the optimum range for any plant, essential elements start to become less accessible and growth suffers. In the case of rhododendrons, a pH level of above 6 or 6.5, for example, starts to inhibit the availability of iron, and at levels of below 4.5 copper becomes less soluble.

Although specialists can be contracted to undertake a detailed soil analysis, this expense is really unnecessary for home gardeners unless severe difficulties are encountered. An inexpensive soil pH test kit makes a valuable long-term investment. In the simplest form, a small sample of soil is mixed with water, then sprinkled with a white powder. A few drops of an indicating solution will change this powder into a colour indicating its specific pH level as matched against a sample card. Distilled water is best as tap water is likely to affect the reading with its own pH, which may be well removed from neutral. Several samples should be taken from various parts of the garden as the pH level can vary somewhat, even over a small area. Battery-operated pH meters are a convenient, though more expensive option, but they are not necessarily any more accurate than the test kits. Once a reasonable idea of the average pH level has been determined, an appropriate course of action can be taken to provide the ideal pH level of between 4.5 and 5.5.

Maintaining a supply of organic matter is the most advisable long-term solution. Compost and other decayed organic matter tend naturally to be acidic, although this will vary according to the nature of the material being applied or composted. After planting, continual application of organic mulch will help maintain a satisfactory pH level.

A shorter-term solution is the application of copper or ferrous sulphate or iron chelates. The yellowing of evergreen azalea leaves, known as 'lime-induced chlorosis', is a particularly good indicator of an iron deficiency caused by the restricted availability of iron, usually as a result of the soil being too alkaline. The plants are equally quick to respond to dilute applications of ferrous sulphate, which provide short-term relief, or iron chelates, which tend to have a longer-term effect.

However, any soil that is inherently alkaline, or has a predominantly alkaline subsoil, will tend to revert to that state over time. If a satisfactory pH level cannot be maintained by organic means, a chemical solution to the problem is one that will have to be monitored regularly and repeated as required.

Mound planting again provides an answer for obviously alkaline soils. The soil level is raised with soil known to be less alkaline – a reasonably permanent answer if the mound is built deeply enough, as the chemicals causing the excess tend not to leach upwards.

A final option if the soil seems to be impossibly alkaline is to grow rhododendrons in containers, where the growing medium is totally under the grower's control. Fortunately rhododendrons can thrive in containers for many years if good conditions are provided, and this may be the last resort for growers stuck with a very heavy clay.

A factor to be seriously considered in some areas is the pH level of the reticulated water supply. Many growers face the prospect of 'hard' or particularly alkaline water and may already be adding water 'softeners' to the weekly washing. While there are stories of growers adding nitric or other acids to the water applied to their rhododendrons, this potentially hazardous approach is not to be recommended lightly. In such areas the ideal solution is to arrange an independent source of water, such as a small dam or tank to collect rainwater from the roof. Such dams should preferably have a plastic liner to avoid absorption of alkalinity from the surrounding soil. If a water supply from pH 5.5 to neutral is not possible, greater attention will be required to the regular application of pH adjusting chemicals and organic matter to the soil.

Humus and organic matter

The soils that rhododendrons naturally grow in are created by the constant breakdown of leaves and other organic matter falling to the forest floor. This material provides a rich source of nutrients and enables the soil to retain moisture well, while providing good drainage at the same time. To imitate these qualities, as much organic matter as possible should be worked into the soil before planting.

This material could be just about anything that is available, so long as it is well decomposed or composted. Fresh, undecayed material should only be applied as a surface mulch. Composts of all kinds, rotted garden shreddings and milder animal manures, such as cow, horse or sheep droppings, thoroughly broken down and free of weed seeds, are all ideal. There is also value in digging in fairly inert materials such as rice hulls, shredded coconut husks and well-rotted shredded bark, to improve the overall texture of the soil before planting. Peat moss was once widely used for soil conditioning, but it is a dwindling resource rising in cost and its use should be reserved for potting and propagating mixes.

Mulching

The soil in the hill and mountain regions that are usually the natural habitat of the rhododendron is normally contained in shallow pockets on a rock substrata or very poor, gravelly soil. Most of the nutrients in these soils are found only in the top few centimetres, and generated mostly by the continuing addition of leaf mulch from plants occupying the site. Rhododendrons have developed their root systems specifically to cope with extracting those nutrients as efficiently as possible.

An understanding of the role of mulching is critical to the successful cultivation of rhododendrons. This is especially so in climates with hot, dry summers, that are otherwise marginal for the success of rhododendrons. In such areas, the regular application of a deep mulch could mean the difference between enjoying these plants or abandoning hope.

The practice of applying a mulch around garden shrubs offers many benefits. A mulch helps retain the constant moisture level that rhododendrons need around their roots. Gardeners enjoying otherwise ideal growing conditions need only apply additional water during dangerously dry spells, and it will be held for far longer in the soil than would be the case without a mulch. A good layer of mulch also helps to maintain lower soil temperatures, closer to those of the original habitat. All of the ericaceous plants prefer a cool root run.

In cold climates, a converse benefit applies, as a mulch can slow the freezing of winter soils and assist them to retain the little warmth they can capture from the sunlight.

A mulch should be deep enough to suppress most weed growth, thereby dramatically reducing the regular maintenance required. Those weeds that inevitably do germinate and emerge are easily removed from a loose mulch by hand, a pleasant enough task as one browses in the garden. On a larger scale, a careful 'spot' spraying on a calm dry day with a general-purpose herbicide such as glyphosate should be sufficient to keep adventitious invaders at bay. Only those weeds impossible to spray without also affecting the specimen plant need then to be pulled by hand. The sprayed weeds can be allowed to die and join the mulch, the root systems decaying to leave tunnels which provide extra drainage in the soil. What must be avoided, considering the close proximity of the root system to the soil surface – ultimately into the mulch itself – is heavy cultivation, such as deep forking. Once a plant is established and its root system is spreading, the soil and mulch must remain as undisturbed as possible, other than by periodic replenishment of the mulch with new material.

A wide range of organic materials is suitable for mulching, and to some extent the final choice can be dictated by whatever is economically available locally, either as a by-product of local agricultural activity, or from the recycling of organic garden and household wastes.

An obvious option is to emulate the natural mulch created by the falling leaves of the plant itself, and a mature rhododendron does become self-mulching over time in this manner. Any decayed leaf matter, particularly that from deciduous trees and other ornamentals, can make a suitable mulch. Tough drought-resistant plants, such as eucalypts and acacias from Australia and South Africa, have adapted to growing on poor soils and the mulches created from their leaves will contain less nutrient matter, and take longer to break down. Their use in mulching will still help to improve soil structure, suppress weeds and regulate temperature and moisture.

Garden centres and landscaping suppliers offer a range of materials prepared specifically for mulching. The bark and timber of a wide range of trees resulting from sawmilling operations is probably the most widely used, and this should be allowed to decompose somewhat before being placed on the garden. Chipped or shredded timber is slow to break down when compared to more nutritious mulches containing plenty of leaf matter, but consequently requires less frequent replenishment, and draws little nitrogen from the soil as it decays. Byproducts of other agricultural industries, such as rice hulls and shredded coconut fibre are gaining popularity as renewable soil conditioners and mulches, over more traditional materials such as peat moss which is expensive and non-renewable. Crushed marble, fine bluestone screenings or scoria are all useful as fine, compact mulches for the rock garden.

Garden or kitchen waste that is too fresh and is applied too thickly as a mulch will have the opposite effect of that desired, depleting the soil of valuable nitrogen as decomposition takes place, and this loss should be compensated for when fertilising. Grass clippings and sawdust should only be applied in a very thin layer, otherwise an impenetrable, anaerobic and possibly deadly mass will be the result. However, after being turned regularly, mixed with other materials and allowed to compost before application, all manner of vegetable waste can become a component of a very effective mulch. And there is certainly no harm in loosely scattering tea leaves or other kitchen scraps over the garden to join the mulch.

The optimum depth of any mulch will depend very much on the density of the materials used and the amount of protection the soil needs. Shaded areas, for example, will need less mulching than exposed spots. If the mulch is sufficiently deep, the soil immediately below it should feel cool and moist several warm days after rain or a good, deep watering. A minimum depth of between 5 and 10 cm should be adequate for most organic materials, depending on their density, while fine gravel or scoria mulches should be laid at least 2.5 cm deep.

Planting

While any plant can be added to the garden at just about any time of the year, there are times that are better than others. Local climate also has a big influence on choosing the ideal planting time. Both evergreen and deciduous plants will be least disturbed by planting them when their growth is at its slowest, normally in midwinter, although there is also a strong argument for planting in autumn so that the plant is settled in well before winter, particularly in cooler areas. Deciduous rhododendrons are often marketed in containers, enabling growers to buy plants in bloom, rather than bare-rooted as is the case with other deciduous plants. Planting can take place at other times of the year, but greater care will be needed in warmer weather to maintain a good water supply and minimise transplant shock.

Ideally, you should choose a forecast period of several calm, overcast, perhaps drizzly or misty days, and try to plant early or late in the day. Avoid planting in hot or windy weather when moisture loss from the leaves through transpiration will be at its greatest. It's also wise to avoid planting when frosts may be expected. If good weather cannot be guaranteed, it is far better to keep the plant in its container, watered and fed, until conditions improve.

The act of planting is simplicity itself, once the soil structure and pH are known to be satisfactory. Just dig a hole a little larger than the original container, drop the plant in and backfill with the surrounding soil. Take care not to plant too deeply – the surface of the original mix should still be just visible before applying the mulch. If anything, the plant may benefit by being positioned slightly above the surrounding surface, but definitely not below. The potted plant and the soil into which it is to go should be thoroughly watered some hours before planting, and the soil mulched straight after to retain that moisture. Any fertiliser used at the planting stage should only be applied as a top dressing. Many growers prefer not to fertilise at this time, but to allow the plant to become accustomed to its new home before applying any fertilisers. Water the plant well again after planting, stand back and wait.

Watering

Much of the water taken up by the roots of a plant is lost through its foliage during the process of transpiration in which plant sheds water excess to its needs. It is vital when growing plants like rhododendrons that they should never dry out and that a reliable supply of moisture is available to the plant at all times. Otherwise the uptake of carbon dioxide, and thence the process of photosynthesis through which the plant manufactures its own food supply in the form of starches and sugars, is reduced. The growth of the plant will be retarded and full recovery may be slow.

In areas where drought is encountered at some time, the rhododendron is one plant that will certainly encounter difficulties. The grower needs to anticipate periods of dry weather and ensure that sufficient water is available to carry the plant through the spell. An adequate moisture supply can also minimise the likelihood of sunburn, particularly to new growth or current season's leaves. At greatest risk are recent transplants or younger plants in their first few years. Particular attention should also be paid to ensuring that moisture levels are maintained during flowering and the following period of vegetative growth.

Plants that just manage to survive the soil drying out may take several years to recover fully, quite a setback to plants already slow to establish themselves and reach a good size and form. It will therefore be worthwhile to pay particular attention to the watering of younger plants, taking care to water the entire area of potential root spread. Older, established plants with larger root systems will be better able to cope with some drying out and partial root loss.

Satisfying the water requirements of any plant goes hand in hand with providing the right soil structure and consequently drainage, and the sensible application of mulches that will greatly assist the soil in retaining available and applied moisture. Some soils, particularly those with a high organic content, may pose difficulties in re-establishment of moisture levels. This difficulty can be demonstrated by attempting to moisten a quantity of dry peat moss, one of the more common soil and potting mix additives used to assist water retention. The dry peat moss appears to virtually repel water applied to it. Proprietary wetting agents can be applied to the soil or mix to restore its ability to hold water.

Watering rhododendrons involves a level of common sense that should be applied to the irrigation of all garden shrubs. Watering in the early mornings or at dusk – times when evaporation rates will be lower – is better, particularly during warm weather, than watering in the heat of the day.

Deep, infrequent watering should be the rule. Wandering around daily, spraying water about with a hose as a knee-jerk reaction to sudden hot spells, will be of little value. Although some water is absorbed by the foliage, water needs to be applied to the soil to soak in well and deeply and not just moisten the first few centimetres of the mulch. In hot, fine weather, heavy overnight dews can provide some relief to drying plants.

In climates where providing enough water is a continuing headache, it makes great sense to install a permanent irrigation system. These days gardeners can take advantage of micro-irrigation systems developed originally by resourceful Israeli horticulturists determined to make their arid land green and productive with a limited water supply. The most efficient delivery of water is achieved using a system of drippers, one or two per plant, which can also be connected to an automatic timer to operate solenoid valves. Such a system is particularly valuable when the garden is likely to be unattended for periods. Some earlier timer models were operated by photoelectric cells and could be set to operate for predetermined periods at either dawn or dusk. Most systems these days, however, are controlled by a computer chip and can be quite sophisticated in their flexibility, delivering water in sequence over several lines for larger gardens, and with great control over timing and duration to provide watering regimens tailored exactly to the needs of any type of planting.

Drippers on thin, flexible lines are particularly useful for watering plants growing in containers and hanging baskets, susceptible as these are to damage through water loss. Micro-irrigation fittings are readily available from hardware stores and garden centres, which can also supply brochures with adequate instructions on planning and installing a system.

Fertilising

Fertilising can never be an exact process, but we can at least try to ensure that sufficient nutrients are available to plants, not just to sustain them, but for them to grow perhaps more vigorously than they would in the wild, and in such good health that they are able to withstand the external hazards they might have to face in their new environment. At the same time, an over-enthusiastic quest for healthy, vigorous growth can lead to serious problems if too much fertiliser is applied and in garden soils these nutrients should already be present in varying quantities.

As well as all the other botanical variations that make each species distinctive, plants have evolved root systems that accommodate the specific soil conditions of their natural habitats that will not be the same as the typical garden soil. Each different species of plant needs to be able to feed on its own particular menu of nutrients and minerals for healthy growth.

Any garden soil will already contain most, if not all, of the nutrients required. What we are trying to do when we fertilise plants is bridge the gap between the amount of each nutrient that is already present in the soil and the amount that is desirable for the optimum growth rate that we seek in any plant that we grow.

There are three major plant foods that are needed by all plants in varying quantities: nitrogen (N), phosphorus (P) and potassium (K). The proportions of these nutrients available in any fertiliser are expressed as the N:P:K ratio. A commercially prepared fertiliser should list on its packaging a ratio such as '9:4:6', which is an indication of the relative proportions of these three main nutrients. This ratio is guide to the suitability of any fertiliser for a particular application. The packaging should also list, if they are present, the proportions of the 'lesser' nutrients – calcium (Ca), magnesium (Mg) and sulphur (S) – as well as the trace elements iron (Fe), manganese (Mn), copper (Cu), zinc (Zn), boron (B), molybdenum (Mo) and chlorine (Cl).

Nitrogen promotes vegetative growth, and a high proportion should be available, for instance, to leafy vegetables, where vigorous vegetative growth is required. Phosphorus is vital for photosynthesis and the protein production which results in new cell growth. Many plants in warm, drought-affected climates such as those of Australia and South Africa, have adapted themselves to impoverished soils which are low in phosphorous, which in many cases can be quite harmful to them if too much is available. Growers in such areas can compensate in regular feeding programs for such a deficiency.

Potassium is used by plants to aid in chemical reactions, circulation of water and disease protection. Calcium is essential for cell division and, although rhododendrons prefer an acid soil, they still have a high calcium need. This can be either added to compost or applied as a top-dressing around the plant in the form of calcium sulphate (gypsum) – which also aids the soil structure – or as calcium phosphate. Both forms have only a minimal effect on the pH level. Magnesium is a component of chlorophyll and is therefore essential for photosynthesis. Sulphur is another element essential for the production of protein. Although the trace elements are absolutely essential for plant growth, they are only required in tiny quantities.

Observation of plants already growing in an area should give some indication of the level of pre-existing nutrients, and be some guide to the amount of additional fertilising that may be required. The availability of these nutrients to plants is critically linked to the soil pH, which is the first thing to get right before worrying about whether they are lacking or not. In suitable growing conditions (good soil structure, mulching, and adequate drainage), little attention need be given to the fertilising of rhododendrons, other than through routine applications of general-purpose fertilisers recommended for use on ornamental trees and shrubs.

Some fertiliser may be dug into the surrounding soil at planting time, but only if the soil is known to be deficient. Particular care should be taken to avoid bringing any fertiliser, particularly of 'synthetic' or 'chemical' origin, into direct contact with the root system of the plant. It is generally wiser to plant without fertilising, and commence a routine of feeding by top-dressing as the plant establishes itself. The compact root system of the rhododendron means that roots take up their nutrients from a smaller volume of soil than is the case with many more vigorous plants. There is little benefit in applying fertiliser beyond the spread of the plant's foliage.

It may often be sufficient to top up the mulch around established plants with an annual dressing of composted organic matter. However, any mulching material is bound to be lacking in some of the nutrients, and while it is decomposing it will draw some nitrogen from the soil, so a light annual top-dressing of a balanced slow-release fertiliser is beneficial. Rhododendrons take up and store much of their nutrient requirements over winter so that they are available for bud formation, flowering and leaf growth in the spring. For this reason, some growers consider an annual fertiliser application is best made in autumn.

Formulations that contain only a selection of lesser and trace elements are also marketed, and these may be applied in addition to basic N:P:K preparations or in combination with organic applications if it is felt these elements may be lacking in the soil, mulch or the primary fertiliser used.

Plants are unable to distinguish between chemicals derived from organic and so-called 'synthetic' sources and the choice between the two types of fertiliser therefore becomes largely philosophical. It is most unlikely that excessive amounts of organic fertilisers will cause harm, while over-enthusiastic application of chemical fertilisers can result in burning back of sensitive feeder roots, inviting disease in the short term, and the build-up of excess salts in the soil in the long run. Suitable organic fertilisers can include fish, bonemeal, a wide variety of composted animal manures, fish emulsion, and domestic composts.

Possibly the most efficient means of fertiliser application these days results from the development of slow-release fertilisers, tiny pellets of fertiliser whose thin degradable plastic coating regulates the release of fertiliser systematically over a predetermined period. Depending on the formulation chosen, an application may last from three to ten months. Plants are able to take up virtually all the nutrients available to them that they need from the soil over an extended period. The leaching that occurs when conventional fertilisers are used is minimised, the dosage can be accurately controlled, and the risk of excessive salt levels is reduced. As with any fertiliser, however, correct application rates must be followed. The nutrient needs of rhododendrons are lower than those of many more vigorously growing plants, so that, if they are used in combination with organic mulches, slow-release fertilisers may be used at rates below the recommendations suggested by the manufacturer for general garden application. This reduction in application rates also accommodates ambient levels of nutrients in the soil.

A wide range of slow-release pellet formulations is now available, each one for a specific purpose. Some only contain the major nutrients – nitrogen, potassium and phosphorus – while others include a complete formulation of lesser and trace elements, a better choice if there is doubt as to whether these elements are adequately available in the soil or from other sources. For rhododendrons planted in normal garden situations, a general-purpose nine-month or ten-month formulation should be applied in autumn through to early spring, and certainly before flower buds begin swelling to open. There are also specific formulations for plants growing in containers, where it is particularly vital that trace elements be included in the fertilising program.

Fertilisers should not be dug in but applied to a mulch to gently percolate into the soil. This will avoid any unnecessary disturbance to the fine roots close to the surface and reduce any risk of fertiliser burn.

Pruning

While rhododendrons do not require an annual pruning ritual in the manner of some ornamental shrubs such as roses, some pruning can be useful to help plants develop the compact form desired for home gardens. Pruning will be necessary from time to time to remove any damaged or diseased growth. 'Deadheading' is a common practice that entails the removal of spent flowers to encourage stronger leaf growth. Rhododendrons growing in typical garden conditions should develop into a naturally balanced and pleasing form without pruning. This assumes that care has been taken by the gardener to provide a good soil structure, ample nutrition and drainage, and that the plant is well sited to receive sufficient light for the variety grown. In their natural environment – more often than not beneath a forest canopy that may shade the plants more than would occur in cultivation – plants tend to be leggy and thin as they strive to reach the limited light. A typical garden plant is likely to have a more open aspect and more compact growth is likely to occur.

It would be a shame not to enjoy such splendid flowers inside, and taking the flowers from rhododendrons for this purpose encourages the new leaf growth that follows flowering. The stem should be just above a leaf node as any excess stem left behind will die back, encouraging the entry of harmful fungi. Cut branches back to a whorl of leaves from which new shoots will arise. Generally, any pruning is best undertaken in early spring or immediately after flowering, before new leaf buds move into growth.

Some varieties of rhododendron are less responsive to pruning than others, but all will suffer some damage well and tolerate the levels of pruning normally required. Many will respond well, shooting away vigorously from latent buds after pruning or dead-heading, resulting in a denser, bushier form. Smooth, peeling bark on some species and their hybrids can indicate slower regrowth or no shooting at all after pruning. As a general rule, avoid unnecessarily removing too much leaf or shoot material from any one point which may cause that portion of the plant to lose vigour and die back.

Tidying up of dead or damaged material can be undertaken at any time and it is wise to routinely check all plants: wounds can be a point of fungal invasion. Large, older plants tend to carry masses of straggly dead branches beneath an outer shell of leaves, and weak shoots that don't make it to the light that should be thinned out regularly. Hollowing out these old plants will reveal beautiful gnarled and twisting trunks of the main branches, and expose new microenvironments for underplanting with shade-loving companions or smaller rhododendron varieties, including azaleas, where there is sufficient light.

An additional benefit of this tidying will be the discovery of older branches that have been held down by the weight of their own leaves in the deep leaf mulch which naturally develops underneath the shrubs. Roots can develop at the point of contact with the mulch and new shoots arise from the stem. Carefully removed with as much root material as possible and some of the original mulch, these can be potted or replanted. This naturally occurring form of reproduction is known as 'layering'. It can easily be encouraged to occur by tying low branches down, and is perhaps the easiest way of reproducing rhododendrons in the home garden.

Vireya rhododendrons can be treated in much the same manner as their cooler-climate relatives. Azaleas, particularly the evergreens, can be pruned more ruthlessly and, once they reach a reasonable size, many of the more vigorous varieties will demand an annual cutting back to keep them manageable. This pruning need not be restricted just to leaf growth. New plants can shoot from vigorous roots close to the surface, and these roots may well need to be cut back regularly. Deciduous rhododendrons should be treated as any other deciduous plant and are safest pruned, if at all, in winter when they are leafless.

Deadheading

Probably the most frequent pruning carried out on rhododendrons is the practice known as 'dead-heading', which is simply the removal of spent flowers. This is not just undertaken for the cosmetic reason of removing unattractive dying flowers, but is also meant to divert the energy the plant would otherwise expend on developing seeds into improved leaf growth and flower formation for the following season. Often several young shoots will be visible emerging around each flower head by the time the flowers are dying off, and removing the old blooms will encourage these to grow more vigorously.

When the flowers are ready for removal, the swelling ovary beneath the bloom should snap off cleanly with just a gentle twist, when held between the thumb and forefinger. Take great care not to disturb the new leaf shoots. If the flowers seem difficult to remove, leave the job for a few days until they snap off more easily.

Deadheading is of the greatest value in assisting young plants to achieve a good dense form. The size and number of plants will probably dictate the amount of deadheading that can be undertaken. Older shrubs will simply become too large to be thoroughly deadheaded, by which time the practice would be of little value anyway.

4
Good neighbours

It is understandable for a gardener to become obsessed with a favourite genus, and while every plant type may have its band of true believers, we should try to avoid a monoculture mentality that limits the specialist's garden to endless variations of the same plant. This may be exciting for the enthusiast, but less so for passers-by and casual visitors. A successful garden needs variety and contrast.

For much of the year, once rhododendrons have completed their flowering, foliage is all that is to be seen. Having achieved some variation of texture, form and colour in the foliage of our chosen rhododendrons, we should look beyond them to a range of other plants to provide further contrasts. These companions can be as transient as bulbs or perennials, or permanent specimen shrubs that flower at different times from the rhododendrons.

Most, though by no means all, rhododendron species are found as shrubs growing in various levels of shade cast by larger trees. To create a similar woodland atmosphere and the right amount of shade, we need to select a framework of suitable trees as a backdrop. For most rhododendron plantings, deciduous trees are preferable – where they can be grown – as they allow winter sunlight to warm the beds, while lightly protecting them from the summer sun. A canopy of evergreens, particularly large conifers, can often be too dense, reducing flowering and forcing plants to become leggy in the search for more light.

Purple foliage seems to work well with the dark green shades of rhododendrons. Japanese maples, smoke bushes (*Cotinus* spp.), the purple filbert (*Corylus maxima* 'Purpurea') and various *Prunus* varieties can provide such colour. The autumn foliage of many deciduous species provides a display of colour when the rest of the garden is subdued. Particularly useful in this respect are the popular liquidambar, the smaller *Nyssa sylvatica*, and most of the maples and oaks.

More often than not, rhododendrons dwell in the misty humidity of mountain rainforests, and including in our plans other plants that enjoy similar conditions will help to create a natural feeling of plants growing with mutual intent

and need. This approach also allows a uniform cultivation regimen to be applied throughout the garden, rather than attempting to accommodate the clashing soil, irrigation or feeding demands of widely different plants. Similarly, rhododendron species and their cultivars originating from exposed sites can enjoy an open rockery position with a cool, acidic root run, and there are many plants that can share such a site with ease.

The first plants to consider are other members of the family Ericaceae, such as heathers, ericas, arbutus, kalmias, enkianthus and pieris, which share many similar needs to rhododendrons for their successful growth. Next to be considered are those plants from other families that will thrive in the same conditions as rhododendrons we are choosing and look 'at home' with or complement them, such as camellias, daphne and magnolias. Finally, consider aesthetic compatibility in terms of contrasting or complementary foliage, and flowering time and colour.

The following plants are suggested as suitable companion plants for the rhododendron, but the list is by no means intended as definitive nor exclusive.

Trees

Acer Many of the maples are useful as structural elements in a rhododendron garden. Cultivars of the Japanese maple, *A. palmatum*, offer a variety of leaf shapes, often delicate and deeply lobed, with many deep purple varieties such as 'Atropurpureum' or 'Crimson King', in a wide range of habits from prostrate to small, delicately branching trees.

Random seedlings of *A. palmatum* are much cheaper than their grafted and named counterparts, and always desirable in form and colouring, if a bit unpredictable. Most I have tried have grown into open, slowly growing, medium-size trees with light green foliage that still manages a spectacular display of colour in autumn. Once the leaves are gone, the winter skeletons of Japanese maples are just as beautiful as the plant in leaf, making a perfect foil for the earliest spring-flowering rhododendrons. They are really 'at home' with azaleas and the two in combination are inseparable components of the traditional Japanese garden.

The box elder, *A. negundo*, and the Norway maple, *A. platanoides*, are among the many larger maples that are useful for their background structure and autumn colour. Members of the Ericaceae family, these delightful small evergreen trees have foliage which is not unlike that of the rhododendron and delicate panicles of white, cream or pink bell-shaped flowers similar to those of the closely related *Pieris* genus. These are followed by clusters of the distinctive red or orange berries that give the genus its common name of strawberry tree. Some, such as *Arbutus canariensis* and *A. glandulosis* are worth growing just for the sensuous bark of their twisting, contorted trunks, peeling and fading each year from green to a colour and texture reminiscent of soft, suntanned human skin.

Betula The sturdy, reliable, quick-growing and ever-popular silver birch, *B. pendula*, along with its weeping (*B. pendula* 'Youngii') and cut-leaved (*B. pendula* 'Dalecarlica') forms, is deservedly one of the most popular of garden trees, providing dappled shade ideal for rhododendrons and lovely textured white bark. Its popularity should not discourage its use and it looks best planted in drifting, casual groups, rather than as single trees, to create a woodland effect. Lower branches can be cut away as growth progresses to provide space for understorey shrub planting.

The Himalayan birch, *B. utilis*, and the variety *jacquemontii*, with dazzling white bark, is less wind-hardy than *B. pendula*, coming from protected valleys (rather than exposed mountainsides) of Kashmir and Nepal, where it is a natural companion to rhododendrons.

Conifers The density of foliage and growth habit of many conifers limit their value as providers of an overhead canopy. However, they can be most useful trees for background planting and windbreaks. Some more open-growing species may still have a niche in a woodland setting, and a good example of this is the delightful, slow-growing, deciduous maidenhair tree, *Gingko biloba*, with its delicate foliage which turns a strong yellow in autumn.

Embothrium A member of the Proteaceae family and a close South American relative of the Australian waratah (*Telopea*) genus, *E. coccineum lanceolatum* enjoys a woodland setting with similar soil requirements to the rhododendron. It has showy bright red flowers not unlike those of the waratah.

Eucalyptus Rhododendrons and eucalypts are a particularly Australian combination that can be applied anywhere that climate is mild enough to permit both plants to be grown. They seem to do really well together. The deep roots of quick-growing eucalypts make little competitive demand on the surface soil that is the rhododendron's footing and larder, and they provide a perfect, dappled midday shade all year from their elevated canopies. The choices of eucalypt are vast, particularly for the Australian gardener, and good nursery advice should be heeded in selection. They can be vigorous, seemingly unstoppable trees, dangerous in the wrong situation.

Nyssa The deciduous tupelo, *N. sylvatica*, from eastern North America and its smaller Chinese counterpart, *N. sinensis*, look good in clumps rather than alone and are both worth growing if just for their fabulous autumn colour.

Prunus There are countless species and cultivars of *Prunus*, including some with just about the best purple and autumn foliage around and spring blossoms in abundance. Included in the genus are all the ornamental and edible plums, cherries, almonds and apricots. The flowering cherry is the tree that springs to mind when we think of Japan, where it has been cultivated, hybridised and revered for centuries.

Quercus The sort of slowly growing tree that we plant for our grandchildren, oaks over time develop a wonderful open structure, their massive, twisting trunks supporting a light canopy with just the right density of shade for many rhododendrons. Worthy of interest are the American scarlet oak, *Q. coccinea*, for its autumn colour, and the rugged Daimyo oak from Japan, *Q. dentata* and its golden foliaged form *Q. dentata* 'Aurea'.

Shrubs

Boronia These small, short-lived, delicate Australian understorey shrubs have much in common with the erica family, enjoying cool, moist, acidic soils and some protection from wind and harsh sun. The popular brown boronia, *B. megastigma*, and the similar red *B. heterophylla* offer a fragrance probably matched only by the daphnes and their delicate foliage makes a good contrast with the broader leaves of the rhododendrons.

Camellia The evergreen camellias share many of the characteristics and requirements of the rhododendron, and are logical growing companions. They are close rivals of the rhododendron in popularity, with similarly vast numbers of cultivars available. Although they come from the Theaceae family, they enjoy the same conditions as the rhododendron and have a similar history, being popularised during the same nineteenth-century plant-hunting boom.

Camellias flower before most of the rhododendrons and their dense, dark green, glossy foliage complements that of rhododendrons well. But too much of this deeply coloured rich foliage together can be somewhat sombre during the flowerless summer months and some other form of light relief is necessary.

The countless popular cultivars of *C. japonica* prefer moist, well-mulched, organic soils and some protection from direct sunlight and wind. The vigorous *C. sasanqua* cultivars can cope with a more open position and are useful for hedges, background screening and wind protection. Beyond the temptation of the showy cultivars, there are species camellias of various forms that should be grown more. *C. reticulata* grows slowly into an open tree of up to 15 m, and can ultimately provide cover for smaller plants growing underneath.

Others of interest are the compact, fragrant *C. fraterna*, the shrubs *C. tsaii* and *C. vernalis*, and small trees such as the yellow-flowering *C. chrysantha*. The best known of all camellias would have to be the tea plant, *C. sinensis,* less showy than other species, but nonetheless a pleasant enough garden shrub.

Correa Members of this Australian genus of small shrubs, similar in form to some evergreen azaleas, love shade and acidic soil. Their delicate, colourful bell-shaped flowers have understandably given them the common name in Australia of native fuchsia.

Corylus From the same family as the birches, these deciduous shrubs and small trees, particularly *C. maxima* 'Purpurea', offer strong autumn colours and decorative interest even in winter when covered by catkins.

Cotinus This small group of deciduous shrubs and small trees is grown mostly for the fabulous deep purple or red foliage of some varieties such as *C. coggygria* 'Purpureus', 'Royal Purple' and 'Velvet Cloak'. Plumes of feathery, pink to purplish flowers fade to smoke-like drifts which give the genus its common names of smoke bush or smoke tree.

Crowea Closely related to the boronias, and enjoying much the same conditions, *Crowea* is another Australian genus of small shrubs worth considering. Best known is *C. exaltata* with delicate light green foliage and masses of tiny pink star-shaped flowers.

Daphne Most members of the *Daphne* genus are prized for their rich fragrance and will thrive in similar conditions to rhododendrons. The ever-popular winter daphne, *D. odora*, is a compact evergreen shrub with flowers that fill the garden with a rich scent when little else is in bloom. It has luxuriant, rich green foliage that mingles well with rhododendrons, and its variegated form makes a striking accent plant in a shadier corner.

D. bholua, from the Himalayas, has various winter-flowering forms, both deciduous and evergreen, while the fully deciduous *D. mezereum* from Europe makes a spectacular sight in winter when masses of highly fragrant, pink to purple flowers cover its bare branches before the leaves emerge.

Enkianthus These are deciduous small trees and shrubs in the Ericaceae family, the best known being *E. campanulatus*, from Japan. They have clusters of cream to pink bell-shaped flowers in late spring and summer, and autumn leaves of reds and golds.

Fuchsia Tolerating a wide range of growing conditions including shade, and available in a vast range of forms, these popular shrubs makes ideal 'disposable' plants because of their ease of propagation, to act as fillers in the rhododendron garden.

Hamamelis Witch hazels are hardy, cool-climate deciduous shrubs that flower fragrantly in winter on wood left bare after a rich yellow display of autumn foliage has fallen. *Hamamelis mollis* grows to 4 m and makes a useful background behind medium-size rhododendrons.

Hydrangea Rather than the big popular 'mop-top' *H. macrophylla* varieties, look out for some of the lesser-grown species with interesting foliage and more delicate flowers, such as the oakleaf hydrangea (*H. quercifolia*) and the blue-flowering *H. aspera*. *H. serrata* has striking white flowers that turn pink, then finally crimson before fading. *H. villosa* has delicate lavender 'lace-cap' type flowers from late summer into autumn, well after the rhododendron blooms have gone.

Loiseleuria procumbens The alpine or trailing azalea is found in alpine and subarctic regions of North America, Europe and Asia, and is so closely related to the rhododendron that it was once included in the genus, or at least the *Azalea* genus. It is an exceptionally hardy evergreen prostrate that forms mats or mounds of foliage and bears rose-pink flowers at the end of its stems from spring to early summer.

Despite its botanical differences, the loiseleuria's cultivation needs are much the same as for the hardiest of the dwarf alpine rhododendrons – sharply drained yet damp, cool, peaty soil in an open, sunny position – and it makes an ideal rock or alpine garden plant. *Photo p. 105.*

Magnolia As well as some magnificent evergreen trees, the genus *Magnolia* includes fragrant deciduous shrubs and small trees that flower in early spring on a stark framework of twisted bare wood in superb contrast to the dark masses of surrounding rhododendron foliage. *M.* × *soulangeana* has large white tulip-shaped flowers tinged with purple, while the more compact *M. stellata* has white starry flowers. *Photos pp. 34, 123.*

Pieris Also members of the Ericaceae family, these evergreen shrubs enjoy identical conditions to most rhododendrons – at least some shade, and peaty, acidic soils. After a profuse springtime display of typically erica-like bell-shaped flowers that give the genus the common name lily-of-the-valley shrub, the new foliage, usually bronze or red, is a further attraction.

Telopea The botanical name for the waratah translates as 'seen from a distance', describing the glowing red flowers of the shadewellers from wet temperate eucalyptus forests in Australia. *T. speciosissima* is the most commonly grown species, but also worth trying is the smaller Tasmanian *T. truncata*, in red and rarer white forms, and a growing number of cultivars such as 'Shady Lady', 'Cardinal', 'Brimstone Blush' and 'Fire and Brimstone', all shades of red, and 'Wirrimbirra White'.

All thrive as understorey plants in the shade and protection of a warmer climate woodland setting. Care must be taken not to use any fertiliser containing phosphorus, which can mean certain death to most proteaceous plants, and the best policy is usually to not feed them at all.

Viburnum Best known of the viburnums would probably be the deciduous snowball trees (*V. macrocephalum* and *V. plicatum*), the guelder rose (*V. opulus* 'Sterile'), and the tough, evergreen *V. tinus*, which makes an excellent, quick-growing dense hedge for wind protection and screening. However, of particular interest as plants worth interspersing among rhododendrons are some of the smaller deciduous shrubs such as *V. davidii*, *V. carlesii* and *V.* × *burkwoodii*, all with delicate sprays of small, highly fragrant, pink to white flowers against a variety of shades and textures of foliage.

Dwarfs and ground covers

Calluna Tough heathers, including the common Scottish heather, *C. vulgaris*, and its many cultivars, look best massed into large drifts in the foreground of borders where they can catch the sun.

Cornus Dogwoods are best known as small, fairly slow-growing deciduous trees with delightful spring flowers, but the creeping dogwood, *C. canadensis*, is a herbaceous perennial whose rosettes of flat leaves cover the ground tightly with a rich mid-green mat.

Erica The namesake of the Ericaceae family, and thus a close relative of the rhododendron, the 'true' ericas make attractive compact shrubs for the foreground with their delicate, feathery foliage and masses of tiny, pink, purple or white bell-shaped flowers. There are a number of vigorous cultivars of the European winter heath, *E. carnea*, such as 'December Red' and 'Springwood White', which are useful as dense, spreading ground covers.

Ferns Clumps of ferns scattered about will add to the rainforest feeling appropriate to a rhododendron habitat. Look for ferns that are climatically appropriate to the growing area. The tree ferns (*Dicksonia antarctica* and members of the genus *Cyathea*), from the rainforests of Australasia, bring an almost prehistoric feeling to the garden, and a palm-like form which provides strong structural contrast with traditional shrubs.

Hedera Away from its native habitat, common English ivy (*H. helix*) can become disastrously invasive ground cover and climber and should be avoided at all costs. There are a number of other useful ivies that pose much less of a problem, such as the variegated form of the Canary Islands ivy, *H. canariensis*, and cultivars of *H. helix* such as 'Pittsburgh', 'Parsley Crested' and 'Tricolor'.

Annuals and perennials

Ajuga A few strategically placed bugle plants will spread out widely on their runners, growing into a carpet of deep purple foliage and flowers.

Clivia With foliage similar to that of the agapanthus, clivias such as *C. miniata* love the shade of temperate and warmer climates, their orange and yellow trumpet-shaped flowers positively glowing in the shade.

Euphorbia Gardeners in warmer climates will know this genus best as the poinsettia, *Euphorbia pulcherrima*, a shrub that can certainly accompany vireyas well in subtropical and tropical gardens. In cooler zones, however, the distinctive bright yellow-green foliage of some of the hardier perennial species provides a strong contrast to the darker foliage of rhododendrons.

Helleborus This is a genus of clump-forming perennials that simply love shady spots in moist, organically rich soils. They have interesting fleshy foliage in various shades of greens and purples, and large clusters of long-lasting and sometimes fragrant, bell-shaped flowers that can seem to glow in the dark, particularly the pale green *H. lividus* and *H. viridus*.

Hosta Grown for their splendid variety of foliage textures and variegations in shades of blues, greens, yellows and creams, the perennial hostas love moist, shady spots with plenty of protection. They can be dug up each year and divided after dying back in winter, and over the years a few pots will provide many new plants.

Hyacinthoides The Spanish bluebell (*H. hispanica*) and its English counterpart (*H. non-scripta*) are ideal for massed planting under deciduous trees, providing a luxuriant blue carpet in spring.

Meconopsis All but one of the members of this genus of cheerful poppies originate from the Himalayas and the neighbouring mountains of China, and are thus natural companions to many rhododendrons. In cheerful shades of blue, yellow and red, they make useful detail plants scattered about the border areas or nestling among rocks in the alpine garden.

Myosotis You may well end up regretting the day you introduced forget-me-nots, regarded by many as just a weed curse, but they are easily ripped out when they get in the way and look wonderful in broad drifts under deciduous trees. They will prolifically self-seed and invade, but will suppress the 'real' weeds and provide an endless drift of delicate blue – and less often, pink – flowers and ground-hugging bright green foliage.

Narcissus Popular, tough, daffodils look their best when they are planted in clumps and drifts under deciduous trees. Varieties can be chosen to deliver their spring cheer from as early as autumn in milder climates through to late spring. Rather than sticking to the obvious popular choices, some of the smaller-flowered species are worth hunting out, particularly the delicate hoop petticoat daffodil, *N. bulbocodium*, very much at home in the alpine garden, and the delightful *N. cyclamineus* and *N. triandrus* with their unusual reflexed petals.

Viola Violets, rather than the popular pansies (*V. wittrockiana*) and violas (*V. tricolor*) which are grown as annual bedding plants, make wonderful creeping ground-covers to spread around shrubs in shadier spots. The delicate *V. hederacea* from Australia forms a dense creeping mat of light green foliage sprinkled with tiny white or purple flowers in spring. There are many delightful forms of the common or sweet violet, *V. odorata*, which are ideal in part or full shade. Some species, such as the bird's foot violet, *V. pedata*, are particularly suited to acid soils and an open position in an alpine or rock garden setting. *V. labradorica* 'Purpurea' has particularly handsome dark purplish foliage that gives a rich deep glow of colour to shaded areas. Like many violets, it can become invasive under favourable conditions. A sufficient depth of mulch, however, should make removal by hand effortless if it starts to become a nuisance.

The Wardian case, developed by Dr Nathaniel Bagshaw Ward, became an invaluable aid in enabling plants collected overseas to withstand the long sea journeys back to Europe. It was a wooden-sided container with a pitched glass roof, totally sealed other than for a couple of small ventilator grilles.

5
Rhododendrons in containers

The compact rootball of the rhododendron makes it ideal for growing in containers for many years. Containers allow inner urban gardeners with the limited space of a courtyard or even just a balcony, to grow rhododendrons. Container planting also offers a viable alternative for those keen to grow rhododendrons where the garden soil is simply too difficult – for example, if it is a heavy clay or impossibly alkaline. Plants in containers have the added bonus of being portable.

They can be moved in and out of the shade, wind or frost as desired, or to be shown off when flowering. For example, growers of vireya rhododendrons in frost-prone areas can move their treasured specimens under cover when frosts threaten, or into the sunlight when the weather permits.

Although rhododendrons could never be employed as houseplants in the long term, container-grown plants may be brought inside for few days at a time to enjoy their blooms. In fact, many evergreen azaleas have been bred specifically for a brief moment of glory as flowering pot plants.

Selecting containers

Just about any pot of about the right size and shape can be suitable for rhododendrons, so long as adequate drainage holes can be provided. As rhododendrons are so shallow-rooting, containers for them do not need to be as deep as one might provide for other plants, although extra depth will assist the flow of water through the pot and the roots will tend to work down through the mix once they have explored the top layers.

Containers for rhododendrons don't need to be particularly large in proportion to the size of the plant. Shrubs as tall as 2 m can happily thrive in pots no wider than 25 or 30 cm. As the foliage spread of the potted plant can be considerably wider than the pot, look for the squatter, wider sort of pot that will provide as much weight and stability as possible. There's nothing more frustrating than having to resurrect potted plants caught by the wind and blown over, with branches broken off and potting mix and valuable fertiliser spilt in all directions.

Terracotta clay is still one of the most popular materials used for containers. It is an earthy, organic material that always looks better and better as the pot ages. However, it is also a very porous material, and much water is lost by evaporation through the sides of the pot, which means that special attention has to be paid to the watering of plants growing in terracotta containers, particularly during warmer months.

Plastic pots, on the other hand, are watertight, which means there is no evaporation from the sides of the pot, although they don't insulate the root ball from the heat of the sun as well as terracotta does. They are also light in weight and easy to handle and wash. A sensible compromise between the two materials is to keep plants in plastic pots that can then be placed inside larger ornamental pots. This gives the plant the benefits of plastic and means that the display can be constantly varied. The air space created between the two pots insulates the inner pot from the direct heat of the sun, maintaining that cool root run essential for rhododendrons. The outer ornamental container must allow drainage of water from the inner pot.

In recent years plastic pots have become available in a wide variety of forms and finishes, including colours that imitate traditional terracotta remarkably well. Another modern development is the plastic pots equipped with a self-watering arrangement, normally a reservoir from which the plant is able to draw its water needs by capillary action over an extended period.

Cast concrete containers, like terracotta, also look much better with age, but they can make a potting mix too alkaline for growing rhododendrons in and should be thoroughly cured or sealed before attempting to plant into them. Other possible containers could include halved wooden barrels or treefern stumps, or logs that have been hollowed out. If aesthetics are not such a critical factor, just about any form of container can be used, just so long as the plants have ample drainage by means of holes in the base.

Tree rhododendron exposed on a high ridge between the Hinku and Honghu valleys, Nepal. (Photo: David Francis)

Solitary *R. arboreum* in flower at Daman in Nepal at 2400 m/7900 ft, where they are cut for firewood. This is the national flower of Nepal, where it is called 'Lali Guras'. (Photo: Malcolm Campbell)

Below: The three garden levels – low-growing rhododendrons and azaleas in the foreground, larger shrubs behind them with a background screening of larger evergreen trees.

Many evergreen azaleas are ideal for container cultivation. (Photo: Mary Moody)

A deciduous magnolia provides a striking contrast R. 'Cornubia'.

Above: A mature, well-structured planting of rhododendrons with mixed deciduous and evergreen trees. (Photo: Mary Moody)

Below: A woodland setting with massed evergreen azaleas in full flower. (Photo: Mary Moody)

Many evergreen rhododendrons are able to endu months of heavy snow or severely cold temperatu

Hanging baskets or pots

A large number of smaller, bushy, spreading varieties of rhododendron, and many azaleas, are quite suitable for growing in hanging baskets or pots. These containers may either be plastic, ideally with their own water reservoirs, or the more traditional wire basket frame lined with one of a number of natural fibrous materials, including sphagnum moss, the bark of various trees and, most recently, even wool. They are best hung in at least partial shade, under a verandah or pergola, or from the branches of trees.

There is no difference in the properties required of the potting mix, although epiphytic varieties ideal for hanging basket use may benefit from a coarser mix. Typical orchid or cactus mixes available from nurseries make ideal, open media for this purpose, after the addition of some organic matter and adjusting the pH to a suitable level.

Potting mixes

Various demands are made on a potting mix used for the long-term growing of rhododendrons. Its structure needs to be sufficiently open to allow good circulation of both air and water around the roots, while at the same time retaining a high level of moisture and providing a solid anchorage for the roots. It should also ideally be chemically inert and free of residual salts, so that controlled fertilising can be undertaken confidently.

There are many approaches and a variety of ingredients used to achieving these ends and standards have been developed for potting mixes in most countries to ensure that the buyer can expect consistency of quality and performance. The most widely used ingredients are shredded, well-composted and sterilised barks and a variety of other materials including peat and sphagnum mosses, coarse sand, fine gravel, scoria, perlite and even polystyrene pellets.

Be wary of supposedly 'superior' mixes claiming to contain fertilisers. The effectiveness of a fertiliser added to a mix will depend greatly on the age of the mix when purchased or used. It makes sense therefore to purchase a cheaper mix and add one's own fertiliser with adjustments to suit specific requirements. A local trustworthy nursery can often supply mixes developed for specific purposes, including azalea and rhododendron mixes, based on local experience, which may prove more appropriate than a 'brand name' mix.

Commercial potting mixes *should* have a neutral pH level and provide an inert growing medium that can be modified at will by the grower to improve drainage, for example, by incorporating a proportion of coarse sand, or to raise the acidity by adding peat moss or some other acidic organic matter, ferrous sulphate or iron chelates. Shredded coconut husks, rice hulls, garden shreddings, peat moss or well-rotted compost can also be incorporated to increase the level of organic matter and water-holding capacity appreciated by rhododendrons. It is possible to purchase mixes labelled as specific for rhododendrons, claiming to be more acidic and containing more organic matter than normal mixes. The extra expense of these mixes, however, seems hardly warranted when general-purpose mixes – abundantly and cheaply available, even at supermarkets – is satisfactory with only minimal modification needed for growing rhododendrons.

With the availability of consistently reliable and inexpensive potting mixes, the effort of preparing one's own mix is also hardly warranted, unless an abundance of suitable materials is cheaply available, or if very large quantities are going to be needed. Most production nurseries rely on commercially produced mixes, rarely preparing their own. Loams used in potting mixes must be sterilised to kill harmful pathogens and weed seeds before use, and domestic ovens can only sterilise small quantities.

A good suitable potting mix for those determined to make up their own could consist of 40 per cent sterilised loam, 40 per cent peat moss, finely shredded coconut fibre or composted rice hulls and 20 per cent coarse sand or fine gravel for drainage. Higher proportions of garden soil or loam, without any clay content, may be used as the size of the pot increases.

Planting into containers

It used to be common practice to place 'crocking', which traditionally consisted of broken terracotta pots, lumps of gravel or charcoal, in the bottom of a container when planting. Plastic pots have multiple drainage holes that should extend to the sides of the pot, and good potting mixes allow ample drainage, rendering this technique somewhat redundant. However, anything that can only assist drainage can do no harm, and crocking should still be included if the potting mix contains a proportion of loam or garden soil. Crocking is also worthwhile when using terracotta pots, which normally have only one small and easily blocked hole in the centre of the base.

Give the plant a good soaking and allow it to drain well before carefully sliding it out of its original container. Make sure the potting mix is damp before use as mixes with a high organic content can be hard to re-wet once they have dried out. Tease the roots a little and position the plant in the potting mix so that the top of the root ball is virtually level with the surrounding mix. Allow just a light covering of the mix to protect the top of the root ball. Leave enough depth from the top of the container to the surface of the mix to facilitate watering by filling the pot to its brim, allowing the water to soak gently down into the mix, without it spilling over. A finely shredded organic mulch or a layer of fine gravel can be applied to the surface of the mix to reduce evaporation, in much the same manner as you would to the garden beds, but take care not to build the mulch up too tightly around the trunk of the plant.

Water the plant after potting at least until some water starts to trickle from the drainage holes. A thorough watering at this time can also help to leach out any residual salts present in the mix.

Potting up

There are no hard and fast rules about when potting up (transferring the plant to a larger pot) should occur, although once every couple of years is not unreasonable. The decision should really be based on regular observation of each plant. At least once a year, knock the plant carefully out of its pot and examine the root ball. If the roots totally fill the pot and the potting mix is hardly visible through the dense mass of fine roots, the plant is pot bound and should be potted up. At the same time look for any invasions of earthworms, ants, crickets or other insects that may have mined their way into the mix, and any signs of fungal activity in the roots.

If the plant appears pot bound, with roots pushing into every corner of the pot, look for a replacement which is 30 to 50 per cent wider than the previous one, or that permits a gap of around 25 to 30 mm around the root ball. Since plants generally do better in pots that do not allow too much room to expand, avoid the temptation to prolong repotting by going to too large a container.

It is also feasible to return the plant to the same container by pruning the roots back a little, gently teasing out some of the old mix from the root ball and repotting with some fresh mix. Regular root pruning in this manner can encourage heavier flowering in some varieties.

Watering plants in containers

It is essential to keep the potting mix moist, though not excessively wet, at all times. Drying out is quickly visible as the leaves droop, and, while this may occasionally be allowed to occur, it will start to set the plant back if it becomes a habit. A plant that has insufficient moisture becomes far more vulnerable to wind damage or sunburn. In hot or windy weather, watering at both dawn and dusk may be necessary.

The risk of potted plants drying out can be minimised by the use of an irrigation system, with drippers attached to long, thin flexible tubes branching off a main feeder line. This can be an ideal arrangement for a number of plants grouped together on a patio or decking and for plants in hanging baskets. The flexible lines allow the pots to be moved about or swapped at will while still guaranteeing a water supply.

Do not be tempted to stand pots in saucers in the hope that the plant can take up the water and thus extend the periods between watering. This will render the bottom of the mix over-saturated and with insufficient air circulating around the roots, giving the plant 'wet feet' and encouraging fungal attack.

If a container does dry out and the potting mix appears to resist absorbing water, the whole pot may be dunked for several minutes, ideally in water containing a wetting agent. These solutions restore the ability of a mix or soil to absorb moisture and may also be applied during watering if a pot appears to partially dry out.

A recent innovation available to growers of plants in containers are re-wetting granules. Although they will add to the cost of the potting mix, they improve the water penetration, absorption and drainage of the mix. They can also reduce the likelihood of some portions of the potting mix drying out and enable better re-wetting without dunking should any such drying out occur.

The granules are best mixed into the potting medium prior to potting. They can also be cultivated into the top 100 mm or so of the potting mix in larger containers, although this practice should be avoided with rhododendrons as the roots close to the surface will surely resent the disturbance.

Feeding plants in containers

As well as simplifying the fertilising of plants grown in garden beds, slow-release fertiliser granules have taken much of the worry out of feeding plants in containers, and there are a number of formulations tailored for this purpose. They normally release nutrients over a period of from three to nine months, and may be applied annually as a top dressing in autumn or winter. Take care that they are not spilt and wasted when watering.

Liquid fertilisers of varying kinds may also be used, but these will need to applied on a regular basis, say, fortnightly or according to directions, throughout the growing season, as they leach away with further watering. They present a greater risk of excess salts building up in the mix than do slow-release pellets, and their long-term use makes a more expensive option.

6
Protecting rhododendrons

Rhododendrons are easy plants to grow, when one considers the effort needed to protect them from pests and diseases. If growing conditions are good, rhododendrons face relatively few threats from the insect world or from the host of debilitating fungi that lurk to inhibit the health of many other garden plants.

Azaleas tend to suffer from more insect and disease problems than other rhododendrons. Vulnerability to such problems varies from one species or cultivar to another, partly depending on the origin of the parent plants and their ability to withstand local conditions. The severity of pest or disease problems will vary also according to geographic location and the macro-environment in which the plants are grown. Plants growing strongly in ideal conditions are better able to withstand pests, so the first line of defence should always be to give your valuable plants the best home. A well planned, diverse garden should develop a balance and harmony of its own in which most pests are limited by natural means. Unnecessary use of chemicals resulting from over-reaction to minor problems can only serve to upset that balance and make the garden ultimately more vulnerable. Carefully watch for any problems that might arise and try to solve them chemically as a last resort.

Insect pests
Rhododendron bug

The rhododendron bug, *Stephanitis rhododendri*, was introduced into England early in the century from North America. Clues to its presence are a yellow mottling of the upper leaf surface and brownish spots on the underside. Some species and cultivars are more vulnerable than others, particularly the North American species *R. catawbiense* and its offspring. The dark brown bugs, about 4 mm long, are most active in late spring and early summer and prefer to feed on the undersides of the leaves of plants exposed to open sunlight. Well-shaded plants are less likely to be affected.

Lighter infestation may be controlled on a small scale by removal of affected leaves and squashing the bugs. Contact insecticides, such as malathion, are effective so long as the undersides of the leaves are thoroughly wetted. When the attack is more serious, the most effective remedy is a systemic insecticide for sucking insects.

Systemic insecticides are applied by spraying them onto foliage and are circulated through the plant in the sap, killing any sucking insects, such as mites, bugs and aphids, that choose to feed on the plant. They can be highly effective in eliminating populations of sucking insects from garden plants. They are more potent than most garden chemicals, however, and great care should be taken in their handling and application. Repeat applications, usually about a fortnight apart, but strictly according to the manufacturer's instructions, will be necessary as new generations of nymphs emerge from their eggs.

Weevils

These are often hard to detect, disappearing during the daylight hours and emerging at night to graze on the leaves of nearby shrubs, taking distinctive neat 'bites' from the margins of leaves. Leaf damage like this is often only superficial and pretty much an aesthetic rather than life-threatening problem. These insects, however, also pose a less visible but more threatening problem. Weevils lay their eggs in the soil and the emerging white grubs feed on the root systems of adjacent plants, often retarding or even killing the plant. This is more of a problem with plants grown in containers, a plant in a pot providing a lifetime's requirements for a weevil that need not wander elsewhere in search of sustenance.

Among the weevils likely to cause problems, depending on local conditions, are the elephant weevil or beetle (*Orthorhinus cylindirostris*), the clay-coloured weevil (*Otiorhynchus singularis*) and the white-fringed weevil (*Graphognathus leucoloma*). The black vine weevil (*Otiorhynchus sulcatus*), attacks plants just below ground level, eating the cambium layer away and cutting off the supply of nutrients.

Control of weevils can be difficult. Some control may be achieved by spraying lower branches and some of the surrounding soil with endosulfan. Carbaryl or other contact insecticides can be effective if the weevils can be found, but the best defence is to maintain vigorous healthy growth by ensuring good growing conditions. Plants in containers can be treated by carefully removing the plant, discarding the potting mix with the larvae and repotting in a clean mix.

Lacebugs or lacewings

The azalea lacebug or lacewing, *Stephanitis pyrioides*, believed by some to be two distinct species, is only a problem to growers of rhododendrons, and in particular, evergreen azaleas. They originated from Asia, where they are kept in check by their natural enemy, *Stethoconus japonicus*, which could prove to be effective in future biological control. The adults are about 4 mm long, black and shiny, and with distinctive lace-like wings that give the bug its name. They lay their eggs on the midrib or larger veins of the leaves or stuck anywhere on the leaf surface. The damage, however, is caused by the tiny nymphs which, upon emerging during spring and summer, congregate on the underside of the leaves, sucking the sap from the plant. The most visible symptom of the presence of lacebugs is a fine white, yellow or grey mottling on the upper surface of the leaves, along with brown sticky spots of excreta on the undersides. Plants with a heavy indumentum on their foliage are less likely to be affected.

Spray applications of a contact insecticide such as malathion will dispose of only those bugs it actually contacts. For a more thorough and enduring eradication, one of the more powerful systemic insecticides, such as dimethoate, is necessary.

Mites

The two-spotted mite, *Tetranychus urticae*, is widely referred to as the red spider or spider mite. It is, however, not a spider but an insect and is only reddish in colour for a portion of its life cycle. It is a widespread garden problem in many areas, particularly in calm, dry conditions, or in confined areas such as greenhouses, conservatories or plants grown indoors, where its natural predators are kept at bay.

The life cycle and behaviour of mites and the resultant symptoms of attack are not unlike those of the lacebug or lacewing, principally a fine mottling or greying of the upper leaf surfaces. The mites are born and live on the undersides of the leaves and are just visible to the naked eye. More visible is the fine webbing they spin and which partly explains their popular name.

Mites prefer a dry environment and rhododendrons, by their very nature, demand a high moisture level, which in itself should reduce the likelihood of serious invasion. In the warmer mainland states, it is possible to control two-spotted mite by releasing predatory mites, *Phytoseiulus persimilis*, which will feed on the offending pests. It should be remembered, however, that if the predators do completely consume a population of two-spotted mites, they too will die out, requiring replenishment on a yearly basis or upon a recurrence of the problem. Check classified advertising sections of gardening magazines for suppliers of predatory mites, which are, unfortunately, best suited to temperate and warmer climates.

The last resort, again, should be a general systemic spray for sucking insects, such as dimethoate, or a specific systemic miticide. Any of the normal contact insecticides will be of little use. Repeat applications will be necessary to control the next generation of mites emerging from eggs already laid at the time of spraying.

Greenhouse thrips

The greenhouse thrip, *Heliothrips haemorrhoidalis*, not to be confused with the greenhouse whitefly, ranges in warmer climates well beyond the limits suggested by its name. These small insects, while not a serious threat to healthy, established rhododendrons, suck sap from the leaves causing a discoloration and, in the case of heavy infestation, some loss of vigour. Leaves may appear silvery or show a dull grey mottling not unlike that left by two-spotted mites, along with tiny dark droppings left by the thrips.

Plants growing in sheltered or excessively shaded spots with restricted air circulation, or in enclosed areas, such as conservatories, shadehouses or glasshouses, are most likely to be affected. So this is another case where the first line of defence should be to improve the growing conditions for the affected plants, at the same time making that environment less hospitable to the pest.

Cut out all of the seriously affected parts of the plant and water the surrounding soil deeply as the thrips prefer drier conditions. Visible infestations can be discouraged by simply hosing the insects off the plants. Spraying the invaders with pyrethrum can be effective, but several thorough attempts will be necessary as only those insects that come into contact with the spray will be killed.

If this simple organic approach is not successful, or if infestations continue, an application of maldison should be effective. Pay particular attention to spraying the underside of the leaves, as such contact sprays will only dispose of those insects that are actually hit by the spray. Repeat the spraying at the intervals recommended by the manufacturer to ensure eradication of those insects yet to hatch. The more potent systemic insecticides mentioned for other sap-sucking pests can be used with care for a more thorough eradication, particularly in the larger garden with many plants to be protected.

Whiteflies

There are many species of whitefly, each with its own particular diet of garden plants. As their names imply, the azalea whitefly, *Pealius azaleae* (syn. *Aleyrodes azalae*) and the rhododendron whitefly *(Dialeurodes chittendeni)* are pests specific to various rhododendrons, particularly smooth-leaved varieties. Their presence is most likely to be indicated by clouds of tiny, moth-like insects bursting into the air when they are disturbed. Whitefly larvae congregate and feed on the undersides of leaves, in the same manner as other sap-sucking insects and causing a similar mottling and discoloration. Eggs are also laid on the undersides of the leaves, from which tiny black nymphs emerge to settle like scale insects in one spot where they feed and progress to flying adulthood.

As they feed, whitefly nymphs leave a sticky residue known as honeydew, which inevitably encourages sooty mould, which appears as blackish smudges in the affected areas. The mould itself is not a problem as it feeds on the honeydew rather than on the host plant.

Small infestations of whitefly should cause little concern and may be largely ignored, or sprayed with a mild contact insecticide, such as one based on pyrethrum. A contact insecticide can be effective if the undersides of the leaves are well sprayed, at about fortnightly intervals to allow for emerging hatchlings. If the whitefly prove particularly persistent, the most thorough control is a systemic insecticide for sucking insects, applied with the same precautions I have mentioned earlier.

Caterpillars

A number of caterpillars are likely to enjoy feeding on the tender young shoots and buds of rhododendrons, the most likely being the appropriately named azalea leaf miner, *Caloptilia azaleella*. These are more likely to be found on azaleas than other rhododendrons. They lay their eggs on the leaf surfaces and the emerging caterpillars proceed to feed between the upper and lower surfaces, leaving ugly patches in their path. As the caterpillars develop, they roll the leaves together with fine webbing for protection and continue harvesting within, usually on the growing shoots rather than on older mature leaves.

In small, accessible gardens, hand removal of the caterpillars may be enough. Spray applications of carbaryl, commencing around September and repeated several times during the growing season, ensuring good contact with the larvae, should be effective.

Aphids

Although aphids are not as closely associated with the rhododendron as with other ornamental plants such as roses, they can be a problem for growers of deciduous azaleas and plants growing in greenhouses. A North American species, *Masonaphis lambersi*, was introduced into Europe in the 1970s, and attacks a number of evergreen cultivars and species, particularly hybrids of *R. ponticum*. The insects are quite visible clustering on buds and young shoots, which become distorted as the infestation continues.

On a small scale, they can be hosed off the affected parts of the plant quite easily. Thorough, repeated applications of a contact insecticide are effective, and if the problem is severe enough, several repeated doses at approximately two-week intervals of a systemic sucking insect killer will eliminate the problem.

Scale

Not normally a major problem for rhododendrons, these curious insects cause their damage by sucking nutrients from a plant beneath a hard, protective, limpet-like shell. Their presence is often first indicated by the appearance of black, sooty deposits caused by the sooty mould which thrives in the honeydew excreted by the scale.

Contact insecticides such as malathion can be effective, but the hard shell of the scale provides the insect with a good defence. White oil has the effect of suffocating the insects while a systemic sucking insect killer, applied several times at about fortnightly intervals, will eradicate the problem thoroughly.

Borers

A variety of borers affect rhododendrons, including the rhododendron borer, *Synanthedon rhododendri*, a highly destructive pest active in the north-east of North America. Borers tunnel into trunks or branches to lay their eggs, destroying at the same time the vital cambium layer so that portions of branches beyond their point of entry wither and die. Their presence is detected by small piles of sawdust ejected from the borer's diggings, and often a neat ring-barking of the branch.

As attacks are mostly random and hard to spot until it is too late, there is often little to be done but to cut off damaged branches below the point of entry and destroy them – hopefully disposing of the eggs at the same time – and accept the occasional unexpected pruning. Don't leave the branch on the shrub to die and fall off. Pouring kerosene or poking a wire into the hole, or spraying with carbaryl can help if the insect can be detected before too much damage is done or before its eggs are laid.

Diseases

Rhododendrons play host to a number of fungal diseases, some of which can be fatal to the plants if left unchecked. Often the presence of a fungus can indicate some inadequacy in cultivation, such as waterlogging or poor ventilation. Plants that are overcrowded or growing in confined areas, such as shadehouses, greenhouses or walled courtyards, are more susceptible to disease than those in open positions with plenty of air circulation.

So too are plants that sit in constantly saturated soil with poor drainage. Rather than resorting to the long-term use of chemicals, the answer may often be to transplant to a better spot or remove some plants from a crowded area to improve the circulation of air.

Diseases can enter any part of a plant through damaged tissue above or below the ground, so regular tidying of any physical damage and the use of sharp, sterilised secateurs for any pruning will help minimise infection. Fungi thrive in the increased moisture of humid areas, where it may be wise to spray preventively on a regular basis throughout the year with a mild and non-toxic fungicide such as copper oxychloride, in the same manner as is the common practice to prevent leaf curl in stonefruits.

Leaf gall

Exobasidium vaccinii or leaf gall is a fungus which attacks young leaf growth on some varieties of evergreen azalea, although it is sometimes also found on flower buds. Spreading quickly in cool, moist weather in spring, it is usually only a cosmetic problem, with little long-term effect on the plant, even if left untreated for some time. Younger plants tend to be more susceptible. The affected parts become distorted, thick and fleshy, turning pale green, and swelling into reddish galls which eventually turn white, when the leaves or buds fall from the plant. In wet weather, when the fungus is most active and spreading, a bloom of white spores forms.

Removing and destroying all the affected parts, ideally before the spores appear and are released, may be sufficient control. If the problem is more serious, spray with a fungicide such as chlorothalonil, copper oxychloride, Bordeaux mixture, zineb or mancozeb about once a month from mid-spring to mid-autumn, while new growth is vulnerable to invasion.

Petal blight

One of the most common worries for the azalea grower is *Oluvinia azaleae*, or petal blight, which mostly affects mid to late flowering rhododendrons, kurume, indica and deciduous azaleas, as well as vireyas and a close relative of the rhododendron, *Kalmia latifolia*. It is mostly a threat during periods of cool, moist or humid weather and could be confused for common grey *Botrytis* mould which attacks and rots damaged fruit. The fungus is first visible on petals as circular, brownish spots one or two millimetres in diameter. These spots quickly spread to transform the whole bloom or truss into a slimy, pale brown mass which eventually dries out, sticking to the surrounding foliage.

The highly virulent nature of the fungus makes control difficult without chemical help. As with other fungi, one important step is to avoid overcrowding plants, thus ensuring adequate ventilation is provided. To help minimise infection, spray with triadimefon as soon as the petal colour becomes evident in the opening buds, and repeat the application at intervals of one or two weeks. Once an infection is obvious, remove and destroy all the affected flowers. In areas where the disease is known to be prevalent, the soil can be drenched with a fungicide during winter.

Root rots

Possibly the most widely spread and serious threat to the rhododendron is root rot, *Phytophthora cinnamomi*. The fungus is widely distributed and survives for long periods, its spores being released and carried in running water or water within the soil when moisture and temperature levels are favourable. When the spore encounter a suitable host, the plant is invaded through any damaged or dying root material and the fungus spreads quickly, destroying the network of fine, fibrous roots that are essential for maintaining an adequate uptake of nutrients and ultimately the plant's survival. The leaves of the plant turn yellow from the consequent lack of nourishment and fall off, and the branches die back from the tips. Sometimes only a portion of a plant may appear to be damaged, and the plant may linger for some time in an obviously unhealthy, depleted state before finally giving up and dying. *R. ponticum* and *R. griersonianum* and their hybrids seem to be particularly vulnerable.

P. cactorum and the relatively rare *P. syringae* are species of root rot whose spores can enter a plant through damaged tissue in rainwater splashed from the soil. Infection results in the dying back of branches, particularly on younger plants.

Honey fungus or armillara root rot, *Armillaria mellea*, enters the root system through dead tissue of a wide range of woody plants and spreads out following the roots, sending up distinctive yellow toadstools in summer. These are usually the first indication of the problem.

Good cultivation practice can go a long way to minimising the potential for root rot. As the fungi enters the plant through damaged or dead root material, care should be taken to avoid any dying back of the root system by ensuring good drainage, avoiding overcrowding of plants and compaction of the surrounding soil or any physical damage to the root system. Excessive use of chemical fertilisers can cause the delicate feeder roots to burn and provide a point of entry for spores.

Aluminium fosetyl, applied to both plants and soil suspected of infection, does not affect these fungi but increase the ability of a plant to resist the disease. Furalaxyl or metalaxyl may be used as soil drenches to be taken up through the roots and can be save a plant if the damage is not too severe. In serious cases, plants should be removed and burned and the soil drenched with a suitable fungicide or sterilised with a solution of formaldehyde.

Phomopsis dieback

Phomopsis fungus, which mostly affects azaleas, causes a slow dying back which can prove fatal over several years. Its presence is indicated by random wilting and yellowing of foliage. Once again, remove and destroy all affected plant parts and spray with a fungicide such as sulphur or copper.

Leaf burn

Pestalotia fungi can cause damage which is not unlike sunburn or fertiliser burn in appearance to the margins and tips of foliage. It spreads out from the point of entry with a dark rim around the perimeter of an area of dead or dying tissue. Like many fungi, it usually invades the plant through damaged leaf tissue. If not checked, the fungus can spread, causing serious damage to foliage and at least a general weakening of the plant. Infection can be minimised by ensuring good ventilation and removing any obviously damaged parts of plants. A variety of fungicides may be used to control its spread, including dichofluanid, prochloraz and benzimidazole.

Bud blast or bud blight

Only some rhododendrons, such as *R. macrophyllum*, are affected by bud blast or blight. It is also more prevalent in certain areas, such as the south of England, than others. The fungus infects unopened flower and leaf buds, which turn brown, black or silvery from early autumn, and prevents them from opening. It can be distinguished from frost damage, which it closely resembles, by the appearance on the buds in spring of fine black filaments, about 1 mm long. Known as coremia, these are the fruiting bodies of the fungus. It normally enters the plant through the egg-laying wounds of otherwise harmless insects such as the rhododendron leafhopper, *Graphocephala coccinea*.

Remove and destroy any affected buds, which will become a source of future infection if left on the plant, and spray new buds in early spring with a copper-based fungicide such as copper oxychloride. Some control of the insects when they are active in spring and summer with a contact insecticide such as malathion will also help reduce the number of entry wounds.

Septoria and Cercosphora

These two closely related fungi share similar symptoms of brown spots on the upper sides of leaves which can spread and join, resulting in the loss of foliage and an ultimate weakening of the plant. It is not usually serious enough to warrant attention, but to minimise infection, spray young foliage with mancozeb or chlorothalonil about once a month during the growing season.

Powdery mildew

A great bane of rosarians and growers of many ornamental and food crop plants, the powdery mildews are species of *Oidium* fungi that has only surfaced in the last two decades as a problem with growers of rhododendrons. Deciduous azaleas and some varieties of evergreen rhododendron, including vireyas growing in sheltered conditions where ventilation is restricted, are known to be susceptible, in particular *R. cinnabarinum* and *R. griersonianum* and their respective hybrids.

Yellow spots first appear on the upper leaf surfaces, followed by spreading layers of whitish infected tissue, mostly on the underside of the leaf, which eventually turns purple as it withers and dies. Powdery mildew thrives in dry, still weather with warm days and cool nights, so the first line of defence is to improve air circulation by increasing the spacing between plants and reducing the density of protective windbreaks.

Treatment is much the same as for powdery mildew in roses. Spray to protect varieties known from past experience to be vulnerable with dinocap, benomyl, triforine, chlorothalonil, prochloraz and, in cooler weather, wettable sulphur, buprimate or clobutouil, at intervals of about six weeks, while triforine is effective in eradicating existing infections.

Rust

There are hundreds of varieties of rust which affect a wide range of food crops and ornamental plants, and several species can be a problem in rhododendrons, particularly vireyas growing in humid conditions. Some that affect rhododendrons are known to use spruce (*Picea* spp.) and hemlock (*Tsuga* spp.) as alternative hosts and are likely to be prevalent where these conifers are also growing. The rust can be identified by the presence of small brown circular spots on the upper sides of leaves and orange or brown spots underneath where the rust-coloured fruiting bodies of the fungus finally emerge. If the disease is left unchecked, a mature plant can become severely disfigured and lose vigour. Younger plants and seedlings can be defoliated and die.

Heavily infested plants are best removed and burnt, while less serious or localised attacks may be treated by first removing all branches bearing damaged foliage and spraying with a fungicide. Sulphur, oxycarboxin, bitertanol, triforine or zineb for lighter infections will protect against rust, while triadimefon is effective for eradication of serious infestation.

Collar rot

Planting too deeply or allowing mulches to build up around the trunk invites various fungal infections which can rot their way into the bark of a rhododendron, particularly younger or recently planted specimens. Nutrients and moisture are carried between the roots and the leaves in the cambium layer of the trunk, just beneath the outer skin of dying bark. Ensure, therefore, when planting rhododendrons that the top of the root ball is at least level with, if not higher, than the surrounding soil, and keep a small area around the trunk clear of mulch, allowing good air circulation.

Damping off

This is a widespread problem encountered particularly when raising plants from seed. It can either be 'pre-emergent', wherein the seed itself is attacked before or after germination, or post-emergent, when the seedling manages to emerge, but rots close to base and eventually dies. It is manifested by a distinctive 'pinching' or narrowing of the stem, and has much the same effect as ring-barking or the collar rot which can occur in established plants. The usual culprits are various *Pythium*, *Rhizoctonia* and *Phytopthora* fungi.

Damping off thrives in the moist conditions needed to encourage germination, and is best controlled by ensuring a seed-raising mix is sterilised and free of disease before use, and by the regular application of a weak fungicide solution, such as benomyl, after the seedling has emerged. Once a seedling has sprouted, the moisture level in the medium should be reduced and adequate ventilation provided.

Nutrient disorders

Difficulties caused by nutrient deficiencies should not pose a problem when the gardener has been keen enough to give rhododendrons their best shot, ensuring an ideal environment with careful siting, soil preparation, mulching, watering and fertilising. Average garden soils will naturally contain trace elements in excess of requirements of most plants, and a well-considered approach to fertilising should ensure that sufficient nutrients are available when and where they are needed.

Plants growing in the restricted environment of containers are particularly vulnerable to nutrient disorders. When looking for a pelletised slow-release fertiliser tailored for container use, check that it includes at least all twelve essential elements, not just nitrogen, phosphorous and potassium (N, P and K). If it doesn't, a solution of the required trace elements should be applied annually if they are not included in the routine fertilising program.

Chlorosis

The most obvious indication of a nutrient deficiency is chlorosis, which simply means a yellowing of some of the foliage. Chlorosis has many causes in many plants, including viruses, insufficient light, drainage problems and lack of certain nutrients. The absence of green colouring in a normally green leaf indicates a shortage of chlorophyll in a leaf which is no longer productive and of much use to the plant.

Apart from the first flush of spring leaves on evergreen azaleas, which turn yellow and drop as part of the normal cycle of growth, chlorosis in rhododendrons usually indicates a deficiency of one or more of four elements essential as nutrients – nitrogen, iron, copper and magnesium. The availability of these elements to plants is closely linked to the acidity or alkalinity of the soil. The missing nutrients may well already be present in abundance, but their availability is blocked by the alkalinity, or less likely, the acidity, of the soil.

The first response, therefore, if a deficiency is suspected, is to check the pH balance, which should ideally fall between 4.5 and 5.5 for the healthy growth of rhododendrons. Traditional remedies for these deficiencies involve adjusting the pH balance, making the elements available to the plant in a soluble form at the same time.

Symptoms of these four common element shortages can look very similar to the untrained eye, and, without going so far as to drown the plant in chemical care, there is no harm in treating for more than one of the suspected deficiencies at the same time.

Nitrogen

Nitrogen is vital for vegetative growth, and a plant that is starved of nitrogen shows an obvious lack of vigour coupled with a general yellowing of the leaves which appears on the older foliage first. A 'quick fix' can be obtained by applying a fertiliser high in nitrogen, such as aluminium or ammonium sulphate, or a weak solution of urea. Be wary of overdoing it, however, as too much nitrogenous fertiliser applied too quickly can easily burn the delicate roots, ultimately causing much greater problems, such as invasion by fungi such as *Phytophthora*.

The best approach, if the pH balance is acceptable, is to examine and adjust the routine fertilising program. If slow-release or general purpose garden fertilisers are used regularly according to their directions, or adequate amounts of organic fertilisers, such as rich composts or blood and bone are provided, enough nitrogen should be available for good growth. If your fertiliser program is appropriate, patience will be rewarded.

Iron

A shortage of available iron is most frequently seen in the younger leaf growth of evergreen azaleas. Known often as 'lime-induced chlorosis' it is probably the easiest of the deficiencies in rhododendrons to identify. A distinctive mottled yellowing appears only between the veins of the leaves, which remain darker. The presence of this distinctive form of chlorosis normally indicates that the soil is too alkaline, with a pH level of over 6, for the plants to take up sufficient iron, even if it is present in the soil.

Where all steps have been taken to provide the correct soil acidity, this imbalance may be caused by some temporary external factor, such as dumping ashes from wood heaters or the runoff from recently installed paths or brickwork. Concrete or mortar is highly alkaline too and can pose a serious threat to acid-loving plants in its vicinity until it is fully cured. Unsealed concrete containers can pose similar problems if they are used for planting too soon after manufacture, the alkalinity of the potting mix being raised by lime leaching out of the concrete as the container cures.

The remedy for a deficiency of iron is normally an application of iron chelates, thoroughly dissolved and watered onto the leaves and into the soil around the plant in several small doses rather than a single strong drenching. Iron sulphate may also be used over extended periods to lower the pH level as well as providing a source of available iron. Test the pH level in the soil regularly, at least a couple of days or more after each chelate or sulphate application and repeat the applications until a satisfactory level is reached. Check the pH balance each year, ideally in late winter before flowering and spring growth starts, and adjust it again if the soil appears to drift naturally over time toward alkalinity.

Copper

One seems to be forever pursuing a goal of greater acidity when preparing and maintaining soils for rhododendrons, but it is still quite possible in some circumstances for the soil to be too acidic, with a pH level below 4.5, for plants to enjoy healthy growth. Composted organic material can sometimes be strongly acidic, and fertilisers such as urea and poultry manure, even when well composted or in pelleted form, can have the effect of lowering the pH below desirable levels. Copper becomes less available as the acidity increases. The symptoms of such a shortage are less obvious, although similar, to those of an iron deficiency, and are more likely to occur when the soil is too acidic rather than excessively alkaline as with iron. There is less contrast between the darker veins and paler leaf tissue and the tips of the leaves tend to remain darker.

Spraying the plant and drenching the soil with a copper oxychloride solution, more normally used as a general purpose fungicide, will provide a supply of available copper. The pH balance can be adjusted over time by careful applications of lime and avoiding acidic fertilisers and composts.

Magnesium

Chlorosis on the foliage of rhododendrons suffering a magnesium deficiency is visible as a yellow marbling first appearing on the oldest of the current season's growth. Magnesium sulphate or Epsom salts can be sprayed onto the foliage, and not just to the obviously affected leaves. It can also be applied to the soil, but use it sparingly as too much at one time can be damaging to the roots.

Other problems
Sunburn

Rhododendrons vary widely in their ability to tolerate the effects of direct sunlight falling on their leaves. Some species and hybrids, particularly compact, smaller-leafed varieties originating from exposed mountain habitats, can tolerate full days of sun, so long as the roots are kept cool and moist with mulch. Others, used to the shade of their woodland origins, may start to suffer if exposed to more than a couple of hours of sunlight glimpsed through the tree canopy.

Excessive sunlight results in a breakdown of the chlorophyll in the leaves, which fade to yellow, developing into darker, spreading reddish patches. Only foliage actually in the sun will be affected, their shadows leaving green imprints on the leaves below, and parts of the plant always in shade unaffected. Unless some sort of shade can be quickly provided, suffering plants should be moved to a more shaded spot.

Sudden hot sunny spells in summer can cause rapid and sometimes disastrous burning of uppermost foliage of varieties that should otherwise cope in their chosen spots. Recently planted specimens are particularly vulnerable in their first year or so until they are established. Planting in autumn and winter will assist plants to establish before the onslaught of summer, and great care must be taken with all rhododendrons in periods of unusually hot weather to ensure they have adequate moisture available to cope with the additional evaporation from the foliage.

Fertiliser burn

Repeated applications of chemical fertilisers over time can result in an excess of soluble salts in the soil. These salts can burn the delicate, fibrous feeder roots, reducing the plant's feeding ability. The symptoms are a browning of the leaf margins and tips known as 'marginal leaf scorch'. The damaged root tissue is then vulnerable to attack of fungi such as *Phytophthora*.

Repeated heavy watering of the soil will help to leach out the excess chemicals. Reduce or cease fertilising with chemical fertilisers and try the organic approach, using composted manures, fish emulsion and blood and bone as fertilisers. Poultry manure, even when in pellet form, should be treated with caution. Slow-release chemical fertilisers should pose no problem if used in the recommended quantities.

Waterlogging

Although soils for rhododendrons must always retain some moisture, the plants also resent an excess of water and lack of air spaces between soil particles. These conditions restrict the uptake of nutrients and invite fungal invasion with the subsequent dying back of the roots. The first clues are slowed growth, dying back of the leaf tips and margins similar to fertiliser burn, followed finally by the collapse of the foliage, which hangs limply while retaining most of its colour – rather than yellowing – before dying.

The only real solution is to relocate the plant – either raising it into a mounded position above the surrounding soil level, or to a new and more freely draining site.

Frost

Emerging flower buds and new foliage of rhododendrons are vulnerable to damage from frost. In their natural habitats, plants will normally only start to flower after the likelihood of frost is over, although it's not too unusual to see plants that have 'jumped the gun' and moved into spring growth losing their initial blooms to a late frost.

Rhododendrons vary widely in their ability to tolerate frost, determined largely by the geographical origin – aspect, latitude and altitude – of the species or hybrid's parentage. The most at risk of their sap literally freezing are the vireya rhododendrons, and early flowering varieties planted in frost-prone areas. Although the occasional frost can often be survived, several successive nights with temperatures below freezing will mean certain death to many varieties. Vireyas and other less hardy rhododendrons should not, therefore, be grown outdoors in exposed spots in areas where the overnight temperature falls repeatedly below zero during winter. Growing plants in containers which can be moved out of harm's way is an obvious solution.

If you can imagine that frost 'falls' vertically, like gentle rain on still nights, susceptible plants can be grown with relative safety under the shelter of overhanging trees and shrubs or tucked close to a building, under wide eaves. Otherwise choose later-flowering varieties. Plants that receive morning sun after frost and dew will be subject to repeated wetting, freezing and thawing, which will do more damage than if allowed to warm up gently through the day.

As frost tends to 'flow' to the lowest point it can, the technique of mound planting can help to raise plants out of danger, while also aiding in providing drainage in difficult soils. Plants grouped fairly closely together also tend to provide mutual protection.

A technique sometimes employed by nurseries to minimise frost damage to stock held outdoors in areas only lightly affected is to operate overhead sprinklers emitting a reasonably fine spray intermittently during nights when a frost is anticipated. Most damage in these areas of light frost will only occur in the period approaching and around dawn, and the application of such a spray at regular intervals helps to melt any ice which forms.

If all else fails, simply covering the plants with sheets of plastic, light cloth sheets or newspapers, will be quite effective, though the coverings obviously should not be heavy enough to damage the plants and should be removed immediately the risk has passed.

Viruses

Rhododendrons are not normally associated with the same sort of viral infections that can affect other ornamental plants, including camellias, or that are exploited in flowers such as tulips. There are reports, however, from North America and Europe of a virus known as necrotic ringspot disease affecting some rhododendrons of the subgenus Hymenanthes, as well as the close relative, *Kalmia latifolia*, manifested by small dead spots on the leaves.

It is also possible that there is a form of leaf mosaic virus, similar to that affecting roses and a number of other plants, which causes a variegation or mottling of the foliage. Another suspected condition with the self-explanatory name of 'little leaf', could affect members of the same subgenus and some vireya rhododendrons.

Little seems to be known internationally of viruses affecting rhododendrons, and there is clearly a need for further research in this area.

7
Creating new plants

One of the great joys of gardening is the propagation of new plants. Apart from the obvious satisfaction of cultivating plants you have nurtured into life yourself, the cost of nursery-bought plants can be sufficient motivation to have a try at growing your own, particularly if large plantings are envisaged over a number of years.

Propagating your own plants allows you to grow varieties that may prove hard to find or to acquire a favourite plant envied in a neighbour's garden. Most gardeners will more than happily share their admired plants with other gardeners and the easiest way to share that pleasure is by offering cuttings.

Vegetative or sexual propagation?
There are two distinct paths to the creation of new plants from old. Both methods occur in nature and each has its pros and cons. Seeds can be collected, germinated and encouraged to grow in conditions emulating those found in nature. Plants grown from seed will not necessarily be the same as their parents, being subject to the whims of genetic variation.

The offspring can be of quite a different habit or colour to their parents. Plants grown from the seed of hybrid plants, even when they are known to be self-pollinated, will result in just about any combination of characteristics of all of the generations of breeding that have culminated in that particular hybrid, good or bad. You may be lucky enough to come up with a worthwhile new hybrid, but the chances are just as good that much of your effort will be wasted on uncertain plants with little to offer.

Species rhododendrons come fairly true to form from seed, but only if the grower is certain that pollen from no other neighbouring species or hybrid has been accepted by the 'mother' plant or seed parent. There will still be unpredictable variations of form, just as would occur with plants growing in the wild. Plants grown from seed take longer to reach flowering. Knowing how to grow new plants from seed becomes vital if you are to consider breeding new varieties. There are many genera, particularly quick-growing species and annual crops, that are better suited to growing from seed.

Alternatively, several techniques, known collectively as vegetative propagation, can be used to prompt pieces of existing plants to grow their own roots and fend for themselves. These methods depend on the ability of plant tissue to set out adventitious roots at a point of wounding. Vegetative propagation is best known as the growing of plants from cuttings of the leaves, stems and sometimes the roots, layering, or division of the root system, as with bulbs or perennials. Most recently we have seen the emergence of micro-propagation or tissue culture, in which microscopic pieces of plant tissue are transformed into vast numbers of plants in test tubes under hygienic laboratory conditions.

Vegetative propagation results in plants which are clones or exact copies of the plants from which they were taken. They will have the same strengths and weaknesses of form, colour, fragrance and habit as the original or parent plant. Plants reproduced vegetatively will establish themselves and flower much more rapidly than their seed-grown equivalents. While tissue culture is in its infancy but expanding in use, cuttings remain the standard method for the commercial production of rhododendrons. Most rhododendrons you will find on sale in nurseries will have been produced from cuttings or, less frequently, grafts using much the same methods that have been employed since the plants first entered western horticulture. Vegetative propagation techniques allow nurseries to guarantee that plants that they sell will be of the colour and form predicted by the grower without having seen it flower.

Many of the smaller-leaved rhododendrons, including vireyas and azaleas, can be struck by taking cuttings, traditionally known as 'slips', using basic home equipment. The larger-leaved elepidote rhododendrons can be more difficult to strike without sophisticated facilities, but are still worth a try. Some, though certainly not all, deciduous azaleas can be difficult to strike, which is why they are often sold as seedlings rather than from cuttings. *R. occidentale* is one deciduous species that will strike fairly readily. Layering, although very limited in the number of plants which can be created, offers an alternative procedure which may succeed with more difficult varieties. Grafting offers yet another method of propagation of varieties that can be hard to strike from cuttings or have unreliable root systems.

If the only material available to propagate from is seed, the time needed to wait for flowering to occur can be greatly reduced by employing a combination of both sexual and asexual or vegetative propagation. Seed is germinated and the seedlings raised in the normal manner, to at least the point of generating two full sets of leaves. Tip cuttings are then struck from the seedlings, which will generate a more vigorous root system more rapidly than seedlings of equivalent age, and flower in an equivalent time to any other cutting.

Equipment

The ideal facility for propagating plants from cuttings, as you would find in commercial nurseries, involves elaborate and expensive glasshouses, misting and timing systems, with thermostatically controlled heated benches to keep the propagating medium warm, providing optimum conditions for encouraging root establishment and growth. However, with a little imagination, much can be done by the home gardener to avoid these costly complications and the level of expenditure and effort will depend on how ambitious the grower is.

Not every gardener can own a properly designed and constructed greenhouse, but there are alternatives for providing a suitable environment for cuttings to strike. These include cold frames, improvised or ready-made, discarded fish tanks or polystyrene fruit boxes wrapped in polythene. Maximum humidity is needed for striking cuttings and this can be achieved either by providing a sealed environment from which moisture cannot escape, or – more desirably – by constantly replenishing moisture in the form of an intermittent, very fine spray, known as 'misting' or 'fogging'. There should be plenty of diffused light to enable photosynthesis to occur, but not direct sunlight, which may burn the cuttings or young seedlings. While bottom heat is desirable, particularly with cuttings taken from some of the larger-leaved varieties, it is not essential. It can be provided using thermostatically controlled heating mats or trays that are designed to sit underneath nursery trays of seedlings or cuttings, with an optimum temperature of about 21°C.

While high humidity is essential for striking cuttings, the opposite is true for raising seed, when humidity would be an invitation to fungal diseases and good ventilation is vital. Particularly damaging are the various forms of 'damping off', which constrict the stems of young seedlings, isolating the roots from the leaves, if not destroying the seed itself before the seedling can emerge.

And, while we'd all love to have a good potting shed, what is needed is a clean, protected working area for the preparation of cuttings and this could just as easily be the kitchen table. It is worth spending as much as possible on a good pair of secateurs, probably the most useful and most used single tool a gardener ever owns. The price tags on some might seem exorbitant, but a good pair becomes a lifelong friend, and the ability to make clean, accurate cuts is essential when taking cuttings as well as pruning.

Grafting knives are rather like small, single-bladed pen knives and are available from horticultural or cutlery specialists. They are useful for trimming and wounding of cuttings, and are particularly worthwhile if grafting is to be considered. To keep these blades sharp, a stone will be required, and some form of sterilising liquid – alcohol, methylated spirits or a household bleach – is needed to sterilise containers and the blades of secateurs and knives between cuts in order to avoid transferring fungal infections from one cutting or plant to another. The same attention to hygiene should also be taken when pruning, although it seldom is.

Beyond these basic items, just about everything else that's needed will probably already be in the inventories of most gardeners or can be improvised with a little imaginative recycling. Containers can be just about anything that comes to hand, so long as drainage is looked after and there's enough room for anticipated growth.

Greenhouses and misting

Why is misting so desirable? Once the cutting has been separated from the rest of the plant, the biggest threat is the loss of moisture through evaporation. By maintaining the atmospheric moisture at close to 100 per cent, this loss will be minimised, and leaf material can continue to photosynthesise without stress through moisture loss. To achieve an effective fog, a greenhouse with a minimum volume of about 8 m^3 or $2 \times 2 \times 2$ m is required.

A small domestic greenhouse can be equipped with fogging misters that can be attached to an existing garden irrigation circuit. High-pressure misters can be obtained from horticultural suppliers and are compatible with domestic irrigation fittings so they are no problem to install. Direct sunlight should be excluded by cladding the greenhouse with a translucent material or by stretching a layer of shadecloth over the structure.

To maintain a suitable level of atmospheric moisture provided by the misters, a dynamic feedback system can be employed, the simplest of which is the traditional balance arm as used widely in commercial propagation. This consists of a pivoted arm with a fine mesh paddle at one end, and an adjustable weight at the other. The paddle becomes lighter as moisture evaporates from it and the arm is tipped back by the counterweight. This activates a mercury switch on the arm connected to a low-voltage solenoid that opens the valve allowing water to pass through to the misters. As the sprays disperse their fine, fog-like mist, moisture builds up on the paddle again, the arm tips back, switching the solenoid off, and the process is repeated endlessly. Once the optimum setting of the counterweight is found through a process of trial and error, the system should maintain itself indefinitely with little further adjustment.

The advantage of employing a dynamic feedback system to control misting is that, once a satisfactory moisture level has been established, it can be automatically maintained without further attention, accommodating variations in temperature and atmospheric humidity.

Balance arms can be purchased from horticultural suppliers, or with a bit of effort, can be constructed with relatively little skill. I have built balance arms using paddles made of brass tubing with a fine sieve mesh soldered to the paddle and a weight adjusted by a grub screw at one end. An inexpensive mercury switch, terminals and a small instrument case can be purchased from an electronics hobby shop, the fine tubing and mesh from a model shop and the whole device can be put together for less than $20. The solenoid valve and transformer necessary to operate the inline tap can be found amongst the home irrigation items at most garden centres or hardware stores.

The sky is the limit as far as more expensive solutions to controlling the propagating environment are concerned. Computerised sensors and controllers are displacing the clumsy but simple balance arms of past years, and the technology of large, commercial greenhouses is awesome when compared with the hopes of the average home gardener. The principles, however, are much the same, and a great deal can be accomplished at home with minimal expenditure.

Cold frames

If you are prepared to accept a lower rate of success with cuttings, they can be struck successfully with much simpler equipment. All that is required is any kind of airtight container of sufficient size to allow about 10 cm depth of propagating medium. There should be holes to allow drainage in the base of the container and access to indirect or diffused light, but not direct sunlight, which can cause evaporation to occur too rapidly.

A cold frame is simply an enclosed container for the raising of seedlings or cuttings. It can be as elaborate as the 'traditional' cold frame, either commercially produced or improvised, for example, with old window-frames, or as basic as a polystyrene fruit box, disused fish tank, ice-cream or margarine container wrapped in plastic.

A number of cuttings can be placed into a small pot, say 100 to 200 mm in diameter, ice cream bucket or margarine container and wrapped in a white plastic bag. Wire supports cut from stiff wire or coat hangers may be used to prevent the plastic bag from touching the cuttings. Once prepared and watered, the cuttings may be left undisturbed, to be opened and checked every so often to see if they have struck.

Bench-top propagating units

Another alternative is the commercially available bench-top propagating box which can be placed anywhere around the home where there is a reasonable level of light. These units plug into the normal mains power supply and can be used for propagating a wide variety of plants from both seed and cuttings. They are equipped with bottom heating, usually controlled by a thermostat, that greatly promotes the ability of cuttings to strike and roots to develop and flourish. A clear lid provides the light-transmitting airtight container in which the moisture level is automatically maintained for cuttings, rather like a terrarium, or vents which can be opened as required to allow ventilation for raising seedlings.

The cost of ready-made units will vary according to size and complexity. Some are as basic as a single-tray unit providing bottom heat only with no thermostatic control, while others can take two trays or more with more precise control over the heat source. At the top end of the scale are large professional units, which can also include misting devices within one self-contained unit.

Propagating media

A medium for striking cuttings needs what seem to be properties that contradict each other. While a high moisture content must be maintained, it should be able to drain freely to be replenished with fresh water, and air must also be available at all times throughout the mix in combination with this moisture. So what is needed is a combination of materials with opposing qualities: something to absorb and retain water, and something else to enable that water to drain and provide air circulation.

Traditionally, media employed for striking cuttings have been based on peat moss, in combination of equal or greater parts of some inert material, normally washed 'sharp' builders' sand, expanded polystyrene or perlite. Peat moss possesses a remarkable ability to absorb and retain moisture. It should be free of lumps and sieved, but not too finely, as peat moss that is too fine can completely fill the spaces between the sand or perlite particles, reducing air circulation dangerously. Typical mixtures for striking cuttings using peat moss include:

3 parts coarse sand : 1 part peat moss
2 parts coarse sand : 1 part peat moss : 1 part perlite

Although it is still regarded by production nurseries as the most reliable material for the job, peat moss is unfortunately a non-renewable resource, rising in cost as it becomes more scarce. Its popularity is now challenged by renewable materials, often the byproducts of other processes which would previously have been discarded. They can perform almost as well as peat moss at much less cost and include finely ground or shredded coconut husks, rice hulls or composted pinebark.

Pinebark has a usefully low pH level of about 5.5 and offers the grower the added bonus of releasing phosphoric acid, which aids in early root development. Vermiculite is a mineral which is expanded by heat to possess excellent water-retaining qualities and can be used as a substitute for peat moss. It is often found in commercial propagating mixes. Its main drawback is its high cost, although for the small quantities needed if only a few plants are to be struck, this may not be a prohibitive factor.

It is also possible to use a standard grade commercial potting mix combined with an inert material such as sharp sand, perlite or vermiculite, although it is best to sieve the mix first to remove larger particles and make it easier to handle.

The sand used for striking cuttings should have coarse particles rather than fine, and can be purchased already 'washed' for propagating purposes. If its cleanliness is in doubt, it can be placed into a clean bucket and a hose run through for ten minutes or so until the overflow runs clean.

While a slow-release fertiliser can be added at this time, it is of no use to the plant until the roots emerge seeking nutrients, when it is time to pot up into a medium containing a fertiliser. Peat moss and pinebark have insignificant nutrient value on their own, while vermiculite contains small amounts of potassium and magnesium and the drainage materials, such as sand and perlite, possess none.

Taking cuttings

Mid summer to early autumn are usually the preferred seasons for taking cuttings of most evergreen rhododendrons including azaleas. On the other hand, cuttings can be taken and struck from vireyas and some species and hybrids (e.g. members of the Maddenia subsection and resulting hybrids) over a longer portion of the year. The optimum time for taking cuttings is therefore not hard and fast, and will vary widely according to the particular variety and local conditions.

Deciduous azalea cuttings should be taken in spring, from soft or semi-ripe wood, once the leaves have developed, allowing sufficient time for the cutting to establish roots before the dormant winter period commences. Cuttings are best taken early or late in the day and prepared as soon as possible after taking them from the plant. If collecting cuttings from another garden, as is often the case, go armed with plastic bags, preferably white rather than clear to avoid burning, and sprinkle a small amount of water in each bag to maintain the moisture level. Label the bags carefully and continue to label the cuttings accurately throughout all stages involved to avoid the frustration of having to wait for plants to flower before knowing what has been grown. Choose healthy, younger plants to take cuttings from in preference to older plants or those showing signs of disease or stress.

Theoretically almost any piece of stem can be used to make a cutting, but it is best to take tip cuttings from new shoots that are still green and flexible, known as 'softwood', with leaves that have fully developed. Softwood pieces should be able to be bent virtually in two between the thumb and forefinger without snapping. This is the most actively growing part of the plant, with cell division at its greatest, and is most likely to be able to establish a root system. Although widely used in commercial propagation, softwood is also the most vulnerable part of the plant and can be easily damaged in handling or if conditions are less than ideal.

If facilities are limited the grower may prefer to work with semi-ripe material from last season's growth. Semi-ripe means softwood which has partly matured but is still just pliable, again with fully developed leaves. Semi-ripe wood should partly bend between the thumb and forefinger before breaking part-way through. Remove any flower buds or avoid taking cuttings from materials which include buds, as they will place an unnecessary drain on the cutting's limited resources. Look for pieces that include only leaf buds or shoots.

The length needed for a tip cutting varies according to the general proportions of the plant, but should rarely be more than 100 to 150 mm long. Cuttings from larger-leaved plants will need to be larger than those from azaleas or smaller-leaved varieties. Try to include about three to five internodes (the spaces along the stem between the nodes or the points at which the leaves join the stem) and a growing tip. The cutting should end immediately below the bottom node from which the roots will emerge – any stem left below it will only die off, providing an opportunity for disease entry. Smaller-leaved varieties can often be simply snapped off the main stem, a small portion of which can be retained, and this is known as a 'heel' cutting.

Carefully pull off the lower leaves to expose the stem, with three or four leaves remaining at the top. With larger-leaved varieties, it is usual to cut the remaining leaves in half, further reducing the leaf area and potential loss of moisture through transpiration, as well as making handling a little easier by reducing the bulk of the cutting.

To further reduce the risk of the cuttings rotting during the weeks awaiting striking to occur, they can be washed gently all over in a general-purpose fungicide such as benomyl. The base of the cuttings of larger varieties should be 'wounded' by making a slice, about 10 mm long, into the bark on either side to expose a greater area of the green cambium layer just beneath the bark from which the roots will form and grow. This is not so necessary with azaleas and the smaller-leaved varieties.

Dip the end of the cutting into a rooting hormone, which, while not guaranteeing that a strike will occur, will greatly enhance the chances and will stimulate those roots that do appear into vigorous growth. The introduction of these hormones, along with improved misting and bottom heating, has greatly improved the ability of propagators to grow more difficult species. Hormones are available in powder, gel or liquid forms, in varying strengths according to the type of wood being used.

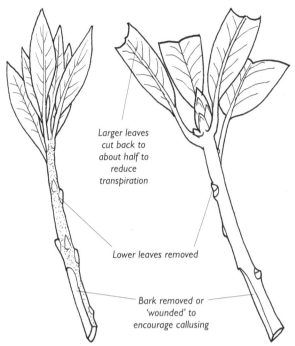

Cuttings of small-leaved (left) and large-leaved (right) evergreen varieties.

The container to be used should be thoroughly cleaned and, ideally, washed in a sterilising agent before filling with the propagating medium. Water the medium well, allowing the water to soak in and drain. Firm the soil down before 'dibbling' a hole for each cutting with a pencil or stick. Place the cutting into the hole and gently firm medium around it.

The cuttings should take anything from six to twelve weeks to strike, depending on the variety and conditions. Striking will be quicker with mist and bottom heat. If the cuttings are kept in a sealed environment, it should be opened about once a week for half an hour or so to rejuvenate the air, rewatered, ideally with a weak solution of fungicide, and resealed. Once striking is believed to have occurred, the easiest way to check on the cuttings' progress is to give one of them a gentle upward tug. If the cutting moves freely and the leaves are still green and healthy, no roots have formed and more time will be necessary. If the leaves appear to be dying back and the cutting can be moved easily, it has probably failed. If the cutting seems to resist an upward pull, it has at least callused and has started root formation. It is this moment, when success seems imminent and all the care and patience has paid off, that has to be one of the most rewarding for a gardener.

Allow a week or so after striking is known to have occurred before carefully removing one of the cuttings to check on the progress of the roots. They should be allowed to form a few roots at least 10 mm long that look as though they are proceeding with confidence before moving the new plants into a protected, but now ventilated, environment. The trick is to keep the cuttings in their humid environment long enough to get the roots established, but not so long as to impede the development of leaf shoots, which will arise some time later than the roots. Once new leaf shoots have appeared, you can be quite confident that you have new plants growing on their own roots that can be potted up into individual containers in a normal potting mix. The greatest risk at this point is damage to the fragile roots during transplanting, so exercise extreme care in handling.

Layering

While the technique of layering plants is not really a commercial proposition, it can be useful for producing a few extra plants in the home garden, as well as for propagating some of the larger-leaved elepidote species and hybrids which may well not strike easily.

This method simulates one of the two ways rhododendrons reproduce themselves in their natural growing environment. As bushes increase in size the foliage remains at the ends of branches that become longer and weightier. There is much futile growth of smaller branches which never receive sufficient light to develop fully and eventually wither off. Some of the lowest of these longer branches become sufficiently weighed down by their own length and crop of foliage that at certain points they rest on the ground and eventually become covered by the mulch of leaves, dead twigs and other organic matter that decays to become the topsoil rhododendron roots thrive in. Adventitious roots form at the site of contact with the mulch and strike into this favourable environment. This branch and root system eventually becomes essentially a new plant in its own right.

Layering can be attempted at any time of year, although autumn is generally considered the best time, allowing the benefit of winter rains to help maintain good moisture levels essential for the layering to succeed.

Select a branch which is low enough to be easily pulled down into contact with the soil. Small slits cut into the bark, parallel to the branch, will aid in root initiation. Dig a shallow trench through the mulch and just into the topsoil. Fill this trench with a cocktail of peat moss, sphagnum moss, leafmould and a little sand to aid drainage. The bark should be wounded by scraping to expose the cambium layer from which the roots will arise, and the application of a rooting hormone to the wound will enhance the chances of a successful strike. Pull the branch down and secure it into this mixture with a peg or two. Tent pegs can be adequate, or you can cut heavy fencing or baling wire into pieces about 30 cm long and bend them into an appropriate shape to fasten the branch into place. Try to position the growing tip of the new shoot as vertically as possible, if necessary by staking and tying it. Recover the portion of branch in the trench with the mulch and keep the area continually moist. Regularly inspect the bundle, not forgetting how fragile the roots are. Allow at least a month or two after roots have started developing, to allow them to become established on their own, before cutting the new plant from its 'parent'.

The new plant, along with its developing root ball, can be planted directly into soil rich in organic matter, ideally including material taken from the parent plant's own mulch. Alternatively, the plant may be nurtured for several months in a container before planting it in the garden.

When rejuvenating older garden specimens, you may well discover ground layering occurring naturally. New growth forming in this manner can be cut and removed in the same manner as artificially layered plants, if you are certain a root system has successfully formed.

Aerial layering

This technique uses the same principles as ground layering, but is useful where there are no convenient branches to pull down to ground level. Rather than the branch coming down to the soil, the soil is taken up to the branch.

A series of small slits is cut into the bark or cambium layer parallel to the branch, or a portion of the bark is removed entirely. The area around the cuts should be moistened well and rooting hormones can be beneficial. Place wet sphagnum moss completely around the branch to a length of about 10 cm and a depth of about 25 mm, and wrap with polythene film. Tie the whole bundle securely at each end to contain the moss and minimise moisture loss. Clear film has the advantage of allowing inspection without unwrapping. Aerial layering takes a little longer than ground layering.

Once a good root system can be seen through the moss under the plastic, the branch can be cut off below the layering and the resulting new plant potted. Raise it in the same manner as any container plant, maintaining moisture levels for a few months before finally planting it out into the garden.

Grafting

The method of propagation least likely to be tackled by the home gardener is grafting, but the keen should not be put off – with a little patience and practice, the two basic grafting techniques useful for propagating rhododendrons are easily mastered and most rewarding. The best tool for the job is the horticultural grafting knife mentioned earlier, kept well honed and sterilised and treated with the greatest respect as cut fingers are often a symptom of novice grafters. Put simply, grafting means the bringing together of two plants to form one in a kind of symbiotic relationship. The plant to be propagated, known as the scion, is joined to a second plant, the rootstock, which is known to be robust and easily propagated, for the mutual benefit of both.

Modern improvements in propagating technology have enabled previously difficult varieties to be struck successfully from cuttings, reducing the commercial need for more costly and labour-intensive grafting. However, grafting still enables some more difficult varieties, including deciduous azaleas, to be propagated with certainty.

Grafting allows the propagator to bring to the scion the desirable qualities of the rootstock, such as pH adaptability and disease resistance. Varieties with dubious root systems can benefit from a union with a vigorous rootstock. *R. degronianum* ssp. *yakushimanum,* for instance, has traditionally been grafted onto the sturdy *R. ponticum,* taking advantage of the latter's superior root system. However, the vigorous, if not weedy, *R. ponticum* has lost favour these days as a rootstock because of its tendency to sucker. It can overtake the scion if suckers are not ruthlessly culled and it has been largely replaced by the hybrid *R.* 'Cunningham's White' and *R. elegans,* which are both reliably strong, easily struck from cuttings and compatible with many likely scions.

The two basic techniques used for grafting rhododendrons are the 'cutting graft' or 'side wedge' and the 'saddle graft'. In both techniques the aim is to bring together as much of the cambium layers of both scion and rootstock as possible, to encourage callusing and a 'union' to form. Both rootstock and scion should be of about the same diameter, typically about 6 to 8 mm, and the optimum temperature to encourage this callusing is around 15 to 20°C. Early spring, as the plants

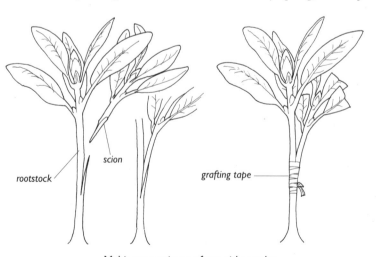

Making a cutting graft or side wedge.

Typical symptoms of 'lime-induced chlorosis'.

R. auritum, a lepidote species from China's Xizang province.

Sunburn damage on the leaves of *R*. 'Unique'.

R. kwayii (syn. *R. agapetum*) from upper Myanmar, takes its name from the famous river.

R. arboreum ssp. *zeylanicum*.

Left: An exercise in foliage contrasts – hostas, rhododendrons against the branches of *Photinia robusta* pruned bare, with a background planting of New Zealand flax, *Phormium tenax*.

52

R. burmanicum. R. ciliicalyx. R. dalhousiae 'Rhabdotum'.
R. forrestii. R. keysii. R. lepidotum.
R. lyndleyii. R. maddenii. R. spiciferum.
R. spinuliferum. R. webstrianum. R. xanthostemon.

move into active growth and sap starts to flow freely, is the best time, although some varieties, including vireyas, can be grafted at other times so long as suitable temperatures can be maintained.

Cutting graft or side wedge

This relatively simple method is the most widely used and has the advantage of producing a plant with the characteristics of one growing on its own root system. A cutting of the desired rootstock is prepared and struck (as described under 'Taking Cuttings', above). The rootstock can be allowed to strike and the graft made later, or both procedures can be undertaken in one operation. A dead straight, downward sloping cut, about 50 mm long, is made into the side of the rootstock. The cut should end about 20 mm from the base of the cutting and extend about halfway into the stem, although all these dimensions may be adjusted according to the size of the plants being grafted.

Cuts of similar size are made on both sides of the scion stem, tapering it to a point, so that it neatly wedges inside the cut on the rootstock, with the edges of both cuts aligning as closely as possible. Care must be taken not to split the rootstock by pushing the scion in too hard. The two pieces are tied together with grafting tape (available from specialist horticultural suppliers) or raffia and the whole assembly struck as a cutting with the union below the surface of the propagating medium. The union should take about six weeks to form, indicated by a swelling callus at the join. Once the union has formed and the cutting has struck, the tape should be removed and the top cut off the rootstock.

Saddle graft

In this technique, which requires a little more precision and dexterity, a young established plant rather than a cutting is used as the rootstock. Converging upward cuts, of similar size to those in the cutting graft, are made into the base of the scion, and top of the rootstock is cut into a wedge of similar shape. The scion cut then sits down over the rootstock, fitting as neatly as possible, and is bound firmly with grafting tape or raffia. Plastic tape helps to maintain the moisture level needed for a union to form. Saddle grafts can be made onto rootstocks growing in the ground, and the graft wrapped in moistened sphagnum moss, secured in clear plastic, in a similar manner to aerial layering.

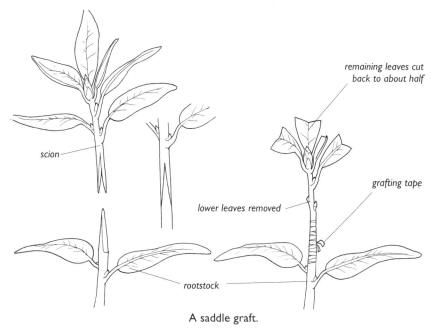

A saddle graft.

Growing rhododendrons from seed

The propagation of rhododendrons by seed is a relatively easy process, requiring only basic equipment and a reasonable amount of care and patience. Reproduction by seed can be used when propagating species rhododendrons, which will reproduce true to form if pollinated with pollen of the same species, either their own or that of another plant. Some species of rhododendron, including many of the deciduous azaleas, are difficult to propagate from cuttings and can often quite reliably come true to form from seed. Seedlings of some species, such as the vigorous R. 'Cunningham's White' are also used commercially as rootstocks for grafted plants.

Rhododendrons are generally self-pollinated by insects moving from flower to flower on the same bush. Species rhododendrons, if flowering on their own, come true with self-pollination. Self-pollinated hybrid rhododendrons, however, will not generally bear a true likeness to themselves, and will tend rather to 'throw back' to characteristics of the parent plants. Some hybrids are sterile and will not set seed at all. Where there are a number of plants flowering at about the same time, there can be no guarantee of self-pollination and a likelihood that the plants grown from their seed will be hybrids of neighbouring plants. This is known as 'open pollination'. Much potential cross-pollination in any mixed group of plants growing together is discounted by the fact that only a few will be flowering at any one time over a three or four month period. Techniques used by breeders to store pollen and determine pollination times allows plants that could never hybridise naturally to do so.

A major drawback of propagating rhododendrons from seed is the long wait a breeder must endure before flowering commences. While dwarf varieties can produce their first flowers in as little as three years, larger plants can take as many as ten to flower. Commercially, reproduction from seed is used for the breeding of new hybrids rather than for large-scale production of known varieties for the nursery trade, where cuttings remain the dominant technique. Plants grown using vegetative techniques will always flower earlier and become established much more rapidly than their seed-grown counterparts.

Collecting seed

After pollination, the seed capsules will enlarge, stay green and remain attached to the flower stalk, rather than drying and falling off if unfertilised. The capsules ripen from late autumn, changing from green to brown as they dry and mature. It can be difficult to tell when they are ready, as their appearance will vary depending on the variety. It is best to leave them on the plant as long as possible, but watch for signs of them opening. They may be picked just before opening and stored in a warm, dry place in paper bags into which the seed will be discharged. It is also possible to tie paper bags, not too tightly, over the capsules on the plant and collect the seed once the capsules have opened, although this method can be frustrated by rainfall. Plastic bags do not allow sufficient ventilation and are likely to destroy the seeds with mould rather than save them.

Seed may also be obtained from friendly plant breeders, specialist suppliers and through membership of a rhododendron society. Seed, but not growing plant material, can usually be imported from one country to another without undue formality, although quarantine requirements vary widely. Seed can be stored safely for a few months if placed in a sealed container in a refrigerator at about 4°C. Label each container well, and it can never be stressed enough that meticulous attention to labelling throughout the growing process is vital.

Media and containers

Seed germination and early growth of seedlings demand similar properties of a growing medium as that used for the striking of cuttings. Fine peat moss or sphagnum moss are the most widely used media for germinating rhododendron seed. Some growers add dolomite limestone at the rate of around 5 mL per litre of moss, to slightly reduce its natural acidity. Others add coarse sand to improve drainage, while loam can also be included. Other materials include shredded vermiculite, perlite, rice hulls or coconut fibre. Finely shredded, well composted pine needles or the foliage of any conifer can be used for organic content, increasing the acidity of the medium.

Loam used for potting or propagating mixes should be sterilised; even supposedly 'clean' garden loams purchased from landscaping suppliers contain spore of potentially threatening fungi. A small quantity can easily be sterilised at home by placing it in an oven-proof container in an oven set at 90 to 100°C for about 30 minutes. This should be long enough to kill harmful pathogens and most seeds. It will also minimise the risk of moss or algae establishing on the medium and smothering the seedlings. The sterilising temperature should not be so high as to burn organic matter, destroying the loam's structure.

All sorts of containers can be used for growing seed, from plastic garden pots or seedling trays to margarine containers and the like, as long as adequate drainage holes are provided. To minimise the risk of fungal infection, thoroughly scrub and rinse any containers, used throughout the process, particularly pots that are being recycled from previous garden use. A final rinse with a household disinfectant or bleach will give the satisfaction of knowing that any diseases will at least have not been carried by the containers used.

Sowing and germinating seed

Highest germination rates result from seed which is sown as soon after collection as possible, and if a suitable environment such as a heated greenhouse is available, this can occur during autumn. However, if no heated environment is available, the emerging seedlings may die off during the colder months and sowing is best delayed until temperatures rise in spring. A minimum temperature of about 16°C is ideal for successful germination and subsequent growing on.

The container should be filled with the chosen growing medium to about 25 mm from the top, watered thoroughly and allowed to drain but not dry out. This first thorough watering prior to sowing the seed is essential as peat moss cakes badly on drying and is difficult to re-wet once it has dried out.

Dry sphagnum moss should be thoroughly dried out and finely sieved. Care should be taken not to shred the moss so finely as to destroy its structure, which effectively retains high quantities of both water and air and provides an ideal environment for germination. This sphagnum moss layer helps reduce the likelihood of 'damping off', which can decimate emerging seedlings. The moss should be sprinkled over the surface of the growing medium to a depth of around 2 or 3 mm.

Scatter the seeds onto this surface layer, press them in gently without covering them, and water carefully with a fine spray. Cover the container with glass or clear plastic film to reduce evaporation and avoid further disturbance until germination has occurred. Keep the container in a warm spot out of direct sunlight.

Germination times vary widely depending on the variety, from as little as ten days to as long as a couple of months. As soon as germination commences with the emergence of the simple seed leaves, remove the cover and water the surface gently as required, always using a trigger spray set to a fine mist to avoid disturbance.

Peat moss contains virtually no nutrients, so a liquid fertiliser, diluted at the recommended standard rate, should be incorporated in the watering solution on a weekly basis, once the first seed leaves have exhausted the seed's own nutrient supply.

Growing on

Shortly after the seed leaves have appeared, the first 'true' leaves emerge, and the plant is now sending its roots down in search of nutrients. If the seedlings are reasonably spaced it is possible to thin them out and keep them for some time in this original container. It is more likely, however, that because of the volume of fine seed produced by rhododendrons, they will be crowded and erratically spaced, and are best pricked out or transplanted into more spacious surroundings. Rhododendron seedlings normally transplant well once the plants are showing healthy growth.

Depending on the type of container being used, several seedlings can be transplanted into one container with spacing of about 25 mm between the seedlings, or they may be potted into individual 'tubes', tiny plastic pots, usually less than 50 mm in diameter, used widely in the horticulture trade. The use of these inexpensive pots at this stage minimises disturbance to the rhododendron's delicate and vulnerable root system when further transplanting takes place.

The same growing medium can be used as for germination, although more sand can be added to further improve drainage. It is also feasible to combine the peat moss, or other organic material, with a commercial potting mix. Feeding can be the same weekly doses of liquid fertiliser as before or slow-release fertiliser pellets sprinkled onto the surface or mixed into the medium before potting.

It is also possible to transplant these seedlings directly into suitably prepared soil in a shaded garden bed, protected from the wind, for growing on until they are large enough to be finally transplanted. I prefer to remain with containers as far as possible, as they allow maximum control over the growing environment and feeding at these critical formative stages.

Breeding rhododendrons

Despite the many fine rhododendron cultivars already available to the gardener, countless enthusiastic breeders all over the world continue to strive for what they believe could be that 'perfect' plant.

A hybrid is a plant resulting from a cross between two species, cultivars or between either, of the same genus. Hybridising occurs in rhododendrons in their natural habitat all the time, as insects rather than other possible vectors, such as the wind, transfer pollen from the flowers of one plant (the pollen parent or donor) to those of another (the seed parent or receptor). The pollination process will also be going on in the home garden, but the lack of ideal conditions and interruptions caused by routine cultivation and maintenance prevents seed from germinating and thriving.

The breeding of new hybrids requires human intervention in a process which is therefore already naturally occurring. The techniques are simple enough to understand, the hard part being the perseverance required. Patience is probably the most important prerequisite before venturing into any program of plant breeding.

A cross will combine characteristics of not only the two parent plants, but those of their respective forbears, and the results are something of a lottery. Any cross will produce a result of some sort and only with the passing of time will the breeder be able to tell whether a new plant has any value. It will take years before it can be seen whether a cross has achieved some improvement in flower quality alone. It takes, of course, even longer to assess characteristics such as growing habit, vigour and disease resistance. Most hybrids produced are discarded, and, like optimistic actors seeking a spot on the stage, a rare few will make it to the point of becoming registered as hybrids, an acknowledgement by the horticultural community that the new variety does in fact offer something unique and the effort has been worthwhile. The time required to see a breeding program reach fruition – if it indeed does – means only a limited amount can be achieved in any one person's lifetime. It is for that reason that much of the breeding that has produced many of the hybrids we grow today can be credited to many generations of nursery families that have carried on the work started by their far-sighted ancestors.

Any program of plant breeding should start out with specific goals in mind and the breeder must be prepared to accept a high proportion of failure. To succeed, a new hybrid should offer a combination of qualities, at least one of which should break some new ground, offering the potential buyer something a little different from, if not better than, what is already available. There is little point, for instance, in perfecting a superior flower colour on a shrub which lacks the disease tolerance of similar proven varieties.

Despite the vast range of colour and form available in the genus, the rhododendron breeder is limited by constraints which merely serve to add to the challenge. For instance, lepidotes cannot be crossed with any of the elepidotes. This limitation restricts colour choices as there are no scarlet lepidotes and no blues and violets in the elepidotes. Evergreen azaleas are virtually impossible to cross with deciduous azaleas, which can themselves be crossed with elepidote rhododendrons. Elepidote rhododendrons can be crossed with deciduous azaleas, but with limited success, the hybrids resulting from these crosses known as 'azaleodendrons'. Vireyas, on the other hand, can only be crossed with other vireyas. The genetic make-up of some hybrids renders them incapable of producing pollen or setting viable seed, and many combinations can result in failures.

Another complication in parent selection is the effect known as 'linkage'. Two (or more) genes controlling different characteristics are linked in such a way that they will always be passed on together. A good example of this effect is the link between fragrance and pale flower colours. Fragrant rhododendrons are usually pale in colour, and attempts to breed deeper colours result in a loss of fragrance.

Any cross includes dominant factors such as flower colour and size. Tall rhododendron genes, for example, will tend to dominate over short genes, while the opposite tends to be true for azaleas where compact growth dominates over taller forms. Serious breeding does require a detailed understanding of the genetic processes involved, well beyond the scope of this book, and the key to breaking some of these restrictive links may lie in future developments in genetic engineering.

It is worthwhile studying the work of other breeders, and looking for varieties that crop up regularly in breeding programs, known to be capable of passing on their desired characteristics. You may be able to identify programs that have already gone some way in search of the same goals, and capitalise on that effort, saving many years' work rather than duplicating work already undertaken.

A greater chance of success in achieving set goals will be attained by going on to at least a second (F^2) generation between hybrids produced from the first cross. This second generation allows a re-combination of characteristics from the original cross, with unexpected, but often valuable results.

If the plants resulting from a cross have all but one of the desired characteristics, the technique of back-crossing can be employed. This involves crossing one of the hybrid plants from either the F^1 or F^2 generations with one of the original parents. Reversing the roles of seed parent and pollen parent may achieve the desired result if the original cross is disappointing. Alternatively, the original parents simply may not be able to deliver the required characteristics in the combination you seek, and this may then prompt you to look for another parent to bring into the program.

Some good hybrids have resulted from hybrids 'selfing' or self-pollinating. However, the pollen parent or donor and the seed parent or receptor are usually selected from different species or cultivars. Ideally, both parents should flower at around the same time or at least within a few weeks of each other. If that is not possible, try to aim for a pollen parent that flowers before the seed parent and store the pollen until the seed parent is ready to receive it. Carefully remove the anthers with tweezers or nail scissors from the stamens from the donor plant as soon as it is about to shed its pollen.

Pollen can be stored in clearly labelled paper bags or envelopes placed in a cool spot for two to three weeks. Breeders exchange pollen with each other in this manner around the globe. For longer-term storage, half-fill gelatine capsules, available from pharmacies, with dried pollen, and label each capsule. Place some silica gel or calcium chloride, also available from pharmacies, to absorb any atmospheric moisture which could encourage mould, then a layer of cotton wool, and then the capsules, in a larger, thoroughly cleaned and preferably sterilised, container in the refrigerator. Pollen dried in this manner will last for up to a year, long enough to be useful for most breeding purposes. For even longer storage, pollen, once thoroughly dried out, can be stored indefinitely in the freezer.

On the seed parent, look for a flower that is on the verge of opening in order to guarantee a mature and unpollinated flower. The abundance of blooms on rhododendron shrubs makes it easy to select ideal flowers to work with, and the pollen is plentiful enough to permit fertilising of a complete truss. Removing flower trusses adjacent to the selected truss will reduce the attraction of the area to insects, but to be sure of no premature fertilising taking place, a light cloth bag can be tied gently over the truss. Watch the stigmas daily as the flowers proceed to open for signs of a stickiness, which indicates they are ready to receive pollen.

Once the stigmas are receptive, carefully remove the petals from the flower to gain access and then cut and discard the stamens so that self-pollination cannot occur. Stamens taken from the donor plant can be gently rubbed over the surface of the stigma, thoroughly covering the surface. Alternatively, use a soft paintbrush to apply the pollen.

In theory, the stigma will not accept any further pollen once it has been pollinated, but tying a muslin bag over the flower truss again will guarantee protection from foreign pollen. Pollination can occur in as little as two hours and the ovary of the seed parent will start to swell visibly within a week or so. Carefully label the pollinated truss for further reference and to avoid accidental dead-heading of the seed parent flowers.

From hereon, it is a matter of waiting for the seed to mature, germinating it and raising the resulting seedlings as described earlier. The waiting and watching begins, but always keep in mind that many lines of hybrids can take several generations to reach the point of just one or two really worthwhile new plants. Parental pride in the new progeny will be difficult to resist and many nondescript plants that probably should be junked will still end up fondly cultivated in a garden somewhere.

Registration

Should one of the seedlings raised from a breeding program show promise, it may be worth naming it and having it registered. As duplication of names must be avoided, all registrations of new hybrids are handled worldwide by one organisation, the Royal Horticultural Society in London, and should be channelled through the registrar of the rhododendron society in your country.

At least two names should be offered, along with details of the parentage, giving pollen and seed parents, a description of the flower and distinguishing characteristics of the foliage or habit of the plant. Try to access as many references as possible to see if the name or names selected have not previously been registered for a rhododendron. It is quite acceptable to use a name already registered for a plant of another genus, but all the names applied to cultivars of each genus must be unique within that genus.

8
The species rhododendrons

Every species rhododendron has a story to tell, conjuring up names such as Hooker, Fortune, Ward and Forrest, the great plant-hunting adventurers. Mysterious and exotic landscapes in distant lands, often difficult to reach, are recalled in the names of places these prospectors discovered each new treasure.

Comparatively few species rhododendrons are grown as garden plants. They have been eclipsed by the showier hybrids that have been bred from them in the search for even more dazzling flowers or other qualities. Rhododendrons in the wild vary widely in form, depending on the environment to which they have adapted. The species which are grown by those seeking something a little less 'common' in their garden shrubs, or for their botanical interest, tend to be propagated from selected forms which have demonstrated a superior habit or flower colour, and are more appropriate for garden use than the 'definitive' forms.

When looking for species rhododendrons, it makes sense to seek plants known to have been propagated from cuttings of these superior forms, rather than having being grown from seedlings, which can vary widely and are often disappointing, if not at least surprising. Cutting-grown plants establish themselves and flower earlier than seedlings.

Often originating in quite different habitats, many species are not easy to cultivate in the domestic garden, or simply are not felt to be attractive enough plants, with straggly forms or poor flowering, at least by hybrid standards. There are, however, many species rhododendrons that should be grown more widely, and that offer the grower endearing qualities other than masses of stunning flowers. Many gardeners are drawn to the quiet, elegant simplicity of their blooms and the more subtle presence of species rhododendrons. Some are sought for the quality of their foliage alone. Of particular fascination can be the new shoots that develop into spires or 'candlesticks' and slowly unfurl to reveal large, deeply textured leaves 30 cm or more in length, in a variety of shapes, surface textures and colours, and often with a luxuriant, felty indumentum, such as *R. falconeri*.

Species rhododendrons growing in a home garden can perform quite differently than they would in their natural habitat – taller species, for example, rarely reaching the heights reached in the wild. Additional nutrients made available by the gardener result in more vigorous growth, and leggier forms can be made more manageable and compact by regular pruning.

Some of the species I have listed may be difficult to obtain but are included here for their botanical significance or the role that they may have played in the creation of hybrid rhododendrons. The species included in this chapter are the evergreen lepidote and elepidote species, those plants that tend to spring to mind as the 'true' rhododendrons, while the vireya and azalea species are to be found in chapters 10, 11 and 12.

There doesn't seem to be an urge to a seek out and revive older cultivars of rhododendron to match the nostalgic 'heritage' rose boom. A number of growers do specialise in collecting and growing species rhododendrons, as much for their botanical and historical interest, as for their often simpler and purer forms than the more popular hybrids that resulted from their discovery.

Lepidote species

Species	Flowers	Notes
ambiguum Triflora China (W Sichuan), in exposed positions on rocks in woodlands and thickets at 2300–4500 m/7500–14 740 ft. E.H. Wilson, 1904 in western Sichuan.	Yellow or greenish yellow, with green spots, widely funnel-shaped, 20–34 mm long, in trusses of 2–7, freely flowering. ML.	Rounded or broad, upright shrub, with attractive, rough bark. Lanceolate, oblong–lanceolate, ovate–lanceolate or elliptic foliage, 23–80 mm long, underside glaucous and scaly. Ht 0.6–5.8 m/2–20 ft, less in cultivation. H3
augustinii Triflora China (Hupeh, Sichuan, Yunnan, Xizang), in woodland margins, thickets and conifer forests, at 1300–3400 m/ 4265–11 150 ft. Augustine Henry, 1886, Hupeh	Lavender blue, with greenish or brownish spots, occasionally white, pink, rose, lilac purple, intense violet, funnel-shaped, 20–43 mm long, in trusses of 2–6. Although variable in the exact shade, this is the closest rhododendron to a 'true' blue. Very freely flowering. ML.	Shrub of variable size, with finely hairy young shoots, lower surfaces of foliage heavily scaly with golden brown hairs. Densely hairy midrib on undersides. Narrowly elliptic to elliptic leaves, up to 120 × 45 mm, on a tall growing bush. Prefers light shade. Named after its discoverer, Augustine Henry, Medical Officer in Chinese Customs in the second half of the 19th century. Great variation of form and characteristics. Ht 1–7.5 m/3–24 ft. H2–3
burmanicum Maddenia Myanmar (Mt Victoria), forest margins at 2700–3000 m/ 8860–9840 ft. Lady Wheeler Cuffe, 1914, Mt Victoria, SW Myanmar. *Photo p. 52.*	Yellow, creamy yellow or greenish yellow, 30–50 mm long, funne–-campanulate, covered with scales, in trusses of 4–6, occasionally 10, freely flowering. M.	Upright shrub with dark green, oblanceolate or obovate leaves, 50–55 mm long, densely scaly underside, with bristly margins. Ht 1–2 m/3–6 ft, up to 1.2 m/4 ft in cultivation. H1-2
calostrotum Saluenensia N & NE upper Myanmar, W China (NW Yunnan, SE, SW Xizang), Assam, Arunachal Pradesh, highlands, open meadows, rocky hillsides and cliffs, at 3000–4800 m/9840–15 750 ft. Kingdon-Ward, 1914, Naung-Chaung, Mwai Divide, NE upper Myanmar.	Magenta, rose crimson, or more rarely pink or purple, often with darker spotting, 13–28 mm long, in trusses of 1–3, sometimes 5. Extremely freely flowering with flowers concealing foliage. M.	Prostrate, mat-forming or more erect shrub. Shiny, dark green foliage, 10–33 mm long, oblong-ovate to almost circular. Prefers an open, well-drained site. Several forms, particularly the compact, freely rosy crimson-flowering variety 'Gigha'. Ht 0.6–0.9 m/2–3 ft. H3–4
carolinianum Caroliniana E USA (N & S Carolina, Tennessee), in woodlands. circa 1810.	Pink or pale, rosy purple, widely funnel-shaped, 20–30 mm long, in trusses of 4–12. Freely flowering from an early age. L.	Compact, rounded shrub with dark green, ovate or ovate-lanceolate foliage, 46–110 mm long, densely scaly underneath. Ht 0.9–2.5 m/3–8 ft (0.9–1.5m/3–5 ft in cultivation). H3
ciliicalyx Maddenia W. China (Yunnan), in rocky hills and woods, at 1800–4000 m/5900–13 120 ft. Abbé Delavay, 1884, Mt. Peechaho, Yunnan. *Photo p. 52.*	White, sometimes with pinkish flush, yellow basal blotch, widely funnel-shaped, 50–60 mm wide and 46–80 mm long, in trusses of 2–4. Freely flowering and fragrant. ML.	Tall, robust shrub, sometimes epiphytic in natural habitat. Dense foliage, narrowly elliptic to narrowly obovate, 70–120 mm long, covered with fine hairs. Distinguished by the fine hairs on the calyx which give the species its name. Ht 0.8–3.0 m/2 ft 6 in.–10 ft. H1–2
cinnabarinum Cinnabarina Himalayas (Nepal, Sikkim, Bhutan, SE Xizang) to N Myanmar, in forests and open hillsides at 2100–4100 m/ 6890–13 450 ft. J.D. Hooker, 1849, Sikkim.	Red to deep orange, through to yellow, usually waxy, tubular-campanulate, 25–35 mm long, in trusses of 3–9. Also red-flowering form. ML.	Tall, shrubby, sometimes straggly, growth. A most distinctive species, with neat, roundish, glaucous green foliage which contrasts well against the flowers. Crushed leaves give off a cinnamon-like fragrance. Quite susceptible to powdery mildew. A number of naturally occurring variations exist. Significant as a breeding parent. Ht 3.0–7.0m/10–21 ft, less in cultivation. H3–4.

Species	Flowers	Notes
concatenens Cinnabarina Himalayas (Xizang) on rocky slopes in rhododendron scrub at 3600–3900 m/11 810–12 800 ft. Kingdon-Ward, 1924, Doshong La, Xizang.	Apricot, tinged with pale purple, tubular campanulate, up to 40 mm long, in trusses of 3–8, freely flowering. ML.	Broadly upright or rounded shrub with large, bluish-green young growth and dark green, glaucous, elliptic or oblong-elliptic leaves, up to 87 × 50 mm, undersides purplish-brown. Ht 1.5–2.1 m/5–7 ft. H3.
cremastum Campylogyna Himalayas, China (NW Yunnan, SE Xizang), at about 3300 m/10 800 ft in open positions. George Forrest, 1917, NW Yunnan.	Light plum rose or bright red, campanulate, 14–20 mm long, in trusses of 1–4. ML	Broadly upright shrub with obovate or oblong-obovate, pale matt green leaves 20–37 × 12–16 mm, scaly underneath. Prefers some shelter. Ht 0.6–1.8 m/2–6 ft. H3
cubitii Maddenia N Myanmar, at around 1500 m/5000 ft. G.E.S. Cubitt, 1909, Bhamo, N Myanmar.	White, or white flushed with rose, widely funnel-shaped, yellow basal botch and brown spotting, 60–80 mm long, in trusses of 2–3. Freely flowering. E.	Upright, spreading shrub with dense foliage. Dark green, deeply textured, oblong-lanceolate leaves, 100 × 30 mm. Smooth, brown, flaking bark on stems and branches. Easy to strike. Ht 1.5–2.5 m/5–8 ft. H1–2
dalhousiae Maddenia Himalayas (Nepal, Sikkim, Bhutan) in forests, rocky hillsides and in trees epiphytically, at 1800–2900 m/5900–8850 ft. J.D. Hooker, 1848, Sikkim. Photo p. 52.	White, cream, creamy white or yellow, 85–105 mm long, tubular campanulate, in trusses of 3–5. R. dalhousiae 'Rhabdotum' (syn. R. rhabdotum) has bold red stripe on each flower. Fragrant and freely flowering. M.	Large, epiphytic or freely growing, open shrub. Young shoots with bristles. Narrowly elliptic foliage, 75–170 mm long, reddish scales on lower surface. Named after Lady Dalhouse, wife of Indian Governor-General. Ht 0.9–3 m/3–10 ft. H1–2
dauricum Rhodorastra E Siberia, Mongolia, N China, Japan. Described by Linnaeus, before 1753.	Pink or violet pink, widely funnel-shaped, 13–23 mm long, in singles or pairs. Freely flowering from an early age. VE.	Easily grown straggling shrub with scaly, pubescent young shoots and densely scaly, dark green, oval to oblong-elliptic leaves 10–35 mm long, rusty brown underneath. Highly variable in the wild. Ht 1.5–2.5 m/5–8 ft. H3–4
dendricola Maddenia Himalayas, SW China (NW Yunnan), N Myanmar, in trees or exposed rocky positions, at 900–3000 m/3000–9840 ft. Kingdon-Ward, 1914, Nwai Valley, N Myanmar.	White, sometimes tinged with pink, with yellow, green or orange blotch, to 70 mm wide, funnel-shaped, in trusses of 2–5. Fragrant. ML	Tall, epiphytic or freely growing, straggly shrub. Leaves 70–120 mm long, narrow elliptic to narrowly obovate, scales on underside. Smooth, dark purple or mahogany red bark. Species sold as R. taronense is now regarded as synonymous with R. dendricola. Ht 1.2–4.5 m/4–15 ft. H1
edgeworthii syn. *bullatum, sciaphilum* Edgeworthia Himalayas (Nepal, Sikkim, Bhutan, Assam, SW China (NW Yunnan, SW Sichuan, E Xizang) upper Myanmar, in exposed, rocky situations, mixed forests and thickets, at 1800–4000 m/5900–13 120 ft. J.D. Hooker, 1849, Sikkim.	White, occasionally flushed with pink, usually with yellow basal blotch, broadly funnel-shaped, 35–65 mm long, in trusses of 2–3. One of the best rhododendron fragrances. ML.	Unusual in having both a brown, woolly indumentum and scales on the undersides of the leaves. Densely woolly branchlets with white or rusty indumentum. Deeply textured, wrinkled foliage, 40–140 × 20–56 mm. Often epiphytic in the wild. Resents heavy soils, needing perfect drainage but ample moisture. Ht 0.3–3.3 m/1–11 ft, normally 1–1.8 m/3–6 ft in cultivation. H2–4

Species	Flowers	Notes
fastigiatum Lapponica W. China (N & C Yunnan), on rocky slopes, moorlands, pine forests, at 3200–4400 m/ 10 500–14 400 ft. Abbé Delavay, 1883, Mt Tsang-chan, Yunnan.	Bright lavender blue to pinkish purple or rich purple, widely funnel-shaped, 10–18 mm long, in trusses of 2–5. ML	Compact, prostrate or cushion-forming shrub. Densely scaly, glaucous grey leaves, 50–160 mm long, broadly elliptic to obovate, lower surface fawn to grey, scaly. Parent of many hybrids. Ht 0.15–1.5 m/6 in–5 ft. H3–4
ferrugineum Rhododendron C Europe (Alps, Pyrenees), described by Linnaeus, before 1753.	Crimson-purple to deep pink, occasionally pale pink or white, 120–170 mm long. Other forms include 'Album' (white), 'Coccineum' (crimson) and 'Glenarn' (deep rose pink). Freely flowering. VL.	Small, upright shrub with erect or rounded growth. Scaly young shoots. Leaves 28–40 mm long, narrowly elliptic to elliptic, margins rolled under, dark green above, reddish brown and heavily scaly below, bristly margins. Ht 0.3–1.5 m/1–5 ft. H3–4
glaucophyllum Glauca Himalayas (Nepal, Sikkim, Bhutan), W China (S Xizang), on rocky ridges in conifer and rhododendron forests at 2750–3660 m/9020–12 000 ft. J.D. Hooker, 1849, Sikkim.	Pink or white flushed with pink, or reddish purple, 14–32 mm long, campanulate, in trusses of 4–10. Freely flowering. ML	Broadly upright, sometimes rounded or spreading shrub. Dark green, glossy leaves 35–60 × 13–25 mm, lanceolate to oblong-lanceolate, narrowly elliptic to elliptic, upper surface dark brownish green, lower surface glaucous, whitish, with scales. Easily grown and suitable for the rock garden. Ht 0.24–1.5 m/9 in–5 ft. H3
hippophaeoides Lapponica W China (NW Yunnan, SW Sichuan), in open grassland to pine forests at 2400–4270 m/ 7785–14 000 ft. Kingdon-Ward, 1913, Chung River, NW Yunnan.	Lavender blue or purplish blue, 10–13 mm long, widely funnel-shaped, in trusses of 3–8. Freely flowering, even when young. ML.	Broadly upright shrub with matt, pale grey-green, oblong leaves, 10–40 × 4–17 mm, undersides densely covered with large, creamy-yellow scales. Suited to the rock garden. Varieties to look for are 'Habba Shan' and 'Bei-Ma-Shan' Ht 0.2–1.2 m/8 in–4 ft, rarely 1.5 m/5 ft. H3–4
impeditum Lapponica W. China (N Yunnan, SW Sichuan) in open grassland, rocky slopes and cliffs, at 3660–4880 m/12 000–16 000 ft. George Forrest, 1910, Lichiang Range, Yunnan.	Violet to purple, 8–15 mm long, broadly funnel-shaped, in trusses of 1–3, occasionally 4. Freely flowering from an early age. M.	Masses of flowers and dense, small, shiny, dark green, scaly leaves, 4–14 × 25–70 mm, on a very compact, much-branched, gound-covering or cushioning shrub. One of the most popular of the smaller rhododendrons, which has been valuable in the breeding of dwarf and prostrate 'blue'-flowered hybrids. Ht 0.1–1 m/4 in–3 ft, usually less. H3–4
intricatum Lapponica W. China (N Yunnan, SW & C Sichuan) in open grassland at 3350–4600 m/11 000–15 100 ft. Abbé Soulié, 1891, Tatsienlu, W Sichuan.	Pale lavender to dark purplish blue, 7–14 mm long, with very short stamens, in compact trusses of 2–10. Unusual flower shape with short, parallel-sided tube and spreading lobes. ML.	Compact, broadly upright and delicately branched habit. Small, matt, greyish green, glabrous leaves 5–20 × 3–10 mm, oblong to elliptic, sometimes almost circular, densely scaly underneath. Fairly fast growing. Ht 0.15–1.5 m/6 in–5 ft, more often below 0.9 m/3 ft. H3–4
johnstoneanum Maddenia India (Manipur, Mizoram, Nagaland, Assam), widespread in open grassland, scrub and forest margins at 1300–3400 m/4260–11 000 ft. Sir George Watt, 1882, Manipur.	Creamy white, usually with a yellow basal blotch, often flushed with pink or purple, 45–60 mm long, funnel-campanulate, in trusses of 2–5. Slightly fragrant. M.	Untidy, upright bush with bristly young shoots, dark green, shiny, elliptic to broadly elliptic leaves, 55–75 mm long, dense greenish brown scales underneath. Smooth, peeling, reddish brown bark. Heat tolerant. Named after wife of Political Agent at Manipur. Varieties include 'DemiJohn' (white, flushed with yellow-green) and 'Double Diamond (pale yellow double flowers). Ht 1.2–4.6 m/4–15 ft. H1–3

Species	Flowers	Notes
keiskei Triflora Japan (C & S), on rocky hillsides at 610–1830 m/ 2000–6000 ft. Miquel, 1866.	Pale yellow, widely funnel-shaped, 14–30 mm long, 16–45 mm wide, in trusses of 2–6. ML.	Usually a low-growing, creeping, twiggy mat, although often more upright in the wild or shade. Dark or olive green leaves, 25–75 × 8–28 mm, lanceolate or oblong-lanceolate to narrowly elliptic, hairy. Lower surface pale green with large scales. Very variable species, with dwarf forms at higher altitudes. Selected forms are available, such as 'Yaku Fairy' (a very dwarf form with large, lemon yellow flowers), and 'Ebino' (a freely flowering dwarf form). Ht 0.3–3 m/1–10 ft. H2–3
keleticum Saluenensia SE Xizang, Yunnan, upper Myanmar, on moist, stony moorland, rocks and cliffs, at 3350–4570 m/11 000–15 000 ft. George Forrest, 1919, SE Xizang.	Purplish crimson with crimson spots, widely funnel-shaped, 16–30 mm long × 38 mm wide, in trusses of 2–3. Freely flowering. L.	Easily grown, dense, flat, creeping, ground-hugging or mound-forming habit, with oblong, elliptic or lanceolate leaves, 7–21 × 3–10 mm, brown or fawn scales underneath. Ht 0.1–0.45 m/4 in–1 ft 6 in. H3
keysii Cinnabarina Bhutan, Assam, S & E Xizang, in conifer, mixed or rhododendron forests at 2400–3600 m/8000–12 000 ft. Nuttall, 1853. *Photo p. 52.*	Small, highly distinctive tubular floowers of red to salmon pink with slightly flared yellow lobes, 15–25 mm long, in axillary racemes of 2–6 florets. VL.	Straggly shrub or small tree to 6 m/20 ft, sometimes epiphytic, its garden habit improved by regular pruning. Elliptic foliage 50–155 mm long × 15–35 mm wide, sometimes larger, with densely scaly lower surfaces. Smooth fawn to brown bark. Variety 'Unicolor' has all-red flowers. H3
kotschyi syn. *myrtifolium* Rhododendron E Europe (Bulgaria, Balkan states, Macedonia, Romania, Russia). Simonkai, 1886.	Crimson purple to deep pink, occasionally pale pink or white, 120–170 mm long. freely flowering. L.	Dwarf, spreading habit – smaller, but otherwise very similar to R. ferrugineum. Scaly young shoots. Shining leaves 28–40 mm long, narrowly obovate, margins rolled under, dark green above, reddish brown and heavily scaly below, bristly margins. Slow growing and not widely cultivated, but a good rock garden candidate. Ht 0.5 m/1 ft 6 in. H3
lepidotum Lepidota Himalayas (widespread), NE Myanmar, W China (Yunnan, S & SE Xizang), amongst rocks, in scrub or grassland and various forest types, at 2440–4880 m/8000–16 000 ft. Before 1835. *Photo p. 52.*	Pink, scarlet, reddish purple or yellow, rotate, 10–17 mm long, in trusses of 1–4. ML.	Very small, rounded, sometimes straggly plant. Young shoots heavily scaly. Small, dark green, scaly leaves, narrowly elliptic or obovate, 6–30 × 3–16 mm. Pale grey-green undersides to leaves with heavy scaling A very widespread and variable species in the wild, and a number of varying forms may therefore be encountered. Drought tolerant. Suited to the rock garden. Ht 0.5–1.5 m/1 ft 6 in–5 ft. H2–3
lindleyi Maddenia Himalayas (Nepal, Sikkim, Bhutan, Assam, S Xizang), in dense mixed forests at 2135–3350 m/7000–11 000 ft. J.D. Hooker, 1848–49, Sikkim. *Photo p. 52.*	Large, white, with or without golden-yellow basal blotch, broadly tubular campanulate, 70–116 mm long, freely produced in trusses of 3–6 or 7, less often 2–12, flowering in 3–5 years from seed. Fragrant. L–VL.	A beautiful, if sometimes straggly or upright shrub, usually epiphytically in treetops and cliff faces. Young foliage sometimes reddish. Long, shiny or matt, dark green, oblong-lanceolate or oblong leaves, pale, scaly and glaucous underneath, 70–160 × 20–50 mm. Likes plenty of moisture and shelter. Named after RHS Secretary and botanist Dr John Lindley. Ht 0.75–3.6 m/ 2 ft 6 in–12 ft, occasionally over 4.0 m/13 ft. H1–2
litangense Lapponica W China (Sichuan, Yunnan), in open pastures to oak forests at 3050–4875 m/10 000–16 000 ft. George Forrest, 1918, Muli mountains, SW Sichuan.	Plum-purple, deep purple to lavender, 10–15 mm long, widely funnel-shaped, in trusses of 1–3. ML.	Fairly fast growing species with broadly upright, erect habit with narrow, glossy, dark green, oblong-elliptic foliage, 13 mm long, dark brown scales underneath. Suited to the rock garden. Ht 0.3–1.2 m/1–4 ft. H3–4

Species	Flowers	Notes
lutescens Triflora W. China (W & C Sichuan, NW Yunnan), in woods, thickets and hillsopes at 800–3000 m/2625–9840 ft. Franchet, 1886, Mupin, W Sichuan.	Pale yellow, with green spots on inside of upper lobes, widely funnel-shaped, small and delicate, 13–26 mm long × 20–45 mm wide, with long, elegant stamens, in trusses of 1–3. Freely flowering. EM.	Attractive, bright bronze red foliage in spring with a further show of colour in autumn. Leaves 50–90 × 13–35 mm, lanceolate to oblong, scaly, particularly underneath. Distinctive, smooth, grey or brown flaking bark. Straggly habit. Prefers a sheltered position. Ht 0.9–6 m/3–18 ft, usually much less in cultivation. H3
maddenii Maddenia Himalayas, Myanmar, SW China, Vietnam, in thickets, scrub and forests at 1520–2750 m/5000–9000 ft. J.D. Hooker, 1849, Choongtam, Sikkim. Photo p. 52.	White, often flushed with pink or purple, and usually with a yellow basal blotch, funnel-shaped, 50–120 mm long × up to 125 mm wide, in trusses of 1–11. Sweetly fragrant. L.	Open, straggling habit in the shade, more compact in the open. Glabrous leaves 60–200 × 25–80 mm, lanceolate, elliptic to broadly obovate, undersides have thick, brownish indumentum on midrib and heavy scaling. Foliage held for 2–4 years. Rough, flaking, sometimes papery, grey-brown bark. Often epiphytic in the wild. Heat and sun tolerant. Ht 0.9–9 m/3–30 ft, usually less. H1–2
maddenii ssp. crassum syn. *manipurense, crassum* Maddenia Assam, N Myanmar, China (W & NW Yunnan, S & SE Xizang), in open positions, woodlands, forests, thickets and rocky slopes at 1600–4200 m/5250–13 750 ft. Sir George Watt, 1882, Japvo, Assam, or Abbé Delavay, circa 1885, Tali Range, W Yunnan.	White, creamy white, or white tinged with pink or red, sometimes with yellow basal blotch, tubular funnel-shaped, 70–100 mm long, in trusses of 3–5. Fragrant. ML.	Robust, broadly upright or spreading shrub or small tree with various forms and sizes in cultivation. Glossy, dark green, shiny, elliptic, oblong-lanceolate to oval leaves, dense covering of dark brown scales underneath, 90–186 × 36–82 mm. Rough bark. Easily struck from cuttings. Ht 0.9–6 m/3–20 ft. H1–3
maddenii ssp. maddenii syn. *polyandrum* Maddenia Himalayas (Assam, Bhutan) in Tsuga forest and rocky situations at 2135–3050 m/7000–10 000 ft. R.E. Cooper, 1914, Chapcha Timpu, Bhutan.	White, or white tinged with pink, or rose pink, usually with a yellowish orange basal blotch, narrowly tubular funnel-shaped, 48–70 mm long, densely scaly on outside, in trusses of 3–6. L.	Broadly upright or spreading shrub or small tree with rough bark and densely scaly branchlets. Glossy, dark green, oblong to lanceolate leaves, 60–120 mm long, densely scaly underneath. Ht 0.9–5 m/3–15 ft. H1–3
megacalyx Maddenia NE India, W China (NW & W Yunnan, E & SE Xizang), NE Myanmar, in rainforests, rocky outcrops and woodlands at 1830–3965 m/6000–13 000 ft. Kingdon-Ward, 1914, Nwai Valley, northeast upper Myanmar.	White or creamy white, occasionally flushed with pink or purple, tubular campanulate, 65–110 mm long, in trusses of 3–6, sometimes 7. Fragrant. ML.	Broadly upright or bushy shrub. Young shoots glaucous, leaves 100–160 mm long, upper surface bullate, bright or olive green, underside covered with dense, golden-brown scales. Very distinctive species, not widely cultivated. Name derived from the large calyx. Ht 1.2–7.6 m/4–25 ft, typically 2.5 m/8 ft in cultivation. H1–2
micranthum Micrantha N China, Korea, Manchuria, in thickets, on cliffs, grassy slopes and exposed ridges, at 1600–3200 m/5250–10 500 ft. Turczaninov, 1837/48, north of Beijing.	White, 4–6 mm long, campanulate, in trusses of 10–28, freely flowering. ML.	Bushy shrub, as broad as high, with shining, dark green foliage 16–50 mm long, oblanceolate, undersides densely covered with large, brown scales. Pale grey to brown bark. A very distinctive species. Ht 0.6–5 m/2–15 ft, typically 1.8 m/6 ft in cultivation. H3–4

Species	Flowers	Notes
moupinense Moupinensia W China (W Sichuan), on rocks, cliffs and woods, and epiphytically on trees, at 2000–3300 m/6560–10 825 ft. Franchet, 1886.	White, sometimes flushed with pink, dark red spots inside, 30–48 mm long × 35–48 mm wide, widely funnel-shaped, in singles or pairs. Also a deep pink form. VE.	Compact, rounded or spreading shrub, sometimes epiphytic in the wild. Bristly young shoots, shiny, mid or dark green, glabrous leaves, 30–40 mm long, narrowly ovate, elliptic or obovate, pale green underside with dense scales and bristles on margins. Very early flowers require some shelter from frost. Ht 0.6–1.2 m/2–4 ft. H3–4
nuttallii Maddenia Himalayas (Bhutan to Assam), upper Myanmar, W China (NW Yunnan, SE Xizang), N India (Manipur, Arunuchal Pradesh), often epiphytically in rainforests, at 1220–4420 m/4000–14 500 ft. T.J. Booth, 1849–50, Duphla Hills, Assam.	Creamy white, with deep yellow blotch, funnel-campanulate, fleshy, 75–135 mm long, with long stamens, in huge trusses of 3–7, occasionally 2–12. Highly fragrant. ML.	Straggly or upright large shrub or small tree with crimson-purple young growth opening to leaves 170–260 mm long, oblong-elliptic or oblong-obovate, upper surface dark green and heavily wrinkled, while lower surface has a pronounced network of veins and a raised midrib. Attractive, dark purplish brown bark. Sun tolerant but prefers shelter from wind. Highly recommended. Ht 1.2–9 m/4–27 ft, often less. H1
pemakoense Uniflora SE Xizang (Tsangpo Gorge) forming carpets on damp, moss-covered rocks, rocky slopes, at 2900–3050 m/9510–10 000 ft. Kingdon-Ward, 1924, Pemakochung, SE Xizang.	Pinkish purple to purple-mauve or violet-pink, tubular campanulate, hairy, 24–35 mm long, in singles or couples, often in sufficient quantity to conceal the foliage. Flowers freely from an early age. EM.	Prostrate, mound-forming or rounded dwarf species with densely branched habit, and bright green or greyish-green, scaly leaves, 13–30 × 5–15 mm, obovate or obovate-elliptic, very dense covering of golden to dark brown scales, particularly thick on undersides. Perfect for rock garden culture but early flowers demand protection from frost. Named after the province in Xizang in which it was discovered. Ht 0.3–0.6 m/1–2 ft. H3
rigidum syn. *caeruleum* Triflora W China (N Yunnan, Sichuan) widespread in open scrub, thickets, forests and their margins, cliffs and rocky slopes, at 800–3550 m/2625–11 650 ft. Abbé Delavay, 1884, Lan-kien-ho, NW Yunnan.	White tinged with pale pink, lilac rose, pinkish violet, sometimes with faint, reddish or olive brown spots, widely funnel-shaped, in trusses of 2–6, freely flowering from an early age. Fragrant. ML.	Normally upright habit, as indicated in its name, with leathery, glaucous, bluish-green, elliptic to lanceolate foliage, 25–68 × 10–32 mm. Ht 0.6–3 m/2–10 ft. H3
rupicola Lapponica W China (NW Yunnan, SW Sichuan), NE upper Myanmar, widespread on rocks, cliffs, open pastures and moors at 3350–4270 m/11 000–14 00 ft. George Forrest, 1910, Lichiang Range, Yunnan.	Deep plum purple to deep magenta red, widely funnel-shaped, 8–18 mm long, in trusses of 2–8. ML.	Cushion, mat-forming or compact rounded shrub with small, densely scaly, elliptic, matt green foliage, distinctive dark brown and yellow scales underneath, 6.5–25 × 40–14 mm. Ideal species for the rock garden. A number of named varieties, including var. *rupicola* (purplish red), var. *chryseum* and var. *muliense* (both yellow). Ht 0.8–1.2 m/2 ft 6 in–4 ft. H3–4
russatum Lapponica W. China (N Yunnan, SW Sichuan), NE upper Myanmar, in stony pastures, rocky slopes, moorland, crevices, cane brakes, rhododendron forests, and forest margins, at 3350–4270 m/11 000–14 000 ft. George Forrest, 1917, Kari Pass, NW Yunnan.	Deep blue-purple, or violet-purple, sometimes with a white throat, widely funnel-shaped, 10–20 mm long, in trusses of 3–6, sometimes up to 14. ML.	Compact rounded, cushion-forming or semi-prostrate straggly shrub with densely scaly branchlets, bristly young shoots and oval to oblong-lanceolate, dark green, matt or shiny leaves, 16–40 mm long, dense reddish brown scales underneath. A number of named varieties, including 'Collingwood Ingram' (taller, purple), 'Keillour' (compact, blue-purple), 'Maryborough' (medium, blue-purple) and 'Night Editor' (twisting foliage, purple). Ht 0.15–1.5 m/6 in–5 ft. H3–4

Species	Flowers	Notes
scintillans Lapponica W China (Yunnan) in marshes and and boggy pastures, alpine moorland, in the margins of oak and conifer forests at 3050–4400 m/ 10 000–14 500 ft. George Forrest, 1913, Lankong-Hoching Pass, Yunnan.	Lavender blue, purplish rose or nearly royal blue, widely funnel-shaped, 10–15 mm long, in trusses of 2–5, freely flowering. ML.	A most worthwhile dwarf species to look for, especially for rockery cultivation. Slender, densely scaly branchlets form an upright, spreading shrub, becoming more leggy in shade, very occasionally cushion-forming, with dark green, heavily scaled, oblong or lanceolate foliage, approx. 13 × 4 mm. Ht 0.15–0.9 m/6 in–3 ft. H3–4
scopulorum Maddenii SE Xizang (Lower Po-Tsangpo Valley), in exposed sites among rocks, in thickets and various forests at 1830–2440 m/6000–8000 ft. Kingdon-Ward, 1924, Tsangpo Gorge, E Xizang.	White, with or without faint pink bands, or apple blossom pink, with or without yellowish orange basal blotch, scaly and finely pubescent all over, widely funnel-shaped, 45–62 mm long, with crinkled margins, in trusses of 2–7. Fragrant. ML.	Broadly upright or bushy shrub, with shiny dark green, grooved, oblong, obovate or oblanceolate leaves, pale green and scaly underneath, 40–82 × 16–36 mm. Ht 0.9–4.5 m/3–15 ft, usually less. H1–2
spiciferum syn. *R. scabrifolium* var. *spiciferum* Scabrifolia W China (W & NW Yunnan, Kweichow, SW Szechuan), widespread in thickets, scrub and pineforests at 1525–3200 m/5000–10 500 ft. Abbé Delavay, 1891, nr. Yunnansen, Yunnan. *Photo p. 52.*	Pink, deep pink, rose or white, widely funnel-shaped, outside scaly, 10–15 mm long, in trusses of 1–4, flowering freely. M.	Low, compact, spreading or upright shrub with pubescent and bristly branchlets and linear to oblong-obovate leaves, 12–35 × 2–13 mm, upper surface scabrid, pale green and with brown scales underneath, recurved margins. Sun tolerant and well suited to rock garden culture. Ht 0.15–1.8 m/6 in–6 ft, more in the shade. H3
spinuliferum Scabrifolia W. China (S Yunnan) in woods and shady thickets at 800–2440 m/2625–8000 ft. Abbé Delavay, 1891, Tonghay, S Yunnan. *Photo p. 52.*	Unusual crimson, brick red or orange, very narrow, erect, tubular flowers, 17–23 mm long, in clusters of 1–5, the filament and style projecting beyond the tube, which fills with a watery solution of nectar. Freely flowering. ML.	Fast-growing, broadly upright, often straggly shrub with bristly and pubescent branchlets, petioles and undersides of leaves, and smooth, dark purple-brown bark. Oblanceolate to obovate foliage, 30–90 × 15–40 mm. An eloquent illustration of the widely divergent form possible within one genus, so far from the conventional concept of a garden rhododendron. Ht 1.5–3 m/5–10 ft. H2–3
taggianum Maddenia W. China (NW Yunnan), NE upper Myanmar, in open conifer forests at 1830–3700 m/6000–12 000 ft. Farrer, 1920, Kum La Bum, NE upper Myanmar.	White, with orange-yellow blotch at base, open, funnel-campanulate, often frilled, 65–95 mm long, in trusses of 2–5, fragrant and freely flowering from 3–4 years. ML.	Broadly upright shrub, sometimes epiphytic in the wild, very similar to *R. lindleyi*, with dark reddish brown, peeling bark and shining, dark green, narrowly elliptic to oblong-elliptic foliage, 85–130 × 25–45 mm. Ht 1.5–3 m/5–10 ft. H1–2
tephropeplum Tephropepla NE India (Arunachal Pradesh), NE Myanmar, W China (NW Yunnan, E, SW Xizang), Assam, on rocks and cliffs, conifer forests and scrub, at 2440–4300 m/8000–14 000 ft. Farrer, 1920, Chawchi Pass, NE upper Myanmar.	Dark or pale rose, pink, crimson-purple, rarely white, campanulate, outside scaly, 18–32 mm long, in trusses of 3–9, freely flowering. ML.	Compact, rounded, bushy or upright shrub with dark green, shining leaves, narrowly elliptic to oblanceolate, 40–100 mm long, densely scaly and glaucous underneath. Distinctive, scaling, brown bark. Spreading forms well suited to the rock garden. Ht 0.3–2.5 m/1–8 ft, usually less. H2–3

Species	Flowers	Notes
trichostomum Section pogonanthum syn. *R. ledoides*, *R. radinum*, *R. hedyosmum*, *R. sphaeranthum* W China (N & NW Yunnan, SW & C Sichuan), very common, in pine and oak forests, stony pastures and meadows at 2400–4300 m/ 7800–14 000 ft. Abbé Delavay, Lankong, W Yunnan, 1887.	Normally white, pink or deep rose, 6–16 mm long, in spherical trusses of 8–20, freely flowering and long lasting. Varieties include var. *ledoides* group (syn. *R. ledoides*): 'Lakeside' and 'Quarry Wood' (white, flushed with reddish purple), 'Rae Berry' (clear pale pink) and var. *radimum* (syn. *R. radinum*) 'Sweet Bay' (white, flushed with rose). L.	A highly variable species, the variations previously being regarded as individual species (eg *R. ledoides* and *R. radinum*) and now as varieties. Normally a compact, often tiny, twiggy, intricately branched, rounded or upright bush with aromatic, narrow, stiff, leathery, dark green, linear, oblong or oblanceolate leaves, 12–30 mm long, undersides scaly and pale brown and margins rolled under. Best in full sun, ideal in rockeries. First introduced by E.H. Wilson, 1908. Ht 0.2–1.5 m/8 in–5 ft. H3
veitchianum Maddenia S & C Myanmar, Laos, Thailand, Vietnam, usually epiphytically, in evergreen jungle, at 900–2400 m/2950– 7875 ft. Thomas Lobb, for Veitch nursery, circa 1850, Moulmein.	Very large and elegant, pure white, usually with yellow basal blotch, often with frilled or wavy margins, openly funnel-campanulate, 60–75 mm long × 125 mm or more wide, in trusses of up to 5, fragrant. ML.	Large, open flowers, borne freely on a broad, upright or spreading shrub with smooth, reddish brown bark. Dark green leaves, obovate or narrowly elliptic, 65– 115 mm long, golden scales on underside. Epiphytic or terrestrial in the wild. Ht 0.9–3.7 m/3–12 ft, usually less. H1
virgatum Virgata Himalayas (Nepal, Sikkim, Bhutan, Assam), W China (W Yunnan, SE Xizang), in varied habitats at 1830–3800 m/ 6000–12 500 ft. J.D. Hooker, 1849, Lachen Valley, Sikkim.	White, pink or mauve, tubular funnel-shaped, 14–39 mm long, outside scaly, in singles or pairs, fragrant. M.	Vigorous, open, upright shrub with long, arching branches, scaly young shoots, dark green, scaly leaves narrowly oblong or oblong-elliptic, 18–80 × 5–20 mm. Easily struck from cuttings. Smaller forms useful in the rock garden. Variety 'Album' is white and less hardy. Ssp. *virgatum* (larger pale to deep pink or mauve), *oleifolium* (white or pink). Ht 0.3–2.4 m/1–8 ft. H1–3
webstrianum Lapponica W. China (NW Sichuan, W Yunnan), in moorlands, boogy pastures, cliffs and rocky slopes at 3300–4900 m/ 10 800–16 000 ft. E.H. Wilson, 1908, Tatsienlu, W Szechuan. *Photo p. 52.*	Pale or rosy purple to deep lavender blue, widely funnel-shaped, 10–20 mm long, in trusses of 1–6. Can be yellow in the wild. M	Upright, intricately branching shrub with tiny, light green foliage 6–15 mm long, ovate or oblong-elliptic, straw-coloured with dense scales underneath. Good, sun and heat tolerant rockery specimen. Ht 0.3–1.5 m/ 1–5 ft. H3–4
xanthostephanum Tephropepla E India (Arunachal Pradesh), NE upper Myanmar, Assam, W China (NW & C Yunnan, E & SE Xizang) in open and sheltered positions at 1830– 4120 m/6000–13 500 ft. Abbé Delavay, 1890, Tsang-shan, Yunnan. *Photo p. 52.*	Bright, lemon, canary or deep yellow, felshy, tubular campanulate, 18–28 mm long, scaly outside, in trusses of 3–5, occasionally 8, freely flowering. ML.	Broadly upright, leggy or bushy shrub, with shiny, brownish green to bright green oblong-elliptic leaves 50–100 mm long, scaly silvery-brown underneath. Attractive, smooth, reddish brown bark. Prefers a reasonably sheltered, woodland environment. A good variety to look for is 'Yellow Garland', with translucent yellow flowers. Ht 0.3–3 m/1–10 ft. H1–2
yunnanense Triflora NE upper Myanmar, W China (W Yunnan, SW Sichuan, Guizhou, SE Xizang) in conifer forests, meadows, rocky slopes, at 1980– 4270 m/6500–14 000 ft. Abbé Delavay, 1883, Houang-li-pin, W Yunnan.	White, pale pink, rose-pink, rose-lavender or lavender, usually densely spotted with red, green or yellow, widely funnel-shaped, 18–34 mm long × 20–40 mm wide, in trusses of 3–5. Very freely flowering. L.	Broadly upright or spreading shrub with scaly branchlets and leaves, oblanceolate to lanceolate, 30– 70 × 12–20 mm. Ideal for woodland setting, and while preferring some shade, is sun tolerant. Widespread and very variable in the wild, according to local conditions, some varieties becoming virtually deciduous. Ht 0.3– 3.6 m/1–12 ft. H3

Elepidote species

Species	Flowers	Notes
aberconwayii Irrorata China (NE Yunnan) 1937, McLaren, Lo Shiueh Mountain, NE Yunnan.	White to pale rose, with crimson or purple spots, saucer-shaped or open campanulate, 28–35 mm long, in trusses of 5–12. Freely flowering. ML.	Thick, glaborous, glossy, rigid, dark green elliptic leaves, 30–60 mm long. Broadly upright growth. Ht 0.3–2.5 m/1–8 ft. H3
adenogynum Taliensia China (SE Xizang, W Yunnan, SW Sichuan) at 3000–4300 m/9480–14 100 ft.	White, flushed with pink or pale pink, 30–45 mm long, funnel-shaped. M.	Shrub or small tree with elliptic or narrow-elliptic leaves, 60–110 mm long, dense spongy covering of yellowish hairs, turning olive brown with age. Glandular petioles and branches. Ht 0.5–4 m/1 ft 6 in–13 ft. H3
arboreum Arborea Himalayas, China, Thailand, S India, Sri Lanka. Photos pp. 33, 85.	Crimson or scarlet, to pink, fleshy, tubular campanulate, 30–50 mm wide. Takes some years to flower, but ultimately freely flowering. Variety 'Album' has white flowers and smaller habit and Ht 3.0–6 m. EM.	Mid-brown, spongy indumentum on undersides of tough leaves up to 200 mm long and equally broad. Wrinkled, glabrous upper surface. Slow-growing tree species, suitable for larger gardens. Rough, peeling bark. Several varieties with variations of colour, leaf form and indumentum. Ht up to 20 m/65 ft, normally less, and much lower in cultivation. H2–3
arboreum ssp. delavayii Arborea W China (W & NW Yunnan), W, C & NE upper Myanmar, in conifer forests at 1500–3500 m/4920–11 500 ft. Abbé Delavay, 1883, W Yunnan. Photo p. 85.	Deep crimson, crimson or scarlet, tubular campanulate, 30–50 mm long, in very compact trusses of 10–30. M.	Broadly upright shrub or tree. Glabrous, lanceolate or oblong-lanceolate leaves, 50–160 mm long, with heavy brown indumentum on undersides which distinguishes this subspecies from the otherwise very similar R. arboreum. Named after its finder. Ht 0.9–12 m/3–40 ft, usually no more than 5 m/15 ft in cultivation. H1–3
arboreum ssp. zeylanicum syn. *zeylanicum* Arborea Sri Lanka, mountainsides at 900–2400 m/3000–7000 ft. Photo p. 51.	Red to crimson, pink forms in the wild, 38–50 mm long. VL.	Slow-growing tree species, developing handsome, gnarled trunks with very rough, corky bark. Dark green, wrinkled, elliptic to elliptic-oblong, leaves, 130 × 50 mm, dense fawn or rusty indumentum underneath. Ht up to 9 m/27 ft. H1–3
arizelum Falconera NE Myanmar, Assam, China (W Yunnan, Xizang), in rhododendron forests, amongst bamboo and scrub at 2400–4400 m/7000–14 500 ft. George Forrest, 1917, west Yunnan.	Pale or deep yellow, or cream, creamy-white or deep rose pink, ventricose campanulate, 30–45 mm long, in large trusses of 12–25. ML.	Rounded, spreading shrub or small tree. Obovate, oval or sometimes oblanceolate leaves, 70–220 × 30–120 mm. Thick, velvety, cinnamon or fawn indumentum on undersides of foliage. Smooth, brown, flaking bark. Ht 1.8–7.5 m/6–25 ft. H3.
barbatum Barbata Himalayas, Wallich, 1829, at Gossain Than, Nepal.	Brilliant scarlet or blood red, occasionally pure white, fleshy, tubular-campanulate, 28–40 mm long, in very compact, rounded trusses of 10–20. EM.	Young shoots have long, stiff bristles. Dark green, glossy, elliptic to oblong, glabrous foliage, 90–190 mm long. Underside pale matt green. Superb, smooth, peeling mahogany-coloured bark. Ht 2.5–18 m/8–60 ft, less in cultivation. H3
beanianum Neriiflora NE India, NE Myanmar, in thickets, forest fringes and granite gullies, at 3000–3300 m/9840–10 825 ft. Kingdon-Ward, 1926, at Seingkhu Wang, Upper Myanmar.	Deep crimson to blood red, 35 mm long, fleshy, tubular campanulate, in trusses of 4–10. M.	Vigorous, open, upright habit, sometimes straggly and tangled. Young growth, branches and petioles covered with bristly hairs and short glands. Leaves 48–100 mm long × 23–45 mm, obovate to elliptic, finely wrinkled upper surface and dense, woolly, brown indumentum underneath. Ht 0.9–3 m/3–10 ft. H3

Species	Flowers	Notes
calophytum Fortunea China (NE Yunnan, W, C & E Sichuan), in woods and forests at 2400–4000 m/ 7870–13 125 ft. Moupin, 1870.	White or pinkish white, with purple spots and basal blotch, 40–60 mm long, widely campanulate, in trusses of 15–30. EM.	Easily grown, long-lived shrub with long, dark green, oblanceolate, glabrous leaves, 140–360 × 40–85 mm. Foliage curls and droops in cold weather. Rough brown bark, and silvery tomentum on young foliage. One of the hardiest large-growing species. Ht 4.5–15 m/15–50 ft. H3
campanulatum Campanulata Himalayas D. Don, 1821, introduced by Wallich, 1825.	White, to pale mauve or pink, normally with purple spotting, open campanulate, 30–50 mm long, in trusses of 6–12. ML.	Multi-stemmed shrub or small tree, with attractive, ovate to broadly elliptic, pale green, glabrous foliage, up to 140 × 250 mm, with a striking, dense cinnamon indumentum on undersides, the leaves held for one year. The dominant shrub in many areas of Nepal and Bhutan, varying widely in form and size according to local conditions. Variety 'Knap Hill' has pale lavender-blue flowers. Ht 0.3–5 m/1–15 ft. H3
campylocarpum Campylocarpa Himalayas, China (Xizang, Yunnan), NE Myanmar, in rocky slopes and mixed forests, at 2900–4200 m/ 9500–13800 ft. J.D. Hooker, 1848, Sikkim	Pale sulphur yellow, occasionally white, and sometimes with basal blotch, 25–40 mm long, campanulate, in trusses of 6–10. Can occasionally be slightly fragrant. ML.	Compact, rounded or sometime leggy and spreading shrub, or even treelike, with grey to brown bark and glabrous leaves 30–100 mm long, orbicular to elliptic. Varies widely in form and size and detail in the wild. Although not heat tolerant, this is one of the best medium-sized yellows. Ht 5 m/15 ft. H3
coelicum Neriiflora W China (W Yunnan), NE Myanmar, in exposed spots on cliffs, rocky slopes at 2750–4250 m/9000–14 000 ft. Kingdon-Ward, 1919, Laktang, NE upper Myanmar.	Deep crimson or scarlet, 35–50 mm long, fleshy, tubular campanulate, in trusses of 6–15. M.	Broadly upright habit. Glandular young shoots, glossy, dark green, obovate to oblong-obovate leaves 60–85 mm long, glabrous above, thick brown indumentum underneath. Ht 0.9–2 m/3–6 ft. H3
decorum Fortunea W. China (Yunnan, Sichuan, Guizhou), NE Myanmar, Laos, in woodlands and open positions at 1800–4500 m/ 5900–14 760 ft. Franchet, 1869, Moupin, W Sichuan.	White to pale pink, with or without green or crimson spots, 35–60 mm long × 38–75 mm wide, funnel-campanulate, in trusses of 8–12. Freely flowering from a very early age. Fragrant. L.	Broad, upright, spreading and sometimes straggly shrub or small tree. Large, oblanceolate to elliptic, glabrous leaves, 60–200 mm long. Self-seeds freely under good conditions. Ht 0.9–15 m/3–50 ft, normally less in cultivation. H3
degronianum syn. *metternichii* Pontica Japan (N Honshu), in woods and thickets up to 1800 m/ 5900 ft. before 1894, Japan. Photo p. 85.	Pink, rose, reddish or occasionally white, darker spots, campanulate, 28–43 mm long, in trusses of 6–15. Freely flowering. ML.	Easily grown, compact, rounded or broadly upright shrub, branchlets covered with whitish tomentosum. Shining, dark green leaves oblong, oblong-elliptic, obovate or oblong-lanceolate, 80–180 × 22–46 mm, deeply veined, felty, fawn indumentum underneath. Ht 0.9–2.5 m/3–8 ft. H3
degronianum ssp. *yakushimanum* syn. *yakusimanum*, *yakushimanum* Pontica Japan (Yakushima Island) in wet, exposed mountainside sites at 1200–1860 m/3930–6100 ft. Nakai, 1921. Photo p. 85.	Rose buds open to pink, then fade to pure white. Campanulate, in compact trusses of 8–12, flowers profusely from quite young. L	Considered one of the finest and sought-after semi-dwarf species, although a slow grower. Low, very compact, spreading, dome-shaped habit. Glossy, dark green leaves, 90 × 38 mm, with recurved margins. Suited to the rock garden. Isolated local colonies in Japan have led to a number of reliable, named varieties. Much used in hybridising and propagates quite easily from cuttings. Ht 0.3–1.2 m/ 1–4 ft. H3

Species	Flowers	Notes
elegantulum Taliensia W China (SW Szechuan), on rocky slopes, woodland and conifer forests, at 3650–3950 m/12 000–13 000 ft. Kingdon-Ward, 1922, Yungning, SW Sichuan.	Cream, flushed with pink, small crimson spots, 30–40 mm long, 50 mm wide, in trusses of 10–20. Takes some years to reach flowering. ML.	Compact habit. Fine, elliptic oblong foliage, 7–13 × 24–35 mm. Light brown indumentum on young shoots, dense, woolly, pink to brown indumentum on undersides of mature leaves. Roughly textured grey-brown bark. Ht 1–1.6 m/3–5 ft. H3
elliottii Parishia NE India, in forests at 2440–2750 m/8000–9000 ft. Sir George Watt, 1882, Mt Japvo, Naga Hills, Assam. *Photo p.85.*	Crimson, scarlet or purple, with darker spots, 40–50 mm long, fleshy, tubular campanulate, in trusses of 9–15. Freely flowering. VL.	Rounded or broadly upright, sometimes straggly shrub or small tree. Young glandular shoots covered with hairs. Glossy, lanceolate to elliptic, glabrous leaves 85–100 mm long. Needs protection from frost. Brilliant red flowers have led to much use in hybridising. Ht 2.4–4.5 m/8–15 ft, 3 m/10 ft in cultivation. H1–3
falconeri Falconera Himalayas (Nepal, Sikkim, Bhutan, W Arunachal Pradesh, Assam), in woodland and dense rainforest at 2440–3350 m/8000–11 000 ft. J.D. Hooker, 1849, Tonglo Mountain, Sikkim	Creamy white, to pink or pale cream, with purple basal blotch, 40–60 mm long, fleshy, campanulate, in large trusses of 12–20. Slightly fragrant, very long-lasting. ML.	Rounded or spreading or columnar tree or shrub. A superb foliage plant with dark matt green leaves, 180–350 mm long, oblanceolate to elliptic, upper surface usually wrinkled, lower surface with heavy, two-layered, white and reddish indumentum. Smooth brown, flaking bark. (white or cream flowers, glabrous foliage). Described by Peter Cox as 'one of the monarchs of the genus or even the plant world.' Ht 3–12 m/10–40 ft. H3
falconeri* ssp. *eximium syn. *R. eximium* Falconera Himalayas (Bhutan, Arunachal Pradesh) on rocky ridges at 2650–3500 m/8700–11 500 ft. Thomas Booth, before 1853, Oola Mountains, Bhutan	Cream, flushed with rose, pale lilac, 45 mm long, fleshy, in compact trusses of 12–20. ML.	One of the best foliage rhododendrons, with dark green, oval to obovate-elliptic, 150–300 × 50–150 mm, foliage. Thick, woolly, cinnamon to rust coloured indumentum on undersides held for first year. Flat-topped habit. Peeling, reddish brown bark. Prefers a moist, shady position. A more persistent indumentum than *R. falconeri* and is regarded by some as a separate species, *R. eximium*. Ht 1.5–9 m/5–30 ft. H2–3
fictolacteum Falconera W China (W Yunnan, Szechuan, E & SE Xizang), NE upper Myanmar, in conifer and rhododendron forests, at 3000–4420 m/9840–14 500 ft. Abbé Delavay, 1886, Lankiung, W Yunnan.	White, to blush pink, pale lilac or rose, blotched and heavily spotted, sometimes frilled, 30–50 mm long, in trusses of 12–25. Freely flowering. ML.	Erect habit with fine foliage and flowers. Very dark green, smooth, shiny, oblong-obovate to oblanceolate leaves, 300 mm long or more, thick, rusty brown indumentum underneath. Young shoots tomentose and rough, grey-brown bark. Ht 1.8–12 m/6–40 ft, usually much lower. H3
forrestii Neriiflora W China (NW Yunnan, Xizang), NE Myanmar, in exposed, rocky sites at 3350–4570 m/11 000–15 000 ft. George Forrest, 1905, Mekong-Salwin Divide, SE Xizang. *Photo p. 52.*	Bright scarlet, very fleshy, tubular campanulate, 30–35 mm long, singly or in pairs. Can be reluctant to flower in cultivation. ML.	Dwarf, creeping, ground-hugging shrub, with prostrate stems up to 600 mm, that often take root as they spread. Rarely more than 100 mm in height. Dense, leathery, dark green foliage 10–28 mm long, obovate to orbicular, upper surface glabrous, lower surface usually purple-red or glaucous green (var. *repens*). A number of distinct forms exist in the wild, including small-leafed varieties that are very slow growing. Influential in the breeding of compact-growing reds. Ht 0.1 m/4 in. H3
fortunei Fortunea E China (widespread), in woods and forests at 600–1200 m/2000–4000 ft. Robert Fortune, 1855, Chekiang, E China.	Pale pink, rose, lilac to almost pure white, 40–60 mm long × 55–70 mm wide, open-campanulate or funnel-campanulate, in trusses of 6–12. Fragrant. L.	Broadly upright, sometimes spreading shrub or tree. Glabrous leaves, matt dark or olive green, glaucous, pale green above, 80–180 mm long, broadly oblanceolate to obovate. Distinctive features include the rough, greyish brown bark, and reddish, bluish or purplish petioles. First hardy rhododendron introduced into England, and widely used in hybridising. Ht 1.8–9 m/6–30 ft, typically around 5 m/15 ft in cultivation. H3

Species	Flowers	Notes
fulvum Fulva W China (SW Yunnan, W Sichuan, SE Xizang), NE Myanmar, on rocky sites, thickets and conifer forest margins, at 2400–4400 m/ 7870–14 400 ft. George Forrest, 1912, Shweli-Salwin Divide, W Yunnan.	White to pink, usually with a dark crimson basal blotch, 25–45 mm wide, campanulate, with or without crimson spots, in compact trusses of 3–15. Freely flowering from an early age. EM.	Rounded shrub or small tree. Young shoots covered with brownish hairs. Beautiful, dark green leaves 80–220 mm long, oblanceolate to ovate, glabrous above, heavy brownish hairy indumentum below. Leaves curl and droop in colder weather. Self-seeds freely in good conditions. Ht 8–9 m/25–30 ft, 0.9–7.5 m/3–25 ft in cultivation. H3
grande Grandia Himalayas (Nepal, Sikkim, Bhutan, Assam), in forests, river banks at 1700–3660 m/ 5500–12 000 ft. Griffith, 1847, Bhutan. *Photo p. 85.*	Pale yellow, lemon yellow, creamy white or white, dark purple basal blotches, 40–70 mm long, fleshy, campanulate, in rounded trusses of 15–25. E.	Loosely branching tree with trunk up to 600 mm diameter on mature specimens, rough, flaking bark. Large, dark green, shining, glabrous leaves 140–300 mm long, elliptic to oblanceolate, silvery-white or fawn indumentum on undersides. Sensitive to wind damage. Ht 3–15 m/10–50 ft. H1–3
griersonianum Griersoniana W China (W Yunnan), NE Myanmar, in open forests, thickets and scrub at 2130–2750 m/7000–9000 ft. George Forrest, 1917, Shweli-Salwin Divide, W Yunnan.	Bright geranium scarlet, deep pink or crimson, sometimes with spots, 55–80 mm wide, tubular campanulate, in trusses of 5–12. Deep red buds. VL.	Loose, rather untidy, leggy, growth habit. Long, conical foliage buds, open to young shoots with a woolly indumentum, glabrous leaves 100–200 mm long, lanceolate, with heavy indumentum beneath, held for 2 years. Rough brown bark. Sun tolerant, but needs protection from frost and responds well to pruning. Long popular as a breeding parent, with enduring offspring including 'Elizabeth', 'Fabia' and 'Vanessa Pastel'. Easily propagated by cuttings and used extensively in hybridisation. Ht 1.5–3 m/5–10 ft. H2–3
griffithianum Fortunea Himalayas (E Nepal, Sikkim, Bhutan, S Xizang, to E Arunachal Pradesh) in mixed forests at 1800–2900 m/ 5900–9500 ft. J.D. Hooker, 1849, Sikkim (Griffith 1850, Bhutan).	White, with or without green spots, or various shades of pale pink, fading to white, even yellowish, 45–80 mm wide, in trusses of 3–6. Normally fragrant. ML.	Sparse shrub or small tree with erect or spreading growth. Glabrous, oblong leaves 100–300 mm long. Flaking, peeling bark. Prefers a level of shelter from wind, sun and frost. Ht 6–10 m/20–33 ft. H2–3
hemsleyanum Fortunea W. China (Sichuan) at 1100–2000 m/3600–6560 ft. E.H. Wilson, 1910, Mt Omei, W Sichuan.	Pure white, or white tinged with rose-pink, yellow-green throat, 45–60 mm wide, campanulate, fragrant, in trusses of 5–10 or	Shrub or small tree with stout, spreading habit and erect branches, dark green, glabrous, ovate to ovate-elliptic leaves, 100–200 mm long, remaining for 2 years. Rough, flaking, greyish-brown bark. Wind tolerant. Ht 3–8 m/10–25 ft. H3
hyperythrum Pontica Taiwan, at 900–1220 m/2950–4000 ft. Hayata, 1913, Mt Shichisei, Taiwan.	White, sometimes pink, with red spots, funnel-campanulate, 35–45 mm long, in trusses of 7–12. Freely flowering. ML.	Compact, rounded or spreading shrub, with glabrous young shoots and dark green, elliptic leaves, 80–120 mm long, pale green underneath. Prefers a reasonable level of shelter. Ht 0.9–2.4 m/3–8 ft. H3
irroratum Irrorata W. China (Yunnan, Sichuan), widespread in various forest types, thickets, scrub or open rocky situations at 1830–3660 m/6000–12 000 ft. Abbé Delavay, 1886, Peetsaolo, NW Yunnan.	White, yellowish white or cream to violet pink, with or without crimson, deep purple or greenish spots, 30–55 mm long, tubular campanulate, pubescent, in trusses of 8–15. Freely flowering from an early age. EM.	Erect or straggling shrub or small tree. Glabrous, pale matt green oblanceolate to elliptic leaves, 70–140 mm long, held for 2–3 years. Light greenish-brown bark. Easily grown species. Variety 'Polka Dot' has pale pink flowers, heavily dotted with purple. Ht 0.9–9 m/3–30 ft. H3

Species	Flowers	Notes
macabeanum Grandia NE India (Nagaland, Manipur) at 2440–3000 m/8000–9840 ft. Sir George Watt, 1882, Mount Japvo, Assam. *Photo p. 85.*	Pale or greenish lemon yellow with deep red or purple blotch, 50–73 mm long, tubular campanulate, in trusses of 12–20. Flowers freely from an early age. ML.	Large, shiny foliage, 130–385 × 80–200 mm, glabrous, broadly ovate to broadly elliptic, with dense, white or fawn indumentum underneath. New growth covered with dense white woolly indumentum, resembles candlesticks. Needs a large garden and self-seeds freely under good conditions. Ht 3–15 m/10–50 ft. H3
magnificum Grandia China (W Yunnan) and NE Mayanmar, in forests and riverbanks at 1500–2400 m/5000–8000 ft. Kingdon-Ward, 1931. *Photo p. 85.*	Crimson purple or rosy purple flowers with crimson blotch at base, 50–75 mm long, funnel–campanulate, in umbels of 12–30 florets. EM.	Large shrub or tree with very large, broadly obovate leaves 200–320 mm long, with thin, fluffy indumentum. 3–18 m/10–60 ft, normaly less (6 m/20 ft) in cultivation. H1–3
makinoi Pontica Japan (C Honshu), in mountain forests at 460–550 m/1500–1800 ft. Before 1925.	Soft pink or rose, with or without red spots, 35–40 mm long, funnel-campanulate, in trusses of 5–8. Freely flowering. L.	Compact, rounded or broadly upright shrub. Young shoots and mature leaves densely hairy. Long, dark green, lanceolate leaves, 50–170 × 8–25 mm, are glabrous above, dense, brown, woolly indumentum underneath. Named after Japanese botanist, T. Makino. Ht 0.9–2.4 m/3–8 ft. H3
niveum Arborea Himalayas (Sikkim, Bhutan), fairly rare, in rocky valleys, on ridges, in Tsuga and bamboo forests at 2900–3660 m/9500–12 000 ft. J.D. Hooker, 1849, Sikkim. *Photo p. 85.*	Lilac, mauve, deep magenta to purple, with or without deep lilac basal blotch, tubular campanulate, 30–35 mm long, in very compact trusses of 15–30. Large oval or oblong flower buds, covered with a rust-coloured tomentum. ML	Broadly upright or rounded shrub or small tree with glabrous leaves, 170–260 mm long, oblanceolate-elliptic, with dense fawn indumentum on underside. Whitish tomentum on young shoots. Pale grey to brown, flaking bark. Ht 2.75–6 m/9–20 ft. H3
ovatum Azaleastrum E, C & S China, Taiwan, widespread on open slopes, forest margins, in dense forests, at 175–2750 m/570–9000 ft. Fortune, 1843, Chusan Island.	White, pink or pale purple, with some crimson-purple spotting, sometimes with yellow basal blotch, rotate, almost flat, 16–26 mm long × 25–30 mm, appearing singly. Reasonably sparse flowering. L.	Erect or bushy habit with bright red or reddish brown young growth. Glabrous, glossy, dark green, broadly ovate to elliptic leaves, 20–48 × 10–24 mm. Pale, glabrous bark. Foliage inclined to chlorosis and prefers protection from frost. Heat tolerant. Sole member of the section Azaleastrum, it was originally called *Azalea ovatum*. Not widely cultivated. Ht 0.9–5 m/3–15 ft. H1–3
peramoenum syn. *arboreum* ssp. *delavayi* var. *peramoenum* Arborea N India (Arunachal Pradesh), W China (W Yunnan), in open forest and thickets at 1600–3400 m/5250–11 150 ft. George Forrest, 1918, Shweli-Sawin Divide, W Yunnan.	Bright cherry red to deep rose crimson, 25–50 mm long × 50 mm wide, in trusses of 15–20. M.	Less tree-like habit than R. *arboreum*, pretty much a narrow-leaved version of R. *arboreum* ssp. *delavayi*. Whitish indumentum on young shoots. Leaves 150 × 30 mm, narrowly lanceolate with white or fawn indumentum underneath. Ht 1.2–12 m/4–40 ft, usually below 4 m/13 ft in cultivation. H1–3
ponticum Pontica East and west Mediterranean (Spain, Portugal, Bulgaria, northern Turkey, Caucasus, Lebanon), in mixed forests from sea level to 1800 m/5900 ft. Described by Linnaeus, 1762, introduced into Britain from Gibraltar, 1763.	Pale mauve or lilac pink, usually with greenish yellow spots, campanulate, 40–50 mm long, in compact trusses of 10–15. VL.	Very hardy vigorous shrub or small tree, dense in the open, leggier in shade. Glabrous, oblanceolate to broadly elliptic young shoots and foliage, 60–180 mm long. Suitable for clipped, formal or informal hedges, or windbreaks. Widely naturalised and now a common part of the landscape in the favourable climate of the British Isles. Used frequently as a rootstock and spreads easily by layering and suckering. Heat and sun tolerant. Named after Mare Ponticum, Latin for Black Sea. Variety 'Ovatum' has distinctive ovate foliage, otherwise as species. Ht 1–8 m/3–25 ft. H4

Species	Flowers	Notes
ponticum 'Variegatum' Pontica	Pale mauve or lilac pink flowers, similar to R. ponticum. VL.	Narrow, creamy-white and green variegated foliage, smaller than R. ponticum. Less vigoruous and invasive than R. ponticum, and with pruning can be kept much more manageable. Ht 1–6 m/1–20 ft. H4
pseudochrysanthum Maculifera Taiwan, as spreading undergrowth in conifer forests at 1800–3900 m/ 5900–12 800 ft. Hayata, 1908, Taiwan.	Pink, with darker lines on outside, spotted crimson inside, campanulate, 30–43 mm long, in trusses of 8–10, eventually freely flowering, after dark pink buds. M.	Slow-growing, rounded or compact habit with dense, rigid foliage, red or grey indumentum on young shoots lingers before falling with maturity. Shiny, dark green leaves ovate to elliptic, recurved margins, 20–80 × 13–38 mm. Prefers a sunny, sheltered spot. Ht 0.3–3 m/1–10 ft. H3
rirei Argyrophylla W. China (Sichuan) in exposed spots within forests at 1200–2200 m/3930–7200 ft. E.H. Wilson, 1904, Mt Omei, Sichuan.	Purple to violet, campanulate, 40–53 mm long, in trusses of 5–10, long-lasting, eventually freely flowering. E.	Rounded, spreading or broadly upright shrub or small tree with attractively long, pointed foliage shoots, rough, brownish-black bark, straight branches and glabrous, olive green leaves, 95–170 mm long, with white indumentum underneath. Early blooms demand shelter from frost. Named after missionary in China, friend of the discoverer, Wilson. Ht 3–16 m/10–50 ft. H3
sidereum Grandia N India (Arunachal Pradesh), upper Myanmar, W China (W Yunnan), Assam, in mixed forests at 2440–3960 m/ 8000–13 000 ft. Captain Abbay, 1912, Tamgam, NE Myanmar.	Creamy yellow to primrose or clear yellow, fleshy, ventricose-campanulate, crimson basal blotch or ring, 50 mm long × 63 mm wide, in open-topped trusses of 15–20, freely flowering. L.	Erect to rounded shrub or small tree with greeny-brown bark, thin branchlets covered with grey tomentum. Matt green, oblong-elliptic to lanceolate leaves, 90–230 × 30–70 mm, with a silvery white to fawn indumentum underneath, drooping in winter. Varying forms in circulation. Ht 1.8–12 m/6–40 ft. H2–3
sinogrande Grandia W China (E, SE Xizang, W Yunnan), Myanmar, in rhododendron and bamboo forests at 3000–4000 m/ 9840–13 120 ft. George Forrest, 1912, Shweli-Salwin Divide, W Yunnan. *Photo p. 85.*	Creamy white, creamy yellow or yellow, with crimson blotch in throat, ventricose-campanulate, 40–60 mm long and fleshy, in large trusses of 15–30. Another form has pale yellow flowers. ML.	Tree or large, broadly upright, rounded shrub with rough bark and the largest foliage of all rhododendrons, which in the wild can be as much as a metre long and 300 mm wide, oblanceolate-elliptic to oblong-oblanceolate. Dark green, wrinkled upper surface, and silvery white, pale brown or tan indumentum on undersides of foliage. Prefers shelter from wind and some shade. Ht 3–15 m/10–50 ft. H1–3
sutchuense Fortunea W China (N Sichuan, Shaanxi, Hubei, Guizhou, Guangxi), in woods, oak and bamboo forests, at 1500–2400 m/ 4920–8000 ft. A. Henry, 1888, W Hubei.	Pale pink to pale mauve, with or without blotch, widely campanulate, 50–75 mm long, in open-topped trusses of about 10, long-lasting. Flowers from an early age. E.	Large, umbrella-shaped shrub with dark green, glabrous, oblong-lanceolate to narrowly oblong-oval leaves, 110–260 mm long, with indumentum on midrib underside, remaining for 1–3 years. Leaves curl and droop during cold or frosty weather. Prefers a woodland environment. Variety (reddish purple, with white centre). Ht 4.6–10 m/15–32 ft. H3
thomsonii Thomsonia Himalayas (Sikkim, Nepal, Bhutan, S Xizang, Arunachal Pradesh), on steep rocky exposed sites, in dense rhododendron, bamboo and conifer forests, at 2440–4270 m/8000–14 000 ft. J.D. Hooker, 1849, Sikkim.	Rich blood red or deep crimson, usually with darker spots, campanulate or tubular campanulate, fleshy, 35–60 mm long, in trusses of 6–13, eventually freely flowering. ML.	Small or large, rounded, spreading or broadly upright shrub or small tree. Distinctive, thick and leathery, rounded, glaucous green foliage, 30–110 mm long, held for one or two years, and attractive, red-brown, fawn or pinkish bark, which peels annually to reveal a smooth skin beneath. Sets abundant seed so appreciates dead-heading. A very variable species in the wild. Ht 0.6–7 m/2–23 ft. H3

Species	Flowers	Notes
ungernii Pontica NE Turkey, Russia (Georgia), in shade amongst deciduous and conifer trees at 800–2200 m/2600–7200 ft. Baron Ungern-Sternberg, 1885, Artvin region, NE Turkey.	White, sometimes flushed with pink, and green spots, funnel-campanulate, up to 35 mm long, in trusses of 12–30, freely flowering. VL.	Broadly upright or rounded shrub or small tree with slightly flaking brown bark. Attractive, dense, woolly, white indumentum on young shoots and undersides of beautiful, dark green oblanceolate to obovate leaves, 90–250 × 28–75 mm, held for 2–3 years. Protect from frost. Ht 1–7 m/3–23 ft, usually less. H3
wallichii Campanulata Himalayas (E Nepal, Sikkim, Bhutan, Arunachal Pradesh), W China (S Xizang), widespread, in various forest types at 2750–4300 m/9000–14 000 ft. J.D. Hooker, 1849, Sikkim. *Photo p. 85.*	White to pale mauve or lilac, with or without darker spots, campanulate, 25–50 mm long, in trusses of 6–10, freely flowering. M.	Easily grown, rounded or broadly upright shrub or small tree with pinkish brown to grey bark. Attractive white indumentum on shoots, remains on undersides of leaves, becoming dark brown with age. Dark, shiny, leathery leaves 70–120 mm long, elliptic to ovate, covered with rough hair tufts underneath, leaves held for 1–2 years. Ht 0.9–6 m/3–20 ft or more. H3
wardii Thomsonia W. China (E, SE Xizang, NW Yunnan, SW Sichuan), widespread, in mixed forests to swampy ground, at 2750–4870 m/9000–16 000 ft. Abbé Soulié, Sie-La, E Xizang, 1895.	Pale yellow to yellow, saucer-shaped, with or without reddish-purple or crimson basal blotch, 24–40 mm long, in loose trusses of 5–14. One of the best yellow species, flowering freely from an early age. L.	Broadly upright or rounded shrub or small tree, very variable in form. Leathery dark green, very rounded, orbicular or ovate leaves, 30–120 mm long, pale green and glaucous underneath, held for 1 or 2 years. Roughly textured greyish brown bark. Used frequently in the development of yellow hybrids. Varieties *wardii* (yellow), 'Ellestee' (lemon yellow with crimson blotch), 'Meadow Pond' (primrose yellow with crimson blotch), 'Puralbum' (white). After the planthunter, Francis Kingdon-Ward. Ht 0.6–8 m/2–25 ft. H3
wightii Grandia/Talensia Himalayas (Nepal, Sikkim, Bhutan), forming spreading dense thickets in exposed positions above the treeline at 3350–4300 m/11 000–14 000 ft. J.D. Hooker, 1848, Sikkim.	Pale yellow to lemon yellow, with red, brown or purple spots, and sometimes a crimson basal blotch, campanulate, 35–45 mm long, in very loose, one-sided trusses of 12–20, freely flowering. ML.	Wide range of forms in the wild, from very compact when more exposed, to open and ungainly, sometimes treelike. Glabrous foliage, broadly elliptic to obovate, 50–250 × 35–65 mm, distinctive dense buff or rust-coloured indumentum on underside, held for 1–2 years. The high altitude of its Himalayan habitat makes it one of the hardiest yellow species, regarded by some (e.g. RGB Edinburgh) as within the Talensia subsection, others say Grandia. Ht 0.6–6 m/2–20 ft. H3
wiltonii Taliensia W. China (W Sichuan), in woods, conifer forests and exposed ridges and cliffs at 2400–3400 m/8000–11 150 ft. E.H. Wilson, for Veitch nursery, 1904, W Sichuan.	White to pink, with or without reddish spots and crimson basal blotch, campanulate, 30–40 mm long, in trusses of 6–10, taking several years to flower, and then not in great abundance. ML.	Broadly upright shrub or bush, dense brown or whitish tomentum on dense branchlets, and light to dark brown bark which becomes rougher with age. Young shoots tomentose for 3–4 years. Olive green, shiny, bullate leaves, oblanceolate to broadly elliptic, 50–120 mm long, with a dense cinnamon indumentum underneath. 'Exbury' form is white, flushed with pink and crimson blotch. 0.9–5 m/3–15 ft. H3

9
The hybrids

Although there are over eight hundred species of rhododendron, only a small number have been seen as having value as garden plants. Many species in their wild state tend to lack the form and physical qualities which could make them of value to horticulture. Others need specific climatic and growing conditions which are difficult to emulate. Some species have at least offered characteristics of interest, such as a particularly strong colour or form of flowers to encourage the breeder to try to blend those qualities with the stronger points of other species to create new and hopefully 'better' plants known as hybrids. In hybridising plants the aim is to create a new blend of growing characteristics with aesthetic appeal – to bring together, for example, the hardiness or tolerance to cold weather of one species with the flower colour and size of another.

The first documented hybrid rhododendron to bloom was a cross made by the Thompson Nursery at Mile End, near London, between a deciduous azalea, *R. periclymenoides* (syn. *R. nudiflorum*) with the much larger evergreen lepidote *R. ponticum*. This hybrid, which was presented to Edinburgh's Royal Botanic Gardens in 1814, was called *R. hybridum* and, at a later date, *R. azaleoides*. It was all the more remarkable in that such a cross would normally be considered to be virtually impossible, one of the rare examples of a successful cross between different Sections of the *Rhododendron* genus, which ignores one of the great genetic limitations facing breeders. A hybrid such as this one, between an azalea and a rhododendron, is known as an azaleodendron. A few successes have been registered over the years and breeders in various countries will continue trying. Most seedlings of these crosses, however, appear to fail, if any viable seed is produced at all. Instead, hybridising more normally tends to try to bring together the characteristics of pre-existing hybrids and species that are broadly similar to each another and within the same Section of the genus, seeking refinement and improvement rather than looking for dramatic change.

At around the same time that the Thompson Nursery was breeding the first azaleodendron, Michael Waterer was beginning to breed rhododendrons at his Knap Hill Nursery at Woking, Surrey. In his first attempted cross, Waterer was trying to blend the pink flower colour he desired of *R. maximum* with the flower size and growing habit of the lilac magenta *R. catawbiense*. This was the beginning of a family dynasty that has become synonymous with the genus. Over several generations, the Waterer family has brought us literally hundreds of great hybrids, including the Knap Hill line of deciduous azaleas and many evergreen rhododendrons that are still strong favourites today. Amongst these are 'Pulcherrimum' (*R. arboreum* × *R. caucasicum*, 1835), 'Mrs R.S. Holford' and 'Sappho' (both of unknown parentage, 1866), 'Pink Pearl' (*R.* 'George Hardy' × *R.* 'Broughtonii', 1867) and 'Lady Eleanor Cathcart' (*R. maximum* × *R. arboreum*, 1926).

Plant hunters continued to come back from further afield with the seeds of new discoveries. The resulting seedlings were patiently nurtured and as each new discovery flowered, often decades later, it was hailed with even greater amazement than the last. The arrival of several species in particular are now seen as landmarks in the hybridising of rhododendrons, each expanding the breeder's palette and sparking new waves of enthusiastic activity. Such was the level of competition between breeders that much secrecy surrounded their efforts to unveil new hybrids at shows.

The parentage of many early hybrids was kept concealed and unfortunately can only be guessed at today.

R. *arboreum*, a tree rhododendron, arrived in England from the Himalayas in 1811, but did not flower for another fourteen years. When it did, the size and perfect globular form of its pure crimson flower trusses could not before have even been imagined. Growing at higher altitudes in tropical areas, R. *arboreum* was frost tender and quite unsuited to English winters. Work began immediately on blending those perfect flowers, the first strong red to become available to breeders, with hardier plants to produce the first red hybrids hardy enough to survive the English winter. One of these plants was a cross between R. *arboreum* and the result of an earlier cross made between R. *catawbiense* and R. *ponticum* to produce 'Altaclarense', a tree form with deep red flowers. In 1835, Michael Waterer crossed R. *arboreum* with R. *caucasicum* to produce 'Nobleanum', which has scarlet flowers with white flushes. And around the same time, R. *catawbiense* was crossed with R. *arboreum* to give us the large-growing, crimson-flowered 'Russellianum'.

In 1850 Sir Joseph Hooker introduced R. *griffithianum* from Nepal and the northern Indian states of Sikkim, Assam and Bhutan. This large plant had fragrant white, pinkish or occasionally yellowish flowers and generous leaves up to 30 cm/1 ft long. In 1855, R. *fortunei* was discovered by collector Robert Fortune in China's eastern Chekiang province, while he was searching for new varieties of tea for the plantations of the British East India Company. Also fragrant, and growing to around 10 m high in its natural habitat, R. *fortunei* was the first truly hardy rhododendron to be introduced into Britain from China. Sir Edmund Loder crossed these two species to create the dazzling 'Loderi' series of hybrids which he introduced in 1901. These tree-like, vigorous hybrids have very large, sweetly scented, lily-shaped flowers in pastel pinks and whites and beautiful foliage.

Nineteenth century hybridising was motivated largely by wealthy landowners with large country gardens seeking larger shrubs and tree-like hybrids. The dark, almost sombre evergreen foliage contrasting with vivid, extravagant flowers appealed perfectly to Victorian tastes. After the First World War, however, the wealth moved closer to the cities, and the rising middle class and the spread of the suburbs caused smaller gardens to become more fashionable. The search was on for more compact plants, an emphasis in breeding which continues today, as the suburban garden reigns supreme.

In 1917, George Forrest discovered R. *griersonianum* growing in the Yunnan province of China, and later again in northern Burma. Forrest named his new find after his friend R.C. Grierson, a British customs official then working in China. Although untidy in its growth habit, the heavy flowering of R. *griersonianum* has found its way into many fine cultivars which endure today, including 'Anna Rose Whitney' (R. 'Countess of Derby' × R. *griersonianum*, 1954) and two of Lord Aberconway's well-known hybrids 'Winsome' (R. 'Humming Bird' × R. *griersonianum*, 1939), and 'Fabia' (R. *griersonianum* × R. *dichroanthum*, 1934).

One of the keys to the breeding of smaller elepidote rhododendrons was the introduction of R. *degronianum* ssp. *yakushimanum* (formerly R. *yakushimanum*) in 1934 by Lionel de Rothschild of Exbury. Discovered thirteen years earlier on the Japanese island of Yakushima, this subspecies offered compact, if slow, growth, with an abundant display of pink to white flowers and the bonus of a whitish beige indumentum on its younger foliage. Rothschild propagated and distributed examples of the species to a number of other gardeners. Its ideal combination of aesthetic qualities, as well as its desirable growing characteristics of hardiness to −20°C/−4°F, reasonable tolerance to direct sunlight and disease resistance, was passed on to many valuable lines of compact hybrids. It is still a popular species in breeding programs today.

Other breeders, both in England and overseas, were experimenting in other directions to produce more compact garden plants. Peter Cox, at Glendoick in Scotland, was breeding compact rhododendrons using R. *ludlowi*. This dwarf species had been discovered in 1936 by Ludlow and Sherriff, growing on a rocky hillside in southeastern Xizang (Tibet), and its discovery opened the way to the breeding of dwarf and compact lepidote rhododendrons.

The Rothschilds of Exbury were just one of a number of famous English family dynasties that have introduced many of the hybrids that are still propagated and grown commercially. That process continues everywhere that rhododendrons can be grown, with breeders in different countries working to produce plants which are appropriate to their climates and gardening habits. In Australia, breeders Victor Boulter, Karel van der Ven and Arnold Teese, based in the favourable climate of the Dandenong Ranges near Melbourne, have introduced a number of successful warmer climate plants that are found in European and American catalogues. New Zealand breeder Edgar Stead has placed several broad-leaved hybrids into the international market, although he is probably best known for the Ilam strain of deciduous azaleas. Hybridising in the United States has been centred towards the western States, the cooler climate of the eastern seaboard restricting the range of plants which could be grown.

Many early cultivars manage to persist in rhododendron catalogues, regardless of fashion trends, because all those years of growing experience have shown them to be ageless and durable. Even after the years of evaluation taken to bring them to registration, newly released hybrids still face a long battle to prove their worth as garden plants and forge an acceptance for themselves in the marketplace. The best of the 'modern' hybrids that have been developed since the 1950s have been in cultivation long enough now to have a track record which justifies their continued appearance in catalogues.

The range of hybrids and species in commercial cultivation at any given time and place is driven as much by market forces and mass appeal as by the particular qualities of an individual variety. The horticultural trade is a business first and no wholesale nursery is going to invest in the propagation of hundreds or thousands of plants that can't pay their way. Growers' catalogues are dictated by the mass appeal of bright, showy flowers, compact manageable growth, site and climatic adaptability, interesting foliage and ease of growth. The result is that most of the thousands of hybrids painstakingly bred and registered over the last two centuries will eventually disappear from view, and as a consequence many very good garden plants are no longer available.

There doesn't seem to be an urge to a seek out and revive older cultivars of rhododendron to match the nostalgic 'heritage' rose boom. A number of growers do specialise in collecting and growing species rhododendrons, as much for their botanical and historical interest, as for their often simpler and purer forms than the more popular hybrids that resulted from their discovery.

Smaller-growing hybrids

Species	Flowers	Notes
Smaller mauves, purples and blues, 0–1 m/0–3 ft		
'Augfast' R. augustinii × R. fastigiatum E. Magor, 1921.	Abundant pale to deep lavender blue, in small trusses of star-shaped flowers. EM.	Small-leafed, compact, dome-shaped shrub with yellowish new growth. Does well in full sun. −18°C/0°F.
'Blue Admiral' Parentage unknown	Bluish mauve. EM.	Fine, dark green foliage. −21°C/−5°F.
'Bluebird' R. intricatum × R. augustinii Lord Aberconway, 1930.	Numerous electric or violet blue flowers, in trusses of 7–10. EM.	Compact, tiny-leafed shrub, wider than tall, prone to chlorosis. Not highly regarded. Strikes easily. −18°C/0°F.
'Blue Tit' R. impeditum lavender form × R. augustinii ssp. augustinii J. C. Williams, 1933. Photo p. 86.	Abundant, grey–blue flowers in trusses of 2–3. EM.	Small, pale green leaves on a compact plant. New growth is yellowish and inclined to be chlorotic. Best flowering in full sun. Susceptible to sucking insect damage. −21°C/−5°F.
'Florence Mann' R. augustinii (or R. rigidum) × 'Blue Admiral' A. Bramley, 1963.	Deep lavender blue or lavender violet. Floriferous. EM.	Heat-tolerant, compact, upright plant, one of the best smaller blue varieties, particularly in warmer climates. Strikes easily. −18°C/0°F.
'Oceanlake' 'Blue Diamond' × 'Sapphire' Arthur Wright Sr. & Jr., 1963/66	Deep violet blue, flattish, 25 mm wide, in trusses of 8. Blooms later and flowers longer than other 'blues'. EM	Small, dense foliage, about 25 mm long, reddish bronze in winter. Sun tolerant. Strikes easily. −21°C/−5°F.
'Peste's Blue Ice' 'Purple Lace' × R. degronianum ssp. yakushimanum F. Peste, 1986.	Deep purplish pink, open to very pale purple with light spotting of deep greenish yellow, 5 very wavy lobes, in domed trusses of 21. M.	Well-branched plant. −18°C/0°F.
'Prostigiatum' R. saluenense ssp. chameunum 'Prostatum' × R. fastigiatum E. Magor, 1924.	Rich deep purple, 25 mm wide, in trusses of 2–3. ML.	Very slowly growing, low, dwarf habit, tiny grey-green leaves. Limited striking success. −21°C/−5°F.

Species	Flowers	Notes
'Ramapo' R. fastigiatum × R. minus var. minus 'Carolinianum' G. Nearing, 1940.	Pinkish violet, smallish in compact trusses, but freely flowering. EM.	One of the hardiest of dwarfs, with attractive, almost circular foliage, 25 mm long, and dusty grey-blue new growth. Deep metallic hue to foliage in winter. Compact, mound-like habit. Sun tolerant, ideal for the rockery, coping well with occasional dry spells. Strikes easily. –32°C/–25°F to –36°C/–33°F.
'Saint Breward' R. impeditum × R. augustinii ssp. augustinii E. Magor, 1962.	Bright lavender violet, darker at margins, in tight, spherical trusses of 26, flowering freely after 5 years. EM.	Small, dense, vigorous, very hardy bush, wider than high. Long, dark foliage, droops unattractively in winter. Strikes easily. –21°C/–5°F to –26°C/–15°F.
'Saint Tudy' R. impeditum × R. augustinii ssp. augustinii E. Magor, 1960.	Lobelia blue, in dome-shaped trusses of 14. Flowers freely after 5 years. EM.	More compact growth and trusses, but otherwise resembles 'Saint Breward', above, from the same cross. –21°/–5°F to –26°C/–15°F

Smaller pinks, 0–1 m/0–3 ft

Species	Flowers	Notes
'April Glow' syn. 'April Showers' R. williamsianum × 'Wilgen's Ruby' Van Wilgens Nursery, 1963/5.	Bright or pale rosy pink with reddish spotting, in trusses of about 10. EM.	Vigorous, semi-dwarf, upright growth, darkish foliage with coppery new growth. –23°C/–10°F.
'Astarte' R. dichroanthum ssp. dichroanthum × 'Penjerrick' Lord Aberconway, 1931.	Salmon pink to apricot, pendulous, cup-shaped flowers, in trusses of about 8. ML.	Low bushy habit. –15°C/5°F to –21°C/–5°F.
'Bow Bells' 'Corona' × R. williamsianum L. de Rothschild, 1934.	Deep pink buds open to cup-shaped, light pink flowers, deeper on reverse, in loose, freely flowering trusses of 4–7. EM.	Reliable, floriferous, rounded plant with medium-sized foliage which is reddish bronze when young. Prefers some shade. Strikes easily. –21°C/–5°F.
'Cilpinense' R. ciliatum × R. moupinense Lord Aberconway, 1927. Photo p. 106.	Blush pink, touched with deeper pink, bell-shaped flowers in trusses of 2–3, very freely flowering. E.	Popular, compact, mound-like shrub with deep forest green, shiny foliage. Protect from sun. Strikes easily. Susceptible to sucking insects. Semi-dwarf. –15°C/5°F.
'Coral Velvet' R. degronianum ssp. yakushimanum × unknown H. Swanson & H. Greer, 1979.	Coral pink, fading to light salmon, long-lasting, 50 mm wide, in open trusses of about 5. EM, sometimes also in autumn.	Japanese seedling once thought to be a form of R. degronianum ssp. yakushimanum. Small, narrow, slightly twisted leaves and thick stems with a velvety indumentum on lower surface. Own roots not very reliable. –26°C/–15°F.
'Doc' R. degronianum ssp. yakushimanum × 'Corona' J. Waterer, Sons & Crisp, 1972.	Rose pink with deeper rims, spots on upper lobes, 35 mm wide, frilled, in rounded trusses of about 9 short-lived flowers. ML.	Vigorous, upright, compact growth. Strikes easily. Not one of the better R. degronianum ssp. yakushimanum hybrids, flowering poorly. –26°C/–15°F.
'Empress Eugenie' Parentage unknown	Blush pink. M.	Small flowers on a low-growing plant.
'Fabia' R. dichroanthum ssp. dichroanthum × R. griersonianum Lord Aberconway and others, c. 1934.	Scarlet, shading to orange tube, in loose, drooping trusses of 7–10 bell-shaped flowers. Also apricot, salmon pink, yellow, orange and tangerine forms. M.	One of the best oranges. A number of forms from Lord Aberconway at Bodnant, Loder at High Beeches and Rothschild at Exbury. Usually neat, compact growth, one dwarf form. Medium-dark green leaves with light indumentum. Easy to strike and heat tolerant. –15°C/5°F.

Cultivar	Flowers	Notes
'Ginny Gee' R. racemosum × R. keiskei 'Yaku Fairy' W. Berg, 1979.	Bright pink buds open to dark pink flowers, shading to shell pink, with white stripes, giving a two-tone effect, 25 mm wide, in groups of 11 buds, each with 4–5 flowers. EM.	A very successful dwarf hybrid, broader than tall, with creeping branches and small, stiff leaves. Easy to strike. Sun tolerant and drought and heat resistant. –23°C/–10°F to –29°C/–20°F.
'Humming Bird' R. haematodes ssp. haematodes × R. williamsianum J.C. Williams, 1933.	Deep pink to cherry red or rose, bell-shaped flowers in loose trusses of 4–5. EM.	Small, dark, leathery, rounded leaves, with slight indumentum, compact, mound-shaped, dense growth. Slow-growing, requires shade. Strikes and grows easily. –15°C/5°F to –18°C/0°F.
'Hydon Dawn' R. degronianum ssp. yakushimanum × 'Springbok' Hydon Nurseries, 1969.	Rhodamine pink, fading to edges, deep purplish pink throat with red-brown spots, frilled, in round trusses of 14–18. Flowers after 3 years. ML.	Vigorous, very compact plant with dark, glossy leaves which have a cream indumentum. Strikes easily and fairly insect resistant. –15°C/5°F to –23°C/–10°F or colder.
'Kimberly' R. williamsianum × R. fortunei ssp. fortunei H. Greer, 1963/64.	Distinctive big, bright purple buds open to light or pastel pink flowers, fading to white, freely flowering. EM.	Attractive moss green, rounded foliage which is hidden under profusion of blooms. Purple petioles. Strikes easily. Enjoys shadier spots. –23°C/–10°F.
'Kimbeth' 'Kimberly' × 'Elizabeth' H. Greer, 1979.	Purplish red buds open to bright rose pink, funnel-shaped, 65 mm wide, in flat trusses of 3–5, flowering profusely from quite young. EM.	Reliable shrub of dwarf, rounded, bushy habit, broader than tall. Yellowish green foliage, bronze when young, held for two years. Strikes easily. –21°C/–5°F.
'Multiflorum' R. ciliatum × R. virgatum ssp. virgatum I. Davies, before 1868.	Pink buds open to pink or blush lilac, tubular flowers held in pairs along the stems, freely flowering. EM.	Small, spreading, compact shrub with long, narrow, olive green, glossy foliage. Strikes easily. –12°C/10°F.
'Olympic Lady' syn. 'White Olympic Lady' 'Loderi King George' × R. williamsianum E. Ostbo & R.W. Clark, 1958.	Pink buds open to pale pink, cup-shaped flowers, fading to white, 100 mm wide, in loose trusses of 4–8. EM.	Compact growth, broader than tall, floriferous, with roundish leaves on reddish petioles. –21°C/–5°F.
'Percy Wiseman' R. degronianum ssp. yakushimanum × 'Fabia Tangerine' Waterer, Sons & Crisp, 1971.	Peach pink, fading to white, pale yellow centre and orange spots, funnel-shaped, in trusses of 13–15, after 2–3 years. ML.	Vigorous, well-branched, compact plant, wider than tall, with shiny, dark green foliage, up to 75 mm long, with no indumentum, despite parentage. Named after its breeder. –15°C/5°F to –18°C/0°F or colder.
'Pink Silk' Hybrid of 'Cilpinense', selfed and re-selfed. A. Teese, 1981.	Pale pink, in trusses of 3 florets. E.	Compact, not particularly vigorous growth, but massed flowers. –15°C/5°F.
'Pirianda Pink' 'Bric a Brac' × unknown hybrid H. Ansell, 1975.	Light cardinal red to deep purplish pink, with white centre, 5-lobed, funnel-shaped, in trusses of 2–3. VE.	Prefers shade. –15°C/5°F.
'Racil' R. racemosum × R. ciliatum N.S. Holland, 1937.	Pale shell pink, in clusters of multiple trusses of 3–4. EM.	Open habit when young, becomes compact with age, small, dark green foliage 45 mm long. Easily propagated from cuttings, but prone to root fungi. –18°C/0°F to –21°C/–5°F.

Species	Flowers	Notes
'Sleepy' R. degronianum ssp. yakushimanum × 'Doncaster', selfed Waterer, Sons & Crisp, 1971.	Red buds open to pink or pale phlox purple flowers, darker at edges, with a deep brownish red blotch, fading finally to off white. Flowers from 2–3 years. M.	Compact, vigorous growth. Long, dark green leaves, purple petioles, stems and buds similar to 'Blue Peter'. Easy to strike. −23°C/−10°F.
'Surrey Heath' [R. facetum × 'Fabia'] × [R. degronianum ssp. yakushimanum × 'Britannia'] Waterer, Sons & Crisp, 1975.	Rose pink with creamy yellow centre, and slight orange spotting, in globular trusses of 12–16. M.	Compact, very dense growth, with distinctive, long, narrow, pointed leaves with whitish indumentum on upper surfaces when young, though none when mature. Strikes easily. −18°C/0°F.
'Valerie Kay' R. degronianum ssp. yakushimanum × 'Leo' Mrs Friedman, 1974.	Bright carmine pink, fading to lighter, frilled lobes, in ball-shaped trusses of 20. M.	Leaves with fawn indumentum, new growth mousey grey. −18°C/0°F.

Smaller reds, 0–1 m/0–3 ft

Species	Flowers	Notes
'Bad Eilsen' 'Essex Scarlet' × R. forrestii ssp. forrestii D. Hobbie, 1965/70.	Cardinal red with faint spotting, in loose trusses of 4–5. Large, pointed, red buds. M.	Vigorous, spreading habit, and small, dull medium green, heavily veined foliage. Easy to strike but resents heat. −23°C/−10°F.
'Baden-Baden' 'Essex Scarlet' × R. forrestii ssp. forrestii D. Hobbie, 1972.	Deep cherry red, waxy, bell-shaped flowers, in flattish trusses of about 6. Freely flowering. M.	Glossy, dark green foliage. Vigorous, compact habit, usually at least twice as wide as its height. Strikes easily but resents heat. −26°C/−15°F.
'Blitz' R. haematodes ssp. haematodes × unknown R.W. Clark, 1945.	Dark red, in loose trusses, freely flowering, including occasional blooms in autumn. M.	Bushy, low, mound-like, compact habit. Fawn indumentum on lower surface of dark green leaves. Heat and sun tolerant. −15°C/5°F.
'Carmen' R. sanguineum ssp. didymun × R. forrestii ssp. forrestii L. de Rothschild, 1935.	Deep bright red, campanulate, waxy flowers, with paler stamens, in trusses of 2–5. Freely flowering from 4–5 years. EM	Broad, sturdy bush with dense, small, dark, glossy foliage. One of the best dwarf varieties. Strikes easily, and prefers some shade. −21°C/−5°F.
'Cary Ann' 'Corona' × 'Vulcan' Wright, Sr. & Jr., 1962.	Coral red, trumpet-shaped flowers in conical trusses of 17. Freely flowering from young. M.	Good, distinctively grooved, dark green foliage. Sun tolerant., easily struck, but susceptible to chewing insects. −15°C/5°F.
'Creeping Jenny' syn. 'Jenny' R. forrestii ssp. forrestii × R. griersonianum Lord Aberconway.	Bright red, fleshy, funnel-campanulate flowers in large, loose trusses of 5–6. EM	Compact, creeping growth, with small, medium green leaves. Strikes easily, but susceptible to mildew. −15°C/5°F to −18°C/0°F.
'Dopey' Probably [R. facetum × 'Fabia'] × [R. degronianum ssp. yakushimanum × 'Fabia Tangerine'] Waterer, Sons & Crisp, 1971.	Glossy red, paler toward margins with dark brown spots on upper lobes, campanulate, 65 mm wide, long lasting, in spherical trusses of about 16, freely flowering from an early age. M.	Compact, vigorous, upright growth, with dull medium green leaves, 100 mm long. Easy to strike. Recommended. −15°C/5°F to −18°C/0°F.
'Dorinthia' R. griersonianum × 'Hiraethlyn' Lord Aberconway, 1938. Photo p. 86.	Clear, shiny red flowers with deep, wavy lobes in loose trusses. M.	Dark foliage with a fawn indumentum underneath. Habit is improved with early pruning. Strikes easily. −15°–21°C/5°F.

Cultivar	Flowers	Notes
'Elisabeth Hobbie' 'Essex Scarlet' × R. forrestii ssp. forrestii D. Hobbie, 1945.	Brilliant scarlet red, with darker red spots, in loose trusses of 5–10. EM.	Popular, low-growing, dense, compact shrub, leggier with age, with deep green, roundish foliage. Strikes easily. –21°C/–5°F.
'Elizabeth' R. forrestii ssp. forrestii × R. griersonianum Lord Aberconway, 1929/39. Photo p. 86.	Bright red, in loose trusses of 6–8 funnel–campanulate flowers 90 mm wide, the masses of flowers often completely concealing foliage. EM, can also bloom randomly in autumn.	A compact plant, broader than tall, with medium green foliage. One of the better dwarf hybrids, and certainly one of the most popular. Sun tolerant and easily struck, but prone to mildew and chewing insects. –18°C/0°F.
'Faith Henty' 'Elizabeth' × 'Earl of Athlone' V.J. Boulter, 1978.	Bright red, in trusses of 5–7 trumpet-like florets, freely flowering. EM.	Compact habit. –15°C/5°F.
'Fireman Jeff' 'Jean Marie de Montague' × 'Grosclaude' L. Brandt & J. Eichelser, 1977.	Bright blood red, with brown spotting and large, bright red calyx in compact trusses of about 10, flowering after 3–4 years. M.	Well-branched plant which is broader than high, leggy without pruning. Medium dull green foliage, with light indumentum, held for 3 years. Strikes fairly easily. –18°C/0°F.
'Mandalay' R. haematodes ssp. haematodes × R. venator L. de Rothschild, 1947.	Deep red, spotted darker red inside, waxy and tubular, in loose trusses. EM.	Low, compact growth habit. Dark, deeply veined foliage with light fawn indumentum underneath. –18°C/0°F to –23°C/–10°F.
'Mars' Uncertain parentage, possibly a griffithianum hybrid J. Waterer, Sons & Crisp, 1928. Photo p. 87.	Deep red, waxy flowers with distinctively contrasting white stamens, in full, rounded trusses of 12–14 florets. ML.	Slowly growing shrub with dark, twisted and ribbed leaves. Highly susceptible to sucking insects and bud blast, and usually performs better in the shade. Parent of many other hybrids. Strikes easily but slowly. –23°C/–10°F.
'May Day' R. haematodes ssp. haematodes × R. griersonianum A.M. Williams, 1932.	Cerise or light orange–scarlet, funnel-shaped, in loose trusses of about 8, freely flowering. EM.	Low-growing, vigorous habit, with medium to dark green leaves, thick, light brown indumentum. Strikes easily. –15°C/5°F.
'Myrtifolium' R. minus × R. hirsutum Loddiges, before 1828.	Purplish rose, spotted with crimson, in clusters of up to 12.	Broad, dome-shaped shrub with dense, rich, dark green foliage, whitish when young, turning bronze red in winter. Heat and sun tolerant. A very old hybrid which should not be confused with the old species R. myrtifolium, now R. kotschyi. –26°C/–15°F.
'Perri Cutten' 'Bambi' × R. arboreum R. Cutten, 1976.	Light red with enlarged pink calyx, in trusses of 20 florets.	Ht 0.75 m.
'Potlatch' 'Thor' × unknown R.W. Clark, before 1983.	Bright scarlet, in large trusses. M.	Small, dense shrub with thick foliage, indumentum on leaves. Similar to 'Thor' (q.v., below). –15°C/5°F.
'Purple Gown' 'Midnight' × 'Coronation Day' K. Van de Ven, 1986. Photo p. 88.	Huge, vivid purplish red, with darker ruby red blotch, in large, compact trusses of 15. M.	Sun tolerant –21°C/–5°F.
'Redwax' syn. 'Red Wax' R. haematodes ssp. haematodes × 'May Day' R. Henny, 1956.	Red, waxy, campanulate flowers, 55–60 mm wide, in very loose trusses of 3–5. M.	Low, dense, spreading plant with deep green foliage, 75 mm long, with heavy tan indumentum underneath, dusty tomentum on new growth. –15°C/5°F.

Species	Flowers	Notes
'Ruby Hart' ['Carmen' × 'Elizabeth'] × R. elliottii W. Whitney, 1956.	Dark blackish red, waxy, 35 mm wide, long-lasting, in very loose trusses of 6–8. Flowers from 2 years. EM.	Low, dense, compact plant as broad as tall, dark green, ribbed, leaves with thick gray-brown indumentum. Strikes easily. –18°C/0°F.
'Scandinavia' 'Betty Wormald' × 'Hugh Koster' M. Koster & Sons, 1950.	Dark crimson or cardinal red, shaded with bronze, with black blotch, funnel-shaped, contrasting white stamens, in large, dome-shaped trusses of 14–18, freely flowering. ML.	Strong medium habit, wider than tall, with medium green foliage up to 175 mm long. Strikes easily. –18°C/0°F.
'Scarlet Wonder' 'Essex Scarlet' × R. forrestii ssp. forrestii D. Hobbie, 1960.	Bright cardinal red, campanulate, with wavy edges, in loose trusses of 4–7. Freely flowering from 2 years. M.	Very popular, vigorous, compact plant with glossy, ribbed, green foliage, twice as wide as tall. Sun and wind tolerant and very easy to strike. –26°C/–15°F.
'Sir Robert Menzies' 'Elizabeth' × R. arboreum 'Bennet's' K. Van de Ven.	Bright red flowers. E.	Very hardy shrub with compact bushy growth and distinctive foliage.
'Thor' R. haematodes ssp. haematodes × 'Felis' L. Brandt, 1961/63.	Geranium like or bright scarlet, with large calyx, in loose trusses of about 7. M.	Compact plant with thick indumentum on underside of dark green foliage. –15°C/5°F.
'Titian Beauty' [R. facetum × 'Fabia Tangerine'] × [R. degronianum ssp. yakushimanum × 'Fabia Tangerine'] Waterer, Sons & Crisp, 1971.	Turkey red, waxy flowers after two years. M.	Neat, erect, very dense, compact habit, with fine, deep green foliage, thin brown indumentum below. Strikes easily. –18°C/0°F.
'Winsome' 'Humming Bird' × R. griersonianum Lord Aberconway, 1939. Photo p. 105.	Rosy cerise, after pointed, reddish buds in winter, in loose trusses of 4–6, flowering when quite young. EM.	Attractive, bushy little plant, with small, pointed foliage, bronze when young, thin indumentum below. Strikes easily. –18°C/0°F.

Smaller whites, 0–1m/0–3 ft

Species	Flowers	Notes
'Bric a Brac' R. leucaspis × R. moupinense L. de Rothschild, 1934.	Small white flowers, with faint pink markings on upper lobes, with contrasting chocolate-coloured anthers. Freely flowering, and very early, one of the earliest to flower. VE.	Small, round, pubescent foliage on an open bush with new foliage bronze. Characteristic shiny, peeling bark on older wood. Strikes easily and heat tolerant. –15°C/5°F.
'Bronze Wing' Parentage unknown A. Teese, 1981.	Creamy white, flushed with pale cyclamen at edges in open-topped trusses. M.	Nicely rounded, compact plant with heavily textured leaves. New foliage an attractive deep bronze red shade. –18°C/0°F.
'Cowbell' R. ciliatum × R. edgeworthii L. de Rothschild.	Large, pure white flowers, in loose trusses. EM.	Fuzzy, dark green foliage. –9°C/15°F to –12°C/10°F.
'Daviesii' Parentage unknown.	White, flushed pink. Large, heavily perfumed, trumpet-shaped flowers. M.	Bushy habit.

Cultivar	Flowers	Notes
'Dora Amateis' R. minus × R. ciliatum Amateis, 1955.	Pure white, lightly spotted with green, 50 mm wide, in loose trusses of 6–8. Extremely free flowering. EM.	Floriferous, low-growing, bushy variety. Dense mid green foliage with bronze highlights if grown in full sun. Fragrant. –26°C/–15°F.
'Fine Feathers' 'Cilpinense' × R. lutescens Lord Aberconway, 1946.	White, with pale primrose yellow, blushed with pink. E.	Straggly growth. Needs shelter from sun, frost and wind. –15°C/5°F.
'Hoppy' R. degronianum ssp. yakushimanum × 'Doncaster' Waterer & Crisp, 1972.	White, with greenish speckling, frilled, in ball-shaped trusses of 18. M.	Vigorous, compact growth with dull green foliage. Easy to strike, susceptible to mildew. –23°C/–10°F.
'Morning Magic' R. degronianum ssp. yakushimanum × 'Springbok' George, 1972.	White, flushed with deep purplish pink, orange-buff spotting on upper lobes, in trusses of 16. M.	A compact plant, wider than high, with dense foliage. –21°C/–5°F.
'Olinda Bells' Unknown parentage, lepidote hybrid raised from open seed from Kew Gardens.	Small., creamy bell-shaped flowers flushed greenish yellow with pastel pink margins in ball-shaped trusses of 4–6.	Compact, hardy plant with small, rounded foliage which hangs down in winter. Ideal for container growth. Yet to be released at the time of writing.
'Phalarope' R. pemakoense × R. davidonianum Peter A. Cox, 1968/69.	Translucent white, slightly flushed with mauve, in trusses of 5. Free flowering. E.	Vigorous, upright, compact habit, with glossy leaves 25 mm long. –23°C/–10°F.
'Princess Alice' R. ciliatum × R. edgeworthii J. Veitch, 1862.	White, tinged with pink. Deep pink buds. Freely flowering. EM.	Dwarf, compact growth, fragrant. Easily struck and sun tolerant. –12°C/10°F.
'Ptarmigan' R. leucaspis × R. orthocladum var. microleucum P.A. Cox, 1965.	White, broadly funnel-shaped, 25 mm wide, in terminal clusters of several trusses of 2–3 flowers. Freely flowering. EM.	Compact, prostrate plant, foliage to 25 mm long, dark, densely scaly underneath. Drought resistant. –21°C/–5°F.
'Rose Elf' R. racemosum × R. pemakoense B. Lancaster, 1954.	White blushed with pink, campanulate. Very freely flowering. E.	Compact, spreading plant, with small, glossy, dark green foliage, bronze in sun. Sun tolerant and drought resistant. –15°C/5°F.
'Sesterianum' R. edgeworthii × R. formosum Rinz, before 1862.	Creamy white. EM.	Medium-sized, dark, glossy foliage, a rather leggy plant helped by regular pruning. Fragrant. –9°C/15°F.
'Snow Lady' Probably R. leucaspis × R. ciliatum. B. Lancaster, 1955	White, unmarked, after white buds, dark anthers, in trusses of 2–5. Freely flowering. EM.	An excellent early white. Dark green, hairy leaves. Sun tolerant. White buds, small-growing plant. Strikes easily. –15°C/5°F.
'Snow Peak' 'Morio' × 'Mrs E.C. Stirling' K. Van de Ven, 1988.	White, with strong purplish red blotch, funnel-shaped, in trusses of 18.	Elliptic foliage.
'Suave' Parentage unknown Emil Liebig, before 1863.	Blush pink to white, campanulate, reverse pink shading to white, in loose trusses. Freely flowering. EM.	Perfumed. Rounded foliage, easy to strike. An old hybrid still in cultivation for good reason. Susceptible to rust. –12°C/10°F.
'White Flare' R. degronianum ssp. yakushimanum × 'Purple Splendour' Photo p. 106.	White, with light yellow flare on dorsal lobe, in good, tight trusses. M.	Small, compact grower with good sun tolerance. Slight indumentum on foliage. –21°C/–5°F.

Species	Flowers	Notes
Smaller yellows, golds and oranges 0–1 m/0–3 ft		
'Apricot Gold' 'Cup Day' × 'Tortoiseshell Wonder' K. Van de Ven, 1987.	Light orange–yellow or apricot, flushed with pink, in trusses of 12 to 15 5-lobed, funnel-shaped flowers.	An attractive shrub with compact growth.
'Australian Cameo' 'Apricot Gold' × 'Lem's Cameo' K. Van de Ven, 1986.	Light orange–yellow flushed with pink. Trusses of 20–24 funnel-shaped flowers.	Oblanceolate foliage 100 × 50 mm.
'Bambi' *R. degronianum* ssp. *yakushimanum* × 'Fabia Tangerine' Waterer & Crisp, 1951.	Yellow flowers tinged with rose, in trusses of 7–9. M.	Dwarf, compact habit. Thin indumentum. –15°C/5°F.
'Chikor' *R. rupicola* × *R. ludlowi* P. Cox, 1962.	Soft yellow, flattish flowers with deeper spots, in trusses of 3–6. M.	Twiggy stems with tiny, slightly shiny leaves on a compact bush resembling a miniature tree. Bronze red foliage in winter. Named after an Asian bird. Resents excessive heat and poor drainage. –18°C/0°F.
'Chrysomanicum' *R. chrysodoron* × *R. burmanicum* Lord Aberconway, 1947. Photo p. 86.	Bright buttercup yellow in trusses of about 8. Freely flowering. EM.	Low growing, compact, spreading bush. Dark green, shiny leaves. Strikes easily. Buds frost-tender if exposed. –12°C/10°F to –15°C/5°F.
'Denise' 'Winter Favourite' × 'Chrysomanicum' V. J. Boulter, 1972.	Apricot pink, shades of yellow and small red blotches. E.	Small-growing plant producing masses of flowers. 8–9 florets. Recommended. –12°C/10°F.
'Fine Feathers Primrose' 'Cilpinense' × *R. lutescens* Lord Aberconway, 1946.	Pale primrose yellow. E.	Straggly growth. Needs shelter from sun, frost and wind. –15°C/5°F.
'Fred Hamilton' [*R. neriiflorum* × *R. griersonianum*] × *R. dichroanthum* H. Lem cross, Van Veen, 1972. Photo p. 86.	Orange-yellow with pink stripe on lobes, spotted with yellow-green, in flattish trusses of 9–12. Reddish-orange buds. ML.	Dense, coarse, elliptic foliage on a wide, well-branched shrub. Sun tolerant. –21°C/–5°F.
'Goosander' *R. ludlowi* × *R. lutescens* Peter Cox, 1981.	Yellow, flattish, 40 mm wide, upper lobe flecked with deep red, in trusses of 3–5. EM.	Named after a European duck. Small, dark green foliage. Bronze red new growth makes an attractive winter plant. –15°C/5°F.
'Grumpy' *R. degronianum* ssp. *yakushimanum* × unknown hybrid Waterer & Crisp, 1971/79.	Orange buds opening to creamy flowers tinged with pink, in rounded trusses of 11. M.	Compact plant, broader than tall, recurved, dull, dark green leaves. –23°C/–10°F.

Cultivar	Flowers	Notes
'Hello Dolly' 'Fabia' × R. smirnowii H. Lem & J. Elliott, 1974.	Yellow, with tinges of orange and rose, 70 mm wide, in loose trusses of 10–11. EM.	Well-branched, sometimes floppy plant with medium dark green leaves with beige indumentum. –23°C/–10°F.
'Jingle Bells' 'Fabia' × 'Ole Olson' H. Lem & J. Elliott, 1974.	Orange, fading to yellow, with red throat. Freely flowering. M.	Low-growing plant with dense foliage. New growth bronze. Sun tolerant. –15°C/5°F to –18°C/0°F
'Lemon Mist' R. xanthostephanum × R. leucapsis R. Scott, 1968. Photo p. 87.	Small, bright greenish yellow, funnel-shaped flowers in trusses of 2–3, freely flowering. EM.	Spreading, compact plant similar but superior in habit to R. xanthostemon. –12°C/10°F
'Medusa' R. dichroanthum ssp. scyphocalyx × R. griersonianum Lord Aberconway, 1936.	Masses of loose hanging trusses of salmon orange flowers, shading on lobes to mandarin red, heavily speckled with light brown. M	Low, bushy, dense, compact plant. Gray-green foliage with a light, woolly indumentum. –21C.
'Moonstone' R. campylocarpum ssp. campylocarpum × R. williamsianum J. Williams, 1933.	Creamy yellow, pink, or cream flushed with pink, bell-shaped flowers in loose trusses of 3–5. Flowers from 3–5 years. EM.	Dense, compact shrub with smooth, flat, oval-shaped leaves. Although it seems to prefer a cooler climate, late frosts can damage early leaf growth. Strikes easily and sun tolerant. –21°C/–5°F
'Ostbo's Low Yellow' 'Fabia' × 'Mrs W.C. Slocock' E. Ostbo, 1960.	Apricot pink buds open to creamy yellow flowers, 110 mm wide, in loose trusses. Starts flowering when quite young. M.	Handsome foliage, 100 mm long, deeply veined, dense growth. –18°C/0°F.
'Patty Bee' 'Yaku Fairy' × R. fletcherianum W. Berg, 1970.	Clear yellow, 5 wavy lobes, openly funnel-shaped to 50 mm wide, in loose trusses of 6 short-lived flowers. EM.	Well-branched plant broader than tall, with fairly large, dark green foliage held for two years, bronze plum coloured in winter. Sun and heat tolerant. Recommended. –23°C/–10°F.
'Princess Anne' syn. 'Golden Fleece' R. hanceanum × R. keiskei W. Reuthe, 1961.	Pale yellow, with faint greenish tint, campanulate, 70 mm wide, in trusses of 8. Very floriferous. EM.	Compact habit, with foliage which changes to various shades of bronze, particularly when young, according to climate. Strikes easily. –21°C/–5°F.
'Roman Pottery' R. dichroanthum × R. griersonianum J.J. Crosfield, 1934.	Pale orange with copper lobes, in loose, drooping trusses. M.	Neat, compact growth. –15°C/5°F.
'Saffron Queen' R. xanthostephanum × R. burmanicum Charles Williams, 1948. Photo p. 105.	Masses of sulphur yellow flowers with dark spotting carried in small trusses of 8–9. EM.	One of the best yellows, a compact shrub with narrow, glossy green foliage to 75 mm long. –7C°/19°F.
'Whitney's Orange' R. dichroanthum × 'Diane' W. Whitney & G. & A. Sather, 1976.	Light orange with darker blotch, spotted and edged in red, in rounded trusses of about 15, long-lasting. Flowers from early age. ML.	A most impressive orange. Another form is deeper orange and unmarked. Slightly twisted foliage, on a sprawling plant, helped by regular heavy pruning. Strikes easily. –18°C/0°F.

Medium-growing hybrids

Species	Flowers	Notes

Medium-size mauves, blues and purples 1–1.8 m/3–6 ft

Species	Flowers	Notes
'Anah Kruschke' R. ponticum seedling or R. ponticum × 'Purple Splendour' Kruschke, A. Wright snr, T. Van Veen, 1972–73.	Reddish purple, with deep purplish red blotch in tight ball-shaped trusses of up to 12. ML.	A very hardy hybrid with lush, fine, glossy, deep green foliage, and dense, compact habit. Heat and sun tolerant. Strikes easily. –26°C/–15°F.
'Anica Bricogne' Possibly a ponticum or catawbiense hybrid L. Leroy, before 1868.	Pale lilac with small golden yellow blotch in medium tight trusses, freely flowering. L.	Low growing, attractive, dense bushy habit, shiny light green leaves. Strikes easily. –23°C/–10°F.
'Black Prince' parentage unknown J. Veitch & Sons, before 1867.	Very dark purple, spotted, freely flowering.	Open habit, hard to strike. Also a red-flowering medium hybrid of same name (q.v.). –15°C/5°F or colder.
'Blue Crown' 'Purple Splendour' × 'Blue Peter' K. Van de Ven, 1981. Photo p. 86.	Deep lilac blue or violet with lighter centre blotched magenta, in trusses of about 20. Freely flowering. ML.	Drooping foliage, often open, sprawling habit. Easy to strike. –23°C/–10°F.
'Blue Diamond' 'Intrifast' × R. augustinii J. Crosfield, 1935.	Violet blue. EM.	Deepest blue of its kind. A compact, dense upright shrub, with tiny leaves which turn bronze in winter. Does best in full sun. Easy to strike. –21°C/–5°F.
'Blue Ensign' R. ponticum hybrid W.C. Slocock, 1934	Pale lavender blue, with prominent dark blotch, in compact, rounded trusses of 15–18. ML.	Dense, spreading growth, more compact and flowers earlier than the similar 'Blue Peter'. –26°C/–15°F.
'Blue Jay' R. ponticum × 'Blue Ensign' H. Larson, 1964/5	Lavender blue or pale violet blue, with pansy violet edges and a blotch of dahlia purple, spotted brown, in small tight trusses of 15. L.	Dense, glossy green foliage. Ball-shaped trusses of 15 florets. Sun tolerant and easy to strike. –23°C/–10°F.
'Blue Peter' Possibly a ponticum hybrid Waterer & Crisp, 1933	Frilly, light lavender blue with large blackish purple blotch, very frilly edges to petals, in abundant, tight, conical trusses of about 15 medium-sized flowers. ML.	A hardy, vigorous shrub which is wider than tall, well-branched but often sprawling habit, with glossy foliage. Tolerates a wide range of situations, including open sunny spots. Easy to strike, heat tolerant and very popular. –26°C/–15°F or colder.
'Colonel Coen' Possibly a ponticum hybrid E. Ostbo, before 1958	Deep purple with darker spots, in dome-shaped trusses. Flowers when young. ML.	Bushy, vigorous shrub with glossy, wrinkled foliage. Easy to strike. –23°C/–10°F.
'Goldflimmer' Believed to be a sport of R. catawbiense or R. ponticum.	Mauve, ruffled. L.	Variegated foliage more striking than 'President Roosevelt' on a sturdier plant, but flowers less attractive. Strikes easily. –23°C/–10°F.
'Humboldt' R. catawbiense × unknown T.J.R. Seidel, 1926.	Pale mauve or light rose purple, with dark flare and dark markings, in ball-shaped trusses. ML.	Vigorous, upright, well-branched shrub, very popular in Germany where it is normally grafted. –26°C/–15°F.
'Lady Decies' R. griffithianum × unknown J. Waterer, before 1922.	Blush lilac or light mauve, with a yellow eye, 100 mm wide in trusses of about 20. ML.	Strong-growing, leggy plant. –18°C/0°F.

Cultivar	Flowers	Notes
'Lavender Girl' R. fortunei × 'Lady Grey Egerton' W.C. Slocock, 1950.	Pale lavender, edges rosy mauve, fading at centre with golden brown spotting on upper lobe, 65 mm wide, in dome-shaped trusses of 16–20. Fragrant and floriferous. M.	Vigorous, wider than tall, with glossy foliage. Sun and wind tolerant. −21° to −23°C/−10°F.
'Lucidium' R. ponticum × unknown Waterer, 1857.	Rosy, purplish lilac, with brown spotting in throat. freely flowering. ML.	Very hardy. Dark, glossy green foliage on a dense, spreading bush. Easy to strike. −18°C/0°F.
'Madame Doumier' parentage unknown.	Deep mauve with black blotch, campanulate, in trusses of 16. L.	Large flower heads. Handsome dark green foliage. Good sun tolerance.
'Mauve Bouquet' parentage unknown. V. Boulter, 1992.	Mauve, with pale yellow flare, campanulate, in rounded trusses of 15. M.	Good sun tolerance.
'Midnight' 'Cup Day' × 'Purple Splendour' K. Van de Ven, 1978. *Photo p. 87.*	Magenta mauve with blackish throat, heavily spotted dark red on upper lobe in rounded trusses of 16 frilled florets. ML.	Very popular and one of the most successful Australian-bred hybrids. Bushy, vigorous, open-growing bush which may need some pruning to maintain a desirable form. Dark green, glossy foliage and richly coloured flowers. Insect resistant and easy to strike. −21°C/−5°F.
'Mrs T. H. Lowinsky' Parentage uncertain, includes R. catawbiense, R. maximum and R. ponticum Waterer, before 1917.	Mauve buds open to pale lilac with orange-brown blotch, widely funnel-shaped, 75 mm wide, in compact trusses of 14. Floriferous. L.	Vigorous, spreading, rounded shrub with dark green glossy foliage, 110 mm long. Strikes easily and heat tolerant. −23°C/−10°F to −26°C/−15°F.
'Murraba' 'Marion' × 'Purple Splendour' V. Boulter, 1972.	Violet, shading lighter, with double yellow-brown blotch on upper lobe, in trusses of about 18 frilled florets. EM	Dense, bushy habit. Heat tolerant, but difficult to strike. −21°C/−5°F.
'Nicholas' R. ponticum × unknown L. de Rothschild, 1965.	Petunia purple, paler toward centre, with white throat and upper segment spotted green, openly funnel-shaped, 80 mm wide, in closely packed trusses of about 19. ML.	Poor, straggly habit, with unattractive, glossy dark green foliage which tends to be rather sparse and prone to chlorosis. −23°C/−10°F.
'Night Watch' 'Cup Day' × 'Purple Splendour' K. Van de Ven.	Lavender, in rounded trusses of 16. M.	Dark green, glossy foliage. −21°C/−5°F.
'Olive' R. moupinense × R. dauricum Stirling Maxwell, 1942.	Orchid pink, with scattered darker spotting, in singles or pairs, borne profusely. VE.	One of the earliest lepidotes to flower, but rather leggy, sparse, upright growth. Strikes easily and fairly heat tolerant. −26°C/−15°F.
'Purple Lace' 'Britannia' × 'Purple Splendour' Holland, before 1969.	Deep purple red or burgundy, paler toward centre, very frilled. ML.	Compact, dense, spreading shrub with glossy green foliage. Strikes easily, but not particularly heat tolerant. −21°C/−5°F.
'Purple Opal' 'Purple Splendour' × unknown V. Boulter, 1981/84.	Purple or deep violet, with dark blotch, campanulate, in trusses of 15 florets. E.	Good sun tolerance.

Species	Flowers	Notes
'Purple Splendour' R. ponticum × unknown A. Waterer, before 1900.	Very dark purplish blue, with black blotch. Dome-shaped to spherical trusses of about 15 large, ruffled flowers. ML	'King of the royal purples', regarded by many as the best purple hybrid raised. Compact, sturdy, upright bush with glossy foliage. Easily propagated and tolerates both sun or shade. Known to be susceptible to root fungi and mildew –21°C/–5°F to –23°C/–10°F or colder.
'Purpureum Elegans' Probably R. catawbiense × R. ponticum H. Waterer, before 1850.	Bluish purple or amethyst violet, marked with green and brown, in dense, rounded trusses of about 16, freely flowering. ML.	An old very hardy favourite, still popular. Sun tolerant and easy to strike. –32°C/–25°F.
'Russautinii' R. russatum × R. augustinii Sir John Ramsden, 1936/7.	Masses of slate blue or lavender blue flowers with darker eye, in trusses of 2–5. Blooms freely at an early age. EM.	Quick-growing, small long foliage similar to parent R. russatum. –21°C/–5°F to –23°C/–10°F.
'Schiller' 'Doncaster' × 'George Hardy' M. Koster & Sons, 1909.	Light rose, fringed. ML.	Free flowering, bearing masses of small to medium flowers.
'Schubert' R. griffithianum × unknown M. Koster & Sons, before 1958.	Lilac with pale blotch at base of flower, in large compact trusses, freely flowering. ML.	Strong, bushy, vigorous habit, more sprawing in the shade. Strikes easily. –26°C/–15°F.
'Susan' Believed to be R. campanulatum ssp. campanulatum × R. fortunei ssp. fortunei. P. Williams, introduced by W. Slocock, 1948. Photo p. 105.	Bluish mauve flowers fade to nearly white with dark margins and purple spots, in rounded trusses of about 12. M	One of the best 'blues', with superb dark, glossy foliage with some indumentum and purple petioles, on a good-looking, quite vigorous plant. Prefers some shade. Disease resistant but hard to strike. –21°C/–5°F.
'Susette' Parentage unknown.	Lavender blue in medium trusses of 15, slow to flower on younger bushes. ML.	Dense, bushy plant which requires some protection for best results. Good sun tolerance. Not a registered hybrid, available in Australia, very similar to 'Susan'.
'William Downing' Parentage unknown Standish & Noble, before 1870.	Rich purplish brown, with large, intense blotch. Floriferous. M.	Attractive dark foliage, strikes easily. Popular in New Zealand.
'Windsor Lad' R. ponticum × unknown Knap Hill Nurseries, before 1958.	Blush lilac with a bold golden yellow eye, in rounded, compact trusses of 16. freely flowering. ML.	Narrow, medium sized, dark foliage on a well-shaped, upright, umbrella-shaped, though sometimes sparse plant. Strikes easily. –23°C/–10°F.
'Winter Beauty' 'Marion' × 'Van Nes Sensation' or 'Lilac Time'. V. Boulter, 1963.	Lilac in bud, fading to pale lilac in flower. Yellow-brown spots on upper lobes, campanulate, in trusses of 15 frilled florets, freely flowering. EM.	Good-looking foliage on a bushy plant which strikes easily. Good sun tolerance. –18°C/0°F.

Cultivar	Flowers	Notes
Medium-size pinks, 1–1.8 m/3–6 ft		
'Admiral Piet Hein' R. fortunei ssp. fortunei 'Sir Charles Butler' × 'Halopeanum' C. van Nes, 1957.	Rosy lilac, fragrant. M.	Can take full exposure in many situations. Insect resistant, glossy foliage. –26°C/–15°F.
'Alexander Dancer' R. catawbiense × unknown A. Waterer, 1865.	Reddish magenta with lighter centre. M.	An old, hardy hybrid, still popular.
'Arthur J. Ivens' R. williamsianum × R. fortunei Hillier, 1944. Photo p. 86.	Persian rose campanulate flowers, marked with crimson, in loose trusses of 5. EM.	Dome-shaped plant with medium-sized, ovate leaves, red petioles and coppery new foliage. Slow to flower, but strikes easily and sun tolerant. –21°C/–5°F to –23°C/–10°F.
'Australian Rainbow' 'Freckle Pink' × 'Apricot Gold' K. Van de Ven, 1992.	Greenish white inside corolla, fading to strong purplish pink at edges, in rounded, ball-shaped trusses of 20–23. M.	Strong, vigorous, bushy growth with young foliage an atttractive bronze. Mature foliage mid-green with paler, yellow–green midrib and occasional flecking. Good sun tolerance.
'Azor' R. griersonianum × R. fortunei ssp. discolor Stevenson, 1927/33.	Usually salmon pink flowers with deep red throat and ruddy brown flecks toward the base, in loose trusses, freely flowering. L.	Not a particularly attractive shrub with upright, straggly growth, foliage which is susceptible to chlorosis. Strikes easily. –15°C/5°F.
'Bacher's Gold' 'Unknown Warrior' × 'Fabia' John Bacher, 1955.	Large salmon pink flowers, fading to yellow centre, blotched with crimson. Cream stamens and brown anthers. ML.	Dense, compact growth with long, light green foliage. Prefers some shade. Insect resistant and strikes easily. –15°C/5°F.
'Bruce Brechtbill' sport of 'Unique' Brechtbill, 1970/74.	Pale pink, with very light yellow throat, in ball-shaped trusses of 10–12, freely flowering from 3–4 years. Similar to, but stronger colour than 'Unique'. EM.	Very compact habit, with beautiful, shiny, rounded foliage, very similar to 'Unique', of which it is a bud sport. Named after the American nurseryman who discovered it. Strikes easily. –18°C/0°F to –21°C/–5°F.
'Buchanan Simpson' R. oreodoxa var. fargesii × unknown Mr & Mrs E. Greig, 1963.	Phlox pink, frilled, with reddish orange speckles in throat, in rounded trusses of 8–10. EM.	Compact plant with sturdy stems and bright green, heavily veined, bullate foliage. –21°C/–5°F.
'Cheer' 'Cunningham's White' × red R. catawbiense hybrid Shammarello, before 1958.	Shell pink, with conspicuous red blotch, freely flowering in conical trusses. Flowers over a long period, from very early to M.	Rounded, compact, mounded growth with glossy, mid-green leaves 10 cm long, held for 3 years. Strikes easily. –23°C/–10°F to –26°C/–15°F.
'Christmas Cheer' R. caucasicum × unknown Methven	Pink in bud, opening to blush pink and fading to very pale pink 50 mm wide. VE.	An old hybrid, one of the very early winter-flowering varieties. Small flower heads on a dense, compact, low-growing bush. Sometimes opens some flowers during autumn. In Europe was traditionally forced into Christmas flowering, hence the name. Sun-tolerant or light shade.
'College Pink' 'Noyo Chief' × unknown G. Smith, 1985.	Rose bengal buds, opening to paler flowers in compact trusses of about 15.	Fine habit and foliage. Strikes easily. Popular in New Zealand. –15°C/5°F.
'Confection' 'Coronia' × 'Dondis' Henny, 1956.	Bright pink to white, funnel-shaped florets in upright trusses of 16.	Compact plant with large, dark green leaves.

Species	Flowers	Notes
'Corry Koster' Probably 'Doncaster' × 'George Hardy' M. Koster & Sons, 1909.	Light pink, heavily spotted with crimson or cherry red flare in throat, frilled margins, in large, loose trusses of about 16, freely flowering. EM.	Rather open-growing, upright habit, sometimes straggly, with erect medium green leaves. Strikes easily. −21°C/−5°F.
'Countess of Haddington' syn. 'Eureka Maid' R. ciliatum × R. dalhousiae J. Parker, 1862.	Pink buds open to white flushed with rose, in very loose trusses of 2–6 narrow, funnel-shaped flowers 75 mm wide, slightly scented and very floriferous. EM.	Neat, compact, flat-topped shrub with large, bright green leaves with hairy edges. Heat tolerant, but prefers the shade, strikes easily. −7°C/19°F.
'Creole Belle' 'Vulcan' × 'Harvest Moon' Thompson, 1982.	Very bright, striking bluish pink with red basal blotch, in full trusses of 10–12, from an early age. ML.	Well-branched, mound-forming plant with smooth, forest green foliage. Strikes easily and insect resistant. −21°C/−5°F.
'Cup Day' 'Fusilier' × 'Albatross' K. Van de Ven.	Deep pink or Tyrian rose, heavily spotted on all lobes, funnel-shaped, in loose trusses of about 12–15. ML.	Open habit with deep green, twisted and curled foliage, 150–170 mm long. Parent of other successful Van de Ven hybrids, including the popular 'Midnight'. −15°C/5°F.
'Dame Pattie Menzies' 'Marion' × 'Mrs Henry Shilson' Karel Van de Ven.	Very strong, bright pink, in good-looking, tight trusses. VE.	Hardy shrub with a good, bushy habit and sun tolerance.
'David Gable' syn. 'Gable's Pink No.1' 'Atrosanguineum' × R. fortunei J. Gable, 1962.	Fuchsine pink, with Indian red basal blotch, 90 mm wide, in large, dome-shaped trusses of about 8. EM.	Good habit, dark green foliage, 170 mm long. Heat and sun tolerant, strikes fairly easily. −26°C/−15°F.
'Dawn's Delight' R. griffithianum × unknown R. catawbiense hybrid J.H. Mangles, before 1884.	Carmine buds open to soft pink flowers, marked with crimson, shading to white with frilly edges in tall, conical trusses. ML.	Stems show the pink tinge of parent R. griffithianum. −15°C/5°F.
'Day Dream' 'Lady Bessborough' × R. griersonianum L. de Rothschild, 1936.	Rich rose buds and flowers, turning creamy pale yellow with a glowing rose eye, then fading to creamy white, in large, loose trusses of about 13. ML.	Loose, straggly habit, becoming more leggy in shade. −15°C/5°F.
'Desert Sun' R. houlstonii × 'Veta' V. Boulter, 1977.	Apricot pink, campanulate flowers in trusses of 16 florets. M.	Compact shrub with fair sun tolerance.
'Double Date' syn. 'Whitney's Double Pink', 'Fastuosum Flore Rosea', 'Toandos Rose' Parentage unknown Whitney, G. & A. Sather, 1975/77.	Deep purplish pink, with deeper throat, in trusses of about 10 double flowers. M.	Sparse, straggly habit, with dense, matt green foliage. Insect resistant. −21°C/−5°F.
'Dutch Marion' syn. 'Marion' 'Pink Pearl' × R. catawbiense 'Grandiflorum' Felix & Dijkhuis.	Large, frilled, deep lilac pink flowers. L.	Strong, attractive foliage. −26°C/−15°F.

Cultivar	Flowers	Notes
'Edith Boulter' 'Marion' × 'Unique' V. Boulter, 1962/63.	Small, soft lilac or lavender to deeper pink with darker edges, frilled, in medium-sized ball-shaped trusses of 15–18, freely flowering. EM.	Very attractive compact, bushy habit with good foliage. Must receive protection from full sunlight to avoid leaf scorch. Difficult to strike. –18°C/0°F to –21°C/–5°F.
'Emasculum' R. ciliatum × R. dauricum Waterer, or Veitch nursery, 1958.	Deep rosy lilac, 50 mm wide, funnel-shaped in trusses of 2 or 3, freely flowering. EM.	Small, lightly scaly leaves and column-like habit. Found in Britain to have poor roots. Sun and heat tolerant. Strikes easily. –23°C/–10°F.
'Ernest Gill' R. fortunei ssp. fortunei × R. arboreum ssp. arboreum. R. Gill & Sons, 1918.	Bright cerise pink, with crimson basal blotch, sometimes can be reluctant to flower. EM.	Handsome foliage, on a dense, very strongly growing plant. –18°C/0°F.
'Fairy Light' 'Lady Mar' × R. griersonianum L. de Rothschild, 1948.	Bright pink or soft salmon pink in loose trusses.	Fast-growing, two forms. Compact habit. –18°C/0°F.
'Flora Markeeta' R. thomsonii × unknown hybrid Flora Markeeta Nursery, 1967/8.	Coral pink buds open to ivory white flowers, flushed with coral and fringed with bright pink, in round trusses of about 10. Slow to start flowering. EM.	Wider than tall, with large, rounded, glossy foliage. –21°C/–5°F.
'Freckle Pink' 'Marion' × 'Midnight' K. Van de Ven, first flowered 1978.	Beautiful, large, pale mauvish pink bell-shaped flowers with red spotting in throat, in trusses of 12, M.	Sun tolerant shrub with compact habit.
'Furnivall's Daughter' Parentage unknown Knap Hill, 1957.	Bright pink with cherry blotch, in full, beautifully-shaped, conical trusses of about 15, freely flowering from 3–4 years. ML.	Larger flowers of a brighter pink than found on 'Mrs Furnivall', as well as a stronger growth habit. Large, bright green, rugose leaves, prone to chlorosis, unreliable roots. –21°C/–5°F or lower.
'Garnet' R. griffithianum × 'Broughtonii' P.D. Williams, 1942.	Deep salmon rose or salmon pink, flushed with red. M.	Upright, spreading habit, normally quite compact. Glossy, dark green foliage. –15°C/5°F
'Goblin' 'Break of Day' × R. griersonianum L. de Rothschild, 1939.	Bright salmon pink, funnel-shaped, 75 mm wide, on loose trusses of 7. ML.	Sark sage green foliage, low-growing, well-formed plant. Susceptible to mildew. –15°C/5°F.
'Goethe' R. catawbiense 'Grandiflorum' × 'Mrs Milner' T.J. Seidel, 1905. Photo p. 87.	Light rose pink flowers with faint pale brown markings. ML.	Very hardy medium grower. –20°F/–29°C.
'Grace' syn. 'George Grace' 'Loderi' × 'Borde Hill' R. Henny, 1943.	Rich, two-tone pink, 115 mm wide, in trusses of 15. EM	Very free flowering.
'Graf Zeppelin' 'Pink Pearl' × 'Mrs C. F. Sargent' C. B. van Nes & Sons, 1958.	Bright, clear pink, blushing darker to edges, in rounded trusses of up to 10 florets. ML.	Very handsome, vigorous plant with outstanding glossy, dark green foliage. Strikes easily, insect resistant and sun tolerant, although prefers some shade. –23°C/–10°F to –26°C/–15°F.
'Happy' 'Pauline' × R. griffithianum Rothschild, 1940.	Pink with darker blotch.	

Species	Flowers	Notes
'Jan Dekens' Parentage unknown J. Blaauw, Boskoop, 1940.	Bright pink, fringed with deeper pink on edges, fading rapidly to pale pink, Upright, compact trusses of large, frilled flowers, freely flowering. ML.	Strong, vigorous plant with boldy curled leaves. Sun tolerant. One of the best of the 'Pink Pearl' hybrids. −21°C/−5°F.
'Jane Rogers' 'Mrs Donald Graham' × 'Mrs R.S. Holford' Endre Ostbo, 1957.	Clear pink, with vibrant deep rose flare. ML.	Dark, medium or large foliage, susceptible to chlorosis, preferring some shade. −21°C/−5°F.
'Kalimna' 'Edith Boulter' × 'Unknown Warrior' V. Boulter.	Pale pink on tips, shading darker pink in centre, yellow-brown spotting on upper lobes, in trusses of 20. Freely flowering. EM.	Dense, compact habit, with twisted foliage. One of the best of the Australian Boulter hybrids. Hard to strike. −18°C/0°F.
'Lady Clementine Mitford' syn. 'Lady C. Mitford' R. maximum × unknown A. Waterer, 1870.	Soft peach pink, darker at edges, with slight yellow eye, in compact, rounded trusses of 16–18. Free flowering. ML.	An old, but still popular hybrid. Handsome, glossy dark green foliage covered with silver hairs when young. Vigorous, dense, spreading, upright growth, broader than tall. Heat and sun tolerant. −21°C/−5°F or cooler.
'Lady Stuart of Wortley' Parentage uncertain, possibly a R. griffithianum hybrid. M. Koster, 1909.	Glowing pink, large, in drooping trusses. ML.	Upright, open habit. −18°C/0°F.
'Lem's Cameo' 'Dido' × 'Anna' H. Lem, 1962. Photo p. 87.	Deep, purplish-pink buds open to apricot cream and pink, small scarlet dorsal blotch, widely funnel-campanulate, in large, ball-shaped trusses of 17–20. Floriferous. M.	An exceptional variety. Rigid, upright plant with rounded foliage shiny, deep green in summer, bright bronzy red when young, Winner of Superior Plant Award, USA. Hard to strike. −15°C/5°F/5°F to −18°C/0°F.
'Lucky Strike' R. griersonianum × 'Countess of Derby' Van Veen Sr., before 1958.	Deep salmon pink, funnel-shaped, 75 mm wide, slightly waxy, in firm, conical trusses of 9. ML.	Upright, spreading, well-brnached plant with dull green leaves, 150 mm long. Heat tolerant but prefers some shade. Insect resistant, but resents over-fertilising. −12°C/10°F to −15°C/5°F.
'Mahmoud' Parentage and origin unknown, before 1958.	Lavender pink with large golden eye. ML.	Open, rounded habit with long, narrow, matt green, slightly concave leaves. Sun tolerant and insect resistant. −18°C/0°F.
'Margaret Dunn' R. fortunei spp. discolor × 'Fabia' Lord Swaythling, 1946.	Apricot flushed with shell pink, openly funnel-shaped, 90 mm wide, in loose trusses of 8–9. Floriferous. ML.	Slim, elliptic foliage to 150 mm long. Strikes fairly easily. A beautiful variety. −18°C/0°F.
'Margaret Mack' 'Marion' × 'Annie E. Endtz' V.J. Boulter, 1965.	Deep rose pink, spotted upper lobe, in large trusses of 15 frilled florets, 80 mm wide and 100 mm deep, widely campanulate. EM.	Twisted, rich green leaves on a strong-growing bush. Straggly and difficult to manage unless in full sun. Hard to strike. −18°C/0°F.
'Maryke' R. fortunei spp. discolor × 'Fabia' Van Veen Sr, 1974.	A beautiful pastel blend of light pink and yellow, 75 mm wide, in dome-shaped trusses of 13–15. ML.	Erect growth, dull olive green foliage. Heat and sun tolerant. Strikes easily. −18°C/0°F to −21°C/−5°F.
'Melba' 'Marion' × 'Van Nes Sensation' V. Boulter, 1972.	Light pink, fading to very light purple in centre, in trusses of 13 frilled florets, freely flowering. EM.	Compact shrub with curling foliage. −21°C/−5°F.

Cultivar	Flowers	Notes
'Mrs Bernice Baker' 'Dawn's Delight' × *R. fortunei* Larson, before 1958.	Large, unusual flowers, rose pink with lighter throat, and reddish pink on wavy lobes, in large, conical trusses. ML.	Hardy shrub with rather open habit and attractive foliage which hangs down after winter. −21°C/−5°F.
'Mrs C. B. Van Nes' 'Princess Juliana' × 'Florence Sarah Smith' C.B. van Nes, before 1958.	Glowing crimson buds open to deep pink, fading to a soft, pretty, pale pink, in compact, rounded trusses of about 12, freely flowering over a long period, but slow to start flowering. E–L.	Dense, low to medium habit, with good-looking medium green, glossy leaves. Prefers some shade. Easy to strike. −18°C/0°F.
'Mrs Furnivall' syn. 'Mrs Furnival' Parentage unknown A. Waterer, 1920.	Light rose pink, paler at centre, with conspicuous deep sienna blotch, widely funnel-shaped, in large trusses of 12–14. ML.	A reliable, slow-growing, handsome, compact, dense variety with dark green foliage 100 mm long. Heat and sun tolerant. Hard to strike. −23°C/−10°F to −26°C/−15°F.
'Mrs Robert W. Wallace' Unknown hybrid × 'George Hardy' M. Koster, 1909.	Soft pink, fading to white, with dark blotch, freely flowering. ML.	Low, compact growth, free flowering. −21°C/−5°F.
'Mundai' 'Nobleanum' × 'Unique' V. Boulter, 1965.	Deep, glowing pink or magenta, deeper spotting on upper lobe, in abundant medium-sized trusses of 20, freely flowering. E.	Dense, compact growth habit, strong grower with pointed foliage. −18°C/0°F.
'Noble Pearl' 'Elizabeth' × 'Kew Pearl' K. Van de Ven.	Salmon pink in loose trusses, freely flowering. EM.	Spreading habit. −15°C/5°F to −23°C/−10°F.
'P. J. M.' syn. 'P.J. Mezitt' *R. minus* × *R. dauricum* P.J. Mezitt, 1939, intro. 1959.	Bright lavender pink, several other forms, in trusses of 4–9, freely flowering from 3–4 years. EM.	One of the hardiest hybrids ever produced, but heat tolerant at the same time. Compact, rounded plant with small, aromatic, rounded foliage, green in summer, mahogany bronze in winter. Sun, wind and drought resistant. −32°C/−25°F.
'Pink Perfection' Possibly a hybrid of *R. griffithianum* or 'Pink Pearl' × 'Cynthia'. R. Gill, before 1900. Photo p. 88.	Pale pink, tinged with lilac, in open, very conical trusses. ML.	Reddish petioles distinguish this hybrid from 'Pink Pearl' which it resembles, leggy growth. A vireya bears the same name. Strikes easily. −18°C/0°F.
'Prince Camille de Rohan' *R. caucasicum* × unknown Waelbrouck, 1855.	Light pink with deep reddish pink or pinkish brown blotch, very ruffled, freely flowering, in dense trusses of up to 20. EM.	Another very old, but still popular hybrid. Vigorous, rounded shrub with slightly twisted, dark, leathery foliage, lighter green areas on leaves and thin indumentum. Strikes easily. −26°C/−15°F.
'Professor Hugo de Vries' syn. 'Hugo de Vries' 'Pink Pearl' × 'Doncaster' L.J. Endtz & Co., 1921/58.	Rich rose buds open to lilac rose, with reddish brown ray, funnel-shaped, in large, loose conical trusses of about 16, freely flowering. ML.	A 'Pink Pearl' hybrid of stronger growth and bearing very large flowers of a deeper colour. Medium open habit, sometimes leggy, and attractive foliage. Strikes easily and resistant to root fungus. −21°C/−5°F.
'Robyn' 'Marion' × 'Van Nes Sensation' V.J. Boulter, c. 1972.	Large, deep lilac flowers, freely flowering. EM.	Bushy habit, regarded as one of the best of the Australian Boulter hybrids, although not registered. Strikes easily. −21°C/−5°F.

Species	Flowers	Notes
'Rocket' 'Cunningham's White' × red *R. catawbiense* seedling A. Shammarello, 1955.	Glowing coral pink, with scarlet blotch, bell-shaped, in flat-topped or conical trusses. E.	Thick, glossy, heavily veined foliage. Easily propagated. Heat and sun tolerant and strikes easily. −26°C/−15°F.
'Rosabel' 'Pink Shell' × *R. griersonianum* A. Waterer, 1865.	Rose red buds open to pale pink and darker veining, shading to pale salmon pink with a dark eye when fully open. Large, trumpet-shaped, in loose trusses.	An early hybrid still popular today.
'Ruby F. Bowman' *R. fortunei* × 'Lady Bligh' Dr Paul Bowman, 1951.	Tyrian rose pink with ruby or blood red throat, in large, full, long-lasting, dome-shaped trusses of 13–15 florets, freely flowering. EM.	Vigorous, open, upright, spreading bush with large, flat, slightly glossy, yellowish leaves 170 mm long, with red petioles. Sun and heat tolerant, insect resistant and strikes easily. −21°C/−5°F.
'Saki' selfed from 'Letty Edwards' V.J. Boulter.	Cream, tinged with pink, in tight trusses. EM.	Open plant with light green foliage. Not easy to strike. −18°C/0°F.
'Sarita Loder' *R. griersonianum* × 'Loderi' hybrid Col. G.H. Loder, 1934.	Dark crimson buds open to deep rose or salmon pink, in loose trusses of 9–11. ML	Upright, open, often leggy plant with long, pointed leaves. Prefers some shade. −15°C/5°F.
'Satin' 'Boule de Neige' × *R. catawbiense*, red form Shammarello, before 1958.	Shrimp pink. ML.	Handsome foliage. A dwarf, red-flowering hybrid of the same name ('Madam de Bruin' × *R. forrestii* ssp. *forrestii*, D. Hobbie) is popular in continental Europe. −29°C/−20°F.
'Scintillation' Parentage unknown, possibly a *R. fortunei* hybrid. Dexter, 1925–42.	Pastel pink with yellowish-brown flare in throat, in large, full, rounded trusses of about 15, freely flowering. ML.	One of the most highly rated American hybrids. Distinctive, deep green, shiny leaves with waxy texture, which droop in the cold, on an easily grown shrub, wider than tall. Fairly easy to strike. Insect resistant and heat tolerant, but prefers some shade. Often used in hybridising. −26°C/−15°F.
'Seta' *R. spinuliferum* × *R. moupinense* Lord Aberconway, 1933. Photo p. 105.	White with bold margins of rose pink, narrowly campanulate, very free-flowering over a long period. E.	Neat-growing bush. −15°C/5°F.
'Spring Glory' 'Cunningham's White' × red *R. catawbiense* hybrid Shammarello, 1955.	Purplish pink, paler toward centre, with crimson or cherry red blotch, in full, rounded trusses. EM, sometimes also in autumn.	Vigorous, compact plant, with attractive foliage, tolerates sun or shade. Strikes easily. −26°C/−15°F.
'Success' 'Fusilier' × 'Albatross' K. Van de Ven, 1965.	Rose bengal, crimson in throat, in loose trusses of about 15 funnel-shaped florets, each 100 mm wide.	Leaves deep green, 170 mm long. Prefers some shade. −15°C/5°F.
'Trude Webster' 'Countess of Derby' selfed Harold E. Greer, 1961.	Clear pink, fading to near white, upper lobe spotted darker, 127 mm wide, in huge conical trusses, freely flowering. ML.	Winner of Superior Plant Award, USA. Strong, vigorous plant with medium green, slightly twisted, glossy foliage, 175 mm long. Strikes easily and sun tolerant. −23°C/−10°F.
'Turkish Delight' Parentage and origin unknown.	Large pink flowers.	Open habit. Ht 1.2 m, −29°C/−20°F.

Cultivar	Flowers	Notes
'Van Nes Sensation' R. fortunei 'Sir Charles Butler' × 'Halopeanum' or 'White Pearl' C.B. van Nes, before 1958.	Light orchid pink, with paler centre, fading to off-white, 7-lobed, reddish spotting in throat, in very large, dome-shaped trusses. Slightly fragrant. M.	Hardy with large flowers, suits exposed positions. Sturdy, compact plant with attractive foliage. Strikes easily, heat tolerant and insect resistant. Often used in hybridising. −21°C/−5°F.
'Virginia Richards' [R. wardii × 'F.C. Puddle'] × 'Mrs Betty Robertson' William Whitney, 1962/65.	Pink, changing to creamy yellow with crimson or red blotch, 115 mm wide, frilled, long-lasting, in trusses of 9–12, very freely flowering from young. M.	Compact plant with superb, dark, glossy foliage. Strikes easily but susceptible to mildew. −18°C/0°F to −21°C/−5°F.
'Willbrit' 'Britannia' × R. williamsianum D. Hobbie, before 1960, reg. 1965.	Bright pink, campanulate, paler toward edges, in trusses of 5–8. ML.	Bushy, rounded, egg-shaped dark green foliage. Resistant to root rot. −15°C/5°F to −23°C/−10°F.
'You Beaut' 'Marion' × 'Van Nes Sensation' V.J. Boulter.	Deep lilac or cyclamen pink in bud, fading darker. E.	Medium trusses of 14–15 florets. Vigorous, bushy, compact, low growth.

Medium-size reds, 1–1.8 m/3–6 ft

Cultivar	Flowers	Notes
'Aunt Martha' R. ponticum × unknown Roy W. Clark, 1958.	Bright red-purple, speckled with gold in centre, in large, full trusses. Floriferous. ML.	Dense, leathery foliage. Vigorous, sun-tolerant plant. −23°C/−10°F.
'Barclayi' R. thomsonii ssp. thomsonii × 'Glory of Penjerrick' R. Fox & S. Smith, 1913.	Large crimson flowers in open trusses. 'Robert Fox' has larger, paler, blood red flowers.	Treelike but not untidy habit, often with red streak to midribs. −10°C/14°F.
'Bastion' 'Bibiani' × R. elliottii L. de Rothschild, 1961.	Dark red with black spots in tight upright trusses. EM.	Attractive bright chestnut young foliage on a tallish plant with loose habit. −12°C/10°F.
'Black Prince' R. thomsonii × 'Romany Chal' Lester Brandt, 1962.	Oxblood red in trusses of 15–16. ML.	Compact, medium-growing bush bearing medium-sized trusses. Free flowering and hardy. Also a mauve-flowering medium hybrid of same name (q.v.). −18°C/0°F.
'Bonfire' Unknown hybrid × R. fortunei ssp. discolor Waterer & Crisp, 1928.	Fiery orange-red, with darker spots, in loose, conical trusses of large flowers, flowers from 4–5 years. ML.	Strong-growing. Dull green foliage can be chlorotic. Heat tolerant and prefers open sunlight. −21°C/−5°F.
'Bulstrode Park' Unknown R. griffithianum hybrid × 'Sefton' C.B. van Nes, before 1922.	Bright scarlet crimson, in large, loose trusses of waxy flowers, freely flowering after 4–5 years. M.	Strong, hardy variety with upright, sometimes treelike growth, narrow, dark green leaves. Strikes easily. −21°C/−5°F.
'Burgundy' 'Britannia' × 'Purple Splendour' Lem, before 1958.	Burgundy red in trusses of 15, freely flowering. ML.	Good habit and foliage. Strikes easily. −26°C/−15°F.
'C.B. van Nes' 'Queen Wilhelmina' × 'Stanley Davies' C.B. van Nes.	Glowing scarlet, in rounded trusses of 12–14 90 mm florets, freely flowering. EM.	Symmetrical, compact bush with matt green, long, narrow foliage, tends to yellow. Prefers some shade and not very heat tolerant. Fairly easy to strike, but susceptible to mildew. −15°C/5°F.

Species	Flowers	Notes
'C.P. Raffil' 'Britannia' × *R. griersonianum* RBG, Kew, 1949.	Deep orange–red in large, rounded trusses. L	Dense, spreading plant with light green foliage 150 mm long, and reddish brown petioles. Named after former curator at Kew Gardens, London. –15°C/5°F to –18°C/0°F.
'Chevalier Felix de Sauvage' *R. caucasicum* × unknown hardy hybrid C. Sauvage, 1870.	Coral rose with prominent dark blotch in centre, frilled, in tight trusses of 9–15 medium-sized florets, freely-flowering. EM.	Compact, low-growing, mound-like bush. –21°C/–5°F.
'Choremia' *R. haematodes* × *R. arboreum* Lord Aberconway, 1933.	Blood red or crimson scarlet, waxy, bell-shaped flowers, with prominent calyx, in small trusses of about 10. E.	Low-growing dense, bushy habit. Neat, dark foliage has silvery indumentum underneath. Strikes easily, but susceptible to root rot. –15°C/5°F.
'Crimson Glory' Parentage unknown Cottage Gardens, Eureka, 1950.	Crimson, long-lasting flowers, freely flowering. ML.	Dark green foliage. –23°C/–10°F.
'Crossroads' Possibly *R. kwayii* × *R. strigillosum* H.L. Larson. Photo p. 86.	Rich cardinal red flowers in full trusses. EM.	Narrow foliage covered with thick bristles. –18°C/0°F
'Earl of Athlone' 'Queen Wilhelmina' × 'Stanley Davies' C.B. van Nes & Sons, 1933.	Bright blood red in full, handsome, dome-shaped trusses of 12–20 campanulate flowers. Very free-flowering. EM.	Open, spreading habit, sometimes ungainly and straggly, with long, narrow, dull, dark green leaves. Not particularly vigorous, and roots inclined to be unreliable. Prefers shade in warmer areas. –18°C/0°F.
'Earl of Donoughmore' *R. griersonianum* × [unknown hybrid × Mrs L.A. Dunnet'] M. Koster & Sons, 1953.	Bright red, with orange glow and bluish hint, in good-looking trusses of 10–15, freely flowering. ML.	Open, often sparse bush, particularly straggly in more shade, with dull green leaves, liable to be chlorotic. Strikes easily. –18°C/0°F to –21°C/–5°F.
'Fire Prince' 'Britannia' × *R. delavayi* K. Van de Ven, 1973.	Brilliant deep or cardinal red, lightly spotted on upper lobe, trusses of 20 frilled florets. EM.	Good-looking strongly growing, hardy, sun tolerant shrub with attractive brownish indumentum on younger foliage.
'Fire Walk' 'Britannia' × *R. delavayi* K. Van de Ven, 1972.	Deep red, in trusses of 14 florets.	Light fawn indumentum on foliage.
'Gibraltar' 'Bibiani' × *R. elliottii* L. de Rothschild, 1939.	Large, impressive, deep blood red, spotted with black, in dome-shaped trusses, normally freely flowering, with a long flowering period. EM.	An excellent rhododendron except for the conspicuous hanging of its otherwise attractive foliage during the colder months. Upright, leggy habit with sparse foliage. Young foliage chestnut. Prefers protection from wind and sun. –12°C/10°F.
'Gill's Gloriosa' *R. griffithianum* × 'Pink Pearl' R. Gill & Son, 1925.	Bright cerise, long-lasting, in rounded trusses. E.	–15°C/5°F.
'Glamour' 'Margaret' × *R. Griersonianum* L. de Rothschild, 1939.	Deep cherry red, flushed with orange, in large, fine trusses of about 10, freely flowering. ML.	Strong, vigorous, spreading plant with uninspiring foliage. –15°C/5°F.
'Goldsworth Crimson' syn. 'Madame Charron' *R. griffithianum* × 'Doncaster' W. Slocock, 1926.	Bright crimson or red, fading in centre, spotted with black, in compact, rounded trusses of 12–16, freely flowering. EM.	Spreading but compact plant with long, glossy, dark green foliage. –18°C/0°F.

Cultivar	Flowers	Notes
'Grace Seabrook' 'Jean Marie de Montague' × R. strigillosum C. Seabrook, 1965.	Currant red at margins, shading to blood red in centre, funnel-shaped, 75 mm wide, in full, tight trusses of 10–15, flowering after 4–5 years. EM.	A very worthwhile hybrid with superb, very large and thick, pointed, dark green foliage, light indumentum on undersides. −21°C/−5°F.
'Gwillt King' R. griersonianum × R. arboreum ssp. zeylanicum Caton Haig, Portmeirion, Wales, 1938.	Large turkey red flowers with spotting on upper lobes.	A vigorous, medium-size shrub.
'Halfdan Lem' 'Jean Marie de Montague' × red 'Loderi' Lem, 1974.	Red buds open to bright red flowers, 80 mm wide, with darker spots on dorsal lobe, in huge, rounded, tight trusses of about 13–14. Flowers fade to pink after a few days. ML.	A very vigorous plant, sometimes sprawling in habit, with deep green leaves, 200 mm long. Behaves better with concerted pruning. −21°C/−5°F.
'Hallelujah' 'Kimberly' × 'Jean Marie de Montague' H.E. Greer, 1976.	Deep rose red, in large, tight trusses of 10–13, flowering from an early age. M	Dense compact plant with large, dark green, downward-curving, thickly textured foliage. Strikes easily. −26°C/−15°F.
'Ibex' R. griersonianum × R. pocophorum L. de Rothschild, 1941.	Bright crimson scarlet with darker spots, funnel-shaped, in dome-shaped trusses, freely flowering. Other forms are rosy carmine or orange–scarlet. EM.	Good-looking, long, thin, dark sage green leaves with dense, brown, felty indumentum on lower surfaces. Easy to strike. −15°C/5°F.
'J. H. van Nes' 'Monsieur Thiers' × R. griffithianum C. B. van Nes, before 1958.	Glowing soft red, lighter in centre, 65 mm wide, with pointed lobes, in compact, conical trusses of 12–14 long-lasting flowers. M.	Compact, upright habit with pale green leaves. Prefers some shade and is easy to strike. −21°C/−5°F.
'Jean Marie de Montague' syn. 'The Honorable Jean Marie de Montague', 'Jean Marie' R. griffithianum × unknown C.B. van Nes, 1921.	Large, bright scarlet flowers in dome-shaped trusses of 10–14, very freely flowering from an early age. The definitive red. Flowers when quite young. M.	One of the best reds. Compact, slow-growing plant with spreading growth, thick, emerald green, sun-tolerant foliage. Prefers some pruning to maintain shape. Strikes easily and heat tolerant. Often used in hybridising. −21°C/−5°F.
'Johnny Bender' 'Jean Marie de Montague' × 'Indiana' C.S. Seabrook, 1960.	Intense bright currant red, with darker dorsal spotting, in tight, ball-shaped trusses of 5–8. M.	Thick, glossy dark green, heavily textured leaves, 150 mm long, with a slight indumentum. −15°C/5°F to −21°C/−5°F.
'Lady Bligh' R. griffithianum × unknown C.B. van Nes & Sons, 1934.	Dark strawberry pink, fading to pastel pink or white, in a beautiful two-toned effect between newer and older blooms. Widely campanulate, 75 mm wide. ML.	Spreading, compact, rounded shrub, wider than tall, with medium green foliage, 150 mm long, held for two years. −21°C/−5°F.
'Lamplighter' 'Britannia' × 'Madame Fr. J. Chauvin' M. Koster & Sons, 1955.	Clear red with salmon glow, large, in tall, conical trusses of 10–12. ML.	Large trusses on a compact, rounded, bushy plant. Medium green, narrow, pointed foliage 150 mm long. Strikes easily. Highly recommended. −18°C/0°F to −21°C/−5°F.

Species	Flowers	Notes
'Langley Park' 'Queen Wilhelmina' × 'Stanley Davies' C.B. van Nes & Sons, before 1922.	Deep red, 65 mm wide, in tight, dome-shaped trusses of 10–15, freely flowering, fading rapidly if in too much sun. ML.	Bushy plant, wider than tall, dark green foliage. Needs some shade. –18°C/0°F to –21°C/–5°F.
'Lord Roberts' Parentage unknown, possibly a R. catawbiense hybrid B. Mason, 1958.	Deep dark red or dark crimson, with a black blotch in tight, ball-shaped trusses, freely flowering from an early age. ML.	Sturdy, erect, medium compact grower, with pointed, glossy, crinkled foliage. Easily propagated and quite hardy. Sun tolerant. –26°C/–15°F.
'Madame de Bruin' 'Prometheus' × 'Doncaster' M. Koster & Sons, 1904.	Bright, clear cerise red, spotted with dark brown, in dense trusses of about 20. ML.	Sturdy, vigorous, tallish growth, light green leaves have conspicuous yellowish midrib. Prefers some shade, not heat tolerant and strikes easily. –23°C/–10°F.
'Manderley' 'Scandinavia' × 'Fabia' G. Slootjes, 1965.	Darker buds open to cardinal red with darker spots, campanulate, in full trusses of 12–13, very freely flowering. M.	New foliage reddish, medium compact, slightly spreading growth. Sun tolerant, but susceptible to insect attack. –21°C/–5°F.
'Markeeta's Prize' 'Loderi Venus' × Anna' Flora Markeeta Nursery, 1967.	Greenish yellow buds open to large, bright scarlet red with darker spotting, 125 mm wide, in trusses of 12, freely flowering. M.	Strongly branching plant, usually broader than tall, with thick, leathery dark green leaves to 150 mm long. Pruning when young will help long-term shape. Insect resistant and does best in full sun. –21°C/–5°F.
'Matador' R. griersonianum × R. strigillosum Lord Aberconway, Lionel de Rothschild, 1945.	Dark orange–red or scarlet red, tubular, in loose trusses of 7–8. EM.	Sparse, upright growth with attractive foliage with thin, woolly indumentum and hairy petioles. –12°C/10°F to –18°C/0°F.
'Max Sye' 'Chevalier F. de Sauvage' × unknown C. Frets & Son, 1935. Photo p. 88.	Dark red with prominent black blotch. ML, sometimes also in autumn.	Open, spreading habit, with grooved foliage. –18°C/0°F to –21°C/–5°F.
'Nova Zembla' 'Parson's Grandiflorum' × unknown hardy dark red hybrid M. Koster & Sons, 1902.	Dark red flowers with darker blotch, in full, compact, ball-shaped trusses. M.	One of the most successful hardier reds, a strong-growing upright plant. with matt, dark green foliage. Better form achieved by pinching out when young. Heat and sun tolerant, but sometimes susceptible to root rot. –29°C/–20°F to –32°C/–25°F.
'Noyo Chief' R. arboreum ssp. nilagiricum × unknown Reuthe Nursery, England, 1966. Photo p. 88.	Clear rose red, broadly campanulate, 65 mm wide, in compact trusses of 16 very showy flowers. EM.	Bronze new growth develops into outstanding, very glossy deep green, deeply ribbed foliage with fawn indumentum on lower surface. –12°C/10°F to –15°C/5°F.
'Old Port' R. catawbiense × unknown, possibly a R. ponticum hybrid. A. Waterer, 1865.	Dark wine red or plum, with blackish crimson markings, in ball-shaped trusses of about 15. M.	Vigorous shrub with medium-sized, dense habit, and glossy, deeply grooved foliage similar to R. catawbiense. Sun tolerant. –26°C/–15°F.
'Peter Koster' 'George Hardy' × 'Doncaster' hybrid M. Koster & Sons, 1909. Photo p. 88.	Dark buds open to bright magenta red with lighter margins, trumpet-shaped, in solid, compact, conical trusses, very freely flowering. ML.	Sturdy, bushy, strong-growing plant, medium to tall-growing, with flattish leaves, light indumentum. Strikes easily. –21°C/–5°F.

Cultivar	Flowers	Notes
'President Roosevelt' Parentage and origin unknown, possibly a sport of 'Limbatum', an *R. arboreum* hybrid. Photo p. 88.	White and bold red edging, giving a very dramatic two-toned effect, frilled, in medium-sized conical trusses of 15–29, very freely flowering, from an early age. EM.	One of the most distinctive and popular of all rhododendrons, with striking variegated foliage and bold flowers. Leaves have irregular bold splashes of yellow. Can be weak and brittle, with a sometimes sprawling, ungainly habit best controlled by pruning. The variegation can be unstable and any branches bearing foliage reverting to plain green should be culled. Strikes easily. –18°C/0°F
'Radium' *R. griersonianum* × 'Earl of Athlone' J.J. Crosfield, 1936.	Bright geranium scarlet, in large, rounded, somewhat loose trusses. ML.	Open, upright habit with glossy leaves to 125 mm. Easily propagated. –15°C/5°F.
'Romany Chai' 'Moser's Maroon' × *R. griersonianum* L. de Rothschild, 1932.	Rich terracotta, speckled with brown, in large, loose trusses. ML.	Upright, open, sometimes straggly plant with large, dark green foliage, often with a bronze tinge. Tolerates heat and strikes easily. Name means 'gypsy child'. Similar to the larger-growing 'Romany Chal' (q.v.) from the same breeder. –18°C/0°F.
'Rosalea' Parentage unknown V.J. Boulter, before 1984.	Light red, shading to pink centre, large, in tight, medium-sized trusses. E.	Strong, compact growth with average foliage held for one year, leading to often sparse appearance. –21°C/–5°F.
'Rubicon' 'Noyo Chief' × 'Kiliminjaro' R.C. Gordon, 1979.	Bright cardinal red, spotted with black inside, in full trusses of 17–18, flowering after 3–4 years. ML	Good habit and beautiful dark, glossy, bullate leaves. Sun tolerant, difficult to strike. –12°C/10°F to –15°C/5°F.
'Scarlet King' 'Ilam Alarm' × *R. griersonianum* E. Stead, before 1947.	Rich scarlet, in trusses of about 12–18, freely flowering. ML.	Attractive shrub with dark green foliage and silvery or white indumentum. Does well in open sun and warm climates and strikes easily. –15°C/5°F.
'The Warrior' syn. 'Warrior' Parentage unknown J. Waterer, 1867.	Light crimson red, with bluish tinge, spotted. ML.	–23°C/–10°F.
'Unknown Warrior' 'Queen Wilhelmina' × 'Stanley Davies' C.B. van Nes, before 1922.	Clear light red, strawberry red or deep rose pink, with brownish markings, in large, domed trusses of 12–18. EM.	Vigorous but straggly and untidy, especially when young, with pointed leaves folding at midrib. Sun tolerant. Very popular. Strikes easily. –15°C/5°F.
'Vulcan's Flame' *R. griersonianum* × 'Mars' B.F. Lancaster, 1958. Photo p. 105.	Bright red, 75 mm wide, in trusses of 12–15, very free-flowering from an early age. ML.	Vigorous, compact plant, with long, deep yellow–green leaves with reddish petioles. Does well in warmer climates, very heat and sun tolerant. Easily propagated. –26°C/–15°F.
'Witchery' 'Mars' × *R. facetum* R. Henny.	Glowing, fiery deep red flowers, in tall trusses, flowering from 4–6 years. ML.	Compact habit with silvery indumentum on new growth. Strikes fairly easily. Not registered. –21°C/–5°F.

Medium-size whites, 1–1.8 m/3–6 ft

Cultivar	Flowers	Notes
'Abby Boulter' V.J. Boulter, 1986.	White, in rounded trusses of 16. E.	Good sun tolerance.
'Adriaan Koster' 'Mrs Lindsay Smith' × *R. campylocarpum* ssp. *campylocarpum* hybrid M. Koster & Sons, 1920.	Creamy white with yellow centre and red spotting, bell-shaped, in compact trusses.	Sturdy, robust, compact growth, with veined foliage. Not particularly heat tolerant. –21°C/–5°F.

Species	Flowers	Notes
'Album Novum' R. catawbiense × unknown L. van Houtte, before 1896.	White with a hint of rose–lilac and greenish yellow spotting, freely flowering. ML.	Vigorous, sturdy, open plant with good-looking foliage. Easy to strike. −29°C/−20°F.
'Anne Teese' R. ciliicalyx × R. formosum A. J. Teese, 1968.	White, flushed purplish pink and striped on outside, in trusses of 3 fragrant florets, freely flowering. EM.	Open, sprawling habit. Easy to strike. −10°C/14°F.
'Award' 'Anna' × 'Margaret Dunn' D. James, F. Mossman & C. Ward, 1972/3.	Pink buds open to white flowers with light yellow flare and margins shaded with pink, fragrant, in ball-shaped trusses of 14, flowering from an early age. ML.	Plant as broad as high, with new growth a greenish copper or bronze. Slightly sparse, especially in shade. Strikes easily. −18°C/0°F
'Belle Heller' R. catawbiense 'Alba' × white R. catawbiense seedling A. Shammarello, before 1958.	Large white flowers with dominant golden yellow blotch in large, globular trusses. M, sometimes also in autumn.	Vigorous plant with good habit and large dark green foliage. Sun and heat tolerant. Strikes easily. −12°C/10°F
'Boule de Neige' R. caucasicum × unknown R. catawbiense hybrid Oudieu, circa 1878.	Small, slightly frilled white flowers with a few yellowish green spots, in medium-sized, compact, rounded trusses. M.	Small flowers on a dense, low-growing, rounded plant with heavily textured light green foliage. An early, easily grown hybrid which is still popular and strikes easily. Parent of many other hybrids. Prefers some shade. −32°C/−25°F.
'Countess of Sefton' R. edgeworthii × Multiflorum' J. Davies, 1877.	Pink buds open to fragrant white flowers, stained with red and fading to pure white, in trusses of 2–4, freely flowering. EM.	Glossy, bullate foliage on a compact bush. Prone to rust. Strikes easily. −12°C/10°F or colder.
'Cunningham's White' R. caucasicum × R. ponticum 'Album' Cunningham, 1830.	Pinkish or pale lavender buds open to small white flowers, with a pale yellow eye in throat, in upright trusses of about 8–20. Flowers after 4–5 years.	A very old and reliable, hardy, fast-growing, spreading shrub with dark green foliage, tolerates a fairly alkaline soil. Strikes easily. −26°C/−15°F.
'Diane Titcomb' 'Marinus Koster' × 'Snow Queen' H. Larson, 1942.	Very large, white flowers with pink edges, in large conical trusses of about 16, flowering from 4–6 years. EM.	Strongly growing, open plant with large, dark foliage. Strikes with moderate ease. −21°C/−5°F.
'Dot' 'Mrs Lindsay Smith' × R. fortunei Lord Swaythling, 1945.	Large, white flowers with red spotting and unusual satin-like texture, in large trusses. M.	Open, upright habit. −23°C/−10°F.
'Dr Stocker' R. caucasicum × R. griffithianum G. Abbey (Veitch & Sons), 1900.	Ivory or creamy white, campanulate flowers 75 mm wide, with light brown and crimson streaks and spotting, in very loose trusses of 6–8. EM.	Plant usually wider than tall, thick, heavily veined foliage. Good pest resistance and strikes easily. −18°C/0°F.
'Elizabeth Titcomb' 'Marinus Koster' × 'Snow Queen' H. Larson, before 1958.	Pink buds open to substantial white flowers, in tall, conical trusses of about 16.	Large, dark, heavy foliage on a sturdy, strong plant. Tolerates sunlight. −18°C/0°F to −21°C/−5°F.

Cultivar	Flowers	Notes
'Fragrantissimum' R. edgeworthii × R. formosum Origin unknown, before 1868. Photo p. 86.	Carmine buds open to white funnel-shaped, very heavily perfumed flowers, tinged with pink and creamy yellow centre, 100 mm wide, in loose trusses of 3–4, flowering when quite young. EM.	Popular variety, usually ungainly, leggy, sparse growth, with dark, glossy, rugose, scaly and hairy foliage. Prune hard for best bush shape, or lends itself to espalier training. Strikes very easily, but can be prone to rust and mildew. –9°/15°F to –10°C/14°F.
'Heatherside Beauty' R. caucasicum × R. arboreum ssp. arboreum Frederick Street, before 1959.	Very pale pink flowers fade to white with dark markings, in large, full, shapely trusses. VE.	One of a number of forms resulting from the same cross, most marketed as forms of 'Nobleanum'. Compact, upright, bushy shrub. Early flowering means buds and flowers susceptible to frost damage. –23°C/–10°F.
'Helene Schiffner' syn. 'Hélène Schiffner' R. arboreum hybrid Seidel, 1893.	Pure white with very faint yellow to brown markings. Unusually dark blackish mauve buds. Upright, tight, dome-shaped trusses of 12–14, flowering when quite young. ML.	Slow-growing bush with stiff, pointed narrow leaves of deep mistletoe green, grey powdery finish and reddish stems and petioles. Strikes easily, sun and heat tolerant. –21°C/–5°F.
'Loder's White' Possibly R. arboreum ssp. cinnabarinum × R. griffithianum J. Mangles, F. Godman (E. Loder), 1911. Photo p. 87.	White, margined with pale lilac and a tinge of yellow and red flecks in throat, in large, conical trusses of about 12 long-lasting, slightly fragrant flowers, freely produced after about 5 years. M.	Possibly the best known and loved of white rhododendrons, often a parent of other hybrids. Vigorous, bushy, compact dome-shaped habit, broader than tall and free flowering. Easily grown, heat tolerant and content in both sun and shade, strikes easily. –18°C/0°F.
'Mount Everest' A form of R. cinnabarinum or R. campanulatum × R. griffithianum W. Slocock, 1930.	Pure white, with brownish red markings, narrow, campanulate, in large, conical trusses. of 10–12. Freely flowering and slightly scented. EM.	Vigorous, dense, medium compact habit with dull green leaves. –21°C/–5°F to –23°C/–10°F.
'Mrs A.T. de la Mare' R. fortunei ssp. fortunei 'Sir Charles Butler' × 'Halopeanum' C.B. van Nes, 1958. Photo p. 88.	White with faint green spotting in throat, in large, loose, dome-shaped trusses of 12–14, slightly fragrant. M.	Good medium bushy habit with glossy foliage. Needs some protection for best results, but can take full exposure in many situations. –26°C/–15°F.
'Mrs J. G. Millais' syn. 'Mrs John G. Millais' Parentage unknown A. Waterer before 1927.	White with conspicuous golden yellow blotch in medium-sized trusses of 14 spectacular flowers. Heavy budding on younger plants. ML.	Vigorous, sprawling, open habit. Named after wife of painter J.G. Millais, writer of early rhododendron texts. Strikes easily. –21°C/–5°F or colder.
'Mrs Lionel de Rothschild' syn. 'Lady de Rothschild' R. griffithianum hybrid A. Waterer, 1931.	White, flushed at first with pink, with crimson blotch, red spotting in throat, in large, firm trusses of about 16. ML.	Shiny foliage, on a dense, floppy, sprawling plant. Strikes easily, but best suited to grafting as own roots unreliable. –18°C/0°F.
'Mrs P. D. Williams' Parentage unknown A. Waterer, 1936.	Ivory white with golden olive brown eye, in compact, rounded trusses, freely flowering. ML.	Young plant may sprawl, but becomes more erect with age. Very dark green, smooth, narrow foliage, up to 140 mm long. Strikes easily. –23°C/–10°F.
'Sir Charles Lemon' Form of R. arboreum ssp. cinnamomeum var. album, or natural R. arboreum × R. campanulatum hybrid J.D. Hooker seed, 1849.	Pure white, faintly spotted with red in throat, in large, conical trusses of about 10, after some years. EM.	Slow-growing, bushy, sometimes tree-like plant with superb foliage. Underside of the large, stiff, leathery, dark green leaves carry a distinctive cinnamon indumentum. Strikes fairly easily. –15°C/5°F to –21°C/–5°F.

Species	Flowers	Notes
'Tyermanii' R. nuttallii × R. formosum Tyermann, 1925.	Creamy white with yellow in throat., in loose trusses of about 4 huge, ruffled flowers. Fragrance resembles nutmeg. M.	Handsome, dark, glossy green foliage. Attractive rich brownish bark on main trunk. –7°C/19°F.
'Wedding Gown' syn. 'Wedding Bells' R. veitchianum × R. burmanicum K. Van de Ven, 1986. Photo p. 105.	White, with yellowish throat, funnel-shaped fragrant flowers in trusses of 5–7. EM.	Open habit, medium, mid-green, obovate foliage. –10°C/14°F.
'White Gold' 'Mrs J.G. Millais' × 'Cheyenne' H. Greer, 1979.	White with brilliant yellow dorsal flare, in dome-shaped trusses of 10–12 reflexed flowers. ML.	Sprawling growth, prefers some shade. –21°C/–5°F.

Medium-size yellows, golds and oranges 1–1.8 m/3–6 ft

Species	Flowers	Notes
'Alison Johnstone' R. yunnanense × R. cinnabarinum Major G. Johnstone, 1945.	Open cream changing to a delicate, light apricot pink, in trusses of 9. EM.	Bushy dense shrub with attractive bluish grey, waxy foliage. –15°C/5°F.
'Apricot Sherbert' 'Comstock' × 'Dido' H. Greer, 1985.	Buffy, apricot-coloured flowers with a large calyx of the same colour.	Mound-shaped plant with long, oval leaves. –15°C/5°F.
'Australian Canary' 'Apricot Gold' × 'Lem's Cameo' K. Van de Ven.	Large trusses of well-formed apricot yellow flowers. ML.	Slow growing hardy bush with compact, dense growth and attractive young bronze foliage.
'Australian Sunset' 'Apricot Gold' × 'Lem's Cameo' K. Van de Ven, 1986. Photo p. 106.	Strong orange–yellow inside, reddish orange outside. Funnel-shaped flowers in trusses of 20–24. M.	Broad, bushy shrub with mid green, medium-sized foliage, a delightful bronze when young.
'Ayers Rock' 'Naomi' × 'Fabia' Alf Bramley, circa 1970.	Light orange, in loose trusses of about 10 florets. ML.	Frost hardy.
'Bodnant Yellow' R. cinnabarinum × Royal Flush' Lord Aberconway, 1944.	Butter yellow to orange–yellow buff with deeper reddish flush in pendulous clusters of about 5. ML.	Compact growth, leaves turn downward. Susceptible to mildew.
'Broughtonii Aureum' syn. 'Norbitonense Broughtonianum' [R. maximum × R. ponticum] × R. molle W. Smith of Norbiton, c. 1830.	Soft yellow, spotted with orange–yellow in small, rounded trusses of 8–16, freely flowering. ML.	An old azaleodendron hybrid. Sparse, rough-textured foliage. Heat tolerant but requires protection from both sun and wind. Heavy pruning when young will guarantee a good garden form. Strikes easily. –21°C/–5°F.
'Butterfly' R. campylocarpum × 'Mrs Milner' W. Slocock, 1940.	Very pale yellow, with red spots on upper lobe, in rounded, loose trusses of 11–15, freely flowering. M.	Can often be sparse and leggy. Easily propagated. Sun and heat tolerant., but susceptible to insect attack, particularly mites and lacebugs. –18°C/0°F.

R. 'Saffron Queen'.

R. 'Seta'.

R. 'Sirius'.

R. 'Susan'.

R. 'Tally Ho'.

R. 'Unique'.

R. 'Vulcan's Flame'.

R. 'Wedding Gown'.

R. 'Winsome'.

Left: The bronze autumn foliage typical of deciduous azaleas.

Right: Loiseuleria procumbens, once classified as an azalea, under a blanket of frost at about 4300 m/14 100 ft in the Everest region of Nepal. (Photo: David Francis)

R. 'Australian Sunset'.

R. 'White Flare'.

R. 'Cilpinense', a good compact pink for shadier spots.

R. 'Azma'.

Cultivar	Flowers	Notes
'C. I. S.' 'Loder's White' × 'Fabia' R. Henny, before 1952.	Orange–yellow, changing to creamy apricot, with bright orange–red throat up to 100 mm wide, in loose trusses of about 9–11, freely flowering. M.	Upright, sometimes ungainly plant, as broad as tall. Sometimes sparse, but can be spectacular. Matt-green leaves distinctively twisted. Strikes easily, prefers light shade, and prone to mildew. –15°C/5°F.
'Canary' unknown hybrid or R. campylocarpum ssp. campylocarpum × R. caucasicum M. Koster & Sons, 1930.	Bright lemon yellow in tight trusses, freely flowering. EM.	Deeply veined, shiny, rounded leaves, a little prone to chlorosis and insect attack. One of the hardiest yellows. Prefers some shade and strikes easily. –23°C/–10°F.
'Caramel Coffee' 'Australian Sunset' × 'Apricot Ice' K. Van de Ven, 1992.	Unusual light orange–yellow flowers, suffusing to light yellowish pink flushed with red on margins, in superb trusses of 15–17 florets. ML.	A most attractive and distinctive hybrid with bushy growth to 1.2–1.5 m/4–5 ft and young foliage an attractive bronze. Sun tolerant. Highly recommended.
'Carita' 'Naomi' × R. campylocarpum ssp. campylocarpum Lionel de Rothschild.	Pink buds opening to pinkish primrose yellow, in loose, flat-topped trusses. EM.	Good habit, more open with age, with rich green, rounded, shiny leaves held for one year. Fairly easy to strike. –15°C/5°F.
'Cinnkeys' R. cinnabarinum ssp. cinnabarinum × R. keysii E. Magor, 1926.	Unusual orange–red tubular flowers with soft yellow lobes. ML.	Dark, glossy, narrow foliage on a vigorous, erect shrub. Strikes easily. –15°C/5°F.
'Creamy Chiffon' Parentage unknown Whitney.	Salmon-orange buds, opening to creamy yellow double flowers, resembling a hose-in-hose azalea. ML.	Compact, dense habit, deep green, rounded foliage. Strikes easily. –21°C/–5°F.
'Crossbill' R. spinuliferum × R. lutescens J.C. Williams, 1933. Photo p. 86.	Masses of unusual yellow tubular flowers flushed with apricot with protruding stamens, blooming over a long period. EM.	Vigorous, slender, erect, fine-leafed variety. New growth bright red. Foliage can be rather sparse and density can be improved with pruning. –15°C/5°F.
'Eldorado' R. valentinianum × R. johnstoneanum L. de Rothschild, 1937. Photo p. 86.	Primrose yellow, in loose clusters of 3–4 medium-sized, funnel-shaped flowers, freely flowering. M.	Open habit, with small, scaly dark yellowish green leaves. Strikes easily. –9°C/15°F to –10°C/14°F.
'Evening Glow' R. fortunei spp. discolor × 'Fabia' T. Van Veen Sr., 1958.	Bright yellow, with prominent calyx, in very loose trusses of about 6. L.	Compact, upright growth with narrow, light green foliage. Usually prefers light shade, but heat tolerant and strikes easily. Susceptible to mildew. –21°C/–5°F.
'Fusilier' R. elliottii × R. griersonianum L. de Rothschild, 1938.	Bright orange–red in medium-sized, open trusses of about 10. Free-flowering from young. ML.	Large, dark leaves with indumentum. Several different forms. –12°C/10°F.
'Golden Star' R. fortunei × R. wardii Don Hardgrove, S. Burns, 1966.	Creamy pink buds open to mimosa yellow, 75 mm wide, with 7 wavy lobes, in ball-shaped trusses of up to 13, freely flowering after 4–5 years. ML.	Easily grown hybrid with habit as broad as tall. Shiny, elliptic foliage held for two years. Strikes easily and fairly insect resistant. One of the most reliable yellows. –18°C/0°F to –21°C/–5°F or colder.

Species	Flowers	Notes
'Golden Torch' Possibly 'Bambi' × ['Grosclaude' × R. griersonianum] Waterer & Crisp, 1972.	Salmon pink buds open to soft yellow, faintly spotted with deeper yellow, in compact trusses of 13–15, from quite young. ML.	Upright, compact habit with medium-sized, dull green leaves held for 3 years. Strikes easily. –18°C/0°F.
'Ilona' R. valentinianum × R. auritum Lionel de Rothschild, 1941.	Pale golden yellow in many small trusses. E.	Early flowering, not particularly hardy.
'Lady Chamberlain' R. cinnabarinum ssp. cinnabarinum × 'Royal Flush' (orange form) Lionel de Rothschild, 1930.	Unusual, bright orange to salmon pink, waxy, tubular to long trumpet shape, in loose, drooping trusses of 3–6, flowering freely after some years. M, sometimes also in autumn.	Upright, very leggy plant, with slender, arching, willowy branches and bluish-green new foliage. Small, smooth, dark green leaves, waxy upper surface, scaly underneath. Strikes with moderate ease. Not heat tolerant and susceptible to rust and mildew, but worth trying. –12°C/10°F to –15°C/5°F.
'Letty Edwards' R. campylocarpum × R. fortunei Col. S.R. Clarke, 1946. Photo p. 87.	Pale pink buds open to primrose yellow in rounded trusses of 9–11. Very free-flowering once established. M.	Rounded, compact growth, medium green leaves 125 mm long. –18°C/0°F.
'Maria's Choice' 'Apricot Gold' × 'Lem's Cameo' K. Van de Ven, 1986.	Dramatic flowers with intense golden throat shading to rich orange with frilled edges, hose-in-hose, in tight trusses of 15–18. Flowers when quite young. ML.	Good habit with young foliage a delightful bronze. Production of stock of this exciting new hybrid under way at the time of writing.
'Mrs Betty Robertson' (syn. 'Mrs Betty Robinson') 'Mrs Lindsay Smith' × unknown hybrid M. Koster & Sons.	Creamy yellow with red blotch in medium to large upright dome-shaped trusses. M.	Neat, compact-growing bush with roughly textured foliage, 100 mm long. Prefers some shade in warmer climates. –21°C/–5°F.
'R. W. Rye' R. chrysodoron × R. johnstoneanum Lord Stair, 1938, intro. 1951.	Primrose yellow, gradually deepening into throat, pendulous, in loose trusses of about 4, freely flowering. EM.	Dark, hairy foliage on an upright plant. Strikes easily and prefers some protection from the elements. –12°C/10°F.
'Ring of Fire' 'Darigold' × 'Idealist' Willard & Margaret Thompson 1984.	Dazzling yellow, with narrow band of orange–red along margins, in flat-topped trusses, flowering when quite young. ML.	Vigorous, compact plant with dense foliage and striking flowers. –18°C/0°F.
'Rothenburg' 'Diane' × R. williamsianum Viktor von Martin, 1972. Photo p. 88.	Light primrose yellow or cream funnel-shaped flowers in fairly loose trusses, flowering from about the fourth year. EM.	Large, very glossy, apple green leaves, on an upright, compact, vigorous plant. Easy to strike. –23°C/–10°F.
'Souvenir of W. C. Slocock' R. campylocarpum × unknown W. Slocock, before 1928.	Deep apricot pink buds open to pale primrose yellow, lightly flushed with apricot pink, with crimson spotting, in compact trusses of about 12, freely flowering once established. M.	Compact shrub with medium green leaves, slight twisting. Prone to mildew and sucking insect attack. Strikes easily and sun tolerant, though some shade preferable in warmer areas. –21°C/–5°F.
'Tortoiseshell Champagne' 'Goldsworth Orange' × R. griersonianum W. Slocock, 1946.	Pale yellow, deeper in centre, tinged with pink, in loose trusses of 11–14, freely flowering from quite an early age. ML.	Vigorous, attractive upright shrub with open habit, normally broader than tall. Prefers milder climates and some shade. Strikes easily. –12°C/10°F to –15°C/5°F.

Cultivar	Flowers	Notes
'Tortoiseshell Salome' 'Goldsworth Orange' × R. griersonianum W. Slocock, 1946.	Biscuit, shaded with pink, otherwise as for 'Tortoiseshell Champagne', above. ML.	Similar to 'Tortoiseshell Champagne', above. Others in the same group include 'Orange', 'Scarlet' and 'Wonder'. –12°C/10°F to –15°C/5°F.
'Trewithen Orange' 'Full House' × R. cinnabarinum ssp. xanthocodon G.H. Johnstone, 1950.	Deep orange-brown, loose, tubular, waxy, soft, in pendulous trusses of about 5, freely flowering from 4–5 years. M.	Erect, sometimes straggly growth with stiff, sea-green foliage. Susceptible to rust and powdery mildew. Strikes easily. –12°C/10°F to –15°C/5°F.
'Unique' R. campylocarpum × unknown W.C. Slocock, 1934. Photo p. 105.	Apricot pink, fading to cream, on medium-sized trusses. EM.	A beautiful, dense, compact grower, one of my favourites. Erect, clover green, oblong foliage. Does well in warmer climates if given some shade. –21°C/–5°F.
'Vanessa Pastel' 'Soulbut' × R. griersonianum Lord Aberconway, 1930.	Buds open brick red, changing to apricot, then deep cream, with darker bronze yellow in throat, to 110 mm wide, 5-lobed, on trusses of 8. A much pinker form also exists. ML.	First R. griersonianum gybrid introduced in England. Upright growth, with long, pointed, moss green foliage, 127 mm long. Long reddish petioles. –15°C/5°F.
'Yellow Hammer' R. sulfureum × R. flavidum J.C. Williams, before 1931.	Very deep yellow, tiny, tubular flowers, in trusses of 2–3. Very free flowering, may flower a second time in autumn. EM.	Vigorous, upright, open growth, with small, narrow, light green, scaly leaves. One of the few yellows to do well in full sun, but flowers will last better in some shade. Prefers constant pinching and pruning to provide a good garden form. Strikes easily. –15°C/5°F.

Larger hybrids

Many of these larger growing hybrids have the potential over time to grow to enormous size. Their growth will be influenced considerably by the conditions prevailing in their particular site, but a shrub which could be described as reaching, say, 2.5 m/8 ft in height and width over ten years, may assume twice that height and considerably greater width over thirty years or more.

Larger mauves, blues and purples 1.8 m/6 ft or more

Cultivar	Flowers	Notes
'Arthur Bedford' syn. 'A. Bedford' Unknown mauve seedling × R. ponticum T. Lowinsky, before 1935.	Light mauve with darker lobes, marked with deep rose madder to almost black, in domed trusses of 11–16 funnel-shaped flowers. ML.	Vigorous, upright habit with long, red-stemmed, glossy green leaves to 150 mm. Regular pinching and pruning valuable to achieve desirable form. Named after Lionel de Rothschild's head gardener. Sun and heat tolerant. –21°C/–5°F.
'Auguste van Geerte' R. ponticum × unknown C. van Geerte, before 1867.	Large purplish red flowers in substantial trusses, freely flowering. Earlier than most ponticum hybrids. M.	Hardy, strong-growing bush. Quite suitable for exposed positions. Strikes easily. –18°C/0°F.
'Bud Flanagan' Unknown × R. ponticum E. de Rothschild, 1966.	Mauve, with large flash of deep chestnut, in huge trusses of 18–20. ML.	–21°C/–5°F.
'Bumble Bee' 'Purple Splendour' × 'Blue Peter' L. & S. King, 1984.	Phlox purple, with large maroon and black eye in centre of dorsal lobe, in trusses of 25–27 five-lobed florets. ML.	Dark, glossy green ovate foliage. –23°C/–10°F.

Species	Flowers	Notes
'Colehurst' R. fortunei ssp. discolor 'Houlstonii' × 'Van Nes Sensation' V.J. Boulter, 1978.	Pale mauve, with creamy-white centre in trusses of about 14 large flowers, freely flowering. EM.	An excellent, strong-growing variety with a tall, vigorous, open habit. –21°C/–5°F.
'Countess of Athlone' 'Geoffrey Millais' × R. catawbiense 'Grandiflorum' C.B. van Nes, 1923.	Purple buds open to large, distinctive, deep lilac flowers, fading to a pale, silvery lilac with greenish-yellow basal markings, widely funnel-shaped, in tight, conical trusses of about 15, freely flowering. ML.	Medium bushy, compact upright habit with glossy, dark green foliage. Easy to strike. Often tolerates full sunlight but prefers some shade in hotter areas. –23°C/–10°F.
'Eleanore' R. rubiginosum × R. augustinii L. de Rothschild, 1937.	Lavender blue, with olive green spots, in clusters of 4–5. Also a violet form. Freely flowering. EM.	Vigorous, upright shrub with ultimately very tall growth and foliage resembling parent R. augustini (q.v.). Tolerates full sun and easily propagated. –12°C/10°F to –15°C/5°F.
'Everestianum' R. catawbiense × unknown A. Waterer, before 1850.	Rosy lilac, spotted in throat, with frilled edges, 50 mm wide, in compact trusses of about 15–20. Freely flowering. ML.	A very old, hardy hybrid, versatile and vigorous, profusely flowering in sun or light shade. Pest resistant and heat tolerant. Strikes easily and often used in hybridising. –26°C/–15°F.
'Fastuosum Flore Pleno' syn. 'Fastuosum Plenum' R. catawbiense × R. ponticum G. Francoisi, before 1846. Photo p. 86.	Pale bluish mauve, with small, greenish brown flare, medium-sized, semi-double, in rather loose trusses of 15–17, freely flowering and long-lasting. ML.	Another durable old variety, still one of the best lavender hybrids. Dense, rounded, compact habit and convex, dull green foliage. Sun and wind tolerant. –26°C/–15°F or colder.
'Joseph Whitworth' syn. 'Sir Joseph Whitworth' R. ponticum × unknown J. Waterer, before 1867. Photo p. 87.	Deep maroon with black spotting, in large, full, rounded trusses of 12–16. Freely flowering. ML.	Hardy grower of medium to tall, compact, bushy habit. Dark leaves with greyish tint. Easily propagated from cuttings. –21°C/–5°F to –23°C/–10°F or colder.
'Madame Cochet' syn. 'Madame Cachet' Parentage unknown, possibly includes R. catawbiense or R. ponticum. Bertin, before 1888. Photo p. 88.	Deep violet lilac with dark yellow blotch, campanulate, freely flowering, in trusses of 15. ML.	Open habit and easy to strike. Good sun tolerance. –21°C/–5°F.

Larger pinks, 1.8 m/6 ft or more

Species	Flowers	Notes
'Albert Schweitzer' Parentage unknown A. van Nes, 1960.	Rose bengal with currant red blotch, in large pyramidal trusses of 13–14 florets. ML.	Upright habit with mediocre foliage, difficult to propagate. Named after German missionary and scholar and popular in continental Europe. –21°C/–5°F.
'Alice' R. griffithianum × unknown J. Waterer, 1910.	Pale rose or frosty pink, fading to almost white, in large trusses of 14–18. Takes some years before the large conical trusses are produced. M.	One of the most popular pink rhododendrons. Fast-growing, dense, bushy, upright habit and glossy, pointed foliage. Needs some pruning to keep in shape, although it may resent too much, so best planted with plenty of room. Named after Mrs Gomer Waterer. Sun tolerant and strikes easily. –21° C/–5°F.
'Anna' 'Norman Gill' × 'Jean Marie de Montague' Halfdan Lem, c. 1952.	Deep reddish pink buds, opening with a reddish flare in throat, giving a two-toned effect which fades to pale pink, in large trusses of up to 12. ML.	Unusual foliage which is heavily textured and deeply veined. New growth bronze. –18°C/0°F

Cultivar	Flowers	Notes
'Anna Rose Whitney' R. griersonianum × 'Countess of Derby' T. Van Veen Sr, W. Whitney, 1954.	Large, deep rose pink flowers an impressive 100 mm across, with light green spotting, in open trusses of 12–21, freely flowering after 4–5 years. ML.	Strong, vigorous, fast-growing shrub which may require pruning to control, with handsome, hairy, fern or dark green foliage 200 × 75 mm. Can tolerate exposure to sun, and in cooler areas can be used for screening, but prefers shade in warmer sites. Strikes easily, resistant to most fungi except powdery mildew. –21°C/–5°F.
'Antoon van Welie' 'Pink Pearl' × R. catawbiense L.J. Endtz & Co.	Deep rose pink with yellowish centre and bluish cast, in large, compact trusses. ML.	Strong, rather open habit, more compact in full sun. Large, thick, waxy leaves. Strikes easily, heat tolerant. –21°C/–5°F.
'Azma' R. griersonianum × R. fortunei J.B. Stevenson, 1933. Photo p. 106.	Soft salmon pink, up to 100 mm wide, in large, loose, rounded trusses. Freely flowering. ML.	Strong-growing, straggly, often sparse, upright variety with long, narrow leaves. Strikes easily. –12°C/10°F.
'Betty Wormald' 'George Hardy' × unknown red hybrid M. Koster & Sons, before 1922.	Pastel pink, with paler centre, and light purple spotting, red buds in huge, conical trusses of 10–12 very large flowers. ML.	Upright, spreading plant with large foliage, needing plenty of room. Strikes easily. –21°C/–5°F.
'Calrose' R. calophytum × R. griersonianum Lord Aberconway, 1939.	Deep rose in bud, opening to pink funnel-shaped flowers.	Large plant with good foliage.
'Corinne Boulter' fortunei ssp. discolor 'Houlstonii' × 'Van Nes Sensation' V.J. Boulter, 1992.	Light purplish pink, campanulate, in rounded trusses of 10–16 florets. M.	Good sun tolerance.
'Coronation Day' 'Pink Shell' × 'Loderi' J. Crosfield, 1937.	Delicate China rose, with crimson basal blotch in large, loose trusses of very large, fragrant flowers (up to 120 mm). E.	Compact habit, needs shelter from wind and sun. Used frequently as parent by Australian breeders Karel Van de Ven and Victor Boulter. Better grafted as own roots unreliable. –18°C/0°F.
'Cotton Candy' 'Marinus Koster' × 'Loderi Venus' J. Henny & Wennekamp, 1961.	Huge pastel pink flowers in tall, loose, conical trusses of 12–18, freely flowering after about 4 years. M.	Handsome dark green foliage, 150 mm long. Vigorous, tolerates full sun but sensitive to wind, resistant to root fungi. –18°C/0°F.
'Dame Nellie Melba' 'Standishii' × R. arboreum Sir E. Loder, L. de Rothschild, 1926.	Bright pink with crimson throat, large flowers in conical trusses of about 12, freely flowering once established. EM.	Dark green, glossy leaves, vigorous, bushy habit with branches weighed down by heavy trusses. Needs some shelter from sun. –15°C/5°F.
'Doctor Arnold W. Endtz' 'Pink Pearl' × unknown hybrid L. Endtz, 1927.	Carmine red, tinted with lilac, frilled, long-lasting, in rounded trusses of 12–14, freely flowering. ML.	Compact, bushy, upright growth with medium green, slightly twisted leaves 150 mm long. Sun tolerant and strikes easily. –21°C/–5°F.
'Elie' 'Cunningham's White' × red catawbiense hybrid A. Shammarello, 1955.	Vibrant deep pink, with red spots, in conical or rounded trusses. EM.	Shiny foliage with vigorous growth which may need pruning to keep shape. Easily propagated. –23°C/–10°F.
'Endsleigh Pink' R. arboreum × unknown Origin unknown.	Pale rose, lightly dotted.	Neat trusses of small flowers. More cold-tolerant than R. arboreum.

Species	Flowers	Notes
'Freisland' R. catawbiense hybrid × 'Pink Pearl' L.J. Endtz.	Pale lilac rose.	An old hardy, large-growing hybrid with distinctive foliage.
'Irene Stead' syn. 'I.M.S.' Selfed 'Loderi' from R. griffithianum × R. fortunei E. Stead, 1958.	Soft pink, fragrant, in huge trusses. Better colour in shade. M.	Upright, tree-like habit, reddish purple petioles and buds. Hard to strike, therefore normally grafted. −15°C/5°F to −18°C/0°F.
'Isabel Pierce' 'Anna' × 'Lem's Goal' H. Lem, L. Pierce, 1975.	Cardinal red buds open to rich pink or rose red, paler in centre, with prominent brown blotch and spots in throat. Narrow stripes of pink from base to edges. Openly campanulate, 100 mm wide, with wavy margins, in trusses of about 9–10 from about 4 years. M.	Upright habit, potentially a very large bush, with glossy, narrow, dark, crinkly, green foliage with a yellowish midvein. Strikes easily. −15°C/5°F to −18°C/0°F.
'Janet Blair' syn. 'John Wister' Parentage unknown C. Dexter, D. Leach, 1962.	Light pink, paler at centre, golden bronze rays on upper lobes, frilled, in large trusses. Free flowering and fragrant. ML.	Vigorous, compact plant, wider than tall, with dense, dark green foliage. Parent of many fine hybrids. −26°C/−15°F.
'Lem's Monarch' syn. 'Pink Walloper' 'Anna' × 'Marinus Koster' H. Lem, 1971.	Very attractive flowers, satin pink to white, with pink margins, in huge, conical trusses after about 4 years. ML.	Large, attractive foliage on a tall, spreading, potentially very large, strongly stemmed plant. Insect resistant and fairly easy to strike. −21°C/−5°F.
'Marion' syn. 'Lord Fairhaven' Parentage unknown Cheal & Sons, 1955.	Two-tone pink, frilled, with yellow centre, in abundant, medium-sized trusses. Flowers over a period of two months. EM.	One of the best early pinks, and used often as a parent by Australian breeders Victor Boulter and Karel Van de Ven in search of of early flowering hybrids. Difficult to strike. Not to be confused with the hybrid known in Australia as 'Dutch Marion'. −21°C/−5°F.
'Mother of Pearl' Sport of 'Pink Pearl' John Waterer, 1925.	Rich pink buds open to large, slightly fragrant, delicate pink, flowers fading to pure white, with faint brownish green spots and pink stamens, in full, conical trusses. ML.	Vigorous plant with good foliage. Identical in habit and foliage to parent 'Pink Pearl'. −21°C/−5°F.
'Mrs Charles E. Pearson' 'Coombe Royal' × R. catawbiense 'Grandiflorum' M. Koster & Sons, 1909. Photo p. 88.	Mauve pink buds open to pale pinkish mauve flowers edged with lavender, with heavy chestnut spotting, in very large, conical trusses of 10–12, freely flowering from 4–5 years. ML.	Vigorous, upright grower, with lush, deep matt green foliage, tolerates heat and sun. Strikes easily. −21°C/−5°F.
'Mrs E. C. Stirling' R. griffithianum × unknown J. Waterer, 1906.	Lilac pink, ruffled medium-sized blooms, shading to mauve margins, in large, heavy conical trusses. Floriferous. ML.	Hardy hybrid of strong, bushy, upright habit, often leggy when younger, spreading with age. Heat and sun tolerant, fairly easy to strike. −21°C/−5°F.
'Mrs G. W. Leak' syn. 'Cottage Garden's Pride' 'Coombe Royal' × 'Chevalier Felix de Sauvage' M. Koster & Sons, 1916. Photo p. 87.	Eye-catching, bright rose pink with deep reddish carmine blotch, crimson markings, in large, upright, conical trusses of about 12, freely flowering once established. EM.	One of the most popular of all rhododendrons, distinctive flowers. Tall, vigorous grower with dull, olive-green foliage. Tolerates sun, shade and heat, strikes easily. Susceptible to sucking insects. −18°C/0°F.

Cultivar	Flowers	Notes
'Noele Boulter' 'Dr Stocker' × 'Cornubia' V.J. Boulter, 1963.	Red or deep purplish pink, fading to soft pink with deeper ruby throat, in tight trusses of 10–14 florets, freely flowering. E.	A good, hardy upward-growing variety. Open, bushy habit, strikes easily. –15°C/5°F.
'Norrie King' 'Mrs G.W. Leak' × R. decorum, pink form S. King, 1984/85.	Fuchsine pink with large maroon flare, in large, broad trusses of 12–15 flowers, freely flowering. EM.	Bushy, spreading habit with average foliage. Easily propagated. –18°C/0°F.
'Our Gem' syn. 'Larnook Gem' Laurie Begg.	Bright pink, with frilled margins, in small, tight trusses. VE.	Strongly growing plant, makes a good hedge. Sun tolerant.
'Pierre Moser' R. caucasicum × unknown Moser & Fils, 1914.	Soft pink star-shaped flowers with lighter centre and wavy edges in rounded trusses, freely flowering from an early age. E.	Compact flowers on long stems, on a bush with straggly, tallish growth. Needs regular pruning to establish and maintain a good garden form. –21°C/–5°F.
'Pink Delight' R. arboreum × unknown R. Gill & Son, 1926.	Pink or white, with deeper rose pink edging. Takes some years to flower. E.	Large-growing with strong, upright habit and foliage resembling R. arboreum. A vireya hybrid (q.v.) has same name. –15°C/5°F.
'Pink Pearl' 'George Hardy' × Broughtonii' J. Waterer, 1897. Photo p. 88.	Deep pink buds open to soft pink, paler at edges with a ray of reddish brown spots, in large, conical trusses. ML.	Very popular, regarded by many as the definitive pink rhododendron, the parent of many other successful hybrids. A strong, fast-growing, open and sometimes spindly shrub, often sparse at the base with age. –21°C/–5°F.
'Puget Sound' 'Loderi King George' × 'Van Nes Sensation' Roy W. Clark, 1958.	Pink, with slight tinge of lilac, very large, ruffled, reflexed and fragrant, in tall, shapely trusses, flowering from an early age. M.	Vigorous, upright habit, with thick, glossy, dark leaves on rosy stems and petioles. Heat tolerant. –21°C/–5°F.
'Rainbow' Unknown hardy Anthony Waterer hybrid × R. griffithianum W.C. Slocock, 1928.	Deep pink edges, white centres in loose trusses. M.	Upright plant as wide as it is tall. Long, glossy, drooping leaves with slightly rough texture. Heat tolerant. –18°C/0°F.
'Satin Glow' 'Loderi King George' × 'Cup Day' K. Van de Ven.	Superb, huge, deep pastel pink flowers in large, open trusses, fragrant and freely flowering. EM.	Sprawling, open growth habit but interesting foliage with reddish purple new growth and stems. Leaves held for one year. Moderate sun tolerance, hard to strike, better grafted. –15°C/5°F.
'Sir Frederick Moore' R. fortunei ssp. discolor × 'Saint Keverne' L. de Rothschild, 1935/37.	Large, frilled, clear pink, slightly fragrant flowers in compact, flat-topped trusses of about 15, freely flowering once established. ML.	Vigorous, upright, sturdy growth and large, dark foliage. Heat tolerant and resistant to sucking insects, but hard to strike. Named after a Director at Glasnevin Botanic Gardens, Dublin. –21°C/–5°F.
'Sirius' R. cinnabarinum spp. cinnabarinum × R. maddenii spp. maddenii. G. Reuthe Ltd, 1973. Photo p. 105.	Bright pink, pendulous, waxy flowers. M.	Dark, glossy foliage on an upright plant with open habit, best in milder climates. –12°C/10°F to –15°C/5°F.
'Souvenir de Dr S. Endtz' syn. 'Dr S. Endtz' 'Pink Pearl' × 'John Walter' L. J. Endtz, 1924.	Rose buds open to rich pink marked with a crimson ray, ruby spots, widely funnel-shaped, 80 mm wide, in domed trusses of 15–17, free-flowering. M.	Vigorous plant, broader than tall, with wavy, dark green leaves 165 mm long. Sun tolerant, insect resistant. Easy to strike. –23°C/–10°F.

Species	Flowers	Notes
'Stead's Pink' Edgar Stead.	Pink bell-shaped flowers in loose trusses.	Hardy shrub with open growth habit.
'Sugar Pink' 'Trude Webster' × unknown hybrid H. Greer, 1979.	Large cotton candy pink or light purplish pink flowers, deeper throat, light brown spotting, 127 mm wide, in tall trusses of about 12, up to 300 mm high. EM.	A strong-growing, upright, vigorous plant. Heavy, smooth, thickly textured deep green leaves and stems, 190 mm long. Strikes easily. –21°C/–5°F.
'Virgo' ['Antoone van Welie' × 'Professor J. H. Zaayer'] × 'Annie E. Endtz' P. van Nes, 1959.	Rose buds open to light pink, fading to white, with large reddish brown spotted blotch, in tall, pyramid-shaped trusses of about 17–18 frilled florets. ML.	A vigorous, open and sometimes spindly bush, bare at base. Large, bright green foliage. –21°C/–5°F.
'Walloper' syn. 'Lem's Walloper' 'Anna' × 'Marinus Koster' H. Lem.	Normally deep pink, in huge trusses, also white and red hybrids. M.	Large, densely foliaged plant, thick leaves, new growth reddish. –21°C/–5°F. A number of hybrids share the same name.

Larger reds, 1.8 m/6 ft or more

'Alarm' Parentage unknown A. Waterer & Godfrey, before 1860.	Deep crimson red with blush pink to white centre, brown markings, small to medium flowers, freely flowering. ML.	Vigorous, sometimes sprawling and untidy growth with uninspiring foliage. Easily propagated from cuttings.
'Bibiani' 'Moser's Maroon' × R. arboreum ssp. arboreum L. de Rothschild, 1934.	Deep bright blood red, waxy, in dense, rounded trusses of about 14, freely flowering. E.	Very glossy, dark green foliage, silvery brown underneath, on a vigorous, upright, compact plant. Not wind tolerant. Easily propagated. –15°C/5°F.
'Bloodline' 'Britannia' × 'Cornubia' K. Van de Ven, 1988.	Strong bright red, tubular campanulate flowers in large, full trusses of 10, flowering from 3 years. EM.	Tall, vigorous, bushy growth, flowers from third year. –15°C/5°F to –18°C/0°F.
'Broughtonii' R. arboreum ssp. arboreum × unknown Broughton, 1835–40.	Bright rosy crimson with darker spots in large, pyramidal trusses of 20–21, freely flowering. M.	A very early, hardy variety of strong, dense, bushy habit. Handsome, narrow foliage tends to yellow slightly if exposed to full sunlight. Easy to strike. –23°C/–10°F.
'Cardinal' R. arboreum ssp. arboreum × 'Barclayi' Lord Aberconway, 1937.	Large scarlet flowers.	Tall, vigorous, tree-like habit.
'Cornubia' R. arboreum red form × 'Shilsonii' R. Barclay Fox, 1912. Photo p. 34.	Blood red in large conical or rounded trusses of about 12. Takes up to 5 years before flowering freely over a long period, but early flowering means blooms are frost susceptible. VE.	Tall, open, but spreading bush. Possibly the most popular very early flowering red. In milder climates, grows to a small tree. Easily propagated. –15°C/5°F.
'Cynthia' syn. 'Lord Palmerston' Parentage unknown Standish & Noble/Sunningdale Nurseries, c. 1856.	Rosy crimson or deep rose pink flowers, 75 mm wide, with deeper crimson markings in huge, showy, conical trusses of up to 24, flowering from quite young. ML.	A particularly hardy, pest-resistant variety. A vigorous grower which develops into a very large bushy, dome-shaped plant. Strong, dark green foliage. Tolerates sun, in which it grows less leggy, or shade and strikes easily. –23°C/–10°F to –26°C/–15°F.

Cultivar	Flowers	Notes
'Damozel' 'A.W. Bright Rose' × R. griersonianum L. de Rothschild, 1936.	Deep ruby red, spotted with darker red, funnel-shaped in many dome-shaped trusses of about 17, freely flowering. ML.	Widely spreading and branching plant with sparse, narrow, dark green foliage. Heat tolerant, strikes easily –18°C/0°F.
'David' 'Hugh Koster' × R. neriiflorum F. Rose, Lord Swaythling, 1939.	Deep or blood red with white anthers and frilly margins, deeply spotted inside, campanulate, in loose trusses of 16–19. EM.	A compact, upright growing bush with dark green foliage. Easily struck, but susceptible to insect attack, and prefers protection from wind and frost. –15°C/5°F or colder.
'Direktor E. Hjelm' 2nd generation R. fortunei hybrid D. Koster, before 1958.	Dark carmine rose with bronze blotch, in flat-topped trusses. ML.	Popular in Europe. Hard to strike. –23°C/–10°F or colder.
'Edith Praed' syn. 'Edith Mackworth Praed' 'Doncaster' hybrid M. Koster & Sons, 1934.	Light red, paler in centre, marked with blackish crimson, in pyramidal trusses of about 13, freely flowering, with attractive buds. EM.	A good, hardy garden plant with upright growth, good background plant. Not to be confused with the very hardy pink-flowering R. maximum hybrid, 'Edith Pride'. –21°C/–5°F.
'Fire Bird' 'Norman Shaw' × R. griersonianum L. de Rothschild, 1938	Glowing salmon red, with bright yellow anthers, in large, full trusses. ML.	Tall, vigorous bush with light green foliage which makes a striking contrast against crimson bracts. –18°C/0°F.
'Gill's Crimson' R. griffithianum × unknown R. Gill & Sons. Photo p. 87.	Bright blood red, long-lasting flowers in tight rounded trusses. EM.	Upright sturdy plant, fairly frost-tender and well suited to warmer climates. –15°C/5°F.
'Grenadier' 'Moser's Maroon' × R. elliottii L. de Rothschild, 1939.	Very deep or cherry red, stained with orange and brown, with black spotting, in rounded trusses of about 12. L.	Very strong, fast-growing plant, ultimately tall and straggly, with large, dark green foliage, indumentum. Prefers shade. –15°C/5°F.
'Hugh Koster' 'George Hardy' × 'Doncaster' hybrid M. Koster & Sons, 1915.	Bright crimson, lighter in centre, black spots, with contrasting pale stamens, medium sized, in rounded trusses of up to 16. ML.	Medium to large grower, with upright, spreading habit and shiny, grooved foliage with wavy margins. Easily struck. Needs shelter from sun. –15°C/5°F.
'Ivanhoe' 'Chanticleer' × R. griersonianum L. de Rothschild, 1941.	Brilliant scarlet, spotted with deeper red, funnel-shaped, in loose, flat-topped trusses. EM.	Tall growth, loose, straggly habit. Easy to strike. Popular in New Zealand. –15°C/5°F.
'Ivery's Scarlet' syn. 'Ivorianum' Parentage unknown, possibly includes R. arboreum and R. ponticum Ivery's Nursery, c. 1850.	Deep red, spotted darker on upper lobes, in small, dense, dome-shaped trusses of 12–14 medium-sized flowers. Long flowering period. EM.	A durable old hybrid which can withstand fully exposed positions, being sun, heat and wind tolerant. Leaves are long, thin and pointed, hanging down in the colder months. Low, spreading habit, arching branches. –12°C/10°F.
'John Waterer' Unknown parentage, possibly R. catawbiense and/or R. ponticum × R. arboreum ssp. arboreum J. Waterer, circa 1860.	Purplish red or rosy crimson, with darker crimson spotting, in trusses of about 18. L.	An old, hardy hybrid, still in cultivation. A vigorous, dense shrub with stiff, leathery leaves, thin indumentum. –21°C/–5°F or colder
'Kaponga' R. arboreum × 'Ivery's Scarlet' B. Holland, 1979.	Red, spotted darker, resembling those of R. arboreum, in tight trusses, over long period. Slow to flower. EM.	Large, pyramidal-shaped, tree-like habit. Named after the breeder's home town on New Zealand's North Island. Hard to strike. –12°C/10°F.

Species	Flowers	Notes
'Lady Grenville' R. ponticum × unknown.	Large, purplish red flowers in large trusses. Earlier than most R. ponticum hybrids. M.	Hardy, strong-growing bush, quite suitable for exposed positions. −18°C/0°F.
'Lighthouse' 'Sir John Waterer' or early flowering pink seedling × R. arboreum 'Bennet's' K. Van de Ven, 1960.	Small, brilliant red flowers in very tight, conical trusses held high above foliage. EM.	Tough shrub with good foliage and open, upright habit, frost and very sun hardy.
'Oklahoma' 'Bellerephon' × 'Tally Ho' L. de Rothschild, 1975.	Currant red, lightly spotted with darker red, with black anthers and stigma, waxy, in large trusses of 20–22. V–VL	−15°C/5°F to −23°C/−10°F.
'Red Admiral' R. arboreum × R. thomsonii J.C. Williams, c. 1947.	Glowing blood red, campanulate, over long period. Several years before flowering. E.	One of the best early reds. Tall, erect, tree-like plant with good foliage held for one year. Easily grown, but not so easy to strike. −12°C/10°F.
'Rodeo' 'Mrs L.A. Dunnett' × R. griersonianum M. Koster & Sons, 1958. Photo p. 88.	Clear light red, with orange flush, in large, conical trusses, freely flowering. ML.	Good foliage and upright habit. Recommended and deservedly popular in Australia. Difficult to strike. −18°C/0°F.
'Romany Chal' 'Moser's Maroon' × R. facetum L. de Rothschild, 1932.	Large, rich, glowing red flowers, faintly spotted with brown, bell-shaped, in very large, rounded trusses of about 12, freely flowering. L.	Loose, open-growing plant that needs constant pruning to keep in shape in the shade it needs. Dark green, recurved leaves, up to 165 mm long, with a slight brownish indumentum. Name means 'gypsy girl', and this hybrid should not to be confused with the same breeder's medium red 'Romany Chai' (q.v.). −15°C/5°F.
'Sir Robert Peel' syn. 'Cornish Red' R. arboreum × R. ponticum A. Waterer, before 1871.	Small crimson flowers, with bluish tinge and darker spotting, in rounded trusses, freely flowering. VE.	One of the hardiest rhododendrons, can be grown in exposed positions, suitable for large hedges, sometimes a street tree in New Zealand. Good, tall, vigorous, bushy habit but uninspiring foliage. Heat and drought tolerant, resistant to root fungi, and strikes easily, making it useful as a rootstock. −15°C/5°F.
'Tally Ho' R. griersonianum × R. facetum J. Crosfield & E. Loder, 1933. Photo p. 105.	Clear orange-red or vermillion, spotted deeper in throat, in compact trusses of 9–14, flowering when quite young. L.	Open, straggly plant with thick, pale brown indumentum on underside of dull green, bullate leaves and covering any new growth. Needs shade, ideal in a woodland setting. Strikes easily. −12°C/10°F.
'Taurus' 'Jean Marie de Montague' × R. strigillosum F. Mossman, 1972.	Attractive deep red winter buds open to orange-red flowers, with cherry red throat, campanulate, 90 mm wide, in rounded trusses of about 16, freely flowering from 4–6 years. EM.	Sturdy and vigorous, upright, dense habit, with thick, deep green, pointed leaves held for 3 years. Insect resistant. Recommended. −18°C/0°F to −21°C/−5°F.
'Volcano' Parentage and origin unknown, before 1970.	Abundant small, dark red flowers. EM.	Medium to large, compact, bushy growth. Easy to propagate from cuttings.

Larger whites, 1.8 m/6 ft or more

'Beauty of Littleworth' R. griffithianum × R. campanulatum J. Mangles, before 1884.	Pure white spotted with dark purple markings in very large, conical trusses of 13–19 flowers up to 120 mm across. Five years to bloom, then freely. M.	A showy, strong, vigorous grower with tall, untidy, leggy habit and large, shiny, dark green foliage, bronze underneath in winter. The sheer weight of its flower trusses can distort growth and initiate layering. Strikes fairly easily. −21°C/−5°F.

Cultivar	Flowers	Notes
'Boddaertianum' syn. 'Croix d'Anvers', 'Gloire d'Anvers' R. arboreum × R. ponticum or R. campanulatum L. Van Houtte, 1863.	Lavender pink buds open to pink flowers, which fade to creamy white, with dark purple blotch and crimson ray, in compact, rounded trusses of 18–22, freely produced and long-lasting. EM.	Possibly a natural hybrid from Sikkim. Very tough and sun tolerant hybrid with a compact, bushy habit. Named after Boddaert, foreman at the van Houtte nursery where it was raised. –18°C/0°F.
'Cearuleum' a form of R. rigidum Origin unknown.	Pure white with olive markings. EM.	Neat, glaucous foliage. –21°C/–5°F.
'Faggetter's Favourite' R. fortunei × unknown W. Slocock, 1933.	Creamy white, flushed pink, fading to white, speckled bronze, in large trusses of 11–13 fragrant flowers after 4–5 years. EM.	Compact, vigorous, upright growth with shiny, drooping foliage. Prefers light shade and hard to strike. –21°C/–5°F.
'Geoffrey Millais' R. griffithianum × unknown Otto Schulz, C.B. van Nes, 1892.	Pink buds open to frilled white flowers flushed pink, with crimson-brown markings, in tall, conical trusses of about 14. ML	Large, vigorous, open shrub, sometimes leggy, with generous, dark green, stiff, glossy foliage. Fragrant. Easy to strike. –21°C/–5°F.
'Mrs Tom Agnew' Parentage unknown J. Waterer, before 1877. Photo p. 87.	Mauve pink buds open to white flowers with yellow–brown flare, in trusses of 16. L.	Small leaves. Heat tolerant. –21°C/–5°F.
'Sappho' Parentage uncertain, possibly R. maximum or 'Smithii Album' hybrid A. Waterer, before 1847.	Distinctive, medium-sized pure white flowers with a striking deep maroon–black blotch, widely funnel-shaped, in large, conical trusses of about 15, freely flowering after 3–4 years. ML.	Popular, hardy, fast growing and rather open, leggy shrub with narrow, dark olive green foliage, requiring regular pinching and pruning to maintain an agreeable shape. Strikes easily. One of the oldest surviving hybrids and often used as a parent. –23°C/–10°F to –26°C/–15°F.
'White Pearl' syn. 'Halopeanum', 'Gauntlettii' R. griffithianum × R. maximum Halope, 1896.	Light pink fading to white, speckled crimson in throat, in tall, conical trusses of 9–12. M.	A very vigorous, large growing, heat tolerant, bushy plant suitable for exposed positions. Dark green foliage with a slightly rough texture. Easy to strike, sometimes a rootstock, often used as a parent. –15°C/5°F or colder.
'White Swan' R. decorum × 'Pink Pearl' J. Waterer & Crisp, 1937.	Satin white, with greenish basal markings, in very large, perfectly formed trusses of 16–19, flowering from an early age. M.	Easily grown, upright, compact shrub with thick, dusty greyish green, concave foliage to 150 mm long. Easy to strike. Although heat tolerant, prefers some shade. –21°C/–5°F.

Larger yellows, golds and oranges 1.8 m or more

Cultivar	Flowers	Notes
'California Gold' 'Else Frye' × 'Eldorado' P. & R. Bowman, 1962/76.	Superb primrose yellow, tubular, flat-faced, very fragrant, funnel-shaped flowers, up to 75 mm wide in trusses of 5–6, freely flowering. E.	A well-branching shrub with spinach green, hairy leaves, silvery scales on undersides. –15°C/5°F.
'Crest' syn. 'Hawk Crest' R. wardii × 'Lady Bessborough' L. de Rothschild, 1940/53.	Deep orange buds open to long lasting, bright primrose yellow flowers, slightly darkening around throat, 100 mm wide, in large, elegant, dome-shaped trusses of about 12, floriferous once established. M.	One of the best yellows, magnificent in bloom. Open, sometimes sparse, upright, tree-like habit with deep green, oval, glossy leaves held for one year. Prefers a woodland setting with some shade. Hard to strike, often used as a parent. –21°C/–5°F.

10
Evergreen azaleas

Still thought of by many as the distinct species they once were, evergreen azaleas are truly rhododendrons, and as such, they share much in common with other plants of the genus. Within the group there is great variety of size, habit and flower, with azaleas to suit a wide range of applications in the landscape, in containers or as bonsai specimens. There are evergreen azaleas hardy enough to tolerate the severest of northern hemisphere winters, and others that thrive in the warmth of the subtropics. They are a most useful and versatile group of plants.

The evergreen azaleas are all found within the various sections of the subgenus Tsutsutsi. Although they are called 'evergreen', when the term is applied here it is not strictly correct. Evergreen azaleas have what are known as 'dimorphic' leaves. New spring growth results in larger, thinner leaves which yellow and die off during autumn, not to be mistaken for some sort of ailment. Summer leaves are thicker and smaller, and it is these leaves which persist on the plant through the winter, giving rise to the claim to being 'evergreen'.

The vast majority of azaleas used as garden plants are hybrids, many with a lineage going back hundreds of years, and often with little accurate record of their true origins. Most of the *Rhododendron* species which resulted in the thousands of evergreen azalea hybrids are not commonly grown. All of them are native to Asia, principally Japan, Taiwan, the Philippines, Korea, central and south-eastern China and southward into central Vietnam.

The azalea has long been held in high esteem in Japan, and, like the camellia, is interwoven in that country's culture, their cultivation being a vital component in traditional landscaping so admired and emulated in the West. As early as 1681, the first Japanese book on horticulture, *Kadan Komoku*, was published, listing some 317 varieties and 15 species. *Kinshu Makura* (Brocade Pillow), an illustrated azalea monograph written by nurseryman Ito Ihei and published in 1692, described a total of 332 azaleas, classifying them into the two traditional groups that relate to flowering time - 171 Tsutsujii and 161 Satsuki azaleas.

The Tsutsujii group includes all those azaleas that flower in early spring or up to 30 days after the spring equinox. Satsuki means the fifth month of the old Japanese lunar calendar, which corresponds to June in Japan or December in the southern hemisphere. Satsukis flower about a month later and include *R. indicum* and *R. eriocarpum* and their hybrids.

Evergreen azaleas were taken into China by Japanese Buddhist monks who, in their travels, were responsible for the circulation of many other genera of Japanese plants into China and elsewhere in the region, including *Camellia japonica, Cryptomeria,* the evergreen azaleas and other *Rhododendron* species. These same monks also brought camellias (including tea), chrysanthemums and peonies, to name a few, back with them into Japan.

R. indicum, a parent of many azaleas including the Satsukis, was first named *Azalea indica* by the Swedish botanist Carl Linnaeus in his *Species Plantarum* of 1783, based on descriptions of plants imported by Dutch merchants almost a century earlier. Most of the azaleas introduced into the West in the early days came from established gardens in Japan rather than as naturally occurring hybrids from the wild and were subsequently given Westernised, often Latin, names. For example, 'Indica Alba' (also known as 'Mucronatum') was introduced into Europe early this century and played its part in early hybridising. It has been known as a cultivated hybrid in Japan for at least 300 years, but is never found in the wild. These first azaleas to be imported and cultivated in the west became known as Indian azaleas. Much hybridisation took place in Europe in the nineteenth century when their popularity as container or greenhouse plants increased.

Interest in the Kurume group of hybrids began during the first World War, again initially for their use as potted specimens. Their cold hardiness, however, quickly found them a place outdoors in the cooler Northern Hemisphere garden. Even more tolerant of the cold are the Kaempferi hybrids, with *R. kaempferi* usually as a parent. Western gardeners were slow to show interest in the Satsukis, but to the Japanese, who have reverently cultivated and hybridised them for hundreds of years, they are the definitive azalea.

Evergreen azalea species

Species	Flowers	Notes
eriocarpum Japan (Ryuku, islands off SW), in woodlands and thickets at 300 m/1000 ft. Photo p. 124.	White to purplish pink, widely funnel-shaped, 30–34 mm long, singly or in pairs. ML	Dwarf or upright shrub, with mid green, elliptic or obovate foliage, 17–40 mm long, summer leaves smaller. Closely allied to R. simsii, and not in commercial cultivation, although significant as a parent of Satsuki azaleas. Ht 0.4–1 m/1 ft 4 in–3 ft.
indicum Japan, southern, rocky banks of streams. Dutch traders, 1680.	Violet to purple, occasionally lavender, broadly funnel-shaped, 35–50 mm long × 45–63 mm wide, in clusters of 1 or 2. Freely flowering, VL.	Densely branched, low, sometimes prostrate, habit. Young shoots covered with brown bristles. Glossy, dark green leaves, narrowly lanceolate to oblanceolate, 18–35 mm long. Closely related to R. simsii, which is sometimes marketed as Azalea indica and R. eriocarpum. Cultivated in Japan for at least 300 years, resulting in many forms. Ht 0.5–1 m/1 ft 6 in–3 ft. H2–3
indicum var. 'Balsaminaeflorum' before 1880.	Salmon red, double flowers. VL.	Dwarf form of R. indicum. Ht 0.1–0.3 m/4 in–1 ft. H2–3.
kaempferi Japan (central Hokkaido to extreme south), open thickets, light woodlands, to 1600 m/ 5250 ft. Charles Maries for Veitch Nursery, 1878. Photo p. 124.	Salmon red, brick red, other shades of red, and, occasionally, white or purple, funnel-shaped, 26–38 mm long × 25–43 mm wide, in trusses of 2–4, sometimes singly. L.	A parent of the Kaempferi hybrids. Densely branching small shrub with red-brown bristles on young shoots. Spring leaves glossy green, lanceolate, elliptic or ovate, 20–50 mm long, summer leaves smaller. Sun tolerant. Previously considered a variety of R. indicum, later R. obtusum, now a species in its own right. Ht 0.9–1.2 m/3–4 ft. H3.
kiusianum Japan (Kyushu) on lava and volcanic ash among grass and low shrubs, on mountains and volcanoes, 600–1600 m/2000–5250 ft. E.H. Wilson sent seed to Arnold Arboretum, USA, 1918.	Rose-purple, purple, red, pink or sometimes white, funnel-shaped, 13–25 mm wide, in trusses of 2–3. VL.	Easily-grown, low, dense, much-branched, often prostrate shrub. Brown hairs on young shoots. Glossy, dark green spring foliage 8–20 mm long, summer leaves smaller. Becomes deciduous at higher altitudes. Nominated by E.H. Wilson as the wild parent of the kurume azaleas, of which he selected 50, known as 'Wilson's Fifty' for introduction to the west. Ht 0.3–1 m/1–3 ft. H3.
macrosepalum 'Linearifolium' Japan (Honshu, Shikoku), common in woodlands, open thickets, 150–400 m/500–1300 ft. Standish, 1860s. Photo p. 123.	Pink, purple or purplish red, up to 38 mm long, widely funnel-shaped, in clusters of 2–6. Fragrant. L.	A garden form or selected sport of R. macrosepalum, long cultivated in Japan. Young shoots covered in grey hairs. Large, linear or linear-lanceolate leaves, hairy, particularly underneath, 38–75 × 20–60 mm. Spring leaves turn crimson-purple in autumn. Ht 0.3–0.9m/1–3 ft. H2–3.
nakaharai Taiwan, at 2,000–2,300 m/6500–7500 ft. G. Nakahara, Japanese collector, 1905, Mt Shichiri, N Taiwan.	Dark red or scarlet, funnel-shaped, 20 mm long × 30–35 mm wide, in trusses of 1–3. VL.	Low-growing, much-branched, twiggy, prostrate habit. Small, dark green, lanceolate to elliptic-obovate foliage, 3–10 × 2–5 mm, pale green underneath. The leaves are monomorphic rather than dimorphic as in other evergreen azaleas, meaning it is a true evergreen, rather than having distinct spring and summer foliage. A sun-tolerant species ideal for the rock garden. Ht 0.1–0.3 m/4 in–1 ft. H3.
oldhamii Taiwan, thickets, cliffs and grassy hills, to 2800 m/9000 ft. Richard Oldham, 1864, Tamsui, Taiwan.	Orange-red to pink, tubular funnel-shaped, 30–54 mm long × 25–60 mm wide, in trusses of 2–4, freely flowering. ML.	Densely branching shrub Young shoots and leaves covered with dense brown bristles. Elliptic or elliptic-oblong foliage, 15–80 × 8–25 mm. Ht 1–3 m/3–10 ft. H1–2.

Species	Flowers	Notes
simsii China, Taiwan, upper Myanmar, Laos, Thailand, widespread in open woodland and thickets at 600–2700 m/2000–8860 ft. c. 1793. *Photo p. 124.*	Purple-crimson or deep rose crimson, widely funnel-shaped, 35–50 mm long, in clusters of 2–3. Freely flowering. L.	Twiggy, densely branching shrub with spring leaves 20–60 mm long, summer leaves small, both densely strigose. Parent of Indian or Indica azaleas in 1850s by Belgian and Dutch breeders, and formerly known as *Azalea indica*. The true *R. indicum* is related but restricted to Japan. Ht 1–2 m/3–6 ft. H1–2.
tashiroi Japan (southern), in evergreen forests at 200–500 m/650–1,650 m. Maximowicz, 1887.	Pale rose purple, spotted with maroon purple, large, funnel-campanulate, 25–35 mm long, in trusses of 2–5. Flowers and leaf whorls emerge from the same terminal bud. L.	Dense shrub or small tree known as 'Sakura tsutsuji'. Brownish, hairy petioles and young growth. Mid-green monomorphic (see *R. nakaharai*, above), elliptic obovate leaves, 35–60 mm long. Named after a Japanese botanist. Not introduced into the USA until the mid-1950s and Europe until the 1970s and still comparatively rare. Ht 2–6 m/6–20 ft, has been recorded in Japan at 10 m/33 ft. H3.

Indica azaleas

Commonly known as Indica or Indian azaleas, these are the most widely grown azaleas in the temperate climates of Australia and New Zealand where the climate does not demand the hardier varieties popular in Northern Hemisphere gardens. While they thrive outdoors in milder climates, their development was motivated by the European market for cut flowers and flowering indoor plants. Consequently the aim of breeders tended to favour characteristics of flower form, size and colour over landscaping attributes.

R. simsii is a densely branching shrub native to western, central and southern China, Taiwan, upper Myanmar, Laos and Thailand, normally growing to no more than two metres in height and with strongly coloured flowers in shades of red, crimson and purple. It is only hardy to −4°C with the result that many of the hybrids are frost tender, and this should be borne in mind when choosing planting sites.

In 1851, three forms of *R. simsii*, named 'Vittata', 'Vittata Punctata' and 'Bealii' or 'Vittata Bealii', were collected from a Shanghai nursery by Robert Fortune and imported into England. The plants were incorrectly named as varieties of 'Indica', leading to the traditional use of the term for this group. The true *R. indicum* species did not apparently play a significant role in hybrid development at this time.

Vigorous breeding activity commenced in Belgium when Fortune's plants arrived there three years later. This development was so rapid that by 1860 the Belgian Indian hybrids, grown for export on a vast scale, had well exceeded the popularity of the earlier English Indian hybrids. The resulting shrubs are of medium size, usually from 1.2 m/4 ft to 2 m/6 ft in height, with dense, branching, bushy growth. Flowers are most commonly singles, although there are also many doubles, semi-doubles and 'hose-in-hose' types.

Hybrid	Flowers	Notes
'Advent Bells'	Strong reddish purple, semi-double. E and autumn.	Medium height.
'Albert Elizabeth'	White with pink edges, double, slightly frilled. ML.	Medium height.
'Aline'	White, large double. M and autumn.	Medium bushy growth.
'Angus Bell'	Orange-red with paler centre, medium single to semi-double. ML.	
'Anniversary Joy'	Pale pink flushed with deep pink, white blotch speckled pale green. Frilled semi-double. M.	Burbank, 1980.

Hybrid	Flowers	Notes
'Baby Jill'	Light lavender pink. Large double hose-in-hose. M, also autumn.	Gold Cup hybrid azalea. Bushy growth to 1 m/3 ft.
'Ballerina'	Pale pink to white, cyclamen edging, medium double. L.	Compact growth.
'Beatrix'	Orange salmon. Medium double. EM, also autumn.	Medium height, spreading height. Early. Sport of 'Paul Schaeme'.
'Bertina'	Yellowish pink, very large single. M, also autumn.	Bushy growth to 1 m/3 ft.
'Beverley Haerens' syn. 'California Snow'	White, large semi-double. E, also autumn.	Medium bushy growth. Sport of 'Avenir'.
'Bonnie McKee'	Mauve, large double. EM.	Bushy, medium growth. Greentree, 1970.
'Break O'Day'	Light salmon pink with rose red spots in throat. Large single. ML.	Medium, vigorous, bushy shrub to 1.5 m/5 ft. Sport of 'California Dawn'.
'Bride's Bouquet'	White double. M.	A Kerrigan hybrid, 'Blushing Bride' × 'Rosebud'. Medium upright habit. Prefers protection from wind and sun.
'California Dawn' syn. 'California Pink Dawn'	Coral rose pink, large single.	Medium, vigorous, bushy shrub to 1.5 m/5 ft.
'California Peach'	Light salmon pink. Large semi-double. EM, also sutmn.	Vigorous bushy growth.
'Cameo'	Salmon pink. Medium triple hose-in-hose. M.	Medium, bushy growth. Holland.
'Carnival'	Rose red. Large single to semi-double. M, spot flowers from autumn, then spring.	Full sun. Tall, bushy growth.
'Carnival Candy'	Scarlet red. Medium to large single. M, spot flowers from autumn, then spring.	Full sun. Medium to tall, bushy growth.
'Carnival Clown'	Bright purple, ruffled. Large single. M.	Full Sun. Low, bushy growth.
'Carnival Queen'	Bright pink. Medium to large semi-double. M, spot flowers from autumn, then spring.	Low to medium, bushy growth.
'Carnival Rocket'	Bright orange red. Medium single. M.	Full sun. Low, bushy growth
'Carnival Time'	Purple. Medium to large single. M. spot flowers from autumn, then spring.	Full sun. Tall, bushy growth to 1.6m/5 ft 3 in.
'Cha Cha'	White, with purplish red-frilled margins. Large double hose-in-hose. M, may also flower in autumn.	Gold Cup hybrid. Bushy growth to 1 m/3 ft.
'Charly' syn. 'Charlie'	Strong purplish red, large double. Autumn, ML.	Low, compact, bushy shrub. Sport of 'Lucie'. K. Glaser, G.F.R., 1978.

Species	Flowers	Notes
'Comtesse de Kerchove'	Soft opal pink, bordered with white. Medium double flower with green calyx. E, spot flowers from autumn, then spring.	J.B. Haerens & Son., Belgium, 1938.
'Coral Wings'	Salmon rose. Medium semi-double hose-in-hose. Spot flowers from autumn, then spring. EM.	Hardy, dense, bushy, compact shrub to 1 m. Sport of 'Red Wings'.
'Crown Jewel'	White, with varying flecks and stripes of salmon. Large semi-double. Spot flowers from autumn, then spring. ML.	Vigorous, bushy shrub to 1.2 m/4 ft.
'Dancer'	Salmon pink. Medium semi-double hose-in-hose. Spot flowers from autumn, then spring. M.	Hardy shrub of medium height.
'De Waele's Favourite'	Pink, with white border. Large double with frilled edge. ML.	Medium, bushy growth. Sport of 'Knut Erwen'.
'Desert Rose'	Strong pink with lighter throat and red flecks. Frilled, semi-double. EM, autumn.	Gold Cup hybrid.
'Desiree'	Strong purplish red. Medium single hose-in-hose.	Dense, bushy growth, medium height.
'Dr. Arnold'	Deep pink with white centre, red blotch. Large single. EM, autumn. Long-flowering.	Medium tall growth, bushy habit. Sport of 'Pink Dream'. Hardy.
'Dr. Bergmann'	Carmine orange with darker throat. Medium semi-double. Spot flowers from autumn, then spring.	Medium bushy growth with upright habit. Dark green, glossy foliage.
'Dr. Koester'	Vivid red double. Spot flowers from autumn, then spring. M.	Medium bushy growth.
'Easter Bonnet'	Lavender pink, fading to white centre, green spots in throat. Large single to semi-double. EM.	Gold Cup hybrid azalea. Medium, bushy growth.
'Elsa Karga' Photo p. 124.	Glowing vivid red. Medium double flower with green calyx. M.	Medium bushy growth.
'Eri Schaeme'	Coral pink, edged with white. Large semi-double. Long flowering from autumn to spring.	Sport of 'Paul Schaeme'. Medium height, bushy habit.
'Eureka'	Deep pink with white margin. Autumn, M. Long-flowering.	Low to medium height, compact bushy habit.
'Fire Magic' syn. 'Feuerzauber'	Orange red, medium single. M.	Dense, bushy growth, medium height.
'Firefly'	Deep red, large double. ML.	Vigorous, bushy growth.

Massed Kurume azaleas form a carpet beneath a magnolia and other deciduous trees.

Kurume azalea R. 'Kelly's Cerise'.

R. *macrosepalum* 'Linearifolium'.

Azaleas

R. eriocarpum.

A pink form of *R. kaempferi.*

Kaempferi azaleas reaching 6 m (18 ft) at Tatebayasi Park, Japan. (Photo: ARS)

R. simsii.

R. 'Elsa Karga'. (Photo: ARS – Arthur W. Headlam)

R. 'Hinode Giri'. (Photo: ARS – Arthur W. Headlam)

R. 'Hinomayo'. (Photo: ARS – Arthur W. Headlam)

Indica azalea *R.* 'Rosali'.

Indica azalea *R.* 'Leopold Astrid'.

R. 'Only One Earth'.

R. 'Phoenicium'.

R. 'Phryne'.

Azaleas

Indica azalea R. 'Pink Ice'.

R. 'Pink Ruffles'. (Photo: ARS – Arthur W. Headlam)

R. 'Princess Maude'.

R. 'Red Wings'.

R. 'Rosina'. (Photo: ARS – Arthur W. Headlam)

R. 'Splendens'. (Photo: ARS – Arthur W. Headlam)

R. 'Early Orange'. (Photo: ARS – Ron Moodycliffe)

R. 'George Reynolds'. (Photo: ARS – Arthur W. Headlam)

R. occidentale.

R. 'Dr Oosthoek'. (Photo: ARS – Arthur W. Headlam)

R. 'Orange Supreme'. (Photo: ARS – Ron Moodycliffe)

R. reticulatum. (Photo: ARS – Arthur W. Headlam)

Vireyas

R. aurigeranum. (Photo: Dr John Rouse)

R. aequabile.

R. ericoides.

R. aurigeranum 'Eureka Gold'. (Photo: Graham Snell)

R. javanicum. (Photo: Dr John Rouse)

R. laetum.

R. 'Highland Arabesque'. (Photo: John Colwill)

R. leucogigas 'Hunstein's Secret'. (Photo: Dr John Rouse)

R. macgregoriae.

R. 'Niugini Firebird'.

R. lochiae. (Photo: John Colwill)

R. orbiculatum. (Photo: Dr John Rouse)

Hybrid	Flowers	Notes
'Flamingo' syn. 'Werner Muckel', 'Pink Lady', 'Werner Proehl'	Purplish red double flowers. Long-flowering.	Medium height with bushy habit. Sun tolerant.
'Gay Paree'	White, with cyclamen border, medium semi-double. M.	A Kerrigan hybrid. Compact, bushy shrub to 1 m/3 ft.
'Goyet'	Vivid red, very large double. Autumn, then M.	Sun tolerant. Medium tall, bushy.
'Gretel' syn. 'John Haerens'	White petals with deep cerise edge and tufted centre, medium double. ML.	Compact growth.
'Guanda Pink'	Strong salmon pink, large double. Long-flowering, autumn–spring.	Medium, bushy growth.
'Gumpo × Polka'	Orange red, large single with wide, wavy petals. Spot flowers from autumn, then spring.	Earlier than the 'Gumpo' hybrids.
'Happy Days'	Light purple, medium double hose-in-hose. Long flowering from autumn to spring.	Vigorous, medium to tall, bushy growth.
'Hellmut Vogel'	Vivid purplish red, semi-double or double flower with green calyx. Longh-flowering, autumn, then M.	Medium, bushy shrub. Popular in Europe for its rapid growth and forcing ability.
'Iceberg'	White, with green throat, semi-double. M.	Vigorous, medium bushy growth. Sport of 'Vervaeneana'.
'Inga'	Purplish pink with white edges, large double. Autumn–spring.	Medium bushy growth. Characteristics as for 'Hellmut Vogel' of which it is a sport.
'James Belton'	Pale pink, suffused with light purple or lavender, deepening towards centre. Single flowers. Blooms 8–9 months of the year.	Hairy foliage. Medium bushy growth to 1.5 m/5 ft. Indica × Schryderii hybrid.
'Janeke'	Orange-red, medium single. M, autumn.	Medium tall growth.
'Jindabyne'	Deep purple or rich violet, semi-double. M.	Medium bushy growth.
'Kandy Kid'	White, speckled pink, medium semi-double. Spot flowers from autumn, then spring, E.	Vigorous, compact shrub to 1 m/3 ft.
'Kelly's Cerise' Photo p. 123.	Purplish red, semi-double to double. Autumn, M.	Medium, bushy growth.
'Knut Erwen'	Cerise red, large double with frilled edges. ML.	Medium bushy growth. Has produced several sports.
'Koli'	Purplish pink with almost white stripes, medium semi-double with an average of two stamens, green calyx. M.	Dense, bushy growth, medium height.
'Kosmos'	Bright pink, very large double. Long-flowering, autumn then M.	Medium bushy growth.

Hybrid	Flowers	Notes
'Laura'	Deep pink, large single with occasional petaloids. Spot flowers from autumn, then spring.	Full sun. Tall, vigorous growth.
'Lavender Rosina'	Pale lavender, large double. Flowers heavily in autumn and again in spring.	Compact growth.
'Lavender Supreme'	Lavender. Large semi-double hose-in-hose. ML.	Vigorous bushy shrub to 1.2 m/4 ft.
'Leopold Astrid' Photo p. 124.	Double white, bordered with rose red and green calyx. Large frilled flowers. Spot flowers from autumn, then spring, M.	Bushy growth. Shiny foliage. Can be grown from cuttings as a small plant. Sport of 'Armand Haerens'.
'Little Beauty'	Vivid purplish red, hose-in-hose.	
'Lucie'	Vivid purplish pink, large double. Long-flowering, autumn to spring.	Flowers very early, autumn–mid season. Low, compact, bushy growth.
'Lucille K'	Red, edged with a fine white line, pointed petals. Ruffled, medium single hose-in-hose. Long flowering from autumn to spring, EM.	Full sun. Vigorous, compact, bushy growth. Sport of 'Red Wings'.
'Madame de Waele'	White, large double with frilled edges. ML.	Medium bushy growth. Sport of 'De Waele's Favourite'.
'Madonna'	White, large semi-double. Autumn–spring. M.	Compact bushy growth, large foliage.
'Mardi Gras'	Red with white edge, medium ruffled single. Occasional flowers from autumn, then M.	Low to medium, upright growth. Compact bushy shrub suitable for pot culture.
'Marylin Monroe'	Pale pink, flecked with pink, double. M.	Medium bushy growth.
'Melissa Ray'	Violet purple, large double. Spot flowers from autumn, then spring, E.	Medium bushy growth.
'Mercury'	Off white to blush pink, large single to semi-double. M.	Low to medium spreading growth.
'Mistral'	Pink, medium single. M.	Full sun. Light fragrance. Medium tall, vigorous.
'Madame Auguste Haerens'	Salmon, bordered with white. Large double. Spot flowers from autumn, then spring. E.	Medium bushy growth. Sport of 'Avenir'.
'Mrs Gerda Kint'	Pink, with white edges. Medium single. Spot flowers in autumn, then spring, ML.	Low, dense, compact shrub with small leaves. Also pink form.
'Mrs Jozef Heursel'	Deep purple, very large semi-double. M.	Medium height, vigorous.
'My Fair Lady'	Salmon pink with white border, large double. Spot flowers from autumn, then spring, E.	Medium bushy growth. Sport of 'Beverley Haerens'.

Hybrid	Flowers	Notes
'Only One Earth' Photo p. 124.	Bright red to deep purplish pink, ruffled, semi-double hose-in-hose. E.	Medium bushy growth.
'Orange Chimes'	Bright orange medium semi-double. Clusters of bell-shaped flowers. Spot flowers from autumn, then spring.	Sport of 'Advent Bells'. Prefers protection from sun and strong winds.
'Orchidflora Alba'	White, large semi-double. Long-flowering, autumn, then M.	Medium bushy growth. Tendency to become straggly, responds well to pruning to retain shape.
'Orchidflora Pink'	Pale pink, edged with white. Large semi-double. Long-flowering, autumn, then M.	as for 'Orchidflora 'Alba'.
'Osta'	Blush pink to white with red throat. Very large single. Spot flowers from autumn, then spring.	Medium bushy growth. Sport of 'Bertina'.
'Osta Red'	Red.	As for 'Osta', of which it is a sport.
'Paloma'	Pure white, large double. Autumn–spring.	Medium bushy growth.
'Paul Schaeme'	Bright salmon red, large double flower with green calyx. Long-flowering, autumn, then E.	Medium bushy growth.
'Phryne' Photo p. 124.	Creamy white, frilled double flowers. M.	Medium bushy growth.
'Pink Dream'	Soft pink, large single. Long flowering from autumn to spring.	Medium bushy growth. Hardy.
'Pink Ice' Photo p. 125.	Vivid pink, flushed purplish pink, double. EM.	
'Pink Ruffles' Photo p. 125.	Salmon pink, edged white with heavily ruffled petals. Large double. Long-flowering, autumn to spring, E.	Medium bushy growth. Blooms tend to be susceptible to fungal attack.
'Pink Tiger'	Lavender pink with purplish red spots in throat. Medium, ruffled single. Ml	Bushy shrub to 1.5 m/5 ft.
'Princess Maude' Photo p. 125.	Bright cerise red, small single. M.	Medium vigorous bushy growth. Amoenum hybrid azalea. Hardy.
'Prize'	Deep pink, medium to large semi-double. Spot flowers from autumn, then spring.	Full sun. Bushy growth 1–1.5 m/3–5 ft.
'Red Line'	White with bright pink markings. Large double. Autumn to spring, E.	Medium bushy growth. Sport of 'Eri Schaeme'.
'Red Poppy'	Glowing deep red, large single semi-double. Autumn, M.	Sun tolerant. Medium, bushy.

Hybrid	Flowers	Notes
'Red Ruffles'	Deep salmon rose with heavily ruffled petal edges. Large double. Long-flowering, autumn to spring, E.	Medium bushy growth. Blooms tend to be susceptible to fungal attack.
'Red Satin'	Dark red, large double, hose-in-hose. M.	Medium bushy growth.
'Red Wings' Photo p. 125.	Strong red, hose-in-hose, ruffled. Long-flowering.	Sun tolerant. Medium, spreading, bushy havit. A very versatile and popular Brooks hybrid.
'Ripples'	Rosy red, ruffled medium double. Long-flowering, autumn to spring.	Compact, bushy shrub, low to medium height. A Kerrigan hybrid azalea.
'Roadrunner'	Deep pink to red, medium single hose-in-hose. ML.	Compact, bushy growth. A Whitewater hybrid.
'Rosa Belton'	White, with a prominent mauve border. Large ruffled single, hose-in-hose, with green calyx. Long-flowering, with spot flowers from autumn, then spring, M.	Medium to tall, bushy growth. An Indica × schryderii hybrid, sport of 'James Belton'.
'Rosali' syn. 'Rosalie' Photo p. 124.	Vivid purplish red, inside a little paler. Large semi-double. M.	Medium upright bushy shrub.
'Rosina' Photo p. 125.	Soft candy pink, medium double. M.	Medium bushy growth.
'Ruth Kirk'	Vermillion pink in bud, marbled paler as single flower opens. E.	Medium bushy habit to 0.6 m/2 ft.
'Ruth Marion'	Mauve cerise with white centre. Medium semi-double, hose-in-hose. M.	Medium height, very compact growth.
'Silver Anniversary'	Delicate pale pink, shading to white tips. Frilled, medium semi-double, hose-in-hose. M.	Medium bushy growth.
'South Seas'	Delicate mauve pink, large semi-double. M.	Medium bushy growth.
'Southern Aurora'	Deep apricot salmon or light reddish orange, muted white, medium double. Spot flowers from autumn, then spring, E.	Medium bushy growth. Sport of 'Comtesse de Kerchove'.
'Southern Sunset'	Vivid red-orange, medium double. No stamens. Spot flowers from autumn, then spring, E.	Medium bushy growth. sport of 'Southern Aurora'.
'Stella Maris'	White, with purplish red blotch. Large semi-double. M.	Medium bushy shrub. Sport of 'Rosali'.
'Sweet Nellie'	Carmine red, medium semi-double to double, hose-in-hose. M.	Medium, spreading, bushy habit.
'The Teacher'	White with rose pink frilled edge, semi-double, hose-in-hose. M.	Medium bushy growth to 1 m/3 ft. Sport of 'Little Girl'.

Hybrid	Flowers	Notes
'Violacea'	Vivid reddish purple. Large double flower with green calyx. Spot flowers from autumn, then spring, EM.	Weak growth and weak wood. Medium spreading growth. Has produced a number of sports. C. Schulz, 1884.
'Violet Ray'	Violet, medium semi-double. Flowers from autumn to spring, M.	Full sun. Medium height, very bushy growth.
'White Bouquet'	White, large semi-double. Autumn, M.	Full sun. Compact, bushy growth to 1 m/3 ft.
'White Orchids'	Pale white with upper half of petals flecked with red. Semi-double. L.	Medium bushy growth. A Mossholder–Bristow hybrid, 1950s.
'White Schaeme' syn. 'Madame Marcel de Paepe'	White, large semi-double. Autumn, M.	Medium bushy growth. Sport of 'Eri' (sport of 'Paul Schaeme').

Rutherford hybrid azaleas

Growers in other countries, including the United States, took the development of the line still further. The Rutherford hybrids, for example, were bred as greenhouse plants for the florists' trade during the 1920s at the Bobbink & Atkins Nursery in East Rutherford, New Jersey. They are larger than the Belgian hybrids, typically 2 to 2.5 m/6 to 8 ft in height. and include many frilled or ruffled varieties in colours from a reddish orange to purple and white.

Hybrid	Flowers	Notes
'Constance'	Moderate purplish pink, with darker blotch. Medium single to hose-in-hose, frilled. EM.	Vigorous bushy growth to 1 m/3 ft.
'Dorothy Gish'	Orange salmon. Medium semi-double hose-in-hose. M.	Medium to tall, bushy habit
'Gloria U.S.A.'	Salmon pink, white with red throat, edged with white. Medium semi-double hose-in-hose. M.	Medium height.
'Louise J. Bobbink' syn. 'L.J. Bobbink'	Vivid purplish red with lighter throat, occasionally whitish, sem-double hose-in-hose, frilled. L.	Full sun. Medium to tall, bushy growth.
'Purity'	Pure white, single to semi-double, hose-in-hose. M.	Bushy growth to 1 m/3 ft. Spot flowers from autumn, then spring.
'Rose King'	Deep rose pink, medium semi-double. Spot flowers from autumn, then spring.	Medium to tall, bushy growth. Sport of 'Rose Queen'.
'Rose Queen'	Deep purplish pink with white throat and dark botch. Medium, semi-double hose-in-hose. Spot flowers from autumn, then spring, E.	Medium to tall bushy growth. The variety 'Improved Rose Queen' has darker double flowers.

Hybrid	Flowers	Notes
'Tickled Pink'	Pink, edged with white. Single to semi-double, hose-in-hose. Spot flowers from autumn, then spring, M.	Full sun. Bushy growth to 1 m/3 ft.
'White Gish'	White with creamy throat. Medium semi-double, hose-in-hose. Spot flowers from autumn, then spring, M.	Compact bushy shrub to 1 m/3 ft. Sport of 'Dorothy Gish'.
'White Prince'	White with red throat, occasionally flushed with pink. Medium, semi-double, hose-in-hose. Spot flowers from autumn, then spring, E.	Medium to tall, bushy growth. Sport of 'Duc de Rohan'.

The Brooks hybrids

Leonard L. Brooks, at Modesto in California, developed by a line of hybrids of similar height and form to the Belgian Hybrids by using various combinations of parentage. The best known of these is probably the popular 'Redwings' (syn. 'Red Wing', 'Red Bird').

Although bred initially as houseplants and too susceptible to frost damage for garden use in much of Europe, they can be grown in temperate climates including most parts of Australia and New Zealand, including the subtropics. The shrubs are generally broader than their height, which can range from 0.5 to 1.5 m/1 ft 6 in to 5 ft. There are already thousands of Indica hybrids, with a huge variety of colours including multi-coloured blooms, frilly doubles and hose-in-hose types, and development of new hybrids continues wherever they are grown.

Southern Indian hybrids

Prosper Julius Berckman, a Belgian nurseryman living at Augusta, Georgia, was a prime mover in the popularising of azaleas in the USA. He initiated a breeding program which resulted in a mixed group of plants that drew on the characteristics of a number of the azaleas that had been imported into the area by the middle of the nineteenth century, including the Belgian hybrids.

Two basic types of hybrid azalea emerged from his program. One group is of plants that are more open and vigorous, typically reaching 1.5–3 m/5–10 ft, and blooming early in the season. The second are slow-growing, dense, compact and late to bloom, largely bearing the characteristics of R. indicum. The sometimes striped flowers in shades of pink, red, dark purple on both types are large (50–80 mm in diameter), mostly single with a few doubles, although never hose-in-hose. Hardier than the Belgian hybrids, they were subsequently used in breeding to develop larger flowers in cold hardy azaleas.

Hybrid	Flowers	Notes
'Alba Magnifica'	White, large fragrant single. M.	Hardy Australian-bred hybrid with tall, bushy, vigorous habit. Full sun.
'Alphonse Anderson' syn. 'George Lindley Taber'	White, flushed with light to purplish pink, rose throat., large single. ML.	Full sun. Vigorous and hardy.
'Concinna'	Deep rose violet, large single. ML.	Full sun. Vigorous upright growth to 2 m/6 ft.
'Duc de Rohan'	Salmon with rose throat., medium single. Spot flowers from autumn, then spring, ML	Full sun. Vigorous compact growth to 2 m/6 ft.

Hybrid	Flowers	Notes
'Elizabeth Lawrence'	Large single, violet. EM.	Full sun. Vigorous, bushy growth to 1.5–2 m/5–6 ft.
'Exquisite'	Lilac pink, fragrant. M.	Full sun. Large single. Tall, vigorous. Sport of 'Magnifica'
'Fielder's White'	Whitish yellow with greenish throat, single. M.	Sun tolerant. Fragrant. Tall, spreading, bushy habit.
'Glory of Sunninghill'	Orange-red, large single. L.	Full sun. Tall, bushy, vigorous growth.
'Jean Alexandra'	Pale pink. EM.	Full sun. Large single to semi-double. Tall, bushy.
'Magnifica'	Rosy violet, large single, slightly fragrant. M.	Full sun. Vigorous, tall and spreading habit.
'Pink Lace'	Light pink with rose throat, petals edged with white. Medium single. Spot flowers from autumn, then spring, ML.	Full sun. Sport of 'Duc de Rohan'.
'Pride of Dorking'	Deep pink or brilliant carmine red. ML.	Full sun. Tall, vigorous, bushy.
'Pride of Dorking' orange form	Bronze red, medium single. ML.	Full sun. Tall, vigorous, bushy.
'Splendens' Photo p. 125.	Salmon pink, large single. M.	Full sun. Tall, vigorous growth.
'White Lace'	White, medium single. Spot flowers from autumn, then spring, M.	Full sun. Vigorous, bushy shrub to 1 m/3 ft. Sport of 'Duc de Rohan'.

Kurume hybrids

Known to the Japanese as Kirishima Tsutsujii, the history of these popular azalea hybrids is also somewhat vague and confused. Some credit the origination of the line to the nineteenth century samurai Motozo Sakamoto, although others suggest that kurume hybrids have been in cultivation for as many as 300 years. The name 'Kurume' is taken from a town on the island of Kyushu, traditionally a major azalea growing area of Japan.

Of the 700 or so recorded hybrids, about 300 are known to survive today. Originally thought to have been bred from R. obtusum, their origins are now considered to be from crosses between R. kiusianum (the Kyushu azalea), R. sataense and probably R. kaempferi. The relatively hardy R. kiusianum is endemic to Kyushu and in the wild is highly variable according to local conditions, though it is often quite prostrate in form and densely branching with masses of pale purple flowers.

Kurume azaleas were introduced into Western horticulture by English plant collector Ernest H. Wilson on expeditions to the Far East working for nurserymen Veitch & Sons during the first World War. Wilson selected fifty of the best Japanese cultivars, which became known as 'Wilson's Fifty'. They were subsequently given Western names before being introduced to the nursery trade. Only a few of these original fifty exist in cultivation today.

Kurumes are hardy to −15°C/5°F, typically medium to tall in habit, and with age can grow to quite a large size, although they can be easily kept in check with regular pruning. They bloom early to mid-season with mostly single flowers, with some hose-in-hose varieties, in a wide range of pinks, reds and purples, with the occasional striped or 'freckled' form. Pure colours and abundant flowering have resulted in the immense popularity of these hybrids.

Kurume hybrids

Hybrid	Flowers	Notes
'Addy Wery'	Strong red with dull orange blotch. E.	
'Adonis'	White. Hose-in-hose, frilled.	
'Aladdin'	Vivid red.	
'Anniversary'	Light to pale purplish pink. Hose-in-hose.	Typical kurume foliage. small bush to 0.6 m/2 ft. 'Mucronatum' × 'Blaauw's Pink'.
'Appleblossom' syn. 'Ho o'	White, tinged with strong pink. Blotch darker, occasional red stripes.	
'Arabian Knights'	Yellowish pink.	
'Azuma Kagami' syn. 'Pink Pearl'	Strong pink, with lighter centre. Semi-double hose-in-hose. M.	Tall, bushy growth. One of 'Wilson's fifty'.
'Bit O'Sunshine'	Light red, small single hose-in-hose. M.	Compact growth.
'Blaauw's Pink'	Soft salmon rose, medium semi-double hose-in-hose. EM.	Medium to tall, bushy growth.
'Christmas Cheer' syn. 'Ima-Shojo', 'Fascination'	Bright crimson red, small single hose-in-hose. Spot flowers from autumn, then spring.	Compact growth, dense, low to medium height. One of 'Wilson's Fifty'.
'Decision'	Light reddish orange.	
'Diane Robin'	Pale cyclamen.	
'Emily Knights'	Bright red, crinkled star-shaped petals, medium single. Spot flowers from autumn, then spring, M.	Vigorous, hardy, bushy shrub 1–1.5 m/3–5 ft.
'Esmeralda'	Pale pink, small single. M.	Vigorous bushy shrub 1–1.5 m/3–5 ft.
'Fairy Queen' syn. 'Aioi'	Almond blossom pink, small semi-double, hose-in-hose. M.	Medium bushy growth.
'Fashion'	Very pale violet, small to medium, hose-in-hose. M.	Bushy compact growth.
'Flora'	Deep yellowish pink, semi-double hose-in-hose.	
'Fred Colbert'	Bright red, small to medium semi-double hose-in-hose. M.	Compact, bushy growth.
'Fude Tsukata'	Pink, paling to greenish white.	
'H. H. Hume'	White, with slight yellow cast in throat. Semi-double hose-in-hose. Spot flowers from autumn, then spring, M.	Beltsville hybrid azalea. Vigorous bushy growth to 1 m/3 ft.
'Hana Asobi' syn. 'Sultan'	Strong, purplish pink.	No. 50 of 'Wilson's Fifty'.
'Happy Birthday'	Cyclamen pink, spotted on upper lobes, hose-in-hose.	

Hybrid	Flowers	Notes
'Harry van de Ven'	Pale cyclamen, hose-in-hose.	
'Hatsu-giri'	Vivid reddish purple, with pink spotting in throat.	
'High Sierra'	White, small to medium, hose-in-hose. M.	Compact, bushy growth.
'Hinode Giri' syn. 'Hino', 'Red Hussar' Photo p. 124.	Vivid purplish red.	No. 42 of 'Wilson's Fifty'. A very common azalea and one of the hardiest.
'Hinomayo' syn. 'Hinamoyo' Photo p. 124.	Strong purplish pink.	Tall, upright growth. An old variety, one of the first to be introduced into western horticulture, about 1910.
'Ima Zuma' syn. 'Chi no Ito'	Pale purplish pink, red stripes, tips darker.	
'Iroha Yama' syn. 'Iro Hayama', 'Dainty'	White, with deep yellowish pink margins.	No. 8 of 'Wilson's Fifty'.
'Jill Seymour'	Pink with red stripes, medium semi-double. M.	Sun tolerant. Medium bushy.
'Kasane Kagaribi' syn. 'Rositi'	Deep yellowish pink. M.	No. 32 of 'Wilson's Fifty'. Low, dense, spreading growth.
'Kimigayo' syn. 'Cherub'	Deep pink, with white throat.	No. 15 of 'Wilson's Fifty'.
'Kirin' syn. 'Daybreak', 'Coral Bells'	Silvery rose pink, small single hose-in-hose. Long-flowering, EM.	Low-spreading, bushy growth.
'Kirishima'	White, with pale red centre.	
'Kojo no Odorikaraka'	Vivid red, small flowers.	
'Komachi'	Pale pink, with darker margin.	
'Kure no Yuki' syn. 'Snowflake'	Pure white, hose-in-hose, large semi-double. M.	No. 2 of 'Wilson's Fifty'. Compact, bushy growth.
'Limelight'	Ivory white, small single, mid-season to late.	Dense habit.
'Little Red Riding Hood'	Orange red, small single. M.	Vigorous, compact growth.
'Miyagino'	Bright rose pink, small single hose-in-hose. EM.	Medium bushy growth.
'Mother's Day'	Vivid red, with feint brown spotting. Hose-in-hose to semi-double.	Very popular.
'Mrs Van de Ven'	Pale pink hose-in-hose.	
'Orange Beauty' syn. 'Tsuta Momiji', 'Cardinal'	Deep red.	
'Osaraku' syn. 'Penelope'	Soft lavender or light purple, suffusing to white throat. Small single. Spot flowers from autumn, then spring.	Medium bushy growth. No. 17 of 'Wilson's Fifty'.
'Popcorn'	Creamy white small double. M.	Dense bushy habit.

Hybrid	Flowers	Notes
'Purple Glitters'	Glowing purple, small to medium single. M.	Full sun. Vigorous compact bushy shrub.
'Rose Glitters'	Rose red, small to medium single. Autumn to spring, M.	Full sun. Highly coloured winter foliage. Vigorous, compact, bushy shrub.
'Rosebud'	Pink.	
'Salmon Beauty'	Deep yellowish pink, with darker throat. Hose-in-hose.	A Domoto introduction.
'Scarlet Gem'	Bright red, small semi-double hose-in-hose, trumpet-shaped blooms. Autumn, M.	Medium bushy growth. Protect from direct sunlight and strong winds.
'Seikai' syn. 'Madonna'	White, semi-double, hose-in-hose.	No. 1 of 'Wilson's Fifty'.
'Seraphim' syn. 'Tancho'	Blush pink, edged with rose, small single hose-in-hose. M.	Medium bushy shrub. No. 6 of 'Wilson's Fifty'.
'Shin Utena' syn. 'Santoi'	White, flushed with strong yellowish pink, and darker blotch.	No. 28 of 'Wilson's Fifty'.
'Show Girl'	Bright salmon orange. Small hose-in-hose. Spot flowers from autumn, then spring.	Dense, bushy growth.
'Suga no Ito' syn. 'Kumo no Ito'	Strong pink, darker centre, hose-in-hose.	No. 31 of 'Wilson's Fifty'.
'Sui Yohi' syn. 'Sprite'	White, flushed pink, and strong pink tips. Hose-in-hose. M.	No. 10 of 'Wilson's Fifty'. Dense, bushy growth.
Takasago' syn. 'Cherryblossom'	White, flushed with deep red, dark spots. Hose-in-hose.	No. 11 of 'Wilson's Fifty'.
'Waka Kayede' syn. 'Red Robin'	Strong red. Small to medium single. M.	Sun tolerant. No. 38 of 'Wilson's Fifty'. Medium to tall, bushy growth.
'Ward's Ruby'	Strong blood red. L.	One of the best reds, although less hardy than other kurumes.

Kaempferi hybrids

Although it is the most common native azalea species in Japan, *R. kaempferi* was only introduced into the USA toward the end of the nineteenth century. In Japan it is widely distributed across the southern islands, growing from sea level to altitudes as high as 1,200 m/3,900 ft. In the colder northern areas of Japan, it becomes deciduous, remaining evergreen in warmer climates. *R. kaempferi* is very similar in appearance to *R. indicum* but has broader leaves, growing to as high as 3 m/10 ft and bearing small trusses of funnel-shaped flowers in shades of red to pink and occasionally white. They are mostly singles, but doubles and hose-in-hose blooms do occur naturally, and one variety, *R. kaempferi* f. *kinshibe*, bears no petals at all.

It was immediately obvious that the new species offered superior cold hardiness, to the Kurume hybrids, withstanding temperatures as low as −20°C/−4°F. In extreme conditions, the Kaempferi hybrids can become virtually deciduous. They typically grow to around 1.2 m/4 ft high with a spread of around 1.5 m/5 ft. The hardiness of *R. kaempferi*, combined with the relative ease with which it could be propagated, meant that it quickly took on a valuable role in the development of a number of groups of hybrids more suitable than the Kurumes for cooler climates. Dutch breeders, looking for hardier evergreen azaleas with large flowers, led the way during the first World War years, resulting in the Vuyk hybrids.

Pennsylvania nurseryman Joseph Gable crossed *R. kaempferi* with the Korean azalea, *R. yedoense* var. *poukhanense*, and with other species and hybrids to produce some of the hardiest of all the evergreen azaleas. The Gable hybrids are of medium size, typically growing to between 2 and 2.5 m/6 and 8 ft and themselves formed the basis of further breeding by other growers seeking perfection in a hardy azalea. Most significant of these was Peter E. Girard of Geneva, Ohio, who started working in the 1940s with the Gable plants with the aim of creating more compact hardy varieties suited to container growing as well as for use in landscaping.

Hybrid	Flowers	Notes
'Fedora'	Deep purplish pink.	*R. kaempferi* × 'Malvatica', van Nes, 1922.
'Herbert Gable' syn. 'Herbert'	Vivid reddish purple, with darker blotch, hose-in-hose, frilled. EM.	A Gable hybrid. Spreading, low to medium height.
'Orange King'	Reddish orange.	Endtz.
'Palestrina'	White, with light greenish yellow blotch.	A Vuyk hybrid.
'Sunrise'	Light reddish orange.	Hooftman, 1939.
'Vuyk's Scarlet'	Deep red.	Aart Vuyk, Vuyk van Nes Nursery, Boksoop, Holland, c. 1954.

Satsuki hybrids

The Satsuki group of evergreen azaleas first developed naturally as interspecific hybrids between *R. indicum* and *R. eriocarpum* and recorded cultivars date back as far as 500 years. *R. indicum* is found growing in rocky crevices in mountainous areas of high rainfall on the southern islands of Japan. It has narrow leaves, five stamens and colours ranging from light reds through to pinks and the occasional white.

Known to the Japanese as Maruba Satsuki, *R. eriocarpum* survives harsh conditions at sea level in gravel or sandy soil on the island of Yakushima, off the southwest of the southern island of Kyushu. The leaves of this dense, low-growing bush are broadly elliptic to obovate and its flowers have eight to ten stamens, with colours ranging from purples through reds to pinks and sometimes white.

The Satsuki group includes all species and hybrids which flower thirty days or so after the rest of the azaleas, the Tsutsujii. Thus they are late in blooming, usually from November to December in Australia, and in warmer areas they may need some protection from the summer sun to preserve the flowers as long as possible.

Larger growing hybrids, predominantly bearing the characteristics of *R. indicum*, are known in Japan as Mie Satsuki, and are valued largely for their foliage when used in traditional landscaping, clipped to resemble and accompany rocks. Flower colour and form are less important with these varieties, the constant clipping removing many of the flower buds. Other smaller-growing varieties are used for container culture and are highly prized as Bonsai specimens, with examples hundreds of years old not uncommon in Japan.

Satsuki azaleas were introduced into the West in the early 1900s, although serious interest in the group didn't occur until the late 1930s and they weren't available widely until the . Satsukis have played an important role in the hybridizing of azaleas, both in Japan and the West. They are moderately hardy, to around −12°C/10°F, and have large single flowers with the unusual attribute that the flower colour can vary from truss to truss on one plant. Normally they are small, spreading bushes growing to between 50 cm/1 ft 6 in and 1 m/3 ft in height, and include the dwarf Gumpo varieties which are useful as rockery plants.

Hybrid	Flowers	Notes
'Gumpo Lavender'	Lavender, large single. L.	Dense, spreading growth to 0.5 m/1ft 6 in. Small foliage.
'Gumpo Pink'	Pink, edged with white. Large ruffled single. L.	Dense, spreading growth to 0.3 m/1 ft. Small foliage.
'Gumpo Salmon'	Salmon pink, large ruffled single. L.	Dense, spreading growth to 0.3 m/1 ft. Small foliage.
'Gumpo Stripe'	White, with mauve-red stripes and flecks, large single. L.	Dense, spreading growth to 0.5 m/1 ft 6 in. Small foliage.

Hybrid	Flowers	Notes
'Gumpo White'	White, with occasional pink flecks, large, ruffled single. L.	Dense, spreading growth to 0.3 m/1 ft. Small foliage.
'Kobai' (Red Plum)	Rose red, with occasional distinct white blotches. Small single with six round, overlapping petals. L.	Low, spreading, bushy growth. 'Sanko no Tsuki' × 'Yatano Kagami'.
'Koryu' (Radiant Willow)	Strong yellowish pink with occasional darker stripes to light pink with white rim, small single with narrowly spaced petals. L.	Low to medium, spreading growth. 'Kozan' × 'Meikyo'.
'Mansaku' (Abundant Harvest)	Salmon pink, with occasional white and deeper pink stripes, medium large single with wavy round petals. L.	Low to medium, upright growth. Sport of 'Honen'.
'Shin-Kyo' (Divine Mirror)	Light salmon pink, coral toward edges, medium single. Variations include white flowers. L.	Medium upright bushy growth. Sport of 'Yata no Kagami'.

Glenn Dale hybrid azaleas

Starting in 1935, Y. B. Morrison, of the US National Arboretum, working at Glenn Dale, Maryland, set out to combine the large flowers of the Southern Indian Hybrids with a higher level of cold hardiness. Another aim was to create plants which flowered during mid-April to mid-June (mid-October to December in Australia), when generally fewer azalea varieties would otherwise be flowering. The plants resulting after World War II varied widely in size from dwarf (1 m/1 ft or less) to 2.5 m/8 ft or more, as well as in flower colour and form, including stripes, flecks and variegations.

Hybrid	Flowers	Notes
'Dimity'	White, with fine purplish-red flecks, medium single. E.	Medium upright growth to 2 m/6 ft. Early. Semi-deciduous. 'Vittata Fortunei' × *R. kaempferi*.
'Favourite'	Deep pink with orange undertone, heavy red blotch. Irregular hose-in-hose. E.	Erect to over-reaching habit. *R. indicum* × 'Momozono'.
'Firedance'	Glowing rose red, large double Autumn, ML.	Broad, spreading growth to 1.5 m/5 ft.
'Revery'	Rose pink, medium single ML.	Full sun. Medium to tall and vigorous.
'Romance'	Rich purplish pink, double hose-in-hose. L.	Upright, spreading shrub to 1.5 m/5 ft.
'Tanager'	Vivid purplish red with dark blotch. EM.	Erect to broad, spreading habit to 1.5 m/5 ft. *R. indicum* × 'Hazel Dawson'.

Inter-group hybrid azaleas

The majority of the azalea hybrids introduced in recent years are crosses between various plants of the earlier groups. This has tended to further blur the distinctions between the types as new combinations of characteristics are sought.

There are many other smaller groups of hybrids other than those I have mentioned, with names like Girard, Carlson, Kerrigan, Black Acres, Pericat, Robin Hill and Shammarello. Most come from breeders in the United States, where interest in azaleas of all types is particularly keen, and each is related to one or more of the better known groups within which they tend to be grouped.

Hybrid	Flowers	Notes
'Dew Drop' syn. 'Nuccio's Dew Drop'	Blush pink to white, flushed green, throat spotted pink. Medium single to semi-double. ML.	A Nuccio hybrid. Vigorous, compact, bushy growth.
'Dogwood'	Red with white edges, or pure white, greenish throat. ML.	Vigorous, bushy growth. Sun tolerant.
'Dogwood Red'	Red, small flowers. ML.	Vigorous, bushy growth. Sport of 'Dogwood'. Sun tolerant.
'Dogwood Variegated'	Bright salmon pink, streaking to white edge, medium single. ML.	Vigorous, bushy growth. Sport of 'Dogwood'. Sun tolerant.
'Dorothy Clark'	Light pink, with light red border, large single. L.	A Harris hybrid. Compact growth to 1 m/3 ft.
'Easter Delight'	Clear orchid purple. Medium to large tubular flowers. Flowers profusely in spring, M.	Full sun.
'Fascination'	Pink, with red border, large single. L.	A Harris hybrid. Compact, medium to tall growth.
'Gloria Still'	Variegated light pink and white, medium single in large trusses. M.	A Harris hybrid. Compact growth to 0.6 m/2 ft.
'Helena'	Strong yellowish pink, with vivid red blotch.	An Eden hybrid. Medium bushy growth to 1.2 m/4 ft.
'Honey Bunch'	White to off-white, salmon pink on tips and edges of petals. Medium hose-in-hose. M.	Medium compact, upright growth.
'Margaret Rowell'	Deep red, large semi-double, hose-in-hose. ML.	Medium height. A Harris hybrid.
'Orange Delight' syn. 'Mrs John Ward'	Bright reddish orange, very large single. Spot flowers from autumn, then spring, L.	Low, dense, vigorous, bushy compact shrub to 0.8 m/2 ft 6 in.
'Phoeniceum' Photo p. 124.	Purplish red or violet rose, single flowers. M.	Introduced into England from Canton in 1824, with the name *Azalea indica*, later *A. punica*, *A. rawsonii* and *A. phoeniceum*. Known only as a garden plant.
'Seagull'	White, spotted with green, large hose-in-hose.	Fragrant. H. van de Ven, 1970.
'Summerland Chiffon'	Light pink, double. M.	Medium small shrub.
'Summerland Mist'	White, ruffled, medium semi-double. Autumn, M.	Medium bushy growth.
'Sweetheart Supreme'	Deep or salmon pink with darker blotch. Medium semi-double frilled hose-in-hose. ML.	A Pericat hybrid. Medium spreading dense growth.
'Teena Maree'	Salmon or yellowish pink, medium semi-double hose-in-hose. Spot flowers in autumn, then spring, M.	Vigorous, medium bushy growth.
'Terra Nova'	Deep pink with white edges, semi-double. Long-flowering, M.	Medium, bushy growth. Sport of 'Hellmut Vogel'.
'Vibrant'	White, with pink border, large single. L.	A Harris hybrid. Small, compact growth to 0.9 m/3 ft.

11
Deciduous azaleas

For gardeners in cooler climates, the deciduous azaleas have their own special magic, as a bare landscape of winter skeletons explodes in masses of dazzling, strongly coloured flowers, to be followed by lush foliage that gently changes colour through the months until falling.

All of the deciduous azaleas belong to the subgenus Pentanthera. While there are a number of species which are native to Europe and Asia, the largest concentration – of some eighteen species – are found in North America, where they are widely known, particularly in the southern states of the USA, as the bush or wild honeysuckle. Interest in growing the North American species was taken up in the first instance by European breeders, Several of these species, *R. calendulaceum*, *R. canadense*, *R. occidentale* and *R. periclymenoides*, have played a major role in the evolution of the deciduous azalea into the modern lines of hybrid garden plants to which we are accustomed today.

A further nine species, including the Japanese azalea, *R. japonicum*, come from Japan. Although there are records showing that Japanese gardeners have cultivated *R. japonicum* for over five centuries, it was regarded as a plant of ill portent and their interest lay in instead the revered evergreen azalea. Three species, including the Chinese or sheep azalea, *R. molle*, originate in China. There is just one deciduous European species, *R. luteum*, the plant credited with the downfall of the Greek army in 401 BC.

In 1680, Bishop Henry Compton grew seed of the swamp azalea, *R. viscosum*, the first North American deciduous azalea to be grown in Europe. The seed had been collected in Virginia by English missionary John Banister, who described the plant as *Cistus virginiana flore et odore Periclymeni*, which translates as 'Virginia rock rose with the flowers and odour of honeysuckle'. Spread widely across eastern and southern North America, this variable and very hardy shrub normally has fragrant, pinkish white flowers and its ease of propagation helps explain its importance in early breeding work.

As is the case with the other rhododendron types, most deciduous azaleas grown these days are hybrids. However, the plant has been regarded as more difficult to propagate from cuttings than evergreen rhododendrons, and consequently are frequently sold as unnamed and unpredictable seedlings. With improvements in propagation techniques, this situation will probably be slowly reversed. While plants grown from the seed of known hybrids can come fairly true, and many of these seedlings can be just as attractive as the named hybrids, it is wise to buy seed-grown plants in containers when they are in flower to be certain of their colour. New hybrid varieties are still being developed in a number of countries, continuing the development of the qualities established in the Mollis, Knap Hill and Exbury lines.

Deciduous azaleas can be grown in any areas where other deciduous plants and most of the evergreen rhododendrons – apart the vireyas – are known to thrive. In these cooler climates they are more tolerant of direct sun than most of the evergreen rhododendrons and azaleas. A deciduous woodland setting is ideal in warmer areas where the flowers can open and bask in the spring sun before the canopy of foliage gives protection to the foliage after flowering.

Although it is a leafless framework over the winter months, the deciduous azalea bursts forth in early spring with a sea of striking blooms which, in many varieties, appears before the first foliage unfolds. They range in colour from pure white, through vivid yellows, oranges and strong reds, and a number of species and many of the hybrids, usually the paler colours, are richly scented. New leaf growth is usually a bright green, settling to a rich bronze, before a final vibrant display of autumn colour before the leaves fall for another year.

Deciduous azaleas can, on the one hand, be treated in the same manner any other deciduous shrub or tree. At the same time their cultivation requirements are virtually the same as for the evergreen species and hybrids. They can be planted or transplanted easily in winter in bare-rooted form, although they tend to be sold in containers. Their lack of foliage in winter needs to be taken into account at the planning stage – too many deciduous plants together can leave a garden rather bare and colourless for several months of the year. But each spring they always manage to surprise and delight with their luxuriant masses of colour followed by superb foliage which seems to look different every day until falling in autumn like a rich sunset.

Species	Flowers	Notes
arborescens USA (W. Virginia–Tennessee, N. Carolina, Georgia, Alabama), woodlands and riverbanks around 1600 m/5250 ft. Michaux, 1795.	White or pink, sometimes with yellow blotch, tubular funnel-shaped, 35–52 mm long × 25–45 mm, in trusses of 3–8, opening with or after leaves. Fragrant. VL.	Bright green, obovate foliage. Easily propagated from softwood cuttings. Ht 0.9–3 m/3–10 ft, occasionally tree-like to 6 m. H3.
atlanticum USA (Delaware to S Georgia), in low altitude pine forests. John Clayton, 1743.	White, or flushed with purple or pink, 30–48 mm long × 25–30 mm, funnel-shaped, with cylindrical tube, in trusses of 4–10. Flowers appear with or just before foliage. Highly fragrant. L.	Bright bluish-green, glabrous leaves, obovate or oblong–obovate, sometimes with indumentum beneath. Strikes easily from softwood cuttings. Ht 0.3–0.6 m/1–2 ft. H3.
canadense USA, Canada (eastern), woodlands, riverbanks, swamps. Before 1756.	Rose purple, occasionally white, 16–20 mm long, rotate–campanulate, in trusses of 3–6, appearing before the leaves. Not fragrant. ML.	Most northerly of the American species. Upright, slender habit. Dull bluish-green, elliptical to oblong leaves, indumentum on underside. Distinctive 5-lobed flowers led to earlier classification by Linnaeus into a separate genus as *Rhodora canadensis*. Moderately easy to strike, prefers a very acid soil, around pH4.5. Ht 0.3–1.2 m/1–4 ft. H3.
japonicum originally *R. molle*. Japan, open grassland to 1000 m/3300 ft. c. 1830.	Orange, yellow, salmon red or brick red, with large orange blotch, widely funnel-shaped, 50–60 mm wide and long, in trusses of 6–12. L.	Oblong-obovate foliage, dark green, turning reddish in autumn. Parent of Mollis azalea hybrids, originally known as *Azalea mollis*. Prefers an open, sunny position. Difficult to strike. Ht 0.6–1.8 m/2–6 ft. H3.
luteum Eastern Europe to the Caucasus, woodland and conifer forests, sea level to 2200 m/7200 ft. Tournefort, on Black Sea, 1700–1702.	Yellow, with darker blotch, tubular funnel-shaped, 32–45 mm long × 38–50 mm wide, in trusses of 7–12, freely flowering from young age and opening before the foliage. Stamens extend beyond corolla. Very strong honeysuckle-like fragrance. L.	Vigorous, spreading, delicately twiggy, sometimes invasive growth, with dark green, oblong to oblong-lanceolate leaves, indumentum on young growth. Strong autumn colouring of red, orange and purple. Widely grown, and used in hybridising many modern deciduous azaleas, including the Ghent hybrids, and used as grafting rootstock for cultivars. Easily propagated from seed or as hardwood cuttings in winter. Ht 0.6–4 m/2–12 ft, usually much less. H3.
molle E. China (incl. Hubei, Zhejiang, Jiangxi), grassland, woodland, foothills. Loddiges Nursery, introduced 1823	Golden yellow, yellow or orange, with large greenish blotch. 43–56 mm long × 50–62 mm wide, widely funnel-shaped, in trusses of 6–12 or up to 20, opening with or before leaves. L.	Stout, upright growth, not particularly vigorous. Mid green, oblong to oblong–lanceolate foliage. Very similar to *R. japonicum*, with which it combined to produce the Mollis hybrids, and, in the 1920s, to produce the Exbury strain of Knap Hill azaleas. Can be difficult to strike. Ht 0.3–1.2 m/1–4 ft. H3.
occidentale W USA (southern Oregon to southern California), banks of streams, marshes, wetlands, from sea-level to 2750 m/9000 ft. Captain Beechey discovered, introduced by William Lobb, 1827. *Photo p. 125.*	White, pink, orange-pink, red or yellow, usually with yellow or orange blotch, tubular funnel-shaped, 42–50 mm or more × 35–50 mm, in trusses of 5–12, sometimes up to 50. Long flowering season, fragrant. L–VL.	Mid to bright green, oblong to oblong–lanceolate foliage which turns bronze, then scarlet, crimson or yellow in autumn, 40–90 mm long. Only azalea species west of the Rocky Mountains. Heat tolerant and moderately difficult to strike. Habit highly variable according to location. Ht 0.6–5 m/2–15 ft. H3.

Species	Flowers	Notes
periclymenoides E USA (Appalachians), in open woodlands, riverbanks up to 1160 m/3800 ft. John Banister, 1725–30.	White, whitish pink or pale purple, tubular funnel-shaped, 26–35 mm long × 25–40 mm, trusses of 6–12, with distinctively long stamens, flowers appear with the leaves. Little or no fragrance. L.	A handsome, much branched shrub with bright green, elliptic to obovate foliage, 30–90 × 13–30 mm. Despite being non-fragrant, its name means 'like honeysuckle'. Used in development of the Ghent hybrids in the early 1800s. Should be more widely grown than it is, but may be hard to find. Ht 0.6–1.8 m/2–6 ft. H3.
prinophyllum syn. *roseum* E USA, Canada (SW Quebec) in open woods, streambanks and hillsides. Before 1787	Pink, purplish pink, occasionally white, with or without brownish red blotch, tubular funnel-shaped, 28–35 mm long × 30–38 mm wide, in trusses of 5–9, opening with the foliage. Strong fragrance reminiscent of cloves. L.	Densely pubescent shoots, buds and petioles, bluish green elliptic to oblong–obovate leaves, 30–70 × 13–30 mm. Should be more widely grown than it is, but may be hard to find. Ht 0.6–2.5 m/2–8 ft. H3.
reticulatum Japan (Honshu, Kyushu, Shikoku), mixed forests and open country, 200–1800 m/ 650–5900 ft. 1832–34, Knight's Nursery, Chelsea. Photo p. 125.	Purple, reddish purple to magenta, funnel-campanulate, short white tube and spreading lobes, 10–28 mm long × 35–50 mm wide, singly or in pairs, occasionally up to 4. Flowers appear shortly before foliage. ML.	Medium-sized, much branching shrub or small, bushy tree, habit varying widely in the wild. Dark green foliage, 15–80 mm long × 7–60 mm wide, broadly ovate or rhombic, with some indumentum, in distinctive terminal whorls of 2–3 leaves. Freely flowering from an early age. Ht 0.9–8 m/3–25 ft. H3.
schlippenbachii Korea (very widespread), E Russia, swampy land and riverbanks. Baron A. von Schlippenbach (Russian naval officer), 1854, N Korea. Photo p. 143.	Pale pink, with reddish brown spots on upper lobe, widely funnel-shaped, 30–40 mm long × 56–80 mm, in trusses of 3–6. Fragrant flowers with or shortly before or after the leaves appear. ML.	Spreading habit, leaves 25–110 × 9–72 mm, slightly pubescent, obovate or ovate, in distinctive terminal whorls of 5, from which the flowers also emerge. Excellent autumn colouring. Prefers a less acid soil, around pH6.5, so may require regular top dressings of calcium. Variety (rhodamine pink, flushed with deeper pink, crimson spots). Ht 5 m/15 ft, usually less. H3.
serpyllifolium Japan (C & S), mixed forests on volcanic soils at 150–800 m/ 500–2,625 ft. Miquel, 1865–66.	Small, delicate, pale rose, pink, funnel-shaped, up to 10–12 mm × 11–15 mm, singly, occasionally in pairs. Also white-flowered variety. Both ML.	Low-growing much branched shrub with flattened brown hairs on young growth, tiny obovate or elliptic leaves, 3–10 mm long × 2–6 mm wide. Ht 0.6–9 m/2–30 ft. H2–3.
viscosum USA (Maine to Florida), swamps and riverbanks. John Banister sent drawing to Bishop Henry Compton of London, c. 1680–91.	White, or white flushed with pink, tubular funnel-shaped, in trusses of 4–9, opening after leaves. Spicily fragrant. VL	Known locally as the swamp honeysuckle, enjoys moist soil conditions. Obovate, elliptic-obovate or oblanceolate, 15–60 mm long. New growth yellowish brown or greyish brown. Much used in early hybridising, easily propagated. Ht 0.9–5 m/3–15 ft. H3.
weyrichii S Japan, S Korea, in open woodland to 800 m/2625 ft. 1853, Heinrich Weyrich, Russian naval surgeon.	Pink, funnel-campanulate, 30–40 mm × 35–60 mm, with a short, narrow tube, in trusses of 2–4. Flowers open with or before foliage, freely flowering. M.	Shrub or small tree. Rounded foliage, 35–80 mm × 15–60 mm, covered with reddish brown hairs when young, in whorls of 2–3 at the ends of the branchlets. Ht to 5 m/15 ft. H2–3.

R. 'Golden Eagle', a Knap Hill hybrid typical of the rich colouring of many deciduous azaleas.

Above: Topiaried kurume azaleas, fifty to sixty years old. (Photo: ARS)

Left: A seedling of *R. schlippenbachii*. (Photo: ARS)

Vireyas

R. rarilepidotum. (Photo: Dr John Rouse)

R. 'Clare Rouse'. (Photo: Dr John Rouse)

R. 'Dresden Doll'. (Photo: Graham Snell)

R. 'Haloed Gold'. (Photo: Graham Snell)

R. 'Magic Flute'. (Photo: Graham Snell)

R. 'Simbu Sunset'. (Photo: John Colwill)

R. tuba.

R. 'Coral Flare'.

Ghent hybrids

In the early 1800s, the Belgian city of Ghent was the centre of azalea breeding in Europe and the first significant work on the hybridising of deciduous azaleas was undertaken by a Ghent baker, P. Mortier. He crossed the fragrant *R. periclymenoides* with *R. calendulaceum* to develop the Mortier plants, a line of extremely hardy, late-flowering, scented hybrids. *R. periclymenoides*, from the Appalachian Mountains and eastern North America, was introduced into Europe from North America in 1734. Commonly known as the pinxterbloom, this very hardy shrub has lightly fragrant, white or pink flowers. The flame azalea, *R. calendulaceum*, is a tall shrub reaching three or four metres, and a native of the Appalachian Mountains of the eastern USA. Although not a fragrant species, it was noted early for the brilliance of its flower colours, which vary widely from creams and yellows through to deep rich reds in various combinations.

Other breeders in Belgium and England continued his work, using various combinations of the Mortier hybrids and species azaleas, and the resulting hybrids from all these efforts are nowadays grouped together as the Ghent hybrids. Among these were the Ornatum hybrids developed by J.R. Gowen of London, crossing *R. viscosum* with *R. luteum*. Known as the Pontic azalea, *R. luteum*, from eastern Europe, has fragrant yellow flowers and was only introduced to European cultivation in 1793, although it has been documented as far back as Ancient Greece.

Ghent breeder M.L. Verschaffelt crossed some of the Mortier seedlings with Gowen's Ornatum hybrids, naming over 100 varieties including a number still in cultivation today, including 'Coccinea Speciosa', 'Glora Mundi' and 'Grandeur Triomphante'. Some of the Mortier seedlings produced double flowers and these were developed into the Rustica hybrids between the 1850s and 1870s.

Although hundreds of Ghent hybrids have been developed, only perhaps a couple of dozen are in wide circulation now, having been superseded by the later groups. They are very hardy, to −20°C/−7°F, and typically grow into large bushes up to 2 m/6 ft in height. They are late flowering with smaller flowers, usually around 50 mm in diameter, than most of the other deciduous hybrids.

Rustica Flore Pena hybrids

In 1890, Belgian grower Charles Vuylsteke introduced the Rustica Flore Pena hybrids, believed to be crosses between the Rusticas (double-flowering Ghents) and *R. japonicum*, the Japanese azalea. At that time, *R. japonicum* was known as *Azalea mollis*, and gave its name to the Mollis azalea hybrids which followed. It is a sturdy, very hardy species found on the Japanese islands of Honshu, Kyushu and Shikoku, with flower colours varying from red to yellow. In all, some 500 varieties were named, a dozen or so remaining in circulation today.

The Rustica Flore Pena hybrids are tall, erect shrubs growing up to 3 m/10 ft in height. They share the hardiness of the Ghents, suiting them well to cooler climates, and they flower, often fragrantly, from mid to late season.

Mollis hybrids

The Mollis hybrids are amongst the most widely grown of deciduous azaleas, and while there is some obscurity about their original ancestry, they largely resulted from breeding between *R. japonicum* from Japan and the yellow-flowering Chinese or sheep azalea, *R. molle*. The group also includes a number of selected forms of *R. japonicum* which are not hybrids at all. In the 1870s, Louis van Houtte, of Ghent, introduced some twenty varieties, some of which are still grown today, including 'Alphonse Lavallee', 'Chevalier de Reali', 'Comte de Quincey' and 'W.E. Gumbelton'. The flowers, some of which are fragrant, range from pale yellow to deep orange.

During the 1880s, another Belgian, Frederik de Coninck, introduced a number of successful hybrids, including 'Anthony Koster', 'Dr. Reichenbach' 'Frans Van der Bom' and 'Hugo Koster', while Dutch breeders released 'Adriaan Koster', 'Mathilda' and 'John Ruskin'. Many of the varieties produced around this time are still being grown fairly widely today.

The Mollis hybrids are typically upright in form, growing to around 2–2.5 m/6–8 ft in height, with a similar spread. The flowers of these hardy hybrids are always singles, and larger and more open than those of the Ghents, usually 50–60 mm in diameter. Some are fragrant, usually the paler shades. They flower from mid spring, somewhat earlier than the Ghents, in a wide range of stronger colours from creams, yellows, oranges and reds. They are not quite as hardy as the Ghent hybrids, more commonly to −15°C, but they are more tolerant of heat, making them useful in the breeding of deciduous azaleas suitable for growing in warmer climates.

Knap Hill and Exbury hybrids

English breeder Anthony Waterer has been called 'the father of the deciduous hybrid azalea'. Several generations of the Waterer family, based at the Knap Hill Nursery, near Woking in Surrey, were responsible for the development of many successful and enduring evergreen rhododendron hybrids, but they are probably best remembered for their work on the breeding of deciduous azaleas.

Waterer's line evolved from breeding with Ghent and Mollis hybrids and at least seven azalea species, including *R. molle*, to produce a line of late flowering plants with large, open, richly coloured flowers. Although the work commenced around the middle of the nineteenth century, they were not finally released until 1925, by Gomer Waterer, grandson of Michael Waterer.

Lionel de Rothschild, a name also behind many important evergreen rhododendron hybrids, owned large gardens at Exbury in the New Forest, Hampshire, and from the early 1920s continued the work on deciduous azaleas started by the Waterer family.

The Knap Hill and Exbury hybrids are usually large, bushy shrubs up to 3 m/10 ft high and 2 m/6 m wide, although there are also some dwarf and spreading varieties. The young foliage often has a distinctive reddish tint, which turns to a brilliant show of colour in autumn. The large, wide, tubular flowers can be as much as 100 mm in diameter, sometimes double, and borne in very large trusses of up to 30 flowers. Colours range from off white through yellows and oranges to vivid reds, and most of the paler shades are fragrant.

Ilam hybrids

New Zealander Edgar Stead, working in the Christchurch suburb of Ilam, which gives the strain its name, combined some of the Knap Hill hybrids with *R. calendulaceum*, *R. viscosum* and *R. molle*, seeking new colours in larger, fragrant flowers. This work was continued from the 1950s by Dr. J.S. Yeates at Palmerston North, who also included Exbury hybrids in his breeding, resulting in the Melford strain.

Among the better known of the Melford hybrids are 'Galipolli' and 'Princess Royal'. Although these hybrids could well be grouped within the Knap Hill and Exbury strains, the term 'Ilam' tends to be applied to all deciduous azaleas bred in New Zealand.

Occidentale hybrids

Discovered in 1827, the Western azalea, *R. occidentale* is the only North American azalea species west of the Rockies, growing at sea level up to 2750 m/9000 ft from California to Oregon. It is quite variable in the wild, its form determined largely by its particular habitat. It can grow to as much as 5 m/15 ft in height, although in cultivation it normally reaches only about half that or less, with a similar width. The attractive flowers, which normally appear with or after the leaves in late spring, are deliciously fragrant, and most often are white or a pinkish white with a deep yellow throat, although there are also yellow, orange and red forms.

Seed from California was sent to the Veitch Nursery in England in the 1850s and the species became significant in European hybridising of deciduous azaleas. The first crosses were made by Anthony Waterer with the Chinese azalea, *R. molle*, resulting in the Albican hybrids. Further crosses between early Occidentale hybrids and Mollis azaleas resulted in a number of successful hybrids being released by English and Dutch nurseries during the 1890s, while American breeders are continuing to experiment with the species and its offspring.

The results of hybridising with *R. occidentale* tend to be large plants, reaching 2.5 m/8 ft high and as wide. They flower fragrantly in mid spring with blooms up to 80 mm across which are normally pale in colour and bearing the yellow to orange throat blotch of the original species. They will tolerate warmer, more humid conditions than the other deciduous azaleas, with an ability to cope with periods of dryness.

Hybrid	*Flowers*	*Notes*
Ghent hybrids		
'Altaclarense' (syn. 'Altaclarens')	White with orange blotch.	*R. molle* × *R. viscosum*.
'Coccinea Speciosa'	Deep yellowish pink, with orange blotch.	L. Sènèclause, before 1846
'Corneille'	Pink, double.	M. C. Vuylsteke, Belgium, 1890.
'Fanny' (syn. 'Pucella')	Pale purplish pink with orange blotch. Long tube, petals revolute. EM.	Tall, upright growth.
'George Reynolds' Photo p. 125.	Yellow.	Knap Hill, raised by A. Waterer, introduced by de Rothschild.
'Narcissiflora' (syn. 'Narcissiflorum')	Light yellow, double. ML.	Tall, upright growth. L. van Houtte, before 1871.
Mollis hybrids		
'Apple Blossom'	Light pink.	
'Carat'	Reddish orange, with orange blotch in trusses of 7–9. M.	(*R. viscosum* × 'Koster's Brilliant Red') × 'Satan'. Fragrant. Broad upright growth. Very hardy.

Deciduous azaleas

Hybrid	Flowers	Notes
'Chevalier de Reali'	Light yellow, fading to off-white. ML.	Selected form of R. *japonicum*. Louis van Houtte, 1875.
'Christopher Wren' syn. 'Goldball'	Brilliant yellow, with strong orange blotch. Large flowers.	
'Dr. M. Oosthoek' syn. 'Mevrouw van Krugten', 'Dr. Oosthoek' Photo p. 125.	Vivid reddish orange, with lighter blotch.	× R. *kosterianum*
'Dr. Reichenbach'	Salmon orange, with moderate reddish-orange blotch.	× R. *kosterianum*. M. Koster & Sons, 1896.
'Early Orange' Photo p. 125.	Reddish orange.	
'Frans Van der Bom'	Strong orange-yellow to moderate reddish-orange.	Frederik de Coninck, Belgium, 1880s.
'Golden Sunlight' syn. 'Directeur Moerlands'	Strong yellow with darker throat.	
'Hortulanus H. Witte' syn. 'H.H. de Witte'	Moderate orange yellow, with strong orange blotch.	× R. *kosterianum* cl., M. Koster & Sons, 1892.
'Koster's Brilliant Red' syn. 'Brilliant Red'	Moderate reddish orange	× R. *kosterianum* cl., M. Koster & Sons, 1918.
'Koster's Yellow'	Strong orange yellow with orange blotch.	× R. *kosterianum* cl., M. Koster & Sons, 1920.
'Lemonora' syn. 'Dr. L.N. Deckers'	Moderate yellow, tinged with pink.	K. Wezelenburg & Son., 1920.
'Mathilda'	Deep pink and deep yellowish pink, shaded red.	P.L. Binken, 1940.
'Queen Emma' syn. 'Koningin Emma'	Light orange yellow, to strong orange, suffused with yellowish pink, strong orange blotch.	

Knap Hill and Exbury hybrids

'Aurora'	Strong yellowish pink, with orange blotch.	Exbury, 1947.
'Avocet'	White, tinged with pink.	Knap Hill.
'Ballerina'	White.	Exbury.
'Balzac'	Reddish orange.	Fragrant. Knap Hill.
'Basalisk'	Deep cream with yellow golden flare on upper petal.	Exbury.
'Berryrose'	Vivid red, blotch vivid yellow, spotted vivid orange.	Fragrant. Exbury.
'Brazil'	Bright tangerine red, slightly frilled.	Exbury, 1934.
'Buzzard'	Pale yellow, tinged with pink.	Fragrant. Knap Hill, 1947.
'Caprice'	Deep pink.	Exbury.

Hybrid	Flowers	Notes
'Cecile'	Vivid red, with vivid orange yellow blotch.	Exbury, 1947.
'Coronation Lady'	Yellowish pink, with orange–yellow blotch.	Knap Hill.
'Crinoline'	White, flushed pink with ruffled edges.	Exbury.
'Double Salmon'	Deep yellowish pink, double.	Knap Hill hybrid × *R. austrinum*.
'Exbury Crimson'	Crimson.	Exbury.
'Favor Major'	Orange–yellow.	
'Fawley'	White, tinged with pink.	Exbury, 1947.
'Firefly'	Vivid purplish red, with slight orange flare.	Exbury, 1947.
'Frills'	Reddish orange, frilled.	Exbury, 1947.
'Gibraltar'	Fringed rich orange, flushed red.	Mid-season. Popular. Exbury, 1947.
'Ginger'	Deep orange	Exbury.
'Glowing Embers'	Vivid reddish orange, with vivid orange blotch.	
'Gog' syn. 'G.O.G.'	Strong reddish orange.	
'Gold Dust'	Deep yellow	Exbury, 1951.
'Golden Dream'	Strong orange or golden yellow	Exbury, 1951
'Golden Eagle' Photo p. 143.	Strong reddish orange, with orange–yellow midrib and vivid orange blotch.	Knap Hill, 1949.
'Golden Horn'	Strong orange yellow.	Exbury, 1947.
'Golden Sunset'	Vivid yellow.	
'Homebush'	Vivid purplish red, semi-double.	A. Waterer, Knap Hill, 1926.
'Kathleen'	Light orange, with darker blotch.	Exbury, 1947.
'Kestrel'	Orange.	Probably a hybrid of *R. calendulaceum*. Knap Hill, 1952.
'Kipps'	Vivid reddish orange, with orange blotch	Exbury, 1943.
'Klondyke'	Deep orange with greenish centre, and orange–yellow blotch.	Exbury, 1947.
'Knap Hill Apricot'	Moderate yellow, early to mid season.	Knap Hill, 1950.
'Knap Hill Red'	Deep red.	Knap Hill, 1948.
'Knap Hill Yellow'	Vivid yellow, tinged with orange.	Knap Hill, 1951.
'Krakatoa'	Orange–red.	Knap Hill.

Hybrid	Flowers	Notes
'Lady Jayne'	Vivid yellow, suffused with reddish orange, and orange–yellow blotch. Wavy petals.	Fragrant. Elliott, 1977.
'Mary Claire'	Light pink with yellow blotch.	Exbury, 1951.
'Mary Lou'	Brilliant orange–yellow, flushed pink on tips of petals.	Ht 0.75 m/2 ft 6 in. 'Ilam' hybrid. H. Van de Ven, 1966.
'Mernda Yellow'	Orange yellow.	
'Orange Supreme' Photo p. 125.	Orange, flushed with deep orange, and mid-orange blotch on upper lobe.	Ht 1.8 m/6 ft. Bronze foliage, red in autumn. Exbury-type seedling. J. Marty.
'Oxydol'	White, with a blotch of yellowish dots.	Exbury, 1947.
'Persil'	White, with pale yellow blotch.	
'Pink Delight'	Pink, with deeper pink edging. Takes some years to flower.	Large-growing with strong, upright habit. Exbury, 1951.
'Red Indian'	Reddish orange with yellow blotch.	Knap Hill, 1951.
'Sandpiper'	Pale yellow, flushed with pink, orange blotch. ML.	Medium to tall growth. Knap Hill, 1941.
'Satan'	Vivid red.	Knap Hill Nursery, sold to W.C. Slocock, 1926.
'Scarlet Pimpernel'	Red.	Exbury, 1947.
'Sonia'	White, flushed with pink.	Exbury, 1951.
'Strawberry Ice'	Strong yellowish pink, veined deeper pink and orange-yellow blotch.	Exbury, 1947.
'Sugared Almond'	Pale pink.	Exbury, 1951
'Sylphides'	Purplish pink, with vivid yellow blotch.	Knap Hill, 1950.
'Toucan'	Pale pinkish white. ML.	Upright, open growth.
'Tunis'	Dark red, reddish orange blotch.	Knap Hill Nursery, sold to W.C. Slocock, 1926.
'Wryneck'	Vivid yellow, edged with pink.	

Ilam and Occidentale hybrids

Hybrid	Flowers	Notes
'Dark Red Ilam'	Dark red.	Ilam, NZ.
'Exquisita'	White flushed pink, with an orange–yellow blotch. Frilled.	Fragrant
'Graciosa'	Pale orange–yellow, suffused with strong pink, orange blotch.	
'Irene Koster'	White, flushed with strong pink.	Fragrant. M. Koster & Sons, circa 1895.

12
Vireya rhododendrons

At the opposite end of the climatic scale to the deciduous azalea come the vireyas, understorey rainforest shrubs found at higher altitudes in tropical jungles, with their distinctive tubular flowers in bold colours – yellow, gold, red and white. Apart from making splendid greenhouse specimens, they can grow outdoors in a wide range of climates, so long as frost can be held at bay.

The Vireya section of the genus *Rhododendron* consists of around 300 species, amounting to almost one-third of all rhododendron species. Most of the section originates from the area known as Malesia – the Malayan archipelago, Indonesia, Borneo, the Philippines, with the largest number coming from New Guinea. As with many of the congregations of cool climate evergreen species from Asia, there is little overlapping of species, most being restricted by geographical influences to quite small areas. Only seven species occur naturally outside Malesia, the northernmost being found in Formosa, and the most southerly occurrences being the two Australian species, *R. lochiae* and *R. notiale*.

Vireyas were initially known as 'Malesian' or 'East Indian' rhododendrons and the plants resulting from their breeding were called 'Javanicum hybrids'. The contemporary botanical name for the section 'Vireya', after Julien Jospeh Virey, French pharmacist and naturalist, had originally been applied to what was thought to be a completely new genus, quite separate from the rhododendron, in 1826.

History

Before the middle of the nineteenth century, rhododendrons in cultivation came from two groups – the large, broad-leaved evergreen varieties, mostly from Asia, and the deciduous azaleas from Japan and North America. By the 1850s, however, a smaller group of plants began to appear in cultivation in England, mainly through the breeding efforts of the influential nurserymen J. Veitch and Sons of Exeter, who employed collectors to travel the globe to seek out and bring back new plants for their nursery. One of these collectors, Thomas Lobb, visited the Malayan peninsula and its surrounding islands in 1843 to collect orchids and other tropical plants. Among those that he brought back to England were the Vireya rhododendrons that became the basis, along with two other species brought back by another Veitch collector, Charles Curtis, for the breeding of the many vireya hybrids the nursery produced over the next fifty years.

Unlike the rhododendrons already in cultivation, these new plants needed heated greenhouses, flowered throughout the year and offered the grower exciting new vibrant flower colours. In their first efforts to hybridise vireya rhododendrons, the Veitch nursery used seven species – *R. jasminiflorum*, *R. javanicum*, *R. brookeanum*, *R. lobbii*, *R malayanum*, *R. multicolor* and *R. teysmannii*, (now regarded as a form of *R. javanicum*). From these plants over five hundred hybrids were bred and flowered.

The first to be named and introduced was 'Princess Royal', a cross between the yellow-orange *R. javanicum* and the white *R. jasminiflorum*. Such is the variability within the Section that the resulting flowers were a delicate rose pink. 'Princess Royal' was then crossed with *R. jasminiflorum*, resulting in a white-flowered cultivar, 'Princess Alexandra', which is still grown today.

Many of the hybrids resulting from the Veitch breeding were discarded, but by 1893 the Veitch catalogue conatined some fifty named varieties. Their popularity in the second half of the nineteenth century was aided by a greater interest in greenhouse cultivation of the exotic plants being introduced from around the world.

This was an exciting time in horticulture as many new exotic species were being discovered and introduced into cultivation. The glass tax, which had sealed many windows across Britain, had been repealed. Coal for heating and cheap labour were plentiful, and advances in greenhouse materials and design enabled the wealthier classes to indulge in the fad of collecting exotic tropical plants. Vireya rhododendrons joined orchids, palms, and even a number of Australian plants, hitherto unseen in the British Isles.

The austerity of the first World War forced a decline in the use of heated greenhouses, and many large collections were dissipated or lost, except for those of a few wealthy landowners and insititutions such as Kew gardens. Most of the original Veitch hybrids have long been lost to cultivation. The depression and another world war did nothing to rectify the situation and interest in the plants correspondingly declined until recent years.

The discovery of gold in New Guinea and the increased availability of aircraft after the Second World War gave access to an untapped wealth of new plants, including rhododendrons – over half the vireya species come from that island alone, with the certainty that there are more to be found.

Although many growers prefer the vireya species, it is the development of new hybrids offering superior flowering and a more acceptable garden habit, that have led to the rising popularity of vireyas, with breeding centred on the warmer, favourable growing areas of Australia and the western United States.

In Australia, much of the work by hybridisers Graham Snell, Dr John Rouse and Dr Bob Withers has used one of the two indigenous species, the red-flowering *R. lochiae* from northeast Queensland. The discovery in New Guinea in 1981 of what is claimed to be the smallest of all rhododendrons, *R. rubineiflorum*, has precipitated a thrust towards smaller plants. Using this species as a parent, Melbourne breeder Brian Clancy has developed a number of hybrids that are ideal for container or hanging basket use.

Habitat

The vireya species and the hybrids they have generated have come from a variety of habitats across a broad area of the tropics. While they are often referred to as 'tropical' rhododendrons, this is not strictly a correct description as most have originated from mountain habitats in tropical areas at altitudes between 2000 and 3000 m/ 6550 and 9850 ft. A typical day in this environment will start with mist and light rain, clear to bright, intense sunlight with high ultra-violet levels, followed by evening showers and night-time temperatures that can fall close to freezing. Rainfall is usually consistent and heavy throughout the year, there is little difference between the seasons and the length of day varies only a few minutes each way at around twelve hours.

While all species can be successfully cultivated in the ground, in their original habitats many plants are forced from the deep shade of the forest floors to find the sunlight they need by growing epiphytically, their small, fibrous root systems clinging tenaciously to accumulations of mosses, lichens and decaying debris wherever they can gain a footing.

Form

The most obvious botanical distinction between the vireyas and other rhododendrons is that the minute seed has thread-like 'tails' which assist in its dispersal by the wind and enable it to reach an often lofty footing in the treetops. Being lepidotes, the leaves of vireyas are covered with scales, always on the underside and often on the upper leaf surface as well. Leaf shapes vary as widely as they do among the other rhododendron sections, although they tend more often than not to be more rounded or elliptical than long and narrow, and when they are mature they usually have smooth and shiny upper surfaces rather than being deeply textured.

It is the flowers, however, that tend to identify a vireya from other rhododendrons. Although they vary widely in form, they are more often than not distinctively trumpet or bell-shaped (campanulate) with a long tube or funnel-like corolla. They range in colour from pure white to deep red, with brilliant yellows, golds and oranges between, along with some delicate pastels. Some, such as *R. carringtonii*, *R. jasminiflorum*, *R. konori* and *R. herzogii*, are deliciously fragrant.

While most species in New Guinea flower there from March to September (September to March in the northern hemisphere), vireyas in cultivation are not as seasonal as are the other sections of the genus. While some flower in spring, others can flower either once or several times, almost at random, throughout the year.

Cultivation

Vireya rhododendrons thrive in much the same environment as other evergreen rhododendrons. They need a similar soil – acidic, well-drained and high in organic matter, and have much the same fertilising and watering needs. A major concern is exposure to frost, and at the same time a need for some direct sunlight, so siting the plants carefully to allow for these requirements is vital. The ideal site in the garden is probably facing east to receive a good morning's sun, under a tree canopy for protection from frost and wind.

In their natural environment vireyas have to compete for light with many other lush rainforest plants and tend therefore to be more straggly in growth than other types of rhododendron. For this reason, more pruning may be necessary to maintain a desirable compact garden form. Pinching back the growing shoots of younger plants will help to ensure a dense, well-branched form. On older plants, cutting back every second new whorl of leaves that emerges will result in several more new shoots emerging from that point in place of one single branch. Vireyas are unlikely to produce new growth from branches without leaves, so cut back only as far as lowest whorl. Once a satisfactory growth habit is achieved, cutting the flowers for indoor use or deadheading them after they are spent will assist in maintaining a good shape. Hybrids which have been bred for garden cultivation will often have a better habit, requiring less pruning to give them an acceptable form and they are usually more freely flowering.

Vireyas are vulnerable to much the same pests and diseases as other rhododendrons. Sap-sucking bugs, such as lacewings, thrips, mites and aphids, can all pose a problem, while the various *Phytophthora* species, powdery mildew, rust and petal blight are fungal diseases shared in common with other Sections of the *Rhododendron* genus.

Vireya rhododendron species

Species	Flowers	Notes
aequabile Sumatra Photo p. 126.	Burnt orange. Small campanulate flowers in trusses from 6 to 12.	New shooots have dark red scales. Compact growth habit.
aurigeranum New Guinea Photo p. 126.	Lemon to yellow and orange, sometimes pure yellow, or flushed with orange, funnel-shaped, 60–70 mm long, in trusses of 8–10.	A tall upright shrub with maginificent flowers and medium-sized foliage, 80–100 × 30–40 mm. Ht 1–2.5 m/3–8 ft.
aurigeranum 'Eureka Gold' Select form of *R. aurigeranum* Photo p. 126.	Extra large, full trusses of beautiful orange and yellow flowers.	Strong, upright growth to about 2 m/6 ft.
brookeanum Borneo	Orange–pink to orange red or orange–yellow with white to yellow throat, often fragrant, in trusses of 5–14.	Large oblong-lanceolate foliage, 120–250 × 35–80 mm. Used by the Veitch Nursery in early hybridising. Ht 2 m/6 ft.
burtii Sarawak	Small, purple red pendulous, bell-shaped flowers.	Dainty, glossy, rounded leaves. Ht 1.75 m/6 ft.
carringtonii E New Guinea	White, beautifully perfumed, tubular flowers in upright trusses. Slow to flower.	Upright, bushy growth with rounded foliage. Ht 1.75 m/6 ft.
christi E New Guinea	Striking bicoloured flowers of yellow, or greenish or lemon yellow, with bright orange-red lobes, curved, tubular.	Small shrub with distinctive, ovate, pointed, almost heart-shaped, leaves, in whorls of 3. Suitable for hanging baskets. Ht 0.75 m/2 ft 6 in.
christianae SE New Guinea	Deep yellow, shading to a glowing orange or salmon, bright orange lobes and yellow throat, widely tubular campanulate, in numerous trusses of 3–4. The form 'Grandiflora' has larger, similarly coloured flowers.	Compact, medium-sized shrub with broadly elliptic leaves, 40–70 × 30–45 mm. Used extensively in Australian vireya hybridising. Ht 3 m/10 ft.
dianthosmum W New Guinea	Pure white, tubular, medium-sized flowers.	Glaucous, bushy foliage, roughly textured leaves. Ht 1.5 m/5 ft.
ericoides Sabah (Mt Kinabalu) Photo p. 126.	Tiny, bright scarlet to purplish red, 15 mm long, tubular, singly or in trusses of up to 3.	Tiny, very dense, heather-like foliage, 4–7 × 1 mm. Not widely cultivated, but would make an interesting rockery specimen. Ht 0.15–3 m/6 in–10 ft.
himantodes Sabah	Exquisite small white flowers, speckled with brown scales.	A beautiful and unusual plant with small, slender, rough foliage covered with brown scales. Upright growth to about 0.5 m/1 ft 6 in or more. Prefers some shade.

Species	Flowers	Notes
jasminiflorum Malaysia, Philippines, Indonesia (Sumatra) 1849.	White, delicate, sometimes flushed with pink, and pink stamens, tubular, 35–45 mm long, in full trusses. Free-flowering. Strong fragrance resembles daffodils.	Var. *punctatum* has conspicuous bright spots in throat. Var. *jasminiflorum* var. *jasminiflorum* has compact growth, white flowers with pink blush. Ovate, obovate-elliptic to elliptic leaves, 25–60 × 15–32 mm, in whorls of 3–5. Small, spreading habit in cultivation, very suited to growing in hanging baskets. Disease and pest resistant. Used in hybridising. Ht 2.5 m/8 ft, usually much less.
javanicum Indonesia (Sumatra, Java), South Pacific islands. Blume. Photo p. 126.	Orange, sometimes yellow, red or scarlet. Rosy throats and distinctive purple stamens, 30–50 mm long, funnel-shaped, fleshy, in trusses of 4–20.	Tall, spreading shrub or small tree with strong, bushy growth. Shiny leaves, elliptic–oblong, 40–200 × 25–60 mm, densely covered in scales which persist until maturity, and in false whorls of 5–8. Several forms, ranging from yellow to red or orange, the tube usually lighter than the lobes. Used frequently in hybridising. Ht 1–3 m/3–10 ft.
javanicum var. *teysmannii*	Pale orange or yellow	Paler orange or yellow flowers and longer, narrower foliage than R. *javanicum*. Ht 1.5 m/5 ft.
konori New Guinea	Large, delicate, pure white or pinkish, orchid-like flowers, 120–160 mm long, funnel-shaped, with 7 petals, in trusses of 5–8, flowering from a height of 0.6–0.9 m, and deliciously fragrant.	A most impressive shrub with very distinctive large, matt green, elliptic foliage, 100–180 × 50–80 mm, with a bluish tinge, and prominent reddish-brown indumentum underneath when young. Slow-growing. Ht 1–4 m/3–13 m.
laetum NW New Guinea Photo p. 126.	Pure golden yellow, shading with age to red, orange or salmon, large, flared, broadly funnel-shaped and fleshy, 65–70 mm wide, in open trusses of 6–8. Flowers when quite young.	Strong, open, narrow, upright growth to 2 m, more if not pruned when young. Name is Latin for 'bright or vivid'. Sun tolerant. Ht 0.5–3 m/1 ft 6 in–10 ft.
lochiae Australia (NE Queensland) Photo p. 126.	Bright scarlet, medium-sized, funnel-shaped flowers, up to 45 mm long × 35 mm, in loose trusses of 2–7.	Distinguished from R. *notiale* (q.v.) by dark red anthers and straight corolla tube. Flowers freely when young, often around Christmas. Medium, compact, spreading to bushy growth. Scaly young shoots. Dull or glossy dark green, broadly obovate leaves, up to 100 mm long, in false whorls, scaly underneath. Suitable for hanging baskets. Despite being slow-growing itself, R. *lochiae* is the parent of a number of floriferous and easily grown hybrids, such as 'Arthur's Choice', 'Overflow', 'Liberty Bar' and 'Tropic Fanfare'. Ht 0.9–1.2 m/3–4 ft.
loranthiflorum Bougainville, New Britain	Creamy white, tubular, with flared lobes, in full trusses, lightly scented.	Light green, glossy foliage. Medium, bushy growth. Ht 2 m/6 ft.
macgregoriae New Guinea Photo p. 126.	Light yellow to dark orange or red, in full trusses of 8–15 small flowers, 20–28 mm, with narrow tube and widely spreading, flattened lobes. Some are fragrant.	Variable to strong, bushy growth, occasionally tree-like in habit. Leaves ovate–elliptic or ovate–lanceolate, 40–80 × 35 mm, in false whorls of 3-4. Probably the most widespread of New Guinea's rhododendrons. Easily grown. Ht 0.5–5 m/1 ft 6 in–16 ft, usually much less.
malayanum S Myanmar, Thailand, Malay Peninsula and Indonesia (Sumatra, Java, Borneo, Celebes) Jack, 1822.	Bright red, rose pink, scarlet crimson or purplish, occasionally salmon red or rose pink, 15–24 mm long, tubular, waxy and glossy, in trusses of 4–8.	Young shoots densely scaly. Leaves oblong–elliptic, shiny green above, reddish beneath with dense covering of scales, 40–150 × 15–30 mm. Uninspiring flowers but worthwhile for the foliage. Ht 5 m/16 ft, usually much less.

Species	Flowers	Notes
multicolor Sumatra	Pale primrose, whitish cream to yellow, rose or fiery red, broadly funnel-shaped flowers, 15–20 mm long, in small, distinctive trusses of 4–6. Can be fragrant.	Medium, bushy growth of fine, slender, lanceolate leaves, 40–70 × 10–15 mm. Suitable for hanging baskets. Ht 0.5–1.5 m/1 ft 6 in–5 ft.
notiale Australia (N Queensland) W. Sayer/Baron von Mueller, 1887.	Bright scarlet, medium-sized, funnel-shaped flowers, up to 45 mm long × 35 mm, in loose trusses of 2–7. Distinguished from R. *lochiae* (q.v.) by its yellow anthers and curved corolla tube.	Medium, compact, spreading to bushy growth. Scaly young shoots. Dull or glossy dark green, broadly obovate leaves, up to 100 mm long, in false whorls, scaly underneath. Suitable for hanging baskets. Ht 1–1.5 m/3–5 ft.
orbiculatum Borneo Photo p. 126.	Quite large, delicate, white or silvery pink orchid-like, salver-shaped flowers, 60–65 mm long, in loose trusses of up to 5, fragrant.	Very distinctive, thick, rounded, orbicular leaves, 40–100 × 40–60 mm, and brittle stems. Suitable for hanging baskets. Ht 0.3–3 m/1–10 ft.
pauciflorum Malayan Peninsula	Small, bright red, waxy, long, narrow tubular campanulate flowers, 15–18 mm long, fairly sparse, singly or in pairs, forming small clusters all over the bush.	Epiphytic in the wild. Obovate, bright green leaves 20–30 × 10–15 mm. Suitable for hanging baskets. Ht 0.5 m/1 ft 6 in.
phaeochitum New Guinea	Soft damask pink, curved, tubular flowers, with flared lobes, forming loose trusses. Lightly perfumed.	Blue–green leaves and russett-coloured tomentum on both sides of new foliage. Suitable for hanging baskets. Ht 1 m/3 ft.
phaeopeplum W New Guinea	Large white flowers with a hint of pink flowers, beautifully fragrant.	Dark green foliage. New foliage is a spectacular reddish brown. Very similar to R. *konori*. Ht 1 m/3 ft or more.
rarilepidotum Sumatra Photo p. 144.	Dark brick red, in full trusses.	Open habit with attractive, glossy, dark green foliage. Ht 2 m/6 ft.
rarum New Guinea	Pretty, pinkish red, crimson, scarlet or blood red, curved, tubular flowers, 25–35 mm long, singly or in pairs.	Dwarf but spreading, straggly, pendant growth and distinctive, very slim, widely lanceolate leaves, 30–70 × 6–10 mm. Despite its name, it is actually common in its own habitat where it is normally epiphytic. Probably does best in a hanging basket. Easily grown. Ht 0.5–1 m/1 ft 6 in–3 ft.
retivenium Borneo	Quite large flowers of clear, soft yellow, with pale stamens.	Long, fleshy, dark, glossy leaves and bushy growth. Benefits from pruning when young. Ht 1.5 m/5 ft.
sessilifolium Sumatra	Soft primrose, medium-sized flowers.	Distinctive, veined, pale green foliage. Ht 1 m/3 ft.
tuba E New Guinea Photo p. 144.	White, very distinctive, long tubular flowers.	Dark green, glossy, ovate foliage. Ht 1.5 m/5 ft.
williamsii Philippines	White, cup-shaped flowers in loose trusses.	Strong, bushy growth. Ht 2 m/6 ft.
zoelleri New Guinea, Moluccas	Large, spectacular brilliant, almost iridescent, pinkish orange to yellow, with yellow throat, in large, open trusses of up to 8.	Bushy, medium-sized, open, sometimes straggly shrub, very similar in form to R. *aurigeranum*. Ht 1.5–2 m/5–6 ft. A West Irian form has slightly smaller flowers and bushier growth.

Vireya hybrids

Hybrid	Flowers	Notes
'Alisa Nicole' [R. lochiae × R. gracilentum] F^2 hybrid G. Snell, 1988.	Cerise pink, bell-shaped flowers in trusses of 2–3 florets. Long-flowering.	Compact bush ideal for shaded rockeries. Ht 0.3–0.5 m/1–1 ft 6 in.
'Anatta Gold' [R. laetum × R. zoelleri] × [R. zoelleri × R. leocogigas] G. Snell, 1988.	Medium-sized flowers with deep gold petals with a burnt orange throat.	Upright habit. Sun tolerant. Ht 1.5–2 m/5–6 ft.
'Aravir' R. konori × ['Pink Delight' × R. jasminiflorum] P. Sullivan, W. Moynier, 1979.	Soft white, beautifully fragrant, in domed trusses of 7–10 tubular, funnel-shaped florets with frilled lobes.	Lovely soft green foliage with velvety growth. Medium spreading growth habit to 1.5 m/5 ft.
'Arthur's Choice' [R. christianae × R. lochiae] F^2 B. Clancy.	Deep bright red or scarlet with darker vivid scarlet on lobes, in trusses of 7 medium-sized tubular, funnel-shaped flowers, about 50 mm wide.	Highly recommended shrub with spreading habit and good green foliage. A distinct improvement on both parents. Medium, spreading habit. Ht 1–1.5 m/3–5 ft.
'Bob's Crowning Glory' R. lochiae × R. leucogigas 'Hunstein's Secret' Dr J. Rouse, 1989.	Rose or deep purplish pink, very large flowers with a lovely perfume, in large trusses of 6–12 florets.	Large leaves are often tipped with rich burgundy. Bushy, spreading growth. Suitable for hanging baskets. Ht 1–1.5 m/3–5 ft.
'Bold Janus' R. leucogigas × R. laetum G. Snell, 1988.	Apricot edged with pink, lightly perfumed, in trusses of about 7 very large flowers.	A tall, elegant shrub with deep green leaves. Ht 1.5-2 m/5-6 ft or more.
'Bonza'	Very deep crimson, neat bell-shaped flowers.	Medium compact growth, glossy foliage, new growth bronze. Ht 1.5 m/5 ft.
'Carillon Bells' R. gracilentum × R. laetum R. Withers, G. Snell, 1983.	Rose pink with salmon throat, bell-shaped flowers hanging in trusses of twos or threes, flowering over a long period.	Small-growing bush, perfect container or basket plant. Ht 0.6 m/2 ft.
'Channon Marie' [R. laetum × R. macgregoriae] × R. zoelleri B. Clancy.	Sunset orange with star-shaped yellow throat, in trusses of 8-11 florets.	Compact habit. Ht 1 m/3 ft.
'Charming Valentino' 'Saint Valentine' × 'Saint Valentine' P. Schick, 1989.	Brilliant crimson bell-shaped flowers, in trusses of 3-4 florets.	Glossy bright green leaves. spreading, bushy growth, good for hanging baskets and group plantings or training as a standard. Ht 0.5-1 m/1 ft 6 in-3 ft.
'Chayya' ['Pink Delight' × R. intranervatum] F^2 B. Clancy, 1991.	A lovely shade of pastel pink with pale buff-yellow throat, in perfect trusses of 13 florets.	An outstanding hybrid, winner of many Australian awards.
'Cherry Liquer'	Medium-sized, fragrant flowers with cherry red and cream petals, pale golden throat.	Bushy upright growth. Should be pruned when younger to maintain shape. Ht 2 m/6 ft.
'Christopher John' R. phaeopeplum × R. zoelleri 'Island Sunset' Dr J. Rouse.	Attractive rose pink, shading to a lemon throat. Very large and delicately scented.	Medium, vigorous and easily grown shrub with good habit. Ht 1.2 m/4 ft.

Fixed	Flowers	Notes
'Clare Rouse' R. christianae × R. laetum D. Stanton, 1979. Photo p. 144.	Bicoloured golden yellow with red–orange lobes, in loose trusses of 5–7 medium to large, bell-shaped florets.	Tall, very bushy habit with strong growth. Ht 1.8–3 m/6–10 ft.
'Coral Flare' R. lochiae × R. laetum D. Stanton, G. Snell, 1988. Photo p. 144.	Coral pink, in trusses of 3–7 medium to large flowers, flowering often throughout the year.	Medium-sized spreading habit. Ht 1–1.5 m/3–5 ft
'Craig Faragher' R. gracilentum × R. jasminiflorum C. Faragher, 1981.	Perfumed, damask pink or mauve pink, lobes pale cyclamen pink, in trusses of 6–8 tubular flowers.	Glossy, bushy, spreading growth. Dwarf spreading shrub suitable for hanging baskets. Shady position. Ht 0.5 m/1 ft 6 in.
'Cristo Rey' [R. macgregoriae × R. zoelleri] × [R. laetum × R. zoelleri] P. Sullivan, W. Moynier, 1985.	Masses of very brilliant orange with maize-yellow centre, in dome-shaped trusses of 6–8 tubular funnel-shaped flowers, 50 mm wide × 75 mm long.	Elliptical foliage, 80 × 40 mm, with medium, compact bushy growth. Ht 1.5 m/5 ft.
'Dr. Hermann Sleumer' R. phaeopeplum × R. zoelleri Reg. T. Lelliot, 1972.	Rose pink or mid red, in trusses of 6 perfumed medium-sized florets.	A naturally occurring hybrid from New Guinea. Large, felty leaves on a medium-sized, bushy, compact habit. Ht 1 m/3 ft.
'Dresden Doll' syn. 'China Doll' R. phaeopeplum × R. zoelleri Photo p. 144.	Deep salmon pink with cream throat.	Waxy, lime green leaves are heavily veined and new leaf growth is soft pink. Good shady position in ground or tub. Ht 1 m/3 ft
'Eastern Zanzibar' R. konori × R. zoelleri W. Moynier, 1989.	Striking, perfumed, medium-sized, crimson-edged buff yellow petals, in trusses of 4–5 florets.	Lush, matt green foliage and bushy growth. Ht 1.5–2 m/5–6 ft.
'Elegant Bouquet'	Beautifully perfumed, creamy-white, large flowers.	Upright bushy growth. Ht 2 m/6 ft.
'Esprit de Joie' R. konori × R. laetum Dr J. Rouse, G. Snell, 1986.	Large fragrant flowers with light orange–yellow tube, and lobes claret inside, light pink outside, in trusses of 4–6 tubular funnel-shaped florets.	Elliptic foliage, 100 × 60 mm, on a shrub with tall, bushy growth habit. Ht 2 m/6 ft.
'Fire Plum' [R. phaeopeplum × R. lochiae] × R. zoelleri	Vibrant cherry plum red, paler throat., medium-sized flowers.	Open, spreading, well-branched bush. Shiny foliage. Ht 1.5 m/5 ft.
'Gardenia Odessy' syn. R. gardenia probably a natural hybrid of R. konori.	Rich cream, in very large, full trusses of up to 28 florets, with a magnificent perfume.	Soft brown indumentum on new foliage. Strong, upright growth. Ht 2 m/6 ft.
'Golden Casket'	Lovely full trusses of soft pastel yellow flowers.	Medium, bushy growth with light green foliage. Ideal for containers. Ht 1.5 m/5 ft.
'Golden Charm' Jury, NZ.	Apricot edged and orange. Small flowers held upright in full clusters amongst a background of shiny foliage.	New foliage pink, deepening to a polished bronze while maturing. Compact, bushy, spreading growth habit. Easily grown. Ht 1 m/3 ft.
'Gossamer White' R. loranthiflorum × R. laetum G.L. Snell, 1991.	Lightly perfumed, yellowish white, soft silky flowers, medium size, in trusses of 5-6 tubular florets.	Bushy growth. Ht 1.5 m/5 ft.

Hybrid	Flowers	Notes
'Great Scent-sation' R. konori × R. lochiae	Fragrant, carmine pink, large bell-shaped flowers.	Strong, spreading bushy growth. Ht 1.5 m/5 ft.
'Haloed Gold' Blumhardt, NZ. Photo p. 144.	Gold with vermillion edging, frilled petals.	Glossy foliage, bushy growth. Sun tolerant. Ht 1.5 m/5 ft, sometimes more.
'Happy Times' [R. laetum × R. aurigeranum] × R. rubineiflorum B. Clancy.	Masses of tangerine red bells in trusses of 3–4 florets, exceptionally freely flowering for up to three months.	Outstanding compact dwarf hybrid. Ht 0.3 m/1 ft × 0.45 m/1 ft 6 in wide.
'Hari's Choice' ['Triumphans' × R. javanicum] × R. leucogigas Strybing Arboretum, 1986.	Vivid crimson, large flowers in very full trusses, lightly perfumed.	Very large, strong leaves, strong, vigorous growth, which benefits from regular pruning. Ht 3 m/10 ft.
'Hendre' 'Arthur's Choice' × R. wrightianum B. Clancy.	Vibrant red flowers in trusses of about four florets.	A very showy, dwarf offspring of R. lochiae. Ht 0.6 m/2 ft.
'Highland Arabesque' R. orbiculatum × [R. laetum × R. aurigeranum] Dr J. Rouse, 1989. Photo p. 126.	Deep cyclamen or silver pink, in trusses of 4–7 elegant, long-lasting orchid-like flowers.	Unusually firm, attractive, rounded leaves. Slender, upright, sometimes spreading growth. Ht 1 m/3 ft.
'Highland Fair' R. phaeopeplum × R. lochiae Dr J. Rouse, 1991.	Light yellowish pink or bright crimson, outer lobes strong red, inner lobes light yellowish pink, in trusses of about 5 florets.	Open bushy growth. Ht 1.5 m/5 ft.
'Highland Peter Pan' R. christianae × 'Sweet Wendy' G.L. Snell, 1989.	Straw yellow, softly tipped with orange, in trusses of 5–6 florets.	Bushy growth. Ht 1.2–1.5 m/4–5 ft.
'Highland White Jade' ['Dr. Hermann Sleumer' × R. herzogii] × [R. laetum × R. aurigeranum] G. Snell, 1988	Highly perfumed, porcelain white flowers with green-lemon throat, in trusses of 4–7 flowers.	Bushy growth with unusual, lightly scented foliage. Ht 1.2–1.5 m/4–5 ft.
'Iced Primrose'	Creamy primrose with a faint hint of pastel green in the throat. Beautifully fragrant, very large flowers.	Large, matt green, upwardly-thrusting leaves. Strong, upright growth, but needs full shade. Benefits from pruning when young. Ht 2 m/6 ft.
'Jean Baptiste' [R. laetum × R. leucogigas] × R. phaeopeplum P. Sullivan, W. Moynier, 1984.	Fragrant, creamy white, large tubular funnel-shaped flowers with petaloids making a full centre, in trusses of 7-9 florets. Very small calyx.	Bushy, upright growth with elliptic, slightly bluish green foliage. Soft indumentum on new growth. Ht 0.9-1.5 m/3-5 ft.
'Johannes' 'Christopher John' × R. wrightianum × R. leucogigas 'Hunstein's Secret' B. Clancy.	Snowy white suffused with deep pink, in open trusses of 6–8, freely flowering throughout the year. Highly fragrant.	Medium habit. Ht 1.5 m/5 ft.
'Juan Diego' 'Carillon Bell's × R. leptanthum B. Clancy.	Red carmine, in trusses of 3-4 bell-shaped florets, very freely flowering.	Dwarf hybrid. Ht 0.45 m/1 ft 6 in.

Hybrid	Flowers	Notes
'Kiandra' R. zoelleri 'Island Sunset' × R. brookeanum B. Clancy.	Glowing, vivid orange–red in trusses of 7–14 florets.	Outstanding, compact, easily grown shrub. Brilliant in sunlight, seems to glow on dull days. Ht 1 m/3 ft.
'Laura Kate' R. superbum × 'Dr. Herman Sleumer' Nancy Caddy.	Striking pastel pink flowers offset with white throat, in trusses of 5–6 superbly scented florets.	Compact habit. Ht 1 m/3 ft.
'Liberty Bar' R. lochiae × R. aurigeranum D. Stanton, 1981.	Deep rose red or mid pink, in large trusses of 10–15 florets, throughout the year.	Medium, upright bushy growth. Ht 1.5–2 m/5–6 ft
'Little Ginger'	Bright orange.	Unusual, narrow, upright foliage. Compact, bushy growth. Ht 0.5 m/1 ft 6 in.
'Little One' 'Sunny' × R. rubineiflorum B. Clancy, 1993.	Mandarin pink, in trusses of 2–3 florets, very floriferous, blooming for up to three months.	An outstanding, compact and floriferous hybrid which increases in bushiness with age. Small, rounded foliage. Ht 0.3 m/1 ft × 0.45 m/1 ft 6 in wide.
'Little Pinkie' [R. lochiae × R. macgregoriae] × R. loranthiflorum G. Snell, 1988.	Masses of dainty, perfumed, soft pink, flowers.	Glossy foliage, compact bushy growth. Ht 1 m/3 ft.
'Littlest Angel' R. lochiae × R. pauciflorum G. Snell, 1983.	Profusion of petite, waxy, deep or cardinal red flowers in trusses of 4 bell-shaped florets.	Compact bushy plant, ideal for hanging baskets. Ht 0.4–1 m/1 ft 4 in–3 ft.
'Lochmin' R. lochiae × R. jasminiflorum T. Lelliot, 1980.	Perfumed, pale cyclamen pink flowers with darker tube, in trusses of 7 tubular florets.	Good for hanging baskets. Medium, spreading, bushy growth. Ht 1 m/3 ft.
'Lovey' R. konori × [(R. phaeopeplum × R. lochiae) × R. zoelleri] Dr J. Rouse, 1990.	Soft damask pink with very pale lemon throat, gently perfumed.	Spreading, bushy growth. Ht 2 m/6 ft.
'Magic Flute' Photo p. 144.	Long, tubular, perfumed white flowers in pendant clusters.	Rounded foliage, bushy growth. Ht 1.5 m/5 ft.
'Marjiam' 'Carillon Bells' × R. wrightianum var. wrightianum B. Clancy.	Vibrant scarlet crimson in trusses of 3-4 florets, very freely flowering.	Very compact, showy shrub. Ht 0.3–0.6 m/1–2 ft.
'Moonwood' syn. 'Moonwind' R. konori × ['Pink Delight' × R. jasminiflorum] P. Sullivan, W. Moynier, 1979.	Yellowish-white, with chrome yellow throat, tubular funnel-shaped, in trusses of 12 fragrant flowers.	Velvety surface to fleshy foliage. Compact, bushy, spreading habit which looks good in rockeries. Ht 1 m/3 ft.
'Nancy Miller Adler'	Soft, blush pink.	Very glossy, low-growing with bushy foliage, ideal for containers. Ht 1 m/3 ft.
'Ne-plus-ultra' R. javanicum × 'Duchess of Edinburgh' J. Veitch & Sons, 1800s.	Bright red with rhodonite throat, in firm trusses of 8–14 tubular funnel-shaped flowers, practically identical to 'Triumphans'.	Medium, vigorous, bushy growth, with waxy elliptic foliage, 140 × 65 mm. Ideal for containers. Ht 0.9–1.5 m/3–5 ft.

Hybrid	Flowers	Notes
'Niugini Firebird' R. laetum × R. javanicum D. Stanton, 1985. Photo p. 126.	Bright scarlet, medium-sized flowers with orange throats.	Strong open growth to about. Sun tolerant. Ht 1.5 m/5 ft.
'Orange Wax' parentage unknown Reg. G. Snell, 1986.	Bright orange inside tube, nasturtium orange outside, vivid Indian orange lobes inside, saturn red outside, in trusses of 5–7 waxy medium-sized flowers.	Tall bushy shrub with elliptic foliage, 90 × 40 mm. Ht 1–2 m/3 ft–6 ft.
'Overflow' [R. christianae × R. lochiae] F2 hybrid B. Clancy.	Rose pink, very freely flowering.	Compact habit. Brother of the popular 'Arthur's Choice' (q.v.). 1 m/3 ft.
'Pacific Shower' [R. lochiae × R. macgregoriae] × R. christianae Donald Stanton, 1989.	Light orange–yellow with deep fire red lobes, in trusses of 10 florets.	Small, spreading or sprawling habit. Suitable for hanging baskets or as semi-groundcovering rockery plant.
'Pastenello'	Fragrant, creamy yellow, large flowers in full trusses.	Strong bushy growth, felty foliage. Best as a garden plant. Ht 1.5–2 m/5–6 ft.
'Pennywhistle' R. macgregoriae × R. bagobonum Dr J. Rouse, 1989.	Bright orange, in trusses of 3–5 florets, freely flowering.	Compact, bushy growth, ideal for containers. Shiny foliage. Ht 0.5–0.6 m/1 ft 6 in–2 ft.
'Pindi Pearl' R. laetum × R. phaeopeplum T. Lelliot, R. Cutten, 1980.	Apricot pink or light orange, flushed pink with yellow centre, in trusses of 6.	Strong, medium, upright growth.
'Pink Delight' Parentage unknown Veitch & Sons.	Carmine rose with pink throat. Very full flower trusses of up to 15 open, medium-sized, bell-shaped flowers. Long-flowering.	A classic old hybrid from the Veitch Nursery with good medium, spreading growth, more wide than high. Very good foliage. An elepidote hybrid rhododendron (q.v.) bears the same name. Ht 1.5 m/5 ft in 5 years.
'Pink Pizazz'	Large, perfumed, bright rose pink with ivory throat.	Tall, strong, bushy growth. Ht 2 m/6 ft or more.
'Pink Poppet'	Rose pink, delicate bell-shaped flowers.	Compact bush suitable for hanging baskets and shady position. Ht 0.75 m/2 ft 6 in.
'Pink Seedling'	Soft pastel pink.	Spreading bushy growth. Ht 1 m/3 ft.
'Pretty Cotton Candy' R. laetum × 'Pink Creeper' Origin unknown, reg. G. Snell, 1989.	Very pale cream with deep rose pink lobes, in trusses of 6–8 florets.	Medium bushy growth. Prefers shade. Ht 1–1.5 m/3–5 ft.
'Primrose Promise'	Soft primrose.	Compact, upright growth good for rockeries and shady position. Ht 0.5 m/1 ft 6 in.
'Princess Alexandra' 'Princess Royal' × R. jasminiflorum J. Veitch & Sons, 1840s.	White, sometimes with a blush of pale pink, in open trusses of tubular, waxy, medium-sized, slightly flared, lightly perfumed florets.	A very early Veitch hybrid with compact, bushy growth. Ht 0.9 m/3 ft.
'Red Prince' Parentage unknown 1800s.	Soft rose-red, in very full, rounded trusses of bell-shaped flowers.	Bushy, spreading growth with elliptic foliage, 90 × 30 mm. Ht 1.5 m/5 ft.

Hybrid	Flowers	Notes
'Robert Bates' [R. zoelleri × R. lochiae] × R. konori J.P Evans, 1987.	Shades of pink with greenish yellow throat, moderately perfumed, in flat-topped trusses of 4–5 flowers, 89 × 89 mm.	Strong bushy growth with elliptic leaves, 102 × 51 mm. American-raised hybrid with R. lochiae parentage. Ht 1.5 m/5 ft.
'Rosie Posie'	Unusual, small, tangerine, balsam-like flowers with lemon centre.	Strong bushy growth. Ideal for containers. Ht 1.5 m/5 ft.
'Rouseabout' R. aurigeranum × R. christianae Dr J. Rouse, 1989.	Bicoloured flowers of deep golden yellow with deep orange lobes, in trusses of 5–8 florets.	Bushy growth. Ht 1.5–2 m/5–6 ft.
'Scarlet Beauty' R. laetum × 'Triumphans' D. Stanton, G. Langdon, 1981.	Bright scarlet–orange with deep yellow or mid orange throat, lobes mid red, in trusses of 13 medium-sized flowers.	Upright, bushy growth. Ht 2 m/6 ft.
'Sebastian'	Strong orange, medium-sized flowers.	Striking reddish-bronze new foliage. Upright, bushy growth. Ht 2 m/6 ft.
'Shantung Pink' [(R. phaeopeplum × R. lochiae) × R. leucogigas] × R. laetum. Dr John Rouse, 1991.	Large, fragrant flowers of an unusual coral/salmon colour in full trusses.	Tall, open shrub with large, deep green leaves, growing to about 2 m/6 ft.
'Shantung Rose' [(R. phaeopeplum × R. lochiae) × R. leucogigas] × R. laetum. Dr John Rouse, 1988.	Fragrant, medium to large flowers of deep rose pink with a hint of orange/gold in the centre.	Tall, open shrub with large, deep green leaves, growing to about 2 m/6 ft.
'Simbu Sunset' R. laetum × R. zoelleri T. Lelliot, E. Perrot, G. Smith, 1983. hoto p. 144.	Large bicoloured flowers of brilliant orange with buttercup yellow centre, in trusses of 4–6 funnel-shaped florets.	Elliptic foliage 80–100 × 40–80 mm. Young stems deep red. Upright growth. Ht 2 m/6 ft.
'Sir George Holford' R. javanicum × unknown J. Veitch & Sons, 1800s.	Orange–yellow, shading to red on margins, in trusses of 8–10 flowers.	Low, spreading bush with attractive foliage.
'Souvenir de J. H. Mangles' R. brookeanum × [R. jasminiflorum × R. javanicum] × R. javanicum Veitch & Sons, 1800s.	Soft coral red or orange–yellow suffused with rose pink, in very full trusses.	Another of the old Veitch hybrids from the 1800s. Very vigorous, bushy growth. Ht 1.5 m/5 ft.
'Strawberry Parfait' R. phaeopeplum × R. zoelleri G. Snell, 1993.	Large, perfumed, strawberry-coloured flowers with softly frilled petals and cream throats.	Strong bushy growth to about 1.5 m/5 ft.
'Sunny' R. christianae × R. macgregoriae B. Clancy, 1984.	Bright orange and yellow. Abundant and very full flower trusses of 7–15 small florets. Flowers in spring.	Abundant and very full flower trusses. Bushy compact growth. Ht 1–1.5 m/3–5 ft.
'Sunset Gold 50' R. aurigeranum hybrid. P. Swisher, 1996.	Spectacular large trusses combining orange, gold and bright yellow flowers.	Open, upright growth to about 2 m/6 ft.

Hybrid	Flowers	Notes
'Sweet Amanda' ['Dr. Herman Sleumer' × R. herzogii] × R. laetum × R. aurigeranum] Origin unknown, reg. G. Snell, 1991.	Fragrant, pale yellow with moderate yellowish pink lobes, in trusses of 5–8 quite large, tubular flowers.	Vigorous, bushy growth, with scented foliage, benefits from careful pruning. Ht 2 m/6 ft.
'Sweet Rosalie' R. konori × R. christianae Reg. G. Snell, 1986.	Perfumed, light rose pink., deep lobes on flowers, in trusses of 5–7 tubular funnel-shaped flowers	Lanceolate leaves 130 × 70 mm. Medium, bushy growth. Ht 2–3 m/6–10 ft.
'Sweet Seraphim' R. loranthiflorum × R. christianae G. Snell, 1986.	Masses of creamy white with delicate pink edges to petals, in trusses of 14 florets, 50 × 45 mm.	Elliptic leaves, 80 × 45 mm, with medium, bushy growth. Ht 2 m/6 ft.
'Sweet Wendy' R. laetum × R. phaeopeplum Dr R. Withers, 1989.	Light orange with rose pink edge to petals, perfumed. Freely flowering.	Medium, bushy growth. Ht 1–1.5 m/3–5 ft.
'Triumphans' [R. brookeanum 'Gracile' × R. longiflorum] × R. javanicum J. Veitch & Sons, 1800s.	Vibrant, glowing scarlet crimson, in trusses of 8–14 blooms, continuously flowering from winter to early spring.	A classic, highly recommended hybrid with larger, upright, open growth, with elliptic foliage 140 × 65 mm. An early evergreen azalea hybrid bears the same name. Ht 2 m/6 ft.
'Tropic Fanfare' R. javanicum × R. lochiae D. Stanton, G. Snell, 1981.	Deep pink or red, in trusses of 8–10 florets of bright waxy flowers.	Medium, spreading growth, suitable for hanging baskets. Ht 1 m/3 ft.
'Tropic Summer' R. aurigeranum × R. macgregoriae D. Stanton, G. Snell, 1981.	Bright bicolour yellow and orange or mid orange, lobes orange–red, in full trusses of 10–12 medium to small florets.	Medium-sized, bushy, upright growth. Ht 2 m/6 ft.
'Tropic Tango' 'Princess Alexandra' × R. laetum Dr J. Rouse, G. Snell, 1984.	Delicate, strong orange–yellow, with nasturtium red lobes, in trusses of 5–8 florets, freely flowering.	Tall open bush with dark, glossy elliptic foliage, 100 × 40 mm. Ht 2 m/6 ft.
'Veronica Maureen' [R. christianae × R. lochiae] × R. zoelleri B. Clancy, 1991.	White, with reddish orange margin and black-tipped stamens, in trusses of about 7 florets.	An outstanding, attractive and appealing compact R. lochiae hybrid. Ht 0.6–1 m/2–3 ft.
'Wattlebird' syn. 'Wattle Bird' R. laetum × R. aurigeranum Dr J. Rouse, 1983.	Bright clear gold yellow, in loose trusses of 7–9 large, open, flared, bell-shaped flowers.	Tall, bushy, upright growth with glossy, ovate leaves, 120 × 30 mm. Ht 2–3 m/6–10 ft.
'Zoe Elloise' 'Dr. Herman Sleumer' × R. zoelleri (Michael Black form) B. Clancy.	Large, brilliantly coloured irridescent orange–red, with star-shaped throat of primrose yellow, in trusses of 6–13 florets.	A very showy and spectacular bush. A back cross to R. zoelleri. Medium growth. Ht 0.6–1.2 m/2–4 ft.

About the plant lists

Flowering times

Southern hemisphere	Abbreviation	Flowering Period	Northern hemisphere
July	VE	Very early	January
August–mid September	E	Early	February–mid March
September	EM	Early–middle	March
Early October	M	Middle	Early April
Late October	ML	Middle–late	Late April
November	L	Late	May
December	VL	Very late	June

Hardiness ratings

There are a number of approaches to defining the ability of plants to withstand low temperatures. Climatic zones that have been developed for the United States and Europe unfortunately differ from each other, which means that to use both systems in the following lists of plants would make the lists unnecessarily cluttered. Throughout the lists I have tried to provide, where they are known, the minimum temperatures in degrees celsius (°C) that the plants are believed to be capable of tolerating.

I have also included, again where they are available, the RHS hardiness ratings for the British Isles, which represent the hardiness of each particular plant, rather than a climatic zone for which it is suitable.

Other abbreviations

Ht	Height
m	metres
ft	feet
in	inches
mm	millimetres
reg.	registered
N	north
S	south
E	east
W	west

Hardiness ratings for the British Isles

H4 Hardy anywhere in the British Isles where conditions favour the growing of rhododendrons.

H3 Hardy in the west and favourable areas near the east and south coasts, but requires some shelter.

H2 Hardy in sheltered gardens on the west coast and occasionally in the south.

H1 Usually in greenhouses or against very well sheltered, shaded walls.

Glossary

acidity — The level of chemical acid or 'sourness' of a soil or a liquid, measured in terms of pressure of hydrogen ions or pH, on a scale of 0 to 14. Rhododendrons do best between pH 4.5 and 6. Soils above 6 start to become too alkaline, while soils below 4.5 become too acidic for the successful growth of most varieties.

adventitious roots — Roots which arise from wounded plant tissue, enabling cuttings and layering to occur. Some plants, such as brambles or ivy (*Hedera* spp.) naturally set out adventitious roots when their stems or branches come into contact with another surface or medium, enabling them to spread or obtain a footing.

aerobic — Where oxygen is present in a healthy soil or medium, conducive to plant growth and beneficial organisms.

alkalinity — Opposite to acidity, *above*.

anaerobic — Opposite of aerobic, when oxygen is not present and a medium is not conducive to plant growth.

apex — End tip, normally of a leaf.

Azaleodendron — Hybrid plant arising from a cross between an azalea and a *Rhododendron* of another subgenus.

Bordeaux mixture — A traditional fungicide prepared from copper sulphate and hydrated lime.

back crossing — Technique employed in breeding, wherein the progeny (F^1 or F^2 generation) are crossed with one of the original parents.

bract — Modified leaf found below and surrounding a flower.

bullate — Irregular surface, as in leaves, giving a blistered, textured appearance.

calyx — Outermost flower parts, consisting of the sepals normally green, and surrounding the corolla *See also* hose-in-hose.

cambium layer — The thin layer of cells between the bark and wood in the trunks and branches of woody trees and shrubs.

campanulate — Bell-shaped, as in flowers.

chlorophyll — Green pigmentation in foliage and stems which enables a plant to manufacture its own food supply in the process of photosynthesis

chlorosis — Yellowing of leaves, normally indicating a soil chemical imbalance, probably one of a number of nutrient deficiencies, most commonly iron, in combination with an alkaline soil. It can also indicate waterlogging.

corolla — Inner whorl of petals, normally the most conspicuous coloured part of a plant, above the sepals and surrounding the stamens and stigma. Petals may be joined, as in rhododendrons and other members of the Ericaceae family, or separate.

cross — The act of hybridising or the result of the fertilising of one species or cultivar with another with the intention of creating a new hybrid.

cultivar — Any plant which is normally only grown in cultivation. As well as hybrid plants created by crossing two known species or cultivars, a cultivar can be a 'sport' or naturally or spontaneously arising mutation of a known species, often a named variety.

dimorphic — Normally a reference to the leaves of many evergreen azaleas, which are produced in two distinct forms: the spring leaves, which often yellow and fall in autumn, and the summer or 'persistent' leaves, which remain on the shrub for at least one year.

double — Flower with multiple sets of petals.

F^1 hybrid — First generation of plants derived from the crossing of two different plants. These plants will not reproduce true to form.

F^2 hybrid — The second generation of plants derived from reproducing between the plants of a first generation of crosses or hybrids. These plants will often possess superior qualities to those of the first generation, or will display characteristics sought by the hybridiser but not evident in plants of the first generation.

floret — Individual flower. In rhododendrons, from two to over twenty or more florets comprise a truss or flower head.

grafting — The process of vegetative propagation achieved by uniting the upper part of one plant (the scion) possessing desirable floral and foliage characteristics, to the stem or root system (rootstock) of another, to the mutual benefit of both. In rhododendrons two methods, the cutting graft or wide wedge and the saddle graft, are employed to enable plants which are reluctant to set roots to be propagated and to provide some plants with inadequate roots with a stronger root system.

grafting knife — Small pocket knife with a curved, folding blade, specifically designed for the cuts required in grafting techniques.

grex — A group of seedlings resulting from the same cross. Genetic variation means each seedling will be different.

hardening off — Allowing a plant to acclimatise to its new environment prior to planting in the garden.

hardiness, hardy — A measure of the ability of a plant to withstand cold temperatures.

heel cutting — Cutting taken from a small side shoot which includes a small portion (or heel) of the main stem from which it was taken.

hose-in-hose — The normally green calyx is enlarged and of the same colour as the corolla, giving the appearance of a double flower. A characteristic of some evergreen azaleas.

hybrid — A plant which results from the breeding of two other plants.

indumentum — Woolly or hairy covering found on the undersides of the leaves and sometimes on young shoots of some varieties.

internode — Length of stem between two nodes.

layering — The process of vegetative propagation in which a portion of stem or branch is exposed to the soil or a propagating medium. Adventions roots form and the new growth arising above these roots can be separated from the 'mother' plant and grown on as a separate plant.

node — Joint in a stem from which leaves or flower buds arise.

open pollination — Reproduction wherein the seed parent plant is able to be pollinated freely by any neighbouring plant.

perlite — Porous material used for water retention and aeration in propagating and potting media, created by heating volcanic glass to a high temperature. It is sterile, has no nutrients and has close to the water-holding capacity of peat, but is also rather expensive.

persistent — Summer leaves of some evergreen azaleas with dimorphic foliage, which remain on the plant for at least one year. The term can also refer to fruit or seed capsules which remain attached to a plant after ripening.

petals — Whorl of flower parts which comprise the corolla. Petals may be joined, as in rhododendrons and other members of the Ericaceae family, or separate.

petiole — Stalk of a leaf connecting it to a stem or branch.

pH — Pressure of hydrogen. The measure of acidity or alkalinity in soil or water. The optimum pH level for rhododendrons is 5.0–5.5, although a range of 4.5–6.0 is acceptable for most varieties.

photosynthesis — The process by which a plant manufactures its own food supply in the form of glucose, by using the energy of sunlight to combine water and carbon dioxide from the air in the presence of chlorophyll.

pollination — Transfer of pollen from the anther of the donor plant or pollen parent (male) to the stigma of the seed parent (female) for the purpose of fertilisation and subsequent reproduction. The donor plant and seed parent may be the same or different plants.

rootstock — The portion of plant comprising the lower half of a graft selected to provide the upper half or scion with a strong, easily striking root system.

saddle graft — Graft in which the a 'V' is cut into the base of the stem of the scion to sit snugly over the rootstock which has been cut into a correspondingly shaped point.

scales — Tiny, multi-celled outgrowths on leaves, stems and sometimes parts of the flowers of lepidote rhododendron species and cultivars which aid in the control of transpiration or water loss from the plant. They take a variety of forms and microscopic examination of these scales can aid the identification of species.

scion — The upper plant or half of a graft comprising desirable foliage or floral characteristics which are grafted to a strong, easily striking root system, the rootstock.

selfing — Reproduction from seed created by a plant pollinating itself.

sepals — The flower parts, normally green, which comprise the segments of the calyx, surrounding the corolla.

side cutting or wedge — Graft in which the scion is inserted into a diagonal cut in the side of the stem of the rootstock.

single — Flower with a single set of petals.

sport — Naturally or spontaneously arising random

mutation of a known species, often a named variety, e.g. *Rhododendron sutchuense* 'Seventh Heaven'. To remain true to the form of the original or parent plant, a sport can only be reproduced by vegetative means.

stamen — The male part of a flower, consisting of an anther, which bears the pollen, supported by the filament.

stigma — The pollen-receiving female part of a flower, held at the end of the style.

strigose — Surface, as in leaves, covered with stiff bristles or hairs.

strike — The successful formation of a root system in various techniques of vegetative propagation. The ability of rhododendrons to strike new roots varies from relatively easy to almost impossible, when grafting becomes the only form of propagation possible.

style — The elongated female part of the flower, connecting the stigma with the ovaries.

subspecies — Naturally occurring and often geographically localised variation of a species which is able to perpetuate itself.

sucker — Unwanted vegetative growth arising from the rootstock of a grafted plant. Suckers should always be removed, as their vigour may overtake that of the scion.

tenderness, tender — Opposite of hardy or hardiness. A tender plant is unlikely to tolerate frosts.

tomentum — Woolly or hairy covering found on the upper surface of the leaves of some varieties, similar to the indumentum on the undersides.

top-dressing — Application of a soil conditioner, mulch, fertiliser or other chemical to the soil surface, rather than being dug into the soil.

transpiration — Process in which a plant expels unwanted water through the leaves, aided in many species and their hybrids by the presence of scales.

truss — Group of from one to twenty or more florets or individual flowers forming a terminal raceme, known in rhododendron parlance as a truss.

tube — The joined petals forming the corollas of many rhododendrons, particularly vireyas, which form a distinctive cylindrical shape.

union — Point in a grafted plant where the scion meets the rootstock to which it is grafted.

variety — Spontaneously arising variation of a species, or sport, which does not naturally reproduce itself, and must be propagated by vegetative means to produce plants which are true to form.

vermiculite — Flaky mineral which is crushed and heated, causing it to expand to many times its original size. Added to propagating and potting mixes for aeration and water retention, it also contains small quantities of magnesium and potassium.

white oil — Petroleum-based solution normally used to control scale insects by suffocation.

Typical rhododendron flower shapes

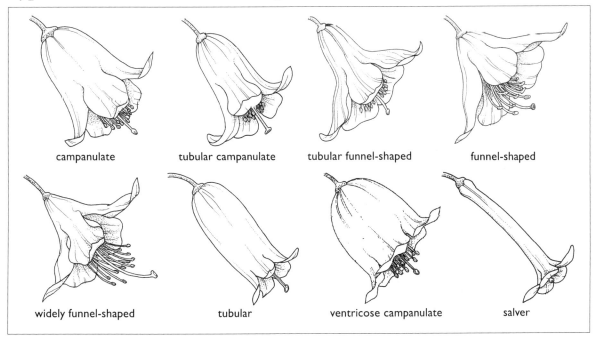

Typical rhododendron leaf shapes

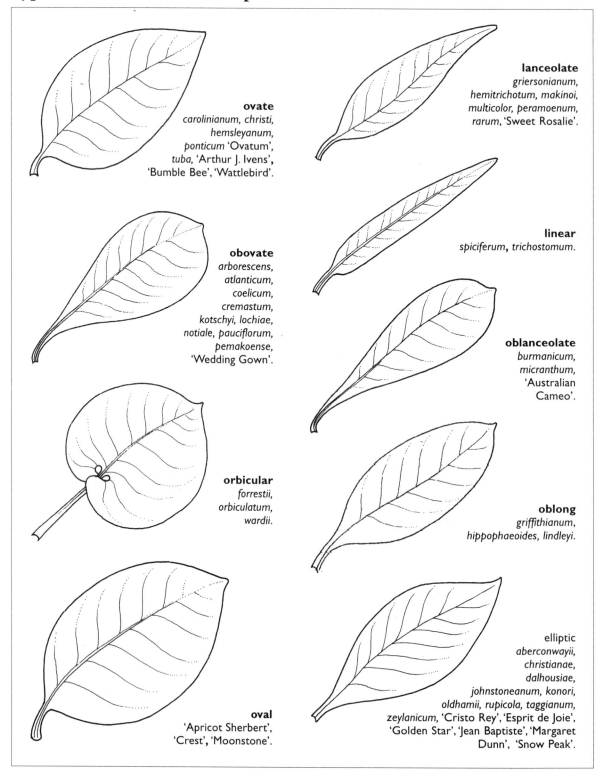

Rhododendron societies

Australia
Australian Rhododendron Society,
PO Box 21,
Olinda, Victoria 3788.

Canada
Rhododendron Society of Canada,
4271 Lake Shore Road,
Burlington, Ontario.

China
Chinese Rhododendron Society,
Kunming Botanical Institute,
Academia Sinica,
Heilongtan,
Kunming, Yunnan.

Denmark
Danish Chapter,
American Rhododendron Society,
Hejrebakken 3,
D K 3500, Vaerloese.

Germany
German Rhododendron Society,
Rhododendron Park,
28 Bremen 17, Marcusallee 60.

New Zealand
New Zealand Rhododendron Society,
PO Box 28,
Palmerston North.

Japan
Japanese Rhododendron Society,
8–5 2–chome, Goshozuka,
Takatsuk, Kawasaki.

Sweden
Swedish Rhododendron Society,
Botaniska Tradgarden,
Carl Skothsbergs Gata 22,
40319 Göteborg.

United Kingdom
The Royal Horticultural Society,
PO Box 313,
London SW1P 2PE.

United States of America
American Rhododendron Association,
14885 SW Sunrise Lane,
Tigard, Oregon 97224.

American Rhododendron Society,
PO Box 1380,
Gloucester, Virginia 23061.

Rhododendron Species Foundation,
PO Box 3798,
Federal Way, Washington 98063–3798.

Index

Entries in bold type indicate a detailed listing, while colour plates are indicated by italic type.

General index

Aberconway, Lord 74
Acer spp. 27, 28
acidity 21, 43
actylandromedal 6
adventitious roots 45
aerial layering 53
air circulation 39
Ajuga spp. 30
Alasakan islands 9
Albican hybrids 146
Aleyrodes azalae 39
alkalinity 21, 43
almonds 28
American Rhododendron Association 167
American Rhododendron Society, 167
andromedotoxin 6
Anenome spp. 8
aphids 39, 152
Appalachian Mountains 145
apricots 28
Arbutus spp. 5, 27, 28
armillara root rot 40
Armillaria mellea 40
Assam 6, 8, 74
Augusta, Georgia 132
Australasia 30
Australia 25, 74, 120, 167
Australian Rhododendron Society 167
azalea lace bug 38
Azaleastrum 9
azaleodendrons 55
back crossing 56
balance arms 46, 47
Balfour, Sir Isaac Bailey 9
bamboo 13
Banister, John 140
bark 18
Belgian Indian hybrids 132, 120
Belgium 120, 145
benomyl 48
Berckman, Prosper Julius 132
Betula spp. 28
Bhutan 6, 74
binomial system 9

Black Sea 7
black vine weevil 37
Bobbink & Atkins Nursery 131
bonsai 137
borers 39
Borneo 6
boron 25
Boronia spp. 28
Botrytis spp. 40
Boulter, Victor 74, 111, 112
box elder 28
breeding 55
Brocade Pillow 118
Brooks Hybrids 132
Brunei 6
bud blast and blight 41
Burma see Myanmar
C. japonica 28, 118
C. sinensis 7
calcium 25
calcium chloride 56
calcium phosphate 25
calcium sulphate 25
California 7
Calluna vulgaris 5, 30
Caloptilia azaleella 39
cambium layer 41
Camellia spp. 7, 27, 28, 29
Canada 167
carbon dioxide 24
caterpillars 39
Caucasus Mountains 6
Chekiang 74
chemical fertilizers 43
cherries 28
China 5, 8, 9, 118
Chinese or sheep azalea 145, 146
Chinese Rhododendron Society, 167
chlorine 25
chlorophyll 25, 42
chlorosis 42, *51*
Clancy, Brian 151
clay 20, 21, 35
clay-coloured weevil 37

climatic zone systems 18, 162
Clivia miniata 30
coconut fibre 54
coconut husks 35
cold frames 46, 47
cold hardiness 18
collar rot 41
compost 22, 25, 35, 43
Compton, Bishop Henry 140
concrete 43
conifers 28
containers 11, 18, 23, 26, 38, 42, 54, 55, 151
copper 25, 42, 43
Cornus canadensis 30
Correa spp. 29
Corylus maxima 'Purpurea' 27, 29
Cotinus spp. 27, 29
Cox, Peter 68, 74
cranberry 5
crocking 35
Crowea spp. 29
Cryptomeria spp. 118
Curtis, Charles 150
cutting graft 50
cuttings 45, 48, 54
Cyathea spp. 30
daffodils 13
damping off 42, 46, 54
Dandenong Ranges 74
Daphne spp. 16, 27, 29
deadheading 26
Dialeurodes chittendeni 39
Dicksonia antarctica 30
dimethoate 38
dogwood 30
drainage 13, 21, 35
East India Company 7, 8
Edinburgh University 9
elephant weevil or beetle 37
elm 13
Embothrium coccineum lanceolatum 28
England 41, 145
English Indian hybrids 120
English ivy 14

Index

Enkianthus spp. 29
epiphytes 35, 151
Epsom salts 43
Erica spp. 27, 30
Eucalyptus spp. 28, 29
Euphorbia spp. 30
Exbury 74, 140, 141, 146
Exobasidium vaccinii 40
ferns 30
ferrous sulphate 35
fertiliser burn 26, 41
fertilisers 24, 25, 26, 35, 41, 42, 43
fish emulsion, 25
flowering cherry 28
fogging 46
forget-me-nots 30
Forrest, George 8, 57, 74
Fortune, Robert 8, 57, 74, 120
fragrant rhododendrons 56, 151
Frederik de Coninck 145
Freesia spp. 13
freezing 18
frost 18, 21, 44, 151, 165
Fuchsia spp. 29
fungi 26
fungicide 48
Gable hybrids 137
Gable, Joseph 136
Gaultheria spp. 5
gentian 15
German Rhododendron Society 167
Germany 167
germinating seed 54
Ghent hybrids 6, 141, 142, 145
Ghent, Belgium 145
Gibraltar 7
Gingko biloba 28
Girard, Peter E. 137
Glasnevin Botanic Gardens, Dublin 113
glass 18
Glendoick, Scotland 74
Glenn Dale hybrid azaleas 138
Gowen, J.R. 145
grafted plants 53
grafting 45, 46, 50
Graphocephala coccinea 41
Graphognathus leucoloma 37
greenhouse thrips 38
greenhouse whitefly 38
greenhouses 39, 46, 150
Grierson, R.C. 74
growing media 55
guelder rose 30
gypsum 21, 25
Hamamelis mollis 29
hanging baskets 35, 151
hardening off 18
hardiness ratings 162
heathers 27, 30
Hedera spp. 14, 30
heel cuttings 48
Heliothrips haemorrhoidalis 38
Helleborus spp. 30
hemlock 41
Himalayan birch 28
Himalayas 6, 29, 74
honey fungus 40
Honshu, Japan 9, 145
Hooker, Sir Joseph 8, 57, 74

Hooker, Sir William 8
Horticultural Society (later RHS) 8
Hosta spp. 13, 30
humus 22
Hyacinthoides spp. 30
Hydrangea spp. 29
Ilam hybrids 74, 146
India 6, 8
indumentum 9, 16, 18, 57
iron 25, 35, 42, 43
iron deficiency 22
irrigation 14, 24, 36
ivy 30
Japan 6, 28, 118, 137, 145, 167
Japanese azalea 145
Japanese maple 27
Japanese Rhododendron Society 167
Javanicum hybrids 150
Kadan Komoku 118
Kaempferi hybrids 18, 118
Kalmia spp. 5, 27, 40, 44
Kashmir 28
Kew gardens 8, 151
Kingdon-Ward, Francis 8, 57, 72
Kirishima Tsutsujii 133
Knap Hill and Exbury hybrids 73, 140, 141, 145, 146
Korea 6
Korean azalea 136
Kurume hybrids 18, 118, 136
Kyushu 9, 137, 145
Kyushu azalea 133
Labrador 7
lace bugs and lace wings 38, 152
layering 26, 46, 49
leaf burn 41
leaf gall 40
leaf mosaic virus 44
lilacs 13
Lilium spp. 8
lily-of-the-valley shrub 29
lime-induced chlorosis 22, 42, 51
Lindley, Dr. John 61
Linnaeus, Carl 9, 118, 141
Liquidambar spp. 27
Lithodora spp. 15
little leaf virus 44
loam 54
Lobb, Thomas 150
Loder, Sir Edmund 74
Loiseleuria procumbens 9, 29, 105
Lonicera spp. 8
Madden, Edward 8
magnesium 25, 42
magnesium sulphate 43
Magnolia spp. 27, 29, *34*
maidenhair tree 28
malathion 37
Malayan peninsula 150
Malaysia 6
Malesian rhododendrons 5
manganese 25
maples 27
marginal leaf scorch 43
Maruba Satsuki 137
Masonaphis lambersi 39
Meconopsis spp. 30
Melbourne 74, 151
Melford hybrids 146

micro-irrigation 24
micro-propagation 45
Mie Satsuki 137
misting 46
mites 38, 152
Mollis azalea hybrids 141, 145, 146
molybdenum 25
mondo grass 13
Morrison, Y. B. 138
Mortier hybrids 145
Mortier, P. 145
mound planting 21
mulches 18, 22, 25
Myanmar (formerly Burma) 5, 6, 8, 74
mycorrhizal fungi 5
Myosotis spp. 30
N:P:K ratio 25
Narcissus spp. 30
necrotic ringspot disease 44
Nepal 6, 28, 74
Nerium oleander 7
New Forest, Hampshire 146
New Guinea 5, 6, 7, 8, 151
New Zealand 74, 120, 146, 167
New Zealand Rhododendron Society, 167
nitrogen 24, 25, 42
North Carolina 6, 8
Norway maple 28
Nuccio hybrids 139
nutrient deficiencies 42
nutrients 24, 55
Nyssa spp. 27, 28
oaks 27
Oidium spp. 41
olive 89
Oluvinia azaleae 40
Oregon 7
organic fertilisers 25
Ornatum hybrids 145
Orthorhinus cylindirostris 37
Otiorhynchus spp. 37
Pealius azaleae 39
peatmoss 35, 47, 48, 54, 55
Pennsylvania 7, 136
perennials 16
periwinkles 14
perlite 47, 54
Pestalotia spp. 41
petal blight 40, 152
pH 21, 35, 42, 43, 50
Philippines 6
phosphorus 24, 25, 29
photosynthesis 24, 25, 46
Phytophthora spp. 40, 42, 43, 152
Phytoseiulus persimilis 38
Picea spp 41
Pieris spp. 5, 16, 27, 28, 29, 41
pinebark 47
pinxterbloom 145
planting 23
plums 28
poison 6, **7**
pollination 55
Pontic azalea 145
Pontic region 7
poppies 30
potassium 25
potting mixes 35
powdery mildew 41, 152

predatory mites 38
Primula spp. 8
propagating media 47
propagating units 47
pruning 26
Prunus spp. 27, 28
PVC (polyvinyl chloride) 13
Pythium spp. 42
quarantine 54
Quercus spp. 28
Rhizoctonia spp. 42
Rhododendron Society of Canada 167
Rhododendron Species Foundation 167
rhododendron borer 39
rhododendron bug 37
rhododendron leafhopper 41
rhododendron whitefly 39
Rhododendrons of Sikkim-Malaya 8
Rhodora canadensis 141
rice hulls 35, 54
rock gardens 14
Rocky Mountains 9
Root rots 40
root invasion 13
root system 13, 20–22, 25, 55, 151
rooting hormones 48
rootstocks 53
Rothschild, Lionel de 74, 109, 145
Rothschilds 74
Rouse, Dr John 151
Royal Botanic Gardens, Edinburgh 73
Royal Horticultural Society (RHS) 8, 162, 167
Russia 9
rust 41, 152
Rustica and Rustica Flore Pena hybrids 145
Rutherford hybrids 131
Sabah 6
saddle graft 50
Sakamoto, Motozo 133
'Sakura tsutsuji' 120
sand 47
Sarawak 6
Satsuki azaleas 118, 137
scales 9, 39, 151
Sea of Japan 6
secateurs 46
sedges 13

seed 46
seed germination 54
seed storage 54
self-pollination 56
Septoria spp. 41
shade houses 39
shadecloth 46
shadehouses 18
Shikoku 9, 145
side wedge 50
Sikkim 8, 74
silica gel 56
slips 45
slow release fertiliser 25, 42, 43, 48, 55
smoke bushes 27
Snell, Graham 151, 155
snowball trees 30
South Africa 25
Spanish bluebell 30
Species Plantarum 9, 118
sphagnum moss 54
spruce 41
Stead, Edgar 74, 146
Stephanitis spp. 37, 38
sterilising 54
Stethoconus japonicus 38
sulphur 25
sunburn 24, 41, *51*
Swedish Rhododendron Society 167
Synanthedon rhododendri 39
systemic insecticides 37
Szechuan 5, 6
Taiwan 6, 9
tea 29
Telopea spp. 28, 29
tenderness 165
terrariums 47
Tetranychus urticae 38
Thompson Nursery 73
thrips 152
Tibet *see* Xizang
tissue culture 45
top-dressing 25
toxicity 7
trace elements 25, 26, 42
Tradescant, John 7
transpiration 18, 24
Transylvania 7

Tsuga spp. 41
Tsutsujii 118, 137
tulips 13
tupelo 28
Turkey 7
Ulmus spp. 13
United States of America 74, 131, 167
US National Arboretum 138
Vaccinum spp. 5
Van de Ven, Karel 74, 111, 112
van Houtte, Louis 145, 147
Veitch, James and Sons 8, 133, 146, 150
vermiculite 48, 54
Verschaffelt, M.L. 145
Viburnum spp. 30
Vietnam 6
Vinca spp 14
Viola spp. 30
Virey, Julien Jospeh 150
Virginia 8
Vuylstekem, Charles 145
waratah 28
Ward, Dr Nathaniel Bagshaw 8, 31
Wardian case 8, 31
water 20
Waterer, Gomer 145
Waterer, Michael 73, 74, 145
watering 24
waterlogging 20, 39
weevils 37
Weigela spp. 8
Western azalea 146
white oil 39
whiteflies 39
whitefringed weevil 37
willows 13
Wilson's Fifty 133
Wilson, Ernest H. 8, 65, 133
wind 151
winter daphne 29
witch hazels 29
Withers, Dr Robert 151
Xenophon 7
Xizang (formerly Tibet) 5, 6, 74
Yakushima 74, 137
Yeates, Dr. J.S. 146
Yunnan 5, 6, 74
zinc 25

Index of rhododendron species

Azalea indica 118, 119, 120
A. mollis 141, 145
A. ovatum 70
A. procumbens 9

aberconwayii **66**
adenogynum **66**
aequabile *126*, **152**
agapetum *51*
albiflorum 9, 10
ambiguum 16, **58**
arborescens **141**
arboreum 6, 8, 5, 16, *33*, **66**, 70, 73, 74, *85*
    'Album' **66**
    delavayii **66**, 70, *85*

delavayi var. *peramoenum* 70
    zeylanicum 16, *51*, **66**
arizelum 15, 16, **66**
atlanticum **141**
augustinii 8, 15, **58**
auriculatum 8
aurigeranum *126*, **152**, 154
    'Eureka Gold' *126*, **152**
auritum 7
azaleoides 73
barbatum 16, **66**
beanianum **66**
brookeanum 15, 150, **152**
bullatum 8, 59
burmanicum **58**, *52*

burtii **152**
caeruleum 63
calendulaceum 7, 145, 146
calophytum **67**
calostrotum **58**
campanulatum 15, **67**
    'Knap Hill' **67**
campylocarpum 8, **67**
camtschaticum 10
canadense 7, **141**
carolinianum **58**
carringtonii 151, **152**
catawbiense 6, 8, 37, 73, 74
caucasicum 8, 73, 74
christi 15, **152**

Index

christianae **152**
ciliicalyx 17, **58**, *52*
cinnabarinum 8, 41, **58**
   roylei 58
coelicum 15, **67**
concatenens **59**
crassum 62
cremastum **59**
cubitii 16, **59**
dalhousiae 17, **59**
   'Rhabdotum' *52*, 59
dauricum **59**
decorum 17, **67**
degronianum 15, **67**, 85
   yakushimanum 15, 19, **67**, 74, 85
dendricola 16, 17, **59**
dianthosmum **152**
dichroanthum 74
edgeworthii 15, 16, **59**
elegans 50
elegantulum 15, 16, **68**
elliottii 8, **68**, *85*
ericoides 15, *126*, **152**
eriocarpum 118, **119**, *124*, 137
eximium 68
falconeri 8, 15, 16, 17, 19, 57, **68**
   eximium **68**
fastigiatum 8, 15, **60**
ferrugineum 6, 7, **60**, 61
   'Album' 60
   'Coccineum' 60
   'Glenarn' 60
fictolacteum 16, **68**
forrestii 5, 8, *52*, **68**
fortunei 8, 16, 17, **68**, 74
fulvum 15, **69**
glaucophyllum **60**
grande 15, 16, **69**, *85*
griersonianum 8, 16, 19, 40, 41, **69**, 74
griffithianum 8, 16, 17, **69**, 74, 92
hedyosmum 65
hemsleyanum 16, 17, **69**
herzogii 151
himantodes **152**
hippophaeoides **60**
   'Bei-Ma-Shan' 60
   'Habba Shan' 60
hirsutum 7
hybridum 73
hyperythrum **69**
impeditum **60**
indicum 118, **119**, 120, 132, 136, 137
   'Balsaminaeflorum' **119**
intricatum **60**
irroratum **69**
   'Polka Dot' 69
japonicum **141**, 145, 147
jasminiflorum 150, 151, **153**
javanicum *126*, 150, **153**
   teysmannii **153**
johnstoneanum 17, **60**
   'Demi-John' 60
   'Double Diamond' 60
kaempferi 118, **119**, *124*, 133, 136
   kinshibe 136
keiskei **61**
   cordifolia 'Ebino', 61
   cordifolia 'Yaku Fairy' 61
keleticum **61**

keysii 52, **61**
kiusianum **119**, 133
konori 151, **153**
kotschyi **61**, 79
kwayii 51
laetum *126*, **153**
lapponicum 6
ledoides see *trichostomum*
lepidotum 52, **61**
leucogigas 'Hunstein's Secret' *126*
lindleyi 52, **61**, 64
litangense **61**
lobbii 150
lochiae 6, *126*, 151, **153**, 154
loranthiflorum **153**
ludlowi 74
lutescens 15, 16, **62**
luteum 6, 7, **141**, 145
macabeanum 9, 15, **70**, *85*
macgregoriae 6, *126*, **153**
macrosepalum 'Linearifolium' **119**, *123*
macrophyllum 41
maddenii 8, 16, 17, 19, *52*, **62**
   crassum **62**
magnificum **70**, *85*
makinoi 15, **70**
malayanum 15, 150, **153**
manipurense 62
maximum 7, 73
megacalyx 17, **62**
metternichii 67
micranthum **62**
molle 8, **141**, 145, 146
moupinense **63**
   'Rubra' 63
multicolor 150, **154**
myrtifolium **61**, 79
nakaharai **119**
nieuwenhuisii 6
niveum 15, 16, **70**, *85*
notiale 6, 153, **154**
nudiflorum 73
nuttallii 15, 16, 17, 19, **63**
obtusum 119, 133
occidentale 7, 45, *125*, **141**, 146
oldhamii **119**
orbiculatum 15, *126*, **154**
ovatum 9, 15, 19, **70**
pauciflorum 15, **154**
pemakoense 8, 15, **63**
peramoenum **70**
periclymenoides 73, **142**, 145
phaeochitum 15, **154**
phaeopeplum 15, **154**
polyandrum 62
ponticum 6, 7, 8, 16, 19, 39, 40, **70**, 74, 97
   'Variegatum' 15, **71**
prinophyllum **142**
prostratum 5
protistum 6
pseudochrysanthum 15, 16, 19, **71**
radinum 65
rarilepidotum **144**, **154**
rarum **154**
reticulatum *125*, **142**
retivenium **154**
rhabdotum see *dalhousiae*
rigidum 17, **63**
rirei 15, **71**

rubineiflorum 5, 151
rupicola 19, **63**
   chryseum 63
   muliense 63
russatum 8, 19, **63**
   'Collingwood Ingram' 63
   'Keillour' 63
   'Maryborough' 63
   'Night Editor' 63
sargentianum 8
sataense 133
scabrifolium var. *spiciferum* 64
schlippenbachii **142**, *143*
   'Prince Charming' 142
sciaphilum 59
scintillans 15, 19, **64**
scopulorum 17, 19, **64**
semibarbatum 9, 10
serpyllifolium 6, **142**
   'Album' 142
sessilifolium 15, **154**
sidereum **71**
simsii 119, **120**, *124*
sinogrande 6, 8, 15, 16, **71**, *85*
sphaeranthum 65
spiciferum 19, *52*, **64**
spinuliferum 16, *52*, **64**
stamineum 9, 10
stapfianum 6
sutchuense **71**
   'Seventh Heaven' 71
taggianum 16, 17, **64**
taronense 59
tashiroi **120**
tephropeplum 16, 19, **64**
teysmannii 150
thomsonii 8, 15, 16, **71**
trichostomum 5, **65**
   'Lakeside' 65
   'Quarry Wood' 65
   'Rae Berry' 65
   'Sweet Bay' 65
tsarongense 8
tuba **144**, **154**
ungernii 15, 16, **72**
veitchianum 16, 17, **65**
virgatum 17, 19, **65**
   'Album' 65
   oleifolium 65
viscosum 7, 140, **142**, 145, 146
wallichii 15, 16, 19, **72**, *85*
wardii 9, 15, 16, **72**
   'Ellestee' 72
   'Puralbum' 72
   'Meadow Pond' 72
webstrianum 19, *52*, **65**
weyrichii **142**
wightii 8, 15, 19, **72**
williamsianum 8, 16
williamsii **154**
wiltonii 15, 16, **72**
xanthostephanum 16, *52*, **65**
   'Yellow Garland' 65
yakushimanum see *degronianum* ssp. *yakushimanum*
yedoense var. *poukhanense* 136
yunnanense 8, 19, **65**
zeylanicum see *arboreum* ssp. *zeylanicum*
zoelleri 15, **154**

Index of rhododendron hybrids

Abby Boulter 19, **101**
Abundant Harvest 138
Addy Wery **134**
Admiral Piet Hein 17, **91**
Adonis **134**
Adriaan Koster (ev. hybrid) **101**
  (dec. azalea) 145
Advent Bells **120**
Aioi **134**
Aladdin **134**
Alarm **114**
Alba Magnifica 19, **132**
Albert Elizabeth **120**
Albert Schweitzer **110**
Album Novum **102**
Alexander Dancer **91**
Alice 19, **110**
Aline **120**
Alisa Nicole **155**
Alison Johnstone 15, **104**
Alphonse Anderson 19, **132**
Alphonse Lavallee 145
Altaclarense (ev. hybrid) 74
  (dec. azalea) **146**
Anah Kruschke 19, **84**
Anatta Gold **155**
Angus Bell **120**
Anica Bricogne 84
Anna 15, **110**
Anna Rose Whitney 15, 19, 74, **111**
Anne Teese 17, **102**
Anniversary **134**
Anniversary Joy **120**
Anthony Koster 145
Anthony Waterer 145, **146**
Antoon van Welie 15, 19, **111**
Apple Blossom (dec. azalea) **146**
Appleblossom (ev. azalea) **134**
Apricot Gold **82**
Apricot Sherbert **104**
April Glow **76**
April Showers 76
Arabian Knights **134**
Aravir 17, **155**
Arnold Teese 74
Arthur Bedford 19, **109**
Arthur J. Ivens 19, *86*, **91**
Arthur's Choice 153, **155**
Astarte **76**
Augfast 19, **75**
Auguste van Geerte **109**
Aunt Martha 15, 19, **97**
Aurora **147**
Australian Cameo 15, **82**
Australian Canary **104**
Australian Primrose 15
Australian Rainbow 19, **91**
Australian Sunset 15, **104**, *106*
Avocet **147**
Award 15, 17, **102**
Ayers Rock **104**
Azaleoides 73, *85*
Azma *106*, **111**
Azor **91**
Azuma Kagami **134**

Baby Jill **121**
Bacher's Gold **91**
Bad Eilsen 15, **78**
Baden-Baden **78**
Ballerina (ev. azalea) **121**
  (dec. azalea) **147**
Balsaminaeflorum *see indicum*
Balzac **147**
Bambi **82**
Barclayi **97**
Basalisk **147**
Bastion **97**
Bealii **120**
Beatrix **121**
Beauty of Littleworth **116**
Bei-Ma-Shan *see hippophaeoides*
Belle Heller 19, **102**
Berryrose **147**
Bertina **121**
Betty Wormald **111**
Beverley Haerens **121**
Bibiani **114**
Bit o'Sunshine **134**
Blaauw's Pink **134**
Black Prince (Veitch) **84**
  (Brandt) **97**
Blitz 15, 19, **78**
Bloodline **114**
Blue Admiral **75**
Blue Crown **84**, *86*
Blue Diamond 19, **84**
Blue Ensign **84**
Blue Jay 19, **84**
Blue Peter 19, **84**
Blue Tit 15, 19, **75**, *86*
Bluebird **75**
Bob's Crowning Glory **155**
Boddaertianum 19, **117**
Bodnant Yellow **104**
Bold Janus 17, **155**
Bonfire 19, **97**
Bonnie McKee **121**
Bonza **155**
Boule de Neige 15, **102**
Bow Bells **76**
Brazil **147**
Break o'Day **121**
Bric a Brac 15, **80**
Bride's Bouquet **121**
Brilliant Red **147**
Bronze Wing 15, **80**
Broughtonii 73, **114**
Broughtonii Aureum **104**
Bruce Brechtbill 15, **91**
Buchanan Simpson **91**
Bud Flanagan **109**
Bulstrode Park **97**
Bumble Bee **109**
Burgundy **97**
Butterfly 19, **104**
Buzzard **147**
C.I.S. **107**
C.B. van Nes **97**
C.P. Raffil **98**
California Dawn **121**

California Gold 15, 17, **117**
California Peach **121**
California Pink Dawn **121**
California Snow **121**
Calrose **111**
Cameo **121**
Canary 15, **107**
Caprice **147**
Caramel Coffee 19, **107**
Carat **146**
Cardinal (ev. hybrid) **114**
  (ev. azalea) **135**
Carillon Bells **155**
Carita **107**
Carmen **78**
Carnival **121**
Carnival Candy **121**
Carnival Clown **121**
Carnival Queen **121**
Carnival Rocket **121**
Carnival Time **121**
Cary Ann 19, **78**
Cearuleum 15, **117**
Cecile **148**
Cercosphora 41
Cha Cha **121**
Channon Marie **155**
Charly **121**
Charming Valentino **155**
Chayya **155**
Cheer **91**
Cherry Liquer 17, **155**
Cherryblossom **136**
Cherub **135**
Chevalier de Reali 145, **147**
Chevalier Felix de Sauvage **98**
Chi no Ito **135**
Chikor 15, **82**
Choremia **98**
Christmas Cheer (ev. hybrid) 19, **91**
  (ev. azalea) **134**
Christopher John 17, **155**
Christopher Wren **147**
Chrysomanicum **82**, *86*
Cilpinense 15, **76**, *106*
Cinnkeys **107**
Clare Rouse *144*, **156**
Coccinea Speciosa 145, **146**
Coccineum *see ferrigineum*
Colehurst **110**
College Pink **91**
Collingwood Ingram *see russatum*
Colonel Coen **84**
Comte de Quincey 145
Comtesse de Kerchove **122**
Concinna 19, **132**
Confection **91**
Constance **131**
Coral Bells **135**
Coral Flare *144*, **156**
Coral Velvet 15, **76**
Coral Wings **122**
Corinne Boulter 19, **111**
Corneille **146**
Cornish Red **116**

Index

Cornubia 114, *34*
Coronation Day 17, **111**
Coronation Lady **148**
Corry Koster **92**
Cotton Candy 19, **111**
Countess of Athlone **110**
Countess of Derby **74**
Countess of Haddington **92**
Countess of Sefton 17, **102**
Cowbell **80**
Craig Faragher 17, **156**
Creamy Chiffon **107**
Creeping Jenny **78**
Creole Belle **92**
Crest **117**
Crimson Glory **98**
Crinoline **148**
Cristo Rey **156**
Croix d'Anvers **117**
Crossbill 15, *86*, **107**
Crossroads *86*, **98**
Crown Jewel **148**
Cunningham's White 50, **102**
Cup Day 15, **92**
Cynthia 19, **114**
Dainty **135**
Dame Nellie Melba **111**
Dame Pattie Menzies 19, **92**
Damozel **115**
Dancer **122**
Dark Red Ilam **149**
David **115**
David Gable 19, **92**
Daviesii 17, **80**
Dawn's Delight **92**
Day Dream **92**
Daybreak **135**
De Waele's Favourite **122**
Decision **134**
Demi-John *see johnstoneanum*
Denise **82**
Denmark **167**
Desert Rose **122**
Desert Sun **92**
Desiree **122**
Dew Drop **139**
Diane Robin **134**
Diane Titcomb 19, **102**
Dimity **138**
Direktor E. Hjelm **115**
Directeur Moerlands **147**
Divine Mirror **138**
Doc **76**
Dogwood **139**
Dogwood Red **139**
Dogwood Variegated **139**
Dopey **78**
Dora Amateis 17, 19, **81**
Dorinthia **78**, *86*
Dorothy Clark **139**
Dorothy Gish **131**
Dot **102**
Double Date **92**
Double Diamond *see johnstoneanum*
Double Salmon **148**
Dr. Arnold **122**
Dr. Arnold W. Endtz 19, **111**
Dr. Bergman **122**
Dr. Hermann Sleumer 17, **156**

Dr. Koester **122**
Dr. L.N. Deckers **147**
Dr. M. Oosthoek *125*, **147**
Dr. Reichenbach 145, **147**
Dr. S. Endtz **113**
Dr. Stocker 15, **102**
Dresden Doll *144*, **156**
Duc de Rohan 19, **132**
Dutch Marion *see* Marion
Earl of Athlone **98**
Earl of Donoughmore **98**
Early Orange *125*, **147**
Easter Bonnet **122**
Easter Delight **139**
Eastern Zanzibar 17, **156**
Ebino *see keiskei cordifolia*
Edith Boulter **93**
Edith Praed **115**
Eldorado *86*, **107**
Eleanore 19, **110**
Elegant Bouquet 17, **156**
Elie **111**
Elisabeth Hobbie **79**
Elizabeth 19, 69, **79**, *86*
Elizabeth Lawrence 19, **133**
Elizabeth Titcomb 19, **102**
Ellestee *see wardii*
Elsa Karga **122**, *124*
Emasculum 19, **93**
Emily Knights **134**
Empress Eugenie **76**
Endsleigh Pink **111**
Eri Schaeme **122**
Ernest Gill **93**
Esmeralda **134**
Esprit de Joie 17, **156**
Essex Scarlet 5, **78**
Eureka **122**
Eureka Gold *see aurigeranum*
Eureka Maid **92**
Evening Glow **107**
Everestianum 19, **110**
Exbury Crimson **148**
Exquisita **149**
Exquisite 19, **133**
Fabia 69, 74, **76**
Faggetter's Favourite 17, **117**
Fairy Light **93**
Fairy Queen **134**
Faith Henty **79**
Fanny **146**
Fascination **134**
Fashion **134**
Fastuosum Flore Pleno 19, *86*, **110**
Fastuosum Flore Rosea **92**
Fastuosum Plenum **110**
Favor Major **148**
Favourite **138**
Fawley **148**
Fedora **137**
Feuerzauber **122**
Fielder's White 19, **133**
Fine Feathers **81**
Fine Feathers Primrose **82**
Fire Bird **115**
Fire Magic **122**
Fire Plum **156**
Fire Prince 15, 19, **98**
Fire Walk 15, **98**

Firedance **138**
Firefly (ev. azalea) **122**
  (dec. azalea) **148**
Fireman Jeff **79**
Flamingo **127**
Flora **134**
Flora Markeeta **93**
Florence Mann **75**
Fragrantissimum 16, 17, *86*, **103**
Frans Van der Bom 145, **147**
Freckle Pink 19, **93**
Fred Colbert **134**
Fred Hamilton 19, **82**, *86*
Freisland **112**
Frills **148**
Fude Tsukata **134**
Furnivall's Daughter **93**
Fusilier 15, **107**
G.O.G. **148**
Gables Pink No.1 **92**
Galipolli **146**
Gardenia Odessy 17, **156**
Garnet **93**
Gauntlettii **117**
Gay Paree **127**
Geoffrey Millais 17, **117**
George Grace **93**
George Hardy **73**
George Lindley Taber **132**
George Reynolds *125*, **146**
Gibraltar (evergreen) 15, **98**
  (dec. azalea) **148**
Gill's Crimson *87*, **115**
Gill's Gloriosa **98**
Ginger **148**
Ginny Gee **77**
Glamour **98**
Glenarn *see ferrugineum*
Gloire d'Anvers **117**
Glora Mundi **145**
Gloria Still **139**
Gloria U.S.A. **131**
Glory of Sunninghill 19, **133**
Glowing Embers **148**
Goblin **93**
Goethe *87*, **93**
Gog **148**
Gold Dust **148**
Goldball **147**
Golden Casket **156**
Golden Charm **156**
Golden Dream **148**
Golden Eagle *143*, **148**
Golden Fleece **83**
Golden Horn **148**
Golden Star **107**
Golden Sunlight **147**
Golden Sunset **148**
Golden Torch **108**
Goldflimmer 15, 16, **84**
Goldsworth Crimson **98**
Goosander **82**
Gossamer White 17, **156**
Goyet **127**
Grace **93**
Grace Seabrook **99**
Graciosa **149**
Graf Zeppelin **93**
Grandeur Triomphante **145**

Great Scent-sation 17, **157**
Grenadier **115**
Gretel **127**
Grumpy **82**
Guanda Pink **127**
Gumpo Lavender **137**
Gumpo Pink **137**
Gumpo Salmon **137**
Gumpo Stripe **137**
Gumpo White **138**
Gumpo x Polka **127**
Gwillt King **99**
H. H. Hume **134**
H.Van de Ven **149**
H.H. de Witte **147**
Habba Shan see *hippophaeoides*
Halfdan Lem 19, **99**
Hallelujah **99**
Haloed Gold *144*, **157**
Halopeanum **117**
Hana Asobi **134**
Happy **93**
Happy Birthday **134**
Happy Days **127**
Happy Times **157**
Hari's Choice **157**
Harry van de Ven **135**
Harvest Moon 15
Hatsu-giri **135**
Hawk Crest **117**
Heatherside Beauty **103**
Helena **139**
Hélène Schiffner 19, **103**
Hellmut Vogel **127**
Hello Dolly 15, **83**
Hendre **157**
Herbert Gable **137**
Herbert **137**
High Sierra **135**
Highland Arabesque 17, *126*, **157**
Highland Fair **157**
Highland Peter Pan **157**
Highland White Jade 17, **157**
Hinamoyo **135**
Hino **135**
Hinode Giri *124*, **135**
Hinomayo *124*, **135**
Ho'o **134**
Homebush **148**
Honey Bunch **139**
Hoppy **81**
Hortulanus H. Witte **147**
Hotei 15
Hugh Koster **115**
Hugo de Vries **95**
Hugo Koster **145**
Humboldt **84**
Humming Bird 74, **77**
Hunstein's Secret see *leucogigas*
Hydon Dawn 15, **77**
I.M.S. **112**
Ibex 15, **99**
Iceberg **127**
Iced Primrose 17, **157**
Ilona **108**
Ima Zuma **135**
Ima-Shojo **134**
Indica Alba **118**
Inga **127**

Irene Koster **149**
Irene Stead 17, **112**
Iroha Yama **135**
Isabel Pierce **112**
Ito Ihei **118**
Ivanhoe **115**
Ivery's Scarlet 19, **115**
J. H. van Nes **99**
James Belton **127**
Jan Dekens 15, 19, **94**
Jane Rogers **94**
Janeke **127**
Janet Blair 17, **112**
Jean Alexandra 19, **133**
Jean Baptiste 17, **157**
Jean Marie de Montague 15, 19, **99**
Jill Seymour 19, **135**
Jindabyne **127**
Jingle Bells 19, **83**
Johannes 17, **157**
John Haerens **127**
John Ruskin **145**
John Waterer **115**
John Wister **112**
Johnny Bender 15, **99**
Joseph Whitworth *87*, **110**
Juan Diego **157**
Kalimna **94**
Kandy Kid **127**
Kaponga **115**
Kasane Kagaribi **135**
Kathleen **148**
Keillour see *russatum* 63
Kelly's Cerise *123*, **127**
Kestrel **148**
Kiandra **158**
Kimberly 15, **77**
Kimbeth **77**
Kimigayo **135**
Kinshu Makura **118**
Kipps **148**
Kirin **135**
Kirishima **135**
Klondyke **148**
Knap Hill see *campanulatum*
Knap Hill Apricot **148**
Knap Hill Red **148**
Knap Hill Yellow **148**
Knut Erwen **127**
Kobai **138**
Kojo no Odorikaraka **135**
Koli **127**
Komachi **135**
Koningin Emma **147**
Koryu **138**
Kosmos **127**
Koster's Brilliant Red **147**
Koster's Yellow **147**
Krakatoa **115**
Kumo no Ito **136**
Kure no Yuki **135**
Lady Bligh **99**
Lady C. Mitford **94**
Lady Chamberlain 15, **108**
Lady Clementine Mitford 15, **94**
Lady Dalhouse **59**
Lady de Rothschild **103**
Lady Decies **84**
Lady Eleanor Cathcart **73**

Lady Grenville **116**
Lady Jayne **149**
Lady Stuart of Wortley **94**
Lakeside see *trichostomum*
Lamplighter **99**
Langley Park **100**
Larnook Gem **113**
Laura **128**
Laura Kate 17, **158**
Lavender Girl 17, 19, **89**
Lavender Rosina **128**
Lavender Supreme **128**
Lem's Cameo *87*, **94**
Lem's Monarch **112**
Lem's Walloper **114**
Lemon Mist **83**, *87*
Lemonora **147**
Leopold Astrid *124*, **128**
Letty Edwards *87*, **108**
Liberty Bar *153*, **158**
Lighthouse 19, **116**
Limelight **135**
Linearifolium see *macrosepalum*
Little Beauty **128**
Little Ginger **158**
Little One **158**
Little Pinkie 17, **158**
Little Red Riding Hood **135**
Littlest Angel **158**
Lochmin 17, **158**
Loder's White 17, 19, *87*, **103**
Loderi **74**
Lord Roberts 19, **100**
Louise J. Bobbink **131**
Lovey 17, **158**
Lucidium **89**
Lucie **128**
Lucille K **128**
Lucky Strike **94**
Madame Auguste Haerens **128**
Madame Cachet/Cochet 19, *87*, **110**
Madame de Bruin **100**
Madame de Waele **128**
Madame Doumier 15, **89**
Madame Marcel de Paepe **131**
Madonna (Indica azalea) **128**
   (Kurume azalea) **136**
Magic Flute 17, *144*, **158**
Magnifica 19, **133**
Mahmoud 19, **94**
Mandalay **79**
Manderley 19, **100**
Mansaku **138**
Mardi Gras **128**
Margaret Dunn **94**
Margaret Mack 19, **94**
Margaret Rowell **139**
Maria's Choice **108**
Marion (Cheal) **112**
   (Felix & Dijkhuis) **92**
Marjiam **158**
Marketeea's Prize 19, **100**
Mars **79**, *87*
Mary Claire **149**
Mary Lou **149**
Maryborough see *russatum*
Maryke 19, **94**
Marylin Monroe **128**
Matador 15, **100**

Index

Mathilda 145, **147**
Mauve Bouquet 19, **89**
Max Sye *88*, **100**
May Day 15, **79**
Meadow Pond *see wardii*
Medusa **83**
Melba **94**
Melissa Ray **128**
Mercury **128**
Mernda Yellow **149**
Mevrouw van Krugten **147**
Midnight **87**, **89**, 92
Mistral **128**
Miyagino **135**
Moonstone 19, **83**
Moonwood 17, **158**
Morning Magic **81**
Mother of Pearl 17, **112**
Mother's Day **135**
Mount Everest 17, **103**
Mrs. A.T. de la Mare 17, *88*, **103**
Mrs. Bernice Baker **95**
Mrs. Betty Robertson **108**
Mrs. C.B. Van Nes **95**
Mrs. Charles E. Pearson 19, *88*, **112**
Mrs. E.C. Stirling 19, **112**
Mrs. Furnivall 19, 93, **95**
Mrs. G.W. Leak 19, **87**, **112**
Mrs. Gerda Kint **128**
Mrs. J.G. Millais **103**
Mrs. John Ward **139**
Mrs. Jozef Heursel **128**
Mrs. Lionel de Rothschild **103**
Mrs. P.D. Williams **103**
Mrs. R.S. Holford **73**
Mrs. Robert W. Wallace **95**
Mrs. T.H. Lowinsky **89**
Mrs. Tom Agnew **87**, **117**
Mrs. Van de Ven **135**
Mucronatum 118
Multiflorum **77**
Mundai **95**
Murraba **89**
My Fair Lady **128**
Myrtifolium 19, **79**
Nancy Miller Adler **158**
Narcissiflora/um **146**
Ne-plus-ultra **158**
Nicholas **89**
Night Editor *see russatum*
Night Watch **89**
Niugini Firebird *126*, **159**
Noble Pearl **95**
Nobleanum 74, **103**
Noele Boulter **113**
Norbitonense Broughtonianum 104
Norrie King **113**
Nova Zembla 19, **100**
Noyo Chief 15, *88*, **100**
Nuccio's Dew Drop **139**
Oceanlake 19, **75**
Odee Wright 15
Oklahoma **116**
Old Port 19, **100**
Olinda Bells 19, **81**
Olive **89**
Olympic Lady **77**
Only One Earth *124*, **129**
Orange Beauty **135**

Orange Chimes **129**
Orange Delight **139**
Orange King **137**
Orange Supreme *125*, **149**
Orange Wax **159**
Orchidflora Alba **129**
Orchidflora Pink **129**
Osaraku **135**
Osta **129**
Osta Red **129**
Ostbo's Low Yellow **83**
Our Gem 19, **113**
Overflow 153, **159**
Oxydol **149**
P.J.M. 15, 19, **95**
Pacific Shower **159**
Palestrina **137**
Paloma **129**
Pastenello 17, **159**
Patty Bee 19, **83**
Paul Schaeme **129**
Penelope **135**
Pennywhistle **159**
Percy Wiseman **77**
Perri Cutten **79**
Persil **149**
Peste's Blue Ice **75**
Peter Koster *88*, **100**
Phalarope **81**
Phoeniceum *124*, **139**
Phryne *124*, **129**
Pierre Moser **113**
Pindi Pearl **159**
Pink Delight (ev. hybrid) **113**
 (dec. azalea) **149**
 (vireya) **159**
Pink Dream **129**
Pink Ice *125*, **129**
Pink Lace 19, **133**
Pink Lady **127**
Pink Pearl (ev. hybrid) 73, *88*, **113**
 (cv. azalea) 134
Pink Perfection *88*, **95**
Pink Pizazz 17, **159**
Pink Poppet **159**
Pink Ruffles *125*, **129**
Pink Seedling **159**
Pink Silk **77**
Pink Tiger **129**
Pirianda Pink **77**
Polka Dot *see irroratum*
Popcorn **135**
Potlatch 15, **79**
President Roosevelt 15, 16, *88*, **101**
Pretty Cotton Candy **159**
Pride of Dorking 19, **133**
Primrose Promise **159**
Prince Camille de Rohan **95**
Prince Charming *see schlippenbachii*
Princess Alexandra 17, 150, **159**
Princess Alice 16, 17, 19, **81**
Princess Anne **83**
Princess Maude *125*, **129**
Princess Royal 146, 150
Prize **129**
Professor Hugo de Vries **95**
Prostigiatum **75**
Ptarmigan **81**
Puget Sound 17, **113**

Pulcherrimum **73**
Puralbum *see wardii*
Purity **131**
Purple Glitters 19, **136**
Purple Gown **79**, *88*
Purple Lace **89**
Purple Opal 19, **89**
Purple Splendour 19, **90**
Purpureum Elegans 19, **90**
Quarry Wood *see trichostomum*
Queen Emma **147**
R.W. Rye **108**
Racil **77**
Radiant Willow **138**
Radium **101**
Rae Berry *see trichostomum*
Rainbow **113**
Ramapo 15, 19, **76**
Red Admiral **116**
Red Bird **132**
Red Hussar **135**
Red Indian **149**
Red Line **129**
Red Plum **138**
Red Poppy **129**
Red Prince **159**
Red Robin **136**
Red Ruffles **130**
Red Satin **130**
Redwings *125*, **130**, 132
Redwax 15, **79**
Revery **138**
Rhabdotum *see dalhousiae*
Ring of Fire **108**
Ripples **130**
Roadrunner **130**
Robert Bates 17, **160**
Robert Fox **97**
Robyn **95**
Rocket 15, 19, **96**
Rodeo *88*, **116**
Roman Pottery **83**
Romance **138**
Romany Chai **101**, **116**
Romany Chal **101**, **116**
Rosa Belton **130**
Rosabel **96**
Rosalea **101**
Rosali *124*, **130**
Rose Elf 19, **81**
Rose Glitters 19, **136**
Rose King **131**
Rose Queen **131**
Rosebud **136**
Rosie Posie **160**
Rosina *125*, **130**
Rositi **135**
Rothenburg *88*, **108**
Rouseabout **160**
Rubicon 19, **101**
Rubra *see moupinense*
Ruby F. Bowman 19, **96**
Ruby Hart 15, **80**
Russautinii **90**
Russellianum 74
Ruth Kirk **130**
Ruth Marion **130**
Saffron Queen **83**, *105*
Saint Breward **76**

Saint Tudy 76
Saki 96
Salmon Beauty 136
Sandpiper 149
Santoi 136
Sappho 73, **117**
Sarita Loder 96
Satan 149
Satin 15, **96**
Satin Glow 113
Scandinavia 80
Scarlet Beauty 160
Scarlet Gem 136
Scarlet King 15, 19, **101**
Scarlet Pimpernel 149
Scarlet Wonder 15, 19, **80**
Schiller 90
Schubert 90
Scintillation 15, **96**
Seagull 139
Sebastian 160
Seikai 136
Seraphim 136
Sesterianum 17, **81**
Seta **96**, *105*
Seventh Heaven *see sutchuense*
Shantung Pink 160
Shantung Rose 160
Sherriff 74
Shin Utena 136
Shin-Kyo 138
Show Girl 136
Silver Anniversary 130
Simbu Sunset *144*, **160**
Sir Charles Lemon 15, **103**
Sir Frederick Moore 17, **113**
Sir George Holford 160
Sir Robert Menzies 19, **80**
Sir Robert Peel 19, **116**
Sirius *105*, **113**
Sleepy 78
Snow Lady 19, **81**
Snow Peak 81
Snowflake 135
Sonata 19
Sonia 149
South Seas 130
Southern Aurora 130
Southern Sunset 130
Souvenir de Dr. S. Endtz 19, **113**
Souvenir de J.H. Mangles 160
Souvenir of W. C. Slocock 19, **108**
Splendens *125*, **133**

Spring Glory 19, **96**
Sprite 136
Stead's Pink 19, **114**
Stella Maris 130
Strawberry Ice 149
Strawberry Parfait 160
Suave 16, 17, **81**
Success 15, **96**
Suga no Ito 136
Sugar Pink 114
Sugared Almond 149
Sui Yohi 136
Sultan 134
Summerland Chiffon 139
Summerland Mist 139
Sunny 160
Sunrise 137
Sunset Gold 50 160
Surrey Heath 15, **78**
Susan *105*, **90**
Susette 90
Sweet Amanda 17, **161**
Sweet Bay *see trichostomum*
Sweet Nellie 130
Sweet Rosalie 17, **161**
Sweet Seraphim 17, **161**
Sweet Wendy 17, **161**
Sweetheart Supreme 139
Sylphides 149
Takasago 136
Tally Ho *105*, **116**
Tanager 138
Tancho 136
Taurus 116
Teena Maree 139
Terra Nova 139
The Teacher 130
The Warrior 101
Thor 15, **80**
Tickled Pink 132
Titian Beauty 80
Toandos Rose 92
Tortoiseshell Champagne 108
Tortoiseshell Salome 109
Toucan 149
Trewithen Orange 109
Triumphans 161
Tropic Fanfare 153, **161**
Tropic Summer 161
Tropic Tango 161
Trude Webster 19, **96**
Tsuta Momiji 135
Tunis 149

Turkish Delight 96
Tyermanii 17, **104**
Unique *51*, 91, **109**
Unknown Warrior 19, **101**
Valerie Kay 15, **78**
Van Nes Sensation 17, **97**
Vanessa Pastel 69, **109**
Veronica Maureen 161
Vibrant 139
Violacea 131
Violet Ray 131
Virginia Richards 97
Virgo 114
Vittata 120
Vittata Bealii 120
Vittata Punctata 120
Volcano 116
Vulcan's Flame 19, **101**, *105*
Vuyk's Scarlet 137
W.E. Gumbelton 145
Waka Kayede 136
Walloper 15, **114**
Ward's Ruby 136
Warrior 101
Wattlebird 161
Wedding Bells 104
Wedding Gown 17, **104**, *105*
Werner Muckel 127
Werner Proehl 127
White Bouquet 131
White Flare 19, **81**, *106*
White Gish 132
White Gold 104
White Lace 133
White Orchids 131
White Pearl 117
White Prince 132
White Schaeme 131
White Swan 117
Whitney's Double Pink 92
Whitney's Orange 83
Willbrit 97
William Downing 90
Windsor Lad 90
Winsome 74, **80**, *105*
Winter Beauty 19, **90**
Witchery 15, **101**
Wryneck 149
Yaku Fairy *see keiskei cordifolia*
Yellow Garland *see xanthostephanum*
Yellow Hammer 19, **109**
You Beaut 97
Zoe Elloise 161